JOHN ADDINGTON
SYMONDS

PHYLLIS GROSSKURTH

John Addington Symonds

A BIOGRAPHY

1724

LONGMANS

LONGMANS, GREEN AND CO LTD
48 Grosvenor Street, London W.1
*Associated companies, branches and representatives
throughout the world*

©   *Phyllis Grosskurth, 1964
First published 1964*

*Printed in Great Britain by
The Camelot Press Ltd., London and Southampton*

FOR
BOB, CHRIS, BRIAN AND ANN
WHO WERE SO VERY,
VERY PATIENT

CONTENTS

ILLUSTRATIONS

Acknowledgements

The photographs are reproduced by permission as follows: *T. H. Green*: Balliol College, Oxford; *Edmund Gosse*: The Brotherton Library, University of Leeds; *Norman Moor*: Clifton College, Bristol; *Graham Dakyns*: Miss Janine and Mr Andrew Dakyns; *Havelock Ellis*: Mme Françoise Delisle; *Henry Sidgwick*: Trinity College Library, Cambridge. *Benjamin Jowett* is from a photograph by H. H. H. Cameron in the Gernsheim Collection and *Dr Vaughan* from a photograph by Elliott & Fry Ltd in F. D. How, *Six Great Schoolmasters*, Methuen & Co. Ltd. With the exception of the photograph of Horatio Brown's house which is by the author, all other photographs are reproduced by permission of the University Library, Bristol.

PREFACE

THIS is a biography of a writer whose name was widely known during his lifetime but who has long since slipped into semi-oblivion. Even among those who know something of the man and his work, John Addington Symonds is remembered generally as a late nineteenth-century aesthete, a minor Pater perhaps, or as one who seemed to suffer particular torment from the religious perplexities of his day.

That such an image of Symonds should survive is the result of certain facts about the man which his family, his friends, and his first biographer, Horatio F. Brown (1895), thought prudent to conceal. No deeper truth was revealed by Van Wyck Brooks's biography in 1914. Consequently, a confused, enigmatic figure hovers on the fringes of literature – and, as Symonds himself remarked in connection with his biography of Michelangelo, to conceal the truth does credit to no one. I have tried to sharpen the focus, to add flesh to the misty outline, and to tell the truth as far as I could reconstruct it.

When Symonds's literary executor, Horatio F. Brown, died in 1926, he bequeathed Symonds's MS. Memoirs to the London Library, with a fifty-year embargo on their release for publication. The story of Symonds's inner life cannot be revealed in Symonds's own words until 1976. I am most grateful to Mr Stanley Gillam, Librarian of the London Library, for allowing me to read this autobiography and to make use of the facts it contains, although without direct quotation. In those cases where the autobiography is cited, the passages have been taken from H. F. Brown's biography of Symonds.

I have also made extensive use of Symonds's voluminous, highly personal letters, which have been scattered widely since his death. These are now being collected and edited by Professor Herbert Schueller and Dr Robert Peters of Wayne State University. In this book I have edited extracts from the letters only to the extent of italicizing titles of books and placing titles of poems within quotation marks for the sake of greater clarity.

The two main repositories of these letters are the University of Bristol and the Dakyns Collection. I wish to take this opportunity to thank all the members of the staff of the Library of the University of Bristol who were so helpful on my many visits, and most particularly the Librarian, J. Shum Cox, for his great kindness and interest in my work. I also want to thank Miss Janine Dakyns and Mr Andrew Dakyns for allowing me to read the more than five hundred letters their grandfather received from his great friend, John Addington Symonds. For permission to publish other unpublished Symonds material I am grateful to The Houghton Library, Harvard University; the Boston Public Library; the University of Texas; The Brotherton Collection, University of Leeds; the British Museum; Colby College; and Mrs Edgar Dugdale. I also wish to thank Mr Charles Feinberg and Professor Schueller for allowing me to summarize the Symonds-Whitman correspondence.

I am grateful to Balliol College for granting me permission to quote from the unpublished letters of Benjamin Jowett; to Mrs George Bambridge for permission to quote part of an unpublished letter by Rudyard Kipling on p. 306 (© Mrs Elsie Bambridge, 1964); to Mme Françoise Delisle for permission to quote from copies of unpublished letters of Havelock Ellis; to Miss Jennifer Gosse for permission to quote from the unpublished letters of Edmund Gosse; to William Heinemann Ltd for allowing me to quote from unpublished letters of A. C. Swinburne; to the Manx Museum and National Trust for allowing me to quote from the copy of an unpublished letter of T. E. Brown; to John Murray Ltd for allowing me to quote from Mrs W. W. Vaughan, *Out of the Past*; to Mr Innes Rose for permission to quote extracts from the unpublished letters of Henry James, and to the Trustees of the Hardy Estate for an extract of an unpublished letter of Thomas Hardy. If I have failed to obtain permission from the executors of any of the letters I have quoted, I apologize with assurances that in every case I have made exhaustive efforts to trace them.

To list the names of all those who have helped me in the preparation of this book does less than justice to my sense of appreciation, particularly to Symonds's granddaughter, Mrs Katharine West, and to Vincent Brome, who spent weary hours reading the MS. and whose many suggestions and criticisms have made it a far better book than it otherwise would have been. I wish Professor Geoffrey Tillotson to know how grateful I am to him for first arousing my interest in Symonds. A further list of those to whom I am indebted must include my good friend, Charles Cunningham, for his unfailing good nature in answering my many queries about Greek quotations; Admiral and Mrs Paul Furse; Iain Fletcher; Timothy 'Arch Smith; Professor Walter Houghton; Paul Mattheisen; Laurence Evans; Donald Weeks; Barry Bloomfield; Professor Herbert Schueller; Robert Peters; Sir Kenneth Clark; Angus Wilson; Charles E. Feinberg; the Hon. Mrs Charles Leaf; C. H. R. Gee; and the US National Library of Medicine.

London.   P. G.

Prologue

On an autumn evening in 1892 a gondola drifted through the lagoons of Venice. Its owner, a middle-aged English writer, lay back absorbed in the melancholy reflections appropriate to his romantic surroundings. He was returning from the Porto del Lido, where each afternoon of that mellow St Martin's summer, his gondolier would tie the boat to one of the *pali*, and there he would sit reading until the light began to fade. On this occasion, still engrossed in the sombre speculations roused by his book, it needed the rough passage of a crowded tourist boat to startle him into wakefulness. Suddenly his attention focused on the extraordinary beauty of the figure sturdily rowing the passing boat, a bronzed *faccino* in the broad black hat and white costume then fashionable with the gondoliers. Slowly the boat drew away, the youth disappeared from view, and the man was left with a sense of deprivation.

It was typical of John Addington Symonds to seize upon a fleeting encounter like this as a revelation of significant truth. The memory of the young gondolier remained so powerfully with him that it grew to represent the symbol of a lost ideal, and in his diary he tried to reinvoke every detail of the scene in terms which seem extravagant to modern sensibilities. He recalled how the boy's lithe agility had flowed into the rhythm of the boat. The boy, in turn, became intricately fused with Symonds's feeling for Venice and his response to the landscape of the lagoons. He remembered the splash of the oars, the pungent odour of air and water, the churches of Venice – S. Giorgio, Redentore, Salute – looming large and dark against the vermilion-streaked sky. His precise mood of melancholy had to be recaptured, 'one of those sad moods, in which all life seems wasted, & the heart is full of hidden want, & one does not even know what one desires, but a sense of wistfulness is everywhere – one of these moods has been upon me several days'.[1] Lines from Pindar had occurred to him : 'Creatures of a day ! What is a man and what is a man not ?' The meditation had been broken by the image of the boy, the

1

crystallization of all beauty. 'I am a soul, he is a soul, we shall never meet', he wrote sorrowfully. 'Each of us has some incalculable doom, and neither of us knows what that doom is.'[2] What the young man's doom was to be we can only guess. Symonds himself was to die five months later.

This episode took place when Symonds was fifty-two years old and seemed to possess much that should make a man happy. He was a well-known literary figure in London, he had a wife and children in a comfortable house in Switzerland, and he could afford to drift at leisure through the lagoons of Venice. By 1892 an impressive body of work lay behind him and his reputation would never stand higher. The riotously catholic nature of his literary production reflected a man with a wide range of interests: poetry, biography, history, aesthetics, science, and philosophy. A study of his favourite poet, Walt Whitman, one of the most congenial pieces of work he had ever undertaken, had recently been completed; he was deeply committed to an investigation of homosexuality in collaboration with Havelock Ellis, and for the past three years he had been absorbed in the writing of his autobiography.

Symonds was undoubtedly given to exaggerating his reactions in purple prose, and his description of the lagoon scene might have been one discarded from *The Picture of Dorian Gray*. Its sensuous elaboration, the connivance at moulding life into art, and his slightly theatrical attitudinizing reveal an important aspect of Symonds's complex personality; yet, while undoubtedly narcissistic, that clearly was not the whole man. The figure depicted in his diaries and autobiography reveals a very different person from the one most people thought they knew. He had an enormous circle of friends – Benjamin Jowett, Robert Louis Stevenson, Sidney Colvin, Leslie Stephen, Algernon Swinburne, Edmund Gosse, Edward Lear, Margot Asquith – and many of these have recorded how he seemed to devour life.

At this period he was a slight, frail man of middle height, with a long lantern face which had something of that false radiance occasionally found in victims of tuberculosis. Although he would die within a few months, his appearance was still youthful, his brown hair as yet unstreaked by grey, his energy apparently undiminished, and even in the languorous atmosphere of Venice he continued to devote a considerable part of each day to his writing. He had become a familiar figure to the English colony in his purple velvet jacket which combined the elegance of the best tailoring with a touch of Bohemian casualness. He was a lover of good conversation and it was characteristic of him to gesticulate freely as some tremendously complicated sentence poured from his lips. Friends were accustomed to the eloquence, the casual erudition, the ready laugh, and the dangerously brandished cigar. He would often pause in mid-sentence, leap to his feet, and pull down a volume to bring a fleeting quotation to heel. A sensualist, he enjoyed good food and fine wine. An aesthete, he responded with equal intensity to the grain of wood, the flow of a Greek statue, or the sound of an organ.

Symonds always declared that life meant more to him than literature. Yet a paradox persisted. The evidence suggests that neither his active life nor his emotional relationships counter-balanced the disappointing literary reputation. At fifty-two he was aware that his success was not proportionate to the immense efforts of a lifetime. Like Arthur Hugh Clough, whom he greatly admired, he had shown early promise which had never completely matured. 'It is very thankless', Symonds wrote to his daughter from Venice during that memorable November. 'On all sides there come pouring in upon me proofs of my achieved renown – the success of my last big book – the sympathy of strangers. And yet I am not happy.'³ Although only a few friends knew it, despite the appearance of frenetic energy, he felt discouraged and tired. Had literature been worth it, had the toil of research and writing and revision produced anything of real value?

'Why do ye toil hither & thither upon paths laborious & peril-fraught? Seek what ye are seeking; but it is not there where ye are seeking it. Ye are seeking a life of beatitude in the realm of death. It is not there.

'And indeed I knew what I was wanting, & at the same time knew that even to want it was vanity, to possess it dust & ashes.

'All these things appertain to the temperament which one calls neuropathic. But they belong also to the artist. In compensation for sensibilities to beauty & powers over language, sound, form, etc., far exceeding those of his neighbours, he is doomed to a life-long ache, a numbing paralyzing pain at the heart, a useless feeble craving, which renders him in some ways weaker, often far more wretched, than the most commonplace of men.'⁴

3

These lines to his daughter were written three days before his encounter with the young gondolier, who seemed the embodiment of all his suppressed cravings.

In middle age Symonds was embittered by the conviction that his talent had been blighted by the strain of accommodating himself to conventional morality. Passionately aware of the possibilities he thought life could offer, he believed that he had never been able to attain complete self-fulfilment because of the constant façade he was forced to maintain. A man hidden behind a mask, a writer who never attained first-rank, he suffered the tormented struggle of a homosexual within Victorian society.

CHAPTER I

Clifton

ON 5 October 1840 John Addington Symonds was born into an earnest Bristol family whose dedicated pursuit of the intellectual life might have provided Matthew Arnold with a sterling example for the middle classes to emulate. All the Symondses were steeped in Culture: their friends were cultivated, their interests were edifying, and their pleasures were purposeful. Although Symonds spent a large part of his life trying to divest himself of this early conditioning, it persisted in clinging to him like a caul.

The commendable activities of his family were directed by Dr John Addington Symonds, the most eminent physician of his time in the West Country. Dr Symonds came from a Nonconformist background and although he had discarded most of its rigid sectarian beliefs, the sobriety with which he conducted every aspect of his life had obvious connections with his early upbringing. Born in Oxford in 1807, he followed a long line of doctors – men who had been debarred from other professions by the University Test Acts – and studied medicine at Oxford and Edinburgh where he received his degree in 1828. After moving to Bristol in 1831 he was elected physician to the General Hospital and Lecturer in Forensic Medicine at the British Medical School. In 1834 he married a beautiful local girl, Harriet Sykes. Two years later he was appointed Lecturer in the Practice of Medicine, a post he held for the next seventeen years, after which he became honorary consulting physician until his death in 1871. He built up an enormous practice not only by his reputation as a skilled physician but also through his forceful personality and impressive intellectual gifts. The romanticized bust of him by the Pre-Raphaelite sculptor, Thomas Woolner,* emphasizes the proud, confident

* The bust was displayed at the Royal Academy in 1872.

5

bearing of a man who could blandly discuss Greek prosody with Gladstone and Tennyson. On the strength of his reputation people from all over England were attracted to Bristol and Clifton. One of these was John Sterling,* and in his *Life* of the essayist, Carlyle refers to the friendship which developed between Dr Symonds and Sterling after the latter moved to Clifton in 1839.[1]

Dr Symonds was remarkable for the breadth of his interests: his son later described him as 'open at all pores to culture, to art, to archaeology, to science, to literature',[2] but his love of literature remained the greatest passion of his life. While still a medical student, he became one of Shelley's earliest admirers. In a letter to Dr Hack Tuke he once expressed the belief that poetry and medicine were closely related, and concluded: 'But I am prosing on poetry. Forgive me; and above all do not betray me. Nine-tenths of the world would not let me prescribe for them if they thought I cared two straws for poetry.'[3] The doctor never failed to rise at six in order to put in two hours of study or writing on some aspect of the arts before he went out to make his morning calls. Culture required work, and both were an integral part of the good Victorian life. An evening with his family meant a reading from the best authors; a *soirée* would often be graced by a recital from Jenny Lind; and a trip abroad would be shamelessly wasted if the historical monuments and great works of art were not duly noted and described in one's diary.

The weeks following the birth of a sickly infant, John Addington, in 1840 were a period of troubled anxiety for the doctor as his wife had already lost three sons during the past two years: premature twins had been stillborn in 1838 and a boy, christened John Abdy Stephenson, had died only the previous year at seven months. Of the two daughters already born to the union, Mary Isabella (Maribella) was delicate and eventually died of consumption, a weakness inherited from Mrs Symonds's family. John Addington, however, surprised everyone by feebly surviving, and he was followed in 1842 by a healthy sister Charlotte. The strain of bearing seven children within ten years was too much for delicate Harriet Symonds and she died of scarlet fever when John Addington was four. At thirty-seven, Dr Symonds became a widower with a young family to rear.

* In 1838 Sterling formed a famous literary group, the Sterling Club, whose members included Carlyle, Tennyson, John Stuart Mill, and Francis Palgrave.

Dr Symonds was devoted to the memory of his wife and he never seems to have entertained the idea of marrying again. The legend clinging to Mrs Symonds said that she was beautiful, tremulous, and infinitely gentle. The description may well be true yet it is inconsistent with the temperaments of most of her female relatives who were assertive, strong-willed women. The only endearing one among them seems to have been her sister, Isabella, who was attracted to Carlyle's friend, John Sterling, but contracted an unhappy marriage with another man, and died young of consumption.

Symonds's only clear recollection of his mother concerned a terrifying experience which they shared when driving in their carriage. On the hill running down from Cornwallis Terrace to the Lower Crescent, the horses suddenly bolted. Recalling the incident in his autobiography in 1889, Symonds still had a vivid recollection of her pale frightened face framed by beautiful golden hair under a pink silk bonnet. Her funeral impressed itself upon him only as a memory of playing with tin soldiers on the nursery floor with his sisters, all of whom were dressed in black, while the grown-ups went off in sad solemnity. Dr Symonds gave him some strands of his mother's hair and for years took him regularly to Arno's Vale Cemetery to lay flowers on her secluded grave, but these occasions aroused no emotion in him and he often felt guilty because he did not feel the requisite sense of loss. Jenny Lind recalled that as a young man he once took her into his father's study and gently removed the cloth covering his mother's bust. However, his memory of her had become so dim that it was an act of gentle piety rather than of any profound feeling.

Nevertheless, although he was not acutely conscious of his loss, the absence of a mother became one of the major factors in the formation of Symonds's character. After his mother's death, her sister, Miss Mary Ann Sykes, moved in to care for the children. A woman of strong character, with a sharp wit and a ready temper, she forcefully inculcated her own prejudices in the children. Very conscious of the fact that she was well-connected, and only too aware of the ambiguous place a doctor occupied in society, she constantly impressed upon the children that they were privileged to be living in luxury, and left them with an uneasy conviction that Symonds was a 'common' name. This lesson made a deep impression

upon John Addington and in later years he would wince with embarrassment if his name were called out in a railway station or a hotel lobby. The
sensitive boy who once wrote to his friend Graham Dakyns that he
longed for love more than anything else in the world, never received the
warmth craved by a child of his temperament. Respect was the emotion
aroused by the formidable figure of his aunt in her lace cap and black silk
gown. While she was fond of John, she could not understand him and she
never became a surrogate mother.

His active imagination caused many misunderstandings between them.
When he started school he passed a house in which the basement grating
was wide enough for him to look down into a cellar where he could see
an old man squatting by a fire, raking up embers, and stirring mysterious
ingredients into a cauldron. Wildly excited by his supposed discovery of a
magician, John wanted to take his sisters to watch the wizard concocting
his magic brew. 'Auntie' grew very stern and ordered him not to tell such
lies. On another occasion he arrived home breathless with a terrifying
tale of having been attacked by robbers, only to be dampened once more
with a severe scolding. Repeatedly his inventive imagination was inhibited
by his well-meaning aunt in her emphasis on the importance of 'truth'.
A general distrust of the imagination as capable of producing only fictions,
as being somehow suspect, is clearly apparent in the mature Symonds
whose natural proclivities tended towards dreams and fantasies which
were constantly repressed by his early conditioning. He was to realize that
only in his poetry could he express his real longings.

One incident throws significant light on his relationship with his aunt.
John kept collections of all sorts of curiosities, and was particularly
attached to a stuffed kingfisher which he even took to bed with him. One
day, on returning from a visit where she had met a little French boy who
shared her nephew's interests, his aunt harangued John until he was
driven to wrap up his treasure and send it off to the unknown boy.
Recalling the experience in his autobiography, Symonds declared that it
was one of the most painful of his entire life. However, 'Auntie's' grim
sense of duty did not entirely muffle a kindly feeling towards him and he
always retained affection for her. Once, in a Christmas letter to Charlotte,
written long after he had gone away from home, he was moved to add a
note of 'greetings to my dear Auntie. I am thinking tonight of our old

8

Clifton home. I see & feel & even smell the winter there – & am so far away from England. Give her my best love, & tell her that the thought of England & the past is always for me connected with a thousand memories of her. I hope for her many years of happy life.'[4]

The only woman who remotely filled the role of mother was the young German governess, Sophie Girard, who joined the family when John was ten. Gay and affectionate, she became the close companion of John and his younger sister Charlotte the year before he left for Harrow. The fact that he had to be separated from this warmth so soon contributed to his hatred of Harrow, and his letters to Charlotte reveal a wistful envy of the happy times she was having with Fräulein Girard.

All other influences paled beside that of his father. Dr Symonds was not another Victorian father of the Canon Butler* type but he was just as dominant in his own conscientious way. Without the help of a wife, he took the duties of rearing his brood with intense seriousness. He had very pronounced views about education which he expressed in an impressive address on 'Habit', delivered to the Bristol Literary and Philosophical Institution in 1853, and so effectively did he instil in his own children the importance of early ingrained habits in the formation of character and the acquisition of accomplishments that this pattern was continued by his son throughout his life. Long before he came under Jowett's influence, John had learned to venerate work.

Although not demonstrative in his affections, Dr Symonds was extremely attached to his only son and took a close interest in all his activities. The boy frequently accompanied his father in his country calls and John loved these excursions through the rolling Somerset downs. When the carriage stopped for his father to enter some low-roofed farmhouse, the boy would wander about the fields, blissfully picking flowers. On the return journey, John usually fell asleep and it would be dark when he was awakened by a carter's shout and the glare of lamps as the carriage re-entered the town.

Something of the flavour of their relationship comes out in a letter written when he was nine to his father during a seaside holiday, on paper embellished with a misty Grecian scene in sepia ink.

* Father of Samuel Butler and the model for Theobald Pontifex in *The Way of All Flesh*.

June 11th 1849.

My dear Papa

I dislike the bathing rather it gets into my nose and mouth so. Two women Bathed me and Mary Bella likes it very much we are now just going to Teignmouth.

I hope you arrived safely and well will come down soon this week.

Is not this pretty paper I am writing on. My stockings were so wet that I did not wear them coming home Edith and Charlotte loke on at us. And we (Mary Bella and I I mean) will look on tomorrow. Write and tell me if you had a pleasant companions in the train. But now good Bye.

Believe me yours affectionty

J<small>AS</small>

PS excuse bad spelling and writing[5]

The father was delighted with the boy's precocious response to the arts, and determinedly set about encouraging his interest in poetry. Before he was old enough to enter Harrow, John had become familiar with many of the works of the major English writers and could recite long passages of verse. One day, when he and his sisters were riding on the rocking-horse which stood on the landing of the attic, they screamed in unison Scott's lines on the death of Marmion.

> With dying hand, above his head,
> He shook the fragment of his blade,
> And shouted 'Victory! –
> 'Charge, Chester, Charge! On, Stanley, on!'
> Were the last words of Marmion.

'Suddenly I ceased to roar', he recalled; 'a resolve had formed itself unbidden in my mind. "When I grow up, I too will be an author."'[6]

Dr Symonds filled his house with objects of art, probably in no worse taste than that of most cultivated Victorian homes. An atmosphere of comfortable opulence was achieved with Brussels carpets, red and white Bohemian glass, heavy draperies, and chairs upholstered in velvet. There were heavy gilt frames surrounding copies of the Italian masters. There were engravings and photographs and illustrated folios over which the preternaturally serious child spent many contented hours. He took drawing lessons for a time but his father, with the realism of the successful, ordered them to be discontinued when it became apparent that he had no natural talent. The pervasive atmosphere of his home always remained with Symonds and many years later he wrote home from Italy to Graham Dakyns: 'I know the stillness of our Clifton home, the silent pictures, the grave books, the light & flowers & undefinable fragrance of perpetual feminine possession. These things I see – see, do I say – feel, handle, live among.'[7]

Music was also intimately connected with his memories of Clifton. The piano formed part of his sisters' education, but John was not allowed to learn as Dr Symonds considered it an unmanly accomplishment. Symonds always regretted this deprivation because he loved music even as a very small child. He associated the airs from Mozart's Masses which Edith often played with the engravings of Correggio's frescoes which hung on the walls of the drawing-room. His earliest memory of all was of his nurse lifting him in her arms in the nave of Bristol Cathedral to see the choristers singing. 'Some chord awoke in me then', he later recalled, 'which has gone on thrilling through my lifetime, and has been connected with the deepest of my emotional experiences. Cathedrals, college-chapels, "quires and places where they sing," resuscitate that mood of infancy. I know when I am entering a stately and time-honoured English place of prayer, that I shall put this mood upon me like a garment. The voices of choiring men and boys, the sobbing antiphones and lark-like soarings of clear treble notes into the gloom of Gothic arches, the thunder of the labouring diapasons, stir in me old deep-centred innate sentiment.'[8]

Dr Symonds entertained a great deal and believed in encouraging his children to move freely among his guests. Soon after his long fair curls had been cut, John was playing *bouts-rimés* or helping with amateur theatricals, but usually he would sit quietly listening to the talk of the eminent men whom his father attracted to his home – men such as Francis Newman, Lord Aberdare, Principal Shairp of St Andrew's, Henry Hallam, Frederick Maurice, and Sir Montagu Macmurdo. Jenny Lind Goldschmidt was a frequent guest, and family legend had it that she once sang so high a note that a Venetian glass on the mantelpiece was shattered. The small boy watched proudly as his dignified father moved assuredly from group to group. Whenever one of the distinguished gentlemen spoke to him he always believed that they were condescending to him for the sake of his father. Dr Symonds seemed to be everything that a man should be and the boy formed a strong resolve to do something some day that would win his admiration.

Beyond the immediate family group were numerous relatives who made up a shadowy backdrop to Symonds's childhood. One who did impinge directly on his life was his grandfather, Dr John Addington Symonds,* who had retired to Clifton many years before. He was a solemn, melancholy old man, who had transmitted to his son his sober sense of duty. None of his children had ever been allowed to dance or to enter a theatre. A Latin scholar, he filled voluminous diaries with Senecan meditations, and when John was only four, he suggested that he teach him Latin. The boy celebrated his fifth birthday by declining Latin nouns to his father, but the lessons did not always proceed harmoniously The usually docile child rebelled when it came to learning the rules of the potential and subjunctive moods: his grandfather declared that he was obstinate and wilful, and refused to teach him any longer. John was propped up on pillows and ordered to write a letter of apology, and the lessons were resumed without further incident.

His relations with his grandfather were not always confined to study. The old man and the small boy often tramped together across the downs, where Dr Symonds would point out plants to him by their Latin names. John's latent emotional responses to nature were aroused by these outings, and, more immediately, he began to develop an interest in botany. Like the youthful Ruskin, he started to collect and classify specimens, and while it never developed into an absorbing hobby, he always retained a keen interest in wild flowers, insisting on knowing their proper names; and his later descriptions of new specimens he had discovered bear the solicitous and accurate detail of a botanical water-colourist.†

He often stayed with his only other surviving grandparent, his maternal grandmother Sykes, a rigidly devout old lady. He dreaded the nights spent in her large creaking house when he would lie awake listening to her intoning, 'Thus saith the Lord: Woe, woe to the ungodly.' Belief in the effectiveness of ejaculatory prayer was invoked in 1848 when he developed an hysterical fear of cholera which was then raging. He went

* Brother of Sir Compton Mackenzie's grandmother.
† His grandson, Admiral Paul Furse, is a distinguished botanical painter.

about mumbling, 'O God, save me from the cholera', a habit of prayer he kept up for years.

Mrs Sykes was a martinet of a woman whose sour attitude to life had been intensified by an incident connected with her husband's death. Symonds's great-grandfather Sykes was a Navy agent who had prospered during the long wars with Napoleon. At his death he left the business to his sons. When Symonds's grandfather was dying of consumption he directed a deed to be drawn up dissolving the partnership in order to bequeath his share in the joint capital to his wife. The deed only awaited his signature when his brother, Admiral Sykes, appeared, demanding to see him on business of great importance. He would allow no one, not even his brother's wife, to be present in the room. When he left, his brother was dead, the deed was unsigned, and the Navy agency passed to him. Admiral Sykes became a very rich man, and Grandmother Sykes, who was left in circumstances far short of what she expected, nursed a hatred of the brother who had defrauded her of her rights, as well as a strong suspicion that he had been guilty of fratricide. The feud affected John Addington to the extent that he believed he would have inherited £500 a year when the Admiral died if his grandmother had not alienated the Admiral by her resentment.

The embittered old woman comforted herself with her stiff-necked brand of religion. As she was leader of the Plymouth Brethren in Bristol,* the group met regularly at her Cornwallis Terrace home. The sharp-eyed child was frequently forced to sit quietly at her lugubrious tea-parties, and was secretly revolted by the Uriah Heep-like characters who unctuously flattered his grandmother. 'It was a motley crew of preachers and missionaries,' he recalled in his autobiography, 'tradespeople and cripples – the women dressed in rusty bombazine and drab gingham – the men attired in greasy suits, with dingy white neckties – all gifted with a sanctimonious snuffle, all blessed by nature with shiny foreheads and clammy hands, all avid for buttered toast and muffins, all fawning on the well-connected gentlewoman whose wealth, though moderate, possessed considerable attractions, and was freely drawn upon.'[9]

* During the 1830s, Francis Newman, who was teaching classics at Bristol College at the time, was a member of the sect, much to the embarrassment of his brother John Henry. Francis Newman was a close friend of Dr Symonds but Symonds never mentions his name in connection with the Brethren, an association which ceased shortly before his birth.

Sometimes he accompanied his grandmother to services at the Blind Asylum which repelled him with its dank piety and 'turbid middle-class Philistinism'. The aesthetic sensibilities of the impressionable boy were offended by the unlovely character of her religion, which seemed to concentrate on long moaning prayers and to exclude entirely the doctrine of Christian love. The only redeeming feature he could remember about the old woman was her passion for flowers.

There was one family outside his relatives who figured in John's early recollections. These were the Sissons – an aged bed-ridden mother, two brothers, and three sisters, all of whom lived comfortably in the Lower Crescent on the revenue of lands which they owned in Cumberland. They were devoted to Dr Symonds who, strangely enough in the circumstances, let John and his sisters call on them occasionally. The children found an eerie fascination in these visits, since the entire family was tainted with varying degrees of madness which revealed itself in an interesting un-predictability of eccentric behaviour. The mother, a loathsome old crone, had toothless gums that dribbled saliva and it was all John could do not to scream when he was lifted up to the bed to kiss her withered cheek. But he was willing to pay this price in exchange for other pleasures. In contrast to the strict discipline of their own home, the children were given the free run of the house which included the privilege of digging out old dresses and hats and decking themselves in extravagant costumes. John's special joy was a collection of minerals belonging to the epileptic sister, Miss Anne, who displayed them as reverently as if they had been the treasures of Aladdin's Cave. He was as much intrigued by the imaginative stories which she wove around her stalactites and fossils as he was by the beauty of the sparkling crystals. Some years later the Sissons were to play an unexpected part in his life.

Immersed in a predominantly female household, John felt uncomfort-able with boys of his own age and shrank from their rough games. However, it did not follow that he was particularly close to his sisters, although a sympathetic bond with Charlotte developed as they grew older. He would help the girls make toffee but his real interests were not theirs, for they could never understand or enter into the world of his fantasies. His defensive indifference to his sisters is revealed by the fact that he never makes more than a passing reference to them in his autobiography, and yet they taunted him mercilessly about his appearance: his snub nose, his mealy complexion, his wide mouth, all were described in unflattering detail. 'Oh, Johnnie, you look as yellow as a lemon this morning !' 'There you go, with your mouth stretching from ear to ear !' He maintained a proud aloofness to this teasing, but embarrassment about his looks made him retire more than ever into his secret world. When he was ten an amateur artist, a Mr Vigor, painted a portrait of him which was considered a very good likeness. A slight, delicately made boy with a mass of soft brown hair and a sensitive mouth, almost feminine in its chiselled outlines, he momentarily turns gentle, inner-directed eyes on the alien adult world.

His father tended to fuss over him like a mother hen and for as long as he could remember it was impressed upon him that he was delicate. Highly nervous, he suffered from chronic diarrhoea, and was subject to all sorts of hidden fears: horrible things were concealed under the bed and he would lie rigid with fright as a disembodied hand beckoned to him from out of the darkness. For a time he dreamt that a corpse was lying in the bed beside him, and he would rise in terror and flee from the room, still asleep, until his father gave orders that he was to be tied to his bed by one ankle, a procedure which would horrify modern psychologists and justify any number of alarming forecasts. It is significant that his mother was the only dead person he had seen. Danger in all reality broke in once when burglars entered their house in Berkeley Square, and managed to get away with a number of his aunt's and sisters' clothes and trinkets. Sensitive, delicately balanced boy as he was, the incident surprisingly did not so much frighten him as arouse in him an admiration for the men's audacity. They were connected with the world of flesh and blood, feeble shadows of the terrors created by his imagination.

Dr Symonds may have coddled his physical weakness, but the boy's instinct told him that his father wished him to be stronger and more manly than he was. When he was eight, in order to offset the influence of a predominantly feminine household, his father decided to send him off to a small day-school run by the Rev. William Knight. Shy and withdrawn, he failed to make any friends but managed to get into some of the same scrapes as the other boys. On one occasion when he was about ten he sold his Latin grammar to a schoolfellow for sixpence. When asked at home where he had lost it, he replied that he did not know; but, stung by conscience, was finally driven to go and confess to his father, whereupon he received a long solemn lecture on the virtue of truthfulness, an intrinsic part of his father's uncompromising moral code.

At his first school he showed no early promise of intellectual ability. His tutor, who was reputed to be a fine scholar, had little understanding of boys. He did nothing to stimulate John, or to overcome his difficulty in mastering arithmetic. A more imaginative teacher, Symonds later believed, might have drawn the obvious conclusions from the boy's easy grasp of geometry, and have approached sums by means of visual symbols instead of the lifeless abstractions his particular temperament resisted. Mr Knight also failed to direct his interest in general reading, although this shortcoming was more than compensated by his father's enthusiasm. The only debt Symonds felt he owed his tutor was Mr Knight's recognition of his excited response to classical literature. Observing that the boy's imagination was aroused by the description of Elysium in the *Aeneid*, he lent him Warburton's *Divine Legation of Moses* which opened 'dim and shadowy vistas for my dreaming thoughts'.[10]

Apart from the predominant role of Dr Symonds, none of the people in John's childhood exerted more than a superficial influence on him. Moving among them, he grazed affectionately against some of them, but by and large he remained dreamily aloof. He had a passionate attachment to his home, but home meant not the family within the house so much as the actual buildings and the grounds surrounding it. The home which he always remembered so lovingly was not 7 Berkeley Square, where he lived until he was eleven. Although this was a solid, handsome house in its way, his memories of it conjured up little except contraction and dreariness, relieved only by the annual miracle of the silvery blossoming of a cherry-tree in the dusty little garden. The home which aroused such passionate devotion in him was Clifton Hill House where Dr Symonds moved his family in June of 1851. Symonds always declared that the period between that memorable June day and May 1854, when he left for Harrow, was the happiest of his entire life.

Many pages of his autobiography are filled with a loving description of Clifton Hill House, which is now used as a hostel for women students of Bristol University. Built in 1747 by a wealthy Bristol merchant, Paul

Fisher, at a time when Clifton was still a country village, it stood high above the great town of Bristol, then second only to London in importance. Paul Fisher had chosen a noble site on which to build his mansion; from its windows he could look down beyond a thickly-wooded hill to the streets and squares of the red-roofed town, interlaced by numerous waterways filled with a myriad of masts among which the spires of St Mary Redcliffe, St Nicholas and St Stephen were almost indistinguishable. The Symonds family could gaze down on much the same vista, for the tall masts still wavered in the hazy sunlight, and from the eastern windows they could enjoy the green hills rolling between Lansdowne and Bath. The Industrial Revolution had only begun to make its encroachments in 1851, and mean little houses had not yet crept up the hill; the smooth Bath stone was still undarkened by the grime of belching chimneys, and the air was clear and fresh. Indeed, there was one distinct improvement since Paul Fisher's day: the trees he had planted in his pleasaunce had grown to noble proportions and to a boy of eleven seemed to touch the sky. 'On that eventful day', Symonds recalled nearly forty years later, 'I entered the solemn front door, traversed the echoing hall, vaulted and floored with solid stone, and emerged upon the garden at the farther end. An Italian double flight of balustraded steps, largely designed, gives access to the gravelled terrace which separates the house from the lawn. For us it was like passing from the prose of fact into the poetry of fairyland.'[11]

John shared his grandmother's pleasure in flowers, a love which could be satisfied in this most enchanting of gardens. Among its many delights were two ponds; in the centre of one stood a fountain shaped like a classical urn, in the other a cupid blew a conch from its perch upon a dolphin. The gardener would amuse the children by making the water rise until it spattered in a myriad of tiny jets on the floating lily-pads to disturb the serenity of the goldfish and drowsy dragonflies. He had happy memories, too, of a kitchen-garden rich in strawberries and currant-bushes, apricots, plums, and peaches. There was also a stable in which his father kept six horses and where for the first time John had a pony of his own. Beyond the garden were the downs which in those days were a wilderness waiting to be explored by a small boy. The only real game he shared with his male cousins was played on the downs where they would attack and defend fortresses, and then fling themselves breathless on a ledge high above the Avon.

Within Clifton Hill House the rooms were wonderfully large and airy after the dark cramped interior of the house in Berkeley Square. The attic held the greatest attraction of all for John and his sisters. It was filled with numerous recesses and from the narrow windows of some of these they could clamber out upon the sloping roof where they had a magnificent view of the town below and, beyond it, hills, woods, trees, and rivers – an aerial vista such as Symonds's friend, Robert Louis Stevenson, later described in 'The Swing'.

These were the memories Symonds recalled when he described his childhood as largely a happy one. In later years the memory of his home invoked in him a mood of *sehnsucht*, and he believed that more than any other influence Clifton Hill House stimulated and enlarged his latent aesthetic responses, which were unusually intense for a boy of his age.

As a child the story which made the deepest impression upon him was Hans Christian Andersen's 'Ugly Duckling'. The empathy he felt for the bird was duplicated in later life in his close identification with those artists with whom he shared a profound bond of sympathy. 'I sympathised passionately with the poor bird swimming round and round the duck-puddle. I cried convulsively when he flew away to join his beautiful wide-winged white brethren of the windy journeys and the lonely meads. Thousands of children have undoubtedly done the same; for it is a note of childhood, in souls destined for expansion, to feel solitary and debarred from privileges due to them.'[12]

Often ill, and left to amuse himself as he lay in bed, he was given the opportunity to develop his imagination, and a tendency towards introspection was intensified. The large window in his bedroom provided the opening to his favourite world. Long after the rest of the household was asleep, he would crouch by his window, absorbed in the patterns of the clouds scudding across the night sky. He watched the changing seasons, lightning and thunderstorms, even a comet once, 'a thin rod of amber white, drowned in the saffron of the sunset'.[13] Sometimes he would wake to watch the dawn and one remained memorable for its connection with his love of flowers. The previous evening he and his sisters had picked autumn crocuses and he had placed them in a bowl outside his bedroom door. When he awoke, his first thought was to run and look at his treasure. The memory was still fresh forty years later: 'a broad, red ray of light fell full upon their lilac chalices, intensifying and translating into glowing amethyst each petal'.[14] In 1887, after having lived in Switzerland for many years, he wrote to his daughter: 'At Davos I sometimes yearn for what I always had at Clifton – the sun rising above a mighty city, flooding wood & pasture & sea-going river, & all the many works of men – the sun setting in glory beyond that strip of sea & low Welsh hills, with the wonderful tenderness of pure yellow spaces & tremulous stars. In a sonnet I printed about the pines at Davos* I condoled with them for never in all their lives of 300 years having seen a sunrise or a sunset. I don't suppose anybody understands what I mean.'[15]

His fantasy world was fed by his reading and by half-understood encounters in the external world. The first poem to stir him deeply was *Venus and Adonis*, which he read before he was ten years old, and he later recalled that it gave 'form, ideality, and beauty to my visions'.[16] In his daydreams he took the part of Venus, and in later years he believed that he had reacted to the poem in the way Shakespeare meant it to be understood. Walking back and forth to school, he would amuse himself by composing a long poem centred about the tale of Apollo's sojourn among mortals in the guise of King Admetus' herdsman. He wondered why the emperors in some of the stories he read kept boys as well as girls in their seraglios, and was puzzled about precisely what it was that those male gods did with the boys they loved. He also found a print of the Praxitelean Cupid which he would gaze at adoringly while his father read poetry aloud in the evenings to the assembled family. Dr Symonds was disturbed by this fixation and suggested that some other statue such as a nymph or Hebe might be more suitable.

Early sexual experiences were sometimes real, sometimes imaginary, and one infused and heightened the other. Among the older boys being prepared by Mr Knight for the university was a big lad who had been sent home from Harrow for some unspecified reason. He would often take John on his knee and one day he suddenly kissed him. John jumped off in agitation, resentment mingling with excited stirrings of unknown danger. The older boy laughed but made no further overtures. 'Wait until

* 'In the Fir Wood', *Vagabunduli Libellus* (Kegan Paul, Trench, and Co., 1884), p. 99.

you go to Harrow', he warned him, 'then you will be some boy's ——.'
But he left the word unsaid, probably out of respect for the child's
innocence.

John's earliest realization that there was some difference between the
sexes was the result of a coarse remark by a nurse when he was out walking
with his sisters. She suddenly told him jeeringly that little boys' penises fell
off when they grew up. So vividly did the experience impress itself
upon his memory that everything connected with the event became
inseparably related, just as all the details surrounding the boy in the
Venetian lagoon were fused many years later: Bristol, its tall spires shining
in the hazy sunlight, and the vulgar jest were always to be associated in
his mind. Not long after this incident he was intrigued by giggling and
whispered conclaves among the maids. He gathered that a man had been
exposing himself in the garden and he was bewildered about why the
incident excited everyone in such a strange way. There was also a rough
servant girl who used to exhibit herself to him and make him touch her,
but his only reaction was a slight distaste. However, when he found a
cousin preparing to have intercourse with her, he was shaken with
disgust, and it is tempting to speculate whether this traumatic experience
could have been one of the contributing factors to his later sexual
patterns. He had further introductions to sex through various male
cousins. Between the ages of eight and eleven he sometimes slept with
one, each holding the other intimately. In bed with another cousin, he
was introduced to *fellatio*. He was not very popular among his more
robust cousins, and as punishment for some imagined offence, they sat
exposing themselves while they forced him to practise *fellatio* on each in
turn.

In his Memoirs he recalls that this latter experience contributed to a
recurrent reverie he had for many years before falling asleep. He half-
dreamt that he was crouched on the floor in the centre of a circle of
robust men, whom he associated with the rough sailors he had seen on the
streets of Bristol. They forced him to serve their wishes, and contact
with their bodies gave him the keenest delight. No woman ever figured
in any of these fantasies. His etherialized erotic daydreams were so
absorbing that they reduced to insignificance any actual experiments he
might make with sex. He had no friends before he went to Harrow and

he later attributed the intensity of this dream-world to the fact that he had no congenial companions of his own age.

Dream-like states, not necessarily sexual, would at times become so overpowering that he sank into a trance, a condition which half-frightened, half-fascinated him. These experiences were marked by a progressive obliteration of space, time, sensation, and all the multitudinous factors which connect one with external reality, culminating in a complete withdrawal from everything except his inner consciousness, the John-ness of John. Gradually he would return to awareness of the world around him, first by a recovery of the power of touch, followed by the rapid influx of familiar sensations.

At eleven, when he was sent off to Harrow to face the outside world, he could not have been less prepared for its brutal impact upon him. Nervous, vulnerable, withdrawn, blanketed by the soft atmosphere of a female household, inspired by the lofty example of a noble father, he was to be as lonely and unhappy as his poor ugly duckling.

CHAPTER II

Harrow

Harrow was a fine, manly place. It was a little world
in itself, and boys were the arbiters of their happiness or
unhappiness in it. A bold, bright boy was sure to be a
favourite, and even a studious retiring boy was never
unkindly treated; but woe betide the sneak and the snob.

Sir William Gregory, *An Autobiography*,
John Murray, 1894, p. 36

In May 1854 'Auntie' and big sister Edith, with a frightened little boy
huddled between them, made the long trip from Bristol to Harrow. When
they set him down at the end of the lane leading to his tutor's house and
the coach started back for London, John ran after it, sobbing hysteric-
ally. Miss Sykes climbed out and managed to quieten him a little. Then
the coach was gone and there was nothing left but to confront this hostile
new world. 'I felt that my heart would break', Symonds recalled more
than thirty years later, 'as I scrunched the muddy gravel, beneath the
boughs of budding trees. . . . But I said to my heart; "I have to be made
a man here."'[1]

Symonds managed to escape the 'ignominy' Trollope suffered at
Harrow,[2] but he hated the school just as passionately. The detachment
into which he had often withdrawn even at home in Clifton became a
habitual defence against his uncongenial surroundings. He was convinced
that he was destined for great things and that some day his real worth
would be revealed to this hostile alien world, whose members seemed
superior to him in every way. His aesthetic awareness set him apart from
his fellows, but he could not match them in stamina, experience, or self-
assertion. He loathed the rough physical contact of games, while the
challenge of competition failed to stir any excitement in him. He could not

throw a ball straight nor even – most humiliating of all – learn to whistle; but he was not an effeminate boy and could run swiftly and jump as high as his chin. Although he was far from robust, his failure in games seems to have been less the result of physical weakness than a reluctance to emerge from his inner world.

Nevertheless, from the outset he viewed Harrow as a place where he must be toughened for manhood. During the first year he often cried himself to sleep, but he knew what his father expected of him and his misery seldom crept into the letters which he wrote to his family every Sunday; yet his homesickness was revealed by his constant loving references to Clifton. 'I should so delight to be at home now', he writes in June 1857, 'and see all the leaves and flowers out. We are suffering great cold here and the poor hawthorns are only just showing some scanty flowers. I wish that you could manage to plant some creeper – Canariensis for instance – on those three little balconies. If sown now in boxes they might be trained all over the iron part and look very pretty.'[3] On another occasion he asked them to send him some leaves from the copper beech-tree in the garden in exchange for some boughs from Byron's elm: 'There is not a single copper beech tree in Harrow.'[4] He was aesthetically starved. In contrast to the downs and woods of Clifton, the heavy clay soil and pastoral landscape of Middlesex oppressed him. He particularly disliked the summer term with 'its all-pervading "buzziness" of heat'. The school itself was ugly and constricting. 'Sordid details, inseparable from a boy's school life in a cheaply built modern house, revolted my taste – the bare and dirty roughcast corridors, the ill-drained latrines, the stuffy studies with wired windows, the cheerless refectory. But these things, I reflected, were only part of life's open-road, along which one had to trudge for one's affairs. . . .'[5]

Scholastically he was so far in advance of those of his own age that he was released from fagging. He later believed this to be unfortunate because fagging would have brought him into closer contact with the other boys. A great deal of his leisure time was spent in writing two long poems which he called 'The Exile' and 'The Toady Tree'. 'I suppose you will not show me *your* "Exile"', he accused Charlotte, 'for fear I should borrow some of your choicest ideas.'[6] One day he arrived back in his room to find the bag containing his poems missing. 'Horror of all horrors! Currey has been up here and seized my most sacred bag of poetry and in it the manuscript of "Toady Tree". It will be read all over the house and then even now I hear it going on underneath. They have just now come to "Exile", and are shrieking over it, I hear, "tissued wet of hazy sky! ! !" "Oh, I am blowed!" roars of laughter, "mumble, mumble" (rather indistinct). "Well, I never heard anything better", "I shall die of laughter." I have often read in books of poets having their poems cut up, but think that none ever underwent a severer test than mine, or any temper a greater trial. To be upon a mental gridiron with the fire immediately below you! to hear your poems and the miseries of your hero read out pompously amid *roars, shrieks, howls*, of laughter. If I was not of the most philosophical temper I should descend. They have now got to the Rhine. Not quite so noisy. Ah! "Yoick, yoick!" "What's this? Oh, I see: George has just tumbled into the Rhine. That's all! I was afraid that it might have been the 'Exile's Apotheosis'." Well, if they are returned I will burn them tragically before the critic's eye (having first reserved a fair copy of the two great poems).'[7]

Even his distaste for games was treated humorously in a letter to Charlotte describing his first experience of football: 'I found out the meaning of certain terms I had not hitherto quite appreciated, such as that of a "squash". A squash is a large collection of boys, about twenty, with the football in the midst of them. They are all kicking it and each other in their endeavours to extricate the ball, and woe to the unlucky wight who falls. He is instantly trampled on by every one. I, to-day, when in a squash, was suddenly propelled by one of the heaviest boys in the school. I rushed forward and stood in a semi-upright position on another boy, whose thigh I was grinding and pounding with my heavy boots, until the ball was hurled out, and then every one came on the ground together. On the whole, there is not so much real danger as I expected, except from great boys dashing their weight against you and using you as a battering-ram or wedge for entering the crushes. It is thus, I imagine, that most accidents occur. I think it a very healthy exercise in fine autumn weather like this, but doubt its good in colder and damper days.'[8]

His sense of inner superiority inevitably made him something of a prig. 'I was so amused yesterday', he told his family, 'with hearing the answers of some of the Sixth Form to our History Paper. They ought really to be ashamed of themselves, for one boy had an idea that "The Tempest" was a political conspiracy and criticized it accordingly. Another declared that Rubens was a celebrated philosopher and learned savant. Another that Galileo was a remarkable divine – very much opposed to the Inquisition's idea of the same man.'[9]

However much the inner core might harden, his frail body was attacked by an increasing variety of colds, boils, and styes, for which his father prescribed liberal doses of nerve tonics, quinine, and strychnine. The boy developed such an acute stammer that the Headmaster, Dr. Vaughan, let him off reading and construing Greek in class, an embarrassment so intense that he dreamed of it years later. An even greater humiliation occurred at a memorable rehearsal for Speech Day in which he was to recite Raleigh's 'Lie'. At the end of the first stanza his mind went blank, and after a couple of minutes of uncomfortable silence, he had to sit down.

At Harrow he did not have the easy gift of making friends effortlessly among his more ebullient schoolmates. Yet there was an air of integrity about him which won the respect of the other boys. Once when he hotly denied the mathematics master's accusation that he had been cribbing, and was given five hundred lines, the other boys shouted, 'Shame!' 'Symonds cannot crib!' In November 1857, although he and his friend Alfred Pretor were a year younger than the Sixth Formers, they were allowed to compete for the Headmaster's Scholarship. When the results were read out, it appeared that Symonds had achieved an easy first, and Pretor had followed in third place.

Harrow   December 5 1857

My dearest Papa

You must prepare yourself for a great disappointment. The Scholarship Examination Lists have been read out. We were all summoned at 5 o'clock to the School Yard where after waiting a short time the Examiner & Dr. V & Westcott appeared on the top of the steps. It was dark & a light having been thrown on the fatal page (imagine my suspense) he cleared his throat & began 'First Class, Symonds, Edwardes, Pretor, etc.' Was not it a pleasant disappointment? I am Head of the School by this Examination & Scholar at the Head Master's gift.[10]

Dr Symonds would not have been quite so pleased if he had been informed of the subsequent events. After the masters had disappeared, the

Head of the School, Henry Yates Thompson, furious because he had lost out to younger boys, grabbed Symonds and Pretor by their collars, and kicking and pushing them, hurled them down the steep steps of the Great School, a scene witnessed by a large crowd of boys. Picking himself up with immense dignity, Symonds announced to Pretor that they were going at once to report the incident to the Headmaster. Pretor protested, but Symonds dragged him along and two bedraggled boys in battered hats and dusty swallow-tail coats suddenly appeared before the startled Dr Vaughan, demanding redress. Symonds declared that unless he received a public apology he would ask his father to withdraw him from the school and that the matter would be made public. His righteous indignation must have impressed Vaughan because the following day Thompson read out an apology before the Sixth Form. Symonds apparently won Thompson's respect as well, because when the older boy left Harrow, he presented Symonds with a handsome edition of the *Ballad of Lenore*.*

Symonds's conduct evinced a remarkable maturity and it is possible that his confidence was based on his knowledge that Dr Vaughan would wish to avoid any further scandal over the monitorial system. Vaughan, who had been one of Dr Arnold's favourite pupils at Rugby, came to Harrow in 1844, determined to mould the school into a counterpart of Rugby. He found a form of the monitorial system already in existence at Harrow but it was his intention to make it more effective, modelling it on the paternal despotism he had known. Like Arnold, he made a special point of forming a close relationship with the Sixth Form in order to imbue these older boys with his own ideals of Christian dedication and service. The monitors in turn were responsible for the conduct of the school by the enforcement of discipline based on these ideals. Unfortunately, there was often a wide discrepancy between lofty ideals and actual practice. When, in 1853, a monitor named Platt gave a younger boy, Stewart, thirty-one cuts with a cane, the boy was so severely injured that he had to have medical treatment, and was subsequently removed from the school. Lord Palmerston, a former Harrovian, was gravely disturbed when *The Times* used the incident for an attack on the monitorial

* Thompson in later life became proprietor of *The Pall Mall Gazette*. He owned a famous collection of illuminated manuscripts whose high quality was maintained by sedulously discarding one item to make way for another more valuable, the entire collection being limited to one hundred specimens. He remembered his old school by donating an art building to Harrow.

system. 'We must now pronounce, without a moment's hesitation', they declared, 'that the monitorial system, as illustrated in the case before us, is entirely indefensible.'[11] Vaughan's reaction was to divest the monitor of his office; yet, at the same time, he dramatically emphasized his faith in the system by increasing the number of monitors from ten to fifteen. He also wrote a public letter to Lord Palmerston in which he defended the monitorial system against an alternative of organized espionage. He maintained that 'faults of turbulence, rudeness, offensive language, annoyance of others, petty oppression, and tyranny' which reflected on the 'gentlemanlike tone of the Houses and of the School' could best be dealt with by the boys themselves. He went on to contend that fagging was a necessary part of the system, since it served as 'a memento of monitorial authority' and was important in creating a system of organized rank best calculated to produce the 'character of an English Christian gentleman'.[12]

In his autobiography, Symonds is highly critical of the system he observed at Harrow. While never a fag himself, he had fags responsible to him and, with his gentle manner, he had difficulty in maintaining discipline. 'I have been having a little trouble with the fags lately,' he wrote home. 'When I called for the night fag the other evening three little boys imitated me, & as this is a most heinous offence I had them sent to the Head of the House who flogged two, & made one go on for four days extra fagging. I should myself think this too severe, but he said it was the proper thing & that I must support my authority and dignity.'[13]

When he became Head of his House – Monkey's – he was very resentful because the housemaster, Rendell, never consulted him and seemed completely indifferent to the management of the House. With one exception, Symonds was contemptuous of most of the masters. His form masters – Cober Adams, Rendell, Ben Drury, Harris, and the Headmaster himself, Dr C. J. Vaughan, failed to encourage or stimulate him in any way. Although he won the Headmaster's Prize and the Botfield Gold Medal for Modern Languages, he regarded his achievement as mediocre and what success he had he attributed to perseverance rather than to competent instruction. None of his teachers seem to have been impressed by him particularly and one of his form masters, Rendell, noted in his report that the boy was 'deficient in vigour both of body and mind'.

Symonds's feelings for Dr Vaughan were mixed from the beginning. Not long after he arrived at Harrow, his turn came to have dinner with the Headmaster and his wife. 'I am just back from dining with Dr V.,' he wrote to his family. 'I enjoyed it excessively, he was so kind and nice. Pretor and Currey, two of my friends, were there & Arkwright, a great acquaintance scarcely a friend, and a Mrs Stanley, sister-in-law to Mrs. Vaughan. I sat at dinner on Dr V's left hand & had a long talk with him. He rather discomforted me by exclaiming as he carved me some beef: "We all of us know how much Symonds wants beef & such things to fatten him. He has a great deal to bear." Why does everybody think I have so much to bear & am so weak?'[14] Always quick to note the deficiencies of adults, he soon perceived that Vaughan's scholarship was thin; moreover, he found him 'somewhat of a hypocrite but a most amusing one'.[14] 'The way in which everything he talks about he makes out to be the most important in the world: how *your* affairs are the most interesting he has ever engaged himself in: how *your* complaints deserve attention before anyone else's amuses me excessively.'[15]

The one outstanding figure whom he almost venerated was the Rev. John Smith, a man regarded by generations of Harrow boys as almost a saint.* Gentle and kindly, he had the faculty of quietly drawing out the shyest boy. He encouraged Symonds's passionate response to poetry, and they often took long walks in the morning or early evening, repeating alternate passages from Shelley, Keats, or Tennyson. 'I think it will be such a nice thing', Symonds told Charlotte, 'when I grow up and have not perhaps so much time as I have now to know some pieces of poetry. . . .'[16] Usually their destination was Smith's mother's home in Pinner, where the hospitable old lady would ply them with heaped bowls of strawberries, jam, tea, and thick country cream. It may have been in the Smiths' home that Symonds acquired his lifelong addiction to cream.

In later years Symonds recalled the academic level of Harrow with contempt. His views tallied with those of Augustus Hare who asserted, 'I may truly say that I never learnt anything at Harrow, and had little chance of learning anything.'[17] Symonds was bitter because he was sent

---

* According to J. G. Cotton Minchin, the most enthusiastic of Harrow's historians, 'Mr John Smith deserved canonisation as much as if his credentials had received the imprimatur of His Holiness the Pope' (*Old Harrow Days*, Methuen and Co., 1898, p. 32).

out into the world without even the rudiments of mathematics and no physical science whatsoever – deficiencies he later tried to remedy for himself. Although he spent long hours on Greek and Latin, he was given little real grounding in their fundamentals and was plucked for Smalls at Oxford in 1859. One would be hard put to it, he claimed, to find five men of eminence who came out of Harrow in the years 1854-8, despite the fact that the boys represented a cross-section of the aristocracy, the landed gentry, and the professional and mercantile classes. The failure lay in the system. In theory athletics were supposed to balance academics, but in actual fact games degenerated into barbarity and lessons were a mechanical routine which could easily be evaded. According to Symonds's view of Harrow, the whole place was rotten to the core: the boys were degraded and the masters ineffectual because there was no guiding spirit to infuse the school with moral energy. All he owed his school, he declared, was the corruption of his moral sense. W. J. Court-hope believed that Symonds was far too hard on Harrow. 'He gained from his school life', he wrote, 'public spirit, good social traditions, mental discipline. . . . Harrow, besides, did much more for Symonds than he is ready to allow, by awakening his intellectual qualities.'[18] Symonds's 'intellectual qualities' were awakened long before he went to Harrow. But proof that his feelings towards his old school were not altogether antagonistic is given in a letter to Gustavus Bosanquet, written shortly after he had gone up to Oxford: '. . . there is no regret in my mind at present but there is a feeling of want and dissatisfaction, a feeling that I might have been nobler and better if I had used the place more lovingly and reasonably. The weakness of my body and indolence of my intellect are both of them legacies of long summer days and hopeless winter evenings spent in despondency at Harrow.'[19] In June 1862, just before taking his degree, he returned to Harrow for a brief visit with Montagu Butler, and again wrote to Bosanquet: 'I cannot tell you how strange it seems to be sitting here in a room looking out upon the street and up to the school gates, watching the boys saunter by dressed as they used to be for Sunday in their white waistcoats and tidy black coats. I am so hugely different. There was never much of the Harrovian in me, but what I had of the ἦδος* of the place seems now obliterated.'[20]

* Surely this is a mis-transcription of ἦθος (Spirit) ?

Symonds did make a few friends at Harrow. The closest of these was Gustavus Bosanquet, a chubby boy with a round face at variance with a long sharp nose. He did not match Symonds intellectually but he gave him a devoted affection, and could make him laugh at incidents which might otherwise have plunged him into the depths of gloom. More than any other friend of his childhood, Gustavus helped him to be a boy. In Clifton, meeting few boys of his own age, his intellectual precocity had been developed at the expense of a normal childhood. With Gustavus he delighted in playing practical jokes, cooking sausages, and calling each other by ridiculous nicknames. Both boys became friendly with another lad, Randall Vickers, not through any pull of personality, but because he aroused their curiosity in Ritualism, a movement in the school not discouraged by Dr Vaughan, who nursed High Church leanings. Half laughing both at Vickers and at themselves, they followed him 'to compline, donned surplices and tossed censers, arrayed altars in our studies, spent spare cash on bits of execrable painted glass to dull our dingy windows, and illuminated crucifixes with gold dust and vermilion'.[21]

In June 1857, Symonds, Bosanquet, and Vickers, were confirmed with three other boys, Alfred Pretor, Charles Dalrymple, and Robert Jamieson. Here again, propinquity created the only bond between them. Jamieson was a powerful raw youth from Glasgow; Dalrymple a well-born, fastidious Scot; and Pretor, the best scholar of the three, was vain and frivolous. Dr Symonds wanted John to be confirmed in Bristol but had been persuaded by Dr Vaughan who 'had found a deeper impression made upon a boy in confirmation here than at home'.[22] Dr Vaughan conducted the preparations for confirmation himself, and the boys were deeply moved by his spiritual exhortations, although Bosanquet was the only one who went on to take holy orders. The intense religious instruction influenced Symonds to become even more devout in his observances, although he later realized that his emotional and aesthetic sensibilities had been inflamed rather than any real spirit of devotion.

Symonds's memories of Harrow present a startling contrast to Vaughan's ambitions for the school. His years at Rugby had left an indelible mark on him and he longed to bring to Harrow the atmosphere of Godliness which Dr Arnold had infused into Rugby. Vaughan had been in the Sixth Form in 1833-4 with two other famous Arnoldians,

W. C. Lake and Arthur Stanley; A. H. Clough had been a year behind him. Dr Arnold followed Vaughan's career with affectionate interest and towards the end of his Cambridge days had written to him from Rugby: 'I am anxious to know your final decision as to profession; but I do not like to influence you. Whatever be your choice, it does not much matter, if you follow steadily our great common profession, Christ's service.'[23] In 1838 Vaughan was bracketed Senior Classic with Lord Lyttelton and was made a Fellow of Trinity College. For a brief period he was vicar of St Martin's in Leicester. On Dr Arnold's death he applied for the Head-mastership of Rugby but lost to Tait by the vote of only one trustee who felt nervous about entrusting the school to a man of twenty-five. How-ever, the following year he succeeded Dr Christopher Wordsworth at Harrow, and it was generally conceded that the knowledge of Dr Arnold's high opinion helped to get him appointed. He was so highly regarded that to a testimonial on his behalf the Dean of Peterborough added a warning not to throw himself away on Harrow.

According to Sir Charles Dalrymple, 'Vaughan was, in every sense, the restorer of Harrow. He re-created the school, and he ranks among the great headmasters of the century.'*[24] On his appointment to Harrow in 1844 there were only sixty boys; but by the time he retired in 1859, the numbers had swollen to four hundred and sixty-nine. When he came to the school, Harrow boys were notorious for drunkenness and disorderly behaviour. One of his first actions was to summon the boys to the Speech Room where he sternly denounced drink as the curse of the school and declared that he was planning to take every measure to ban it, including expulsion of any offender. After Dr Vaughan's death, at a meeting held to promote a memorial to him, Lord John Hamilton said that 'his soft, quiet manner was the screen to a reservoir of great reserve power; his soft voice gave expression to the ideas of an inflexible will; and his genial, cultured utterances were the expressions of a saintly man, slow to wrath, but who, if he found himself face to face with wrongdoing, was fearless in his denunciation and punishment.'[25] The portrait of him by Richmond which hangs in the library at Harrow is that of a strikingly handsome man, of graceful bearing, with eyes frank yet strangely veiled. How

---

* The *D.N.B.* echoes this belief: 'During the last dozen years of his rule it is probable that no school stood higher than Harrow.'

different it is from Symonds's critical schoolboy observation: 'Such a funny small man he is! A little shorter than I am but with such a big head & enormous nose of a brazen colour, like an antique knocker. . . .'[26] In later years Vaughan said of those with whom he had to deal at Harrow that 'he had found the boys always fair, the Masters sometimes, the parents never, and as for widows he had sometimes been tempted to reconsider his objections to suttee'.[27] His imperturbability was unshakeable: on one occasion he calmly continued to read prayers as a boy writhed in an epileptic fit on the floor in front of him. His main object at Harrow seems to have been to deepen its spiritual life. He enlarged the chapel, of whose innumerable services Symonds wrote to his family, 'Do you not think 4 services, 3 sermons, and 1 school are too much in this hot weather?'[28] Vaughan's sermons were famous and Sir Charles Bruce, the Governor of Mauritius, declared that forty years later he still trembled at the memory of a sermon preached by the Headmaster on the text 'Cast forth that evil person from among you.'[29]

Such is the picture which tradition ascribes to Harrow under Dr Vaughan. In his Memoirs Symonds gives a very different description of conditions there. The hypersensitive boy who had been over-protected by an indulgent family was not only stifled by its intellectual confinement and repelled by its ugliness but stunned by its sexual immorality as well. The combination of brutality and lust made him fear that he had stumbled into the land of the Yahoos. The etherialized erotic daydreams in which he had indulged in Clifton seemed to belong to another world. It was the common practice for every good-looking boy to be addressed by a female name; he was regarded either as public property or as the 'bitch' of an older boy. After a predominantly feminine household, the talk seemed to Symonds incredibly obscene, and he could not help seeing innumerable scenes of crude carnality. One particularly horrific memory was associated with a flabby-cheeked, sensual-mouthed boy, whose lovers, for some reason unknown to Symonds, had turned against him. These older boys, some of them monitors, knocked their victim to the floor, exposed him, and kicked him brutally. From then on, whenever he appeared in any part of the school, they spat at him, cursed him and shied books at him, until he ran away, whimpering with misery. During Symonds's first year several advances were made to him, but when they were consistently rebuffed, he was left alone. He constantly reflected on the degradation he saw around him. The monitors were supposed to be leaders of the school, yet they displayed the most degrading brutality to their unfortunate victims. Was this what the 'real' world was like?

One day a master caught a compromising note passing between two boys. The note was handed to the Headmaster who summoned the entire school to the Speech Room. Without revealing the cause of the occasion, Sir Charles Dalrymple later described the tension of the scene: 'The stillness was phenomenal, and the impression produced by the words, addressed to the school generally, and to the culprit in particular, cannot be exaggerated.'[30] Vaughan read the letter aloud, forbade the use of female names, and ordered flogging and lines for the offenders. When it was all over, with stern solemnity he pushed back his chair and the school filed out in silence.

In his Memoirs, Symonds relates that in January 1858 Alfred Pretor sent him a note informing Symonds that he was having a love affair with Dr Vaughan. Symonds's first reaction was incredulous disbelief, but doubt was completely dispelled when Pretor showed him a number of passionate love-letters the Headmaster had written to him. An intricate complex of emotions followed: horror that he had received the Sacrament from Vaughan while kneeling side by side with Pretor; contempt for Vaughan's lack of taste in being attracted to a boy as frivolous as Pretor; disquiet that such a man should be in supreme command of nearly five hundred boys; and all these reactions were, in turn, engulfed by a profound pity for an eminent man gripped by such a devastating passion.

Symonds was in the habit of taking his essays to the Headmaster's study. Sitting side by side on a sofa which he knew to be the setting of amorous scenes between Vaughan and Pretor, the boy trembled with agitation one day when Vaughan began gently to stroke his thigh, a gesture to which he would have attached no importance before Pretor's revelations. Remembering Dr Vaughan's moving exhortations before Confirmation classes, he began to be deeply perplexed about religion. Until his final year in Harrow, he had resisted all the allurements of the senses he saw around him, largely because he was sickened by their vulgarity. Now he began to make tentative explorations into this dangerous territory. He became infatuated with a handsome boy whose hymn book he stole from chapel, but he never worked up enough courage to speak to him. In his final year he almost succumbed one night to the advances made to him by a boy in his bedroom. The horror once aroused in him by the sexual activities of his schoolfellows was gradually muted into a detached cynicism. He withdrew even deeper into himself and not a hint of the vicious atmosphere or of his discoveries about Dr Vaughan was communicated to his family. The letters during this period continue to be filled with requests for 'inexpressibles' or wails of anguish for a cancelled half-holiday.

In March 1858 he spent a week-end in London in the Regent's Park home of a Mrs Bain. After returning from a comedy at the Haymarket, he retired to his room where he took up Cary's crib of Plato which they were then reading in the Sixth Form. He turned by chance to the 'Phaedrus' and was soon so caught up that he continued to read until he had finished it. He then began the 'Symposium' and the sun was shining on the garden outside his window when he finally closed the book, his eyes heavy but all his senses alert. Here was the expression of his own idealized conception of love, a reassuring proof that there could be a love between men different from the sordid unfeeling lust of his schoolmates. With the onset of puberty he had become increasingly aware that his proclivities tended only towards his own sex, a realization that filled him with guilty uneasiness. He always remembered this night as a turning-point in his life. The cynicism which followed the Vaughan episode was arrested by the beauty of the relationships described by Plato.

At the end of the summer term, when he was only seventeen, a year younger than most of the boys in the Sixth Form, Dr Symonds decided to remove him from Harrow, as he believed that another year at the school might prove even more injurious to his health. Symonds was only too happy to leave the place, and at Balliol, which he entered as a Commoner that autumn, he was able to shake off Harrow associations because Dr Vaughan encouraged most of the boys to go on to Cambridge. Shortly before he left, Symonds wrote to Charlotte: 'I shall go to Oxford as if I had never been here as far as friends go. It is all Dr. V's malign influence which is turned entirely in favour of Cambridge.'[31]

Nevertheless, even at Oxford, he continued to brood about Dr Vaughan. In the summer of 1859 he went on a reading party to Whitby with the Corpus Professor of Latin, John Conington, who had shown a great deal of interest in him. As they were walking along the cliffs together one day, Symonds impulsively blurted out the story which he had previously hinted to him. Conington was horrified. He urged him to return immediately to Clifton and show his father Pretor's letter and the diaries he had kept at Harrow. Symonds realized the wisdom of Conington's advice, yet he was deeply troubled because it meant violating Pretor's confidence. Then, too, he was unhappily aware that he had no right to sit in judgment on Dr Vaughan, particularly when he knew that he shared his inclinations. However, knowing that his father believed such tendencies to be a mark of moral weakness, he was determined to suppress or sublimate them in himself, and he came to the conclusion that such hypocritical behaviour as Vaughan's only encouraged the vice at Harrow and depraved boys who otherwise might have led normal sexual lives. Once he had confided in Conington there was no turning back, and he found a measure of consolation in such rationalizations.

Dr Symonds proved no more difficult to convince than Conington had been. He immediately sent a letter off to Vaughan, intimating that he had proof of his relationship with Pretor and that there would be no public exposure if he resigned at once. Dr Vaughan travelled down to Clifton, inspected Pretor's letter, and admitted that he had no alternative but to agree to Dr Symonds's terms. A few days later he was followed by his wife, Catherine, the sister of his old Rugby friend, Arthur Stanley, a cultured woman who was remembered by many Harrovians for her kindness to the boys. Mrs Vaughan flung herself on her knees before Dr Symonds. She confessed that she knew that her husband was subject to this weakness but begged Dr Symonds to have mercy upon him because it had never interfered with his useful service to the school. Dr Symonds was profoundly moved by the suffering of this unhappy woman, the daughter of the Bishop of Norwich and sister of the then Professor of Ecclesiastical History at Oxford, soon to be made Dean of Westminster. But he was adamant in his decision.

During the late summer, correspondence flowed in and out of Clifton Hill House as to the steps which Dr Vaughan was to take towards his resignation. The Headmaster was represented by his brother-in-law and by Hugh Pearson, afterwards Dean of Windsor, both of whom fully supported Dr Symonds in his decision. Dr Symonds also confided in Professor Conington throughout the negotiations. The affair was already known to a number of people through the babbling of the indiscreet Pretor. However, when the situation threatened to explode, Pretor sent off indignant letters about Symonds's perfidy to Dalrymple and Jamieson. Although Symonds believed that he was right to have confided in his father, he later came to see that he should have informed his friends of what he intended to do. None of the three ever spoke to him again.

On 16 September 1859 Dr Vaughan sent a circular to the parents announcing his intention to retire: 'I have resolved after much deliberation, to take that opportunity of relieving myself from the long pressure of those heavy duties and anxious responsibilities which are inseparable from such an office, even under the most favourable circumstances.'[32] On Sunday evening, 4 December, he preached his final sermon in the school chapel. Its title was 'Yet Once More' and one passage, charged with emotion, seemed to be directed at the Symondses, father and son: 'How am I to say those last words, *Finally, brethren, farewell*? I know not. I would fain postpone them; but until when? . . . How can I sever myself, even in imagination, from this place? What will it be when it has been done? Three months ago it seemed to be possible: the clearest and most decisive judgment dictated it: but to-day it is hard to execute. . . . Some of you lately left us: they can tell something, but not all, of what presses upon me to-day. They had scarcely been mixed up as I have been with the permanent life of this place. They had another home all the time. Their gladdest associations were with that other home all the time: and when they left this place, they had life all before them. Some are going now, with me: yet even they can know but a portion of my parting. . . .'[33] After the service Vaughan stood on the steps of the chapel to shake hands with every boy. Years later Percy Thornton wrote: 'Those present . . . can never forget the scene. Each youth who grasped the extended hand and heard the half-suppressed farewell passed into the great world a willing witness of the wisdom that raised Harrow out of misfortune and guided her truly in prosperity.'[34] Two nights later a large group of Harrow men feasted Dr Vaughan at a farewell banquet in London at the Freemasons' Tavern. The Headmaster made a moving speech in which he declared that he believed a man had outlived his usefulness after fifteen years of service. His self-sacrifice was enthusiastically applauded and his favourite ex-pupil, Montagu Butler, succeeded him at only twenty-six years of age. 'I feel now', Vaughan wrote to Mrs Butler, 'that I shall live here over again in my beloved successor – the only person whom I could have borne to think of in my vacant study, or in charge of my beloved Sixth Form.'[35]

After leaving Harrow, Dr Vaughan became vicar of Doncaster. One of Dr Symonds's stipulations had been that he was never again to accept any important ecclesiastical post, an injunction supported by Stanley and Pearson. Perhaps Vaughan hoped that Dr Symonds would not implement his threat. In any event, in 1863 he accepted Lord Palmerston's offer of the Bishopric of Rochester. According to Symonds's account, he was ambitious for a seat in the House of Lords. As soon as Dr Symonds heard the news, he sent off a telegram warning Vaughan of public exposure of the scandal unless he resigned immediately. Within a week of his acceptance, Vaughan advised Lord Palmerston that, on further consideration, he felt it incumbent to withdraw. Two resignations within four years sent tongues buzzing that there was something sinister afoot. Pearson later told Symonds that at the time, when he was vicar of Sonning-on-Thames, Bishop Samuel Wilberforce visited him and warned him that he would become his enemy if he did not reveal the truth to him. Pearson refused, but not long afterwards Wilberforce returned to tell him triumphantly that a lady sitting next to him at a dinner-party had divulged the whole story! At Doncaster, Vaughan's chief interest lay in the preparation of young men for ordination. In 1869 he became Master of the Temple and in 1879 he was appointed Dean of Llandaff (by this time Dr Symonds had been dead for eight years), and until his death in 1897 he divided his time between the two posts. After Stanley's death, the Queen offered him the Deanery of Westminster, but this honour he declined.[36] Shortly before his death a letter from him was read out at a Harrow dinner in which he expressed his undying love for the school and his regret that he had not been kind enough to the boys. When he was dying, he left explicit instructions that all his papers were to be destroyed and that no life of him was ever to be written.

Symonds avoided the embarrassment of a meeting with Vaughan by never returning to Harrow for such public occasions as Speech Days. For some time Stanley extended invitations to him to visit him in his rooms at Christ Church and later to the deanery at Westminster. Although he felt uncomfortable with Stanley, he always accepted these invitations; for Dr Symonds wanted his son's friendship with Stanley to be public knowledge in case the scandal ever broke. While a number of people were aware of the Pretor-Vaughan affair through Pretor's thoughtless boasting and because of the sizeable group involved in the Symonds negotiations, the secret never became public property, largely through the determined efforts that were made to suppress it. R. E. Prothero's collection of Dean Stanley's correspondence* gives no letters between him and Vaughan during the fateful period; which suggests that none except those concerned with Vaughan's resignation were available to fill the gap. Horatio Brown, Symonds's literary executor, omits the entire episode in the Memoirs from his biography, and passes over the period with the terse comment: 'The autobiography of the Harrow period is not copious.' Apparently Dr Symonds did not want Charlotte to know about the unpleasant business because, in September 1859, Symonds wrote to his sister: 'Do you see by the papers that Dr Vaughan has resigned the Head Mastership of Harrow? It will be a great blow to the school I fear, as well as a loss to some old Harrovians. I wonder if he will hereby more easily get a Bishopric.'[37] However, he did talk fairly freely about the matter – to Vaughan's nephew, T. H. Green, when he married Charlotte in 1871; to close friends like H. G. Dakyns; he hinted at it to Dr Percival of Clifton College, and probably to others. Symonds brooded over it for the rest of his life. The following letter indicates that he and Dakyns had been discussing it:

August 12 1866.

My dear Graham

In answer to your question about Harrow – I do not think the school is a bit better than it was when Vaughan left it: probably it is still the worst on a

* An indication of what Stanley's attitude to the affair would be is given in Geoffrey Faber's *Jowett* (Faber & Faber, 1957) in which he quotes Stanley's biographer that Stanley, as a boy, shrank 'from the coarseness and vice that stain school-life' and the extract from his last sermon in Westminster Abbey a week before his death, in which he exalts purity: 'Purity from all that defiles and stains the soul—filthy thoughts, filthy actions, filthy words—we know what they are without an attempt to describe them ... of all the obstacles which can intervene between us and an insight into the invisible and the Divine, nothing presents so coarse and thick a veil as the indulgence of the impure passions which lower our nature' (pp. 121, 122).

Sophie Girard

Miss Sykes—'Auntie'

Charlotte Symonds (Mrs T. H. Green)   Maribella Symonds (Lady Strachey)

'The Ladies of Clifton Hill House'

Clifton Hill House

The drawing-room

large scale in England. Butler, though amiable, is a vain & shallow man, excitable, fond of popularity & eager (as was the case with Vaughan) to keep up the external prosperity of the School at the cost of concealing any of its internal corruptions. One master alone, whose name is Smith, I believe to be wholly above the temptations w^h induce other men to cry peace when there is no peace for the sake of their pockets. He told me things that c^d hardly be credited of the supineness & ostrich like hiding of their heads in sand to w^h self interest has brought many of the older masters* who, convinced of the impurity of their boys refuse to take proper remedies.

As to the boys themselves, they are drawn from the lower aristocracy & the moneyed classes for the most part; idleness, plethoric wealth, hereditary stupidity & parvenu grossness combining to form a singularly corrupt amalgam. The seeds of vice, sown long ago in this fruitful soil continue to propagate themselves like mushrooms on a dunghill. A cousin of mine, Sir Thomas Abdy, not long ago settled at Harrow for the benefit of his sons' education, took a house, etc. etc. Within 3 months he took them away & threw up his establishment, simply because he found the immorality of the School enormous. He has lived for many years in France & Germany & has had much experience of foreign Schools; but he has never met with any *worse* than Harrow among the most corrupt of French Academies. Do not publish this letter abroad, but use it discreetly.

Yrs ever aff

J. A. SYMONDS

* Of the youngest masters I know nothing.[38]

It is interesting to compare Symonds's attitude to the boys in this letter with that in the MS. Memoirs. In the latter he describes them as the progeny of England's best stock who had been corrupted by evil associates. There may be two explanations for this contradiction. The Memoirs were intended as propaganda for a passionately partisan point of view and by 1889 his attitude had undergone significant changes so that the boys appeared to him in a far more attractive light. In 1866 he was not a practising homosexual, and was still very much under his father's influence. Furthermore, he always felt slightly uneasy about his part in the affair; and it was easier to feel morally indignant about a man who had smirched purity than about one who was handling soiled goods. The tightrope Symonds was walking made it necessary for him to adopt some curiously ambivalent moral stances.

Symonds's account of Dr Vaughan's resignation is so very extraordinary

D   39

that one is puzzled as to how it could have been hushed up success-fully. However, the Victorians were extremely skilful at pushing skeletons into closets and it was not the sort of incident that would be related in one of the gossipy books of reminiscences which were churned out by the dozen in the late nineteenth century. There seems no reason to doubt Symonds's version in which he narrates a credible sequence of events, and he certainly lacked the inventive powers to construct such a bizarre story. Extreme truthfulness and candour were outstanding characteristics of the man and he would have no cause to lie in his autobiography which he knew would never be published in his lifetime.

Despite all the public eulogies, Symonds was not alone in his estimation of Dr Vaughan as underhand and untrustworthy. In 1860, when Butler became Headmaster, Henry Sidgwick (who had not yet met Symonds) wrote to Roden Noel: 'I think he only wants experience to carry on Vaughan's system of delicate and unremittingly careful management thoroughly well; and he will add this important advantage that no one will ever fancy him insincere.'[39] Despite Vaughan's bland manner, many remembered him for his remorseless sarcasm and mordant wit.[40] L. A. Tollemache speaks of his 'secretive quality'. 'In truth', he asserts, 'there was no art to find the construction of Vaughan's mind either in his face or his voice. There was an element of inscrutability in him. His mother-in-law, Mrs. Stanley, told my father that she herself did not understand why he first accepted and then declined Lord Palmerston's offer of a bishopric.'[41] Symonds was contemptuous of his intellectual abilities, an opinion shared by L. A. Tollemache and Kenelm Digby, although Dr Butler maintained that he had a real feeling for literature. After Vaughan's death, Charles Dalrymple, (by then a baronet and an M.P.) who, as a boy, had been privy to the whole affair, contributed an affection-ate eulogy to his former Headmaster in a book of essays on Harrow.[42] However, the tribute is couched in vague, conventional terms so there is no means of judging its sincerity.

Few seem to have known the actual feelings of the man who, during his tenure at Harrow, preached a sermon on the loneliness of sin. 'And if such be the loneliness of repentance,' he reflected, 'what must be the loneliness of remorse, which is repentance without God, without Christ, and therefore without hope; the sense of sin unconfessed and unforsaken, only felt as a weight, a burden, and a danger! If repentance is loneliness, remorse is desolation. Repentance makes us lonely towards man; remorse makes us desolate towards God. That is indeed to be alone, when . . . not only earth is iron, but also heaven brass. From such loneliness may God in His mercy save us all through His son Jesus Christ.'[43]

CHAPTER III

Oxford

DURING the Easter holidays of Symonds's last term at Harrow he attended service with his family one Sunday in Bristol Cathedral. While the anthem was being sung, he was startled by the exquisite quality of the voice belonging to the young chorister sitting opposite him. It had the piercing melancholy of wood-wind, and for the rest of his life Symonds was reminded of Willie Dyer's voice whenever he heard the pure notes of a clarinet. He walked home in a dream, still haunted by the etherial sounds. He passed a troubled night, possessed by the memory of the boy, and rose at dawn to lean out of his window and gaze down at the dreaming town where he knew Willie somewhere lay asleep. Determined to get in touch with him, he contrived to learn his name and address, and impulsively wrote asking for his picture which he directed him to send to A.B., C.P.O. After the picture arrived, Symonds, more anxious than ever to know the boy, arranged a meeting in the Cathedral Cloisters at 10 a.m. on 10 April. With his extraordinary memory for every detail connected with the more profound experiences of his life, years later Symonds could reinvoke the immediacy of the encounter by his recollection of the clock striking the hour and the swallows darting about in the spring sunshine. In his Memoirs, when he came to describe how he shyly took Willie's hand, Symonds confessed that he was so agitated by the memory of the incident that he could hardly hold his pen.

The friendship lasted for more than a year. Willie was three years younger than Symonds, he shared none of his intellectual interests, and yet Symonds became so romantically attached to him that everything else in life was relegated to second place. The final term at Harrow passed in dreams of what he and Willie would do when he returned to Clifton. 'He is such a dear little boy', he wrote to Charlotte, 'and when I come home I intend to ask him sometimes to come & drink tea & sing to us.'[1] He devoured Greek literature with its tales of passionate male friendship but neglected his studies. However, Willie helped to reconcile him to Harrow and even to find beauty in it. He began to appreciate the physique of young bathers and to recognize the grace of the cricketers – all of whom reminded him of Willie. Most important of all, Willie enabled him to realize the idealized love which had stirred him in Plato. The relationship remained for many months tremulously romantic, and more than a year passed before they did more than touch hands; until one day, lying side by side in Leigh Woods, something much more definite happened. They kissed. The experience was recalled by Symonds as the most rapturous of his entire life, and he dreamt of it repeatedly in the course of the years to come.

During his first year at Oxford, his thoughts were still centred on Willie in Clifton, and he seized every opportunity to travel home to see him. The piquancy of the relationship was sharpened by the secrecy with which it had to be conducted. Symonds knew only too well how his father would react if the slightest suspicion of such an attachment arose. However, during the Vaughan negotiations in the late summer and early autumn of 1859, Symonds and his father had grown very close, and finally he was driven to open his heart to him about Willie. Gravely, Dr Symonds tried to impress upon him the number of people who might suffer if he did not break off the intimacy: first, his sister Maribella who had recently married Sir Edward Strachey; second, Edith, about to be married to a well-known Bristol barrister, Charles Cave; third, Dr Symonds, whose name had never been touched by scandal; fourth, John himself, whose prospects might be marred by a relationship with the son of a tailor; and finally, the effect of lost reputation on Willie must be considered.

The arguments were overwhelming. For the second time in his life Symonds had betrayed a confidence, a treachery in his eyes more serious than his breach of faith with Pretor, because he genuinely loved Willie. The experience also left him with a slight bitterness towards his father, although he realized that Dr Symonds had logic and common sense on his side. Publicly the relationship was formally terminated but privately he deceived his father and continued to see Willie clandestinely for years.

They usually met in churches where Willie was playing the organ, and Symonds gave the organist of Bristol Cathedral fifty pounds to start his friend on a musical career. He was probably thinking of Willie when he wrote the poem entitled 'What Might Have Been', included in a pamphlet, *Rhaetica*, privately printed in 1878:

> What might have been, what might have been!
>   Is there a sadder word than this?
> Are any serpent's teeth more keen
>   Than memories of what we miss?
>
> The wreaths we might have worn, if but
>   Our feet had found the fields of May,
> Instead of jolting down the rut
>   Of traffic on life's hard high-way!
>
> The love we might have known, if we
>   Had turned this way instead of that;
> The lips we might have kissed, which he
>   For whom they parted, pouted at!
>
> The joys we might, when blood was young,
>   Have garnered in a goodly sheaf;
> The summer songs we might have sung,
>   While still our life was but in leaf!
>
> What might have been, what might have been!
>   Sad thought, when age before us lowers,
> And dark is the December scene,
>   And fallen even autumn's flowers!

In the autumn of 1858, when he was not quite eighteen, Symonds entered Balliol as a Commoner. He had left Harrow behind without regret and he now approached Oxford with comparative indifference. The freedom of University life suited his temperament because, in its relaxed atmosphere, he could withdraw even deeper into himself. At Oxford the dichotomy between the image he presented to the world of a courteous, earnest young intellectual, and the turbulent, troubled heart he hid from its uncomprehending gaze, developed into an habitual defence.

With his emotional problems always seething in the back of his mind, he flitted from interest to interest like any other wealthy undergraduate with an income of three hundred and fifty pounds a year. His uncle, Dr Frederick Symonds, kept a concerned eye on his health and comfort. He sent round to his rooms three enormous pictures – Landseer's 'Sanctuary' and 'Stags Fighting' – '& somebody else's Fighting Stags. They will look well though not the pictures I much care for.'[2] Undecided whether he should join the newly-founded University Rifle Corps which was being formed to defend the town in case of invasion, Symonds wrote: 'The cost of uniform etc will be about £10. I wonder whether it would be worth [while?] to take this trouble upon me: I like the idea, but do not know about time & expense.'[3] In the end it was not the time and expense that ended his abortive military training but the boredom of drilling, and his sword was soon deposited at home in Clifton. He entered Maclaren's gymnasium but did not progress beyond jumping and vaulting. Riding was the only exercise in which he took real pleasure and he had his own horse during his last year. In a quite different field, one memorable evening he heard Dickens read *A Christmas Carol* and the trial scene from *Pickwick Papers*, but unfortunately left no record of his impression of Dickens. One of his greatest joys was the opportunity of hearing good music and many of his letters to Charlotte were filled with enthusiastic accounts of concerts he had attended.

Talk remained the greatest time consumer in Oxford – languid conversation in canoes drifting along the Cherwell, vigorous debate on cross-country hikes, and colloquy late into the night in undergraduates' rooms. In February 1859 he wrote to Charlotte: 'On the whole, I find it difficult to know what to do about acquaintances here. One has either to keep up a great number, or lose several that one would like to have. . . . At Harrow I existed almost without associates till very late, and now I begin to despise myself because I find how much I care to have them, and how much sacrifice this care is likely to produce.'[4] For a short time he and a Scotsman, Edward Urquart,* trailed along after Randall Vickers' ritualistic sentimentalities, but when Symonds realized that Urquart was becoming inordinately fond of him, he broke off the connection. Nor did the Ritualistic phase last long. By June of his first year he was declaring loftily to Charlotte: 'I had thought the tractarian humbug had died, and given way to philosophical cant of infidelity; but it seems that the very dregs

* Urquart later became a country parson.

and offscourings of Oxford youth still rock themselves upon this nonsense.'[5]

After the limitations of Harrow, he was suddenly confronted with an exciting choice of new friends such as Lyulph Stanley, A. O. Rutson, W. R. W. Stephens, W. J. Courthope, and Gustavus Bosanquet's brother, Cecil.* Stanley intrigued him as the most fascinating of these new acquaintances. 'He is a strange rattling creature this Stanley', Symonds told his sister, 'the type of muscular-intellectual young Oxford',[6] and, he might have added, one of the few people who were able to enliven Jowett's lugubrious breakfast-parties.

In his second year Symonds began to entertain at breakfast and wine parties, and his father's advice was sought on the purchase of wine. 'I think they seemed to like my wine (from the Peninsular W.D.) very much,' he reported, 'for I had 6 bottles of claret, 3 of port, 3 of sherry, drunk.'[7] On another occasion he had 'a very intellectual breakfast: Conington, Rutson, Green, Tollemache, Dicey, Lyulph Stanley, and Puller.† I find these breakfasts formidable things: for there is a succession of meats, all of which I have to dispense, to change plates, and keep people going with fresh forks and knives etc. It is not the custom for any scout to be in attendance, so that the host has to do all the menial offices. You would be amused to see these intellectual men with fried soles and sauces, proceed to a cutlet, then taste a few sausages or some savoury omelette, and finish up with buttered cake or toast and marmalade. Up to the sweet finale, coffee is the beverage: tea, coming when hunger has abated, prolongs breakfast ad infinitum.'[8]

---

* The Hon. L. S. Stanley was a cousin of Arthur Stanley. He later showed great interest in various social activities and was the St. Mary-le-bone member of the London School Board (1867-85) and M.P. for Oldham (1880-5). He succeeded to the title of Lord Sheffield in 1909.

Stephens was Dean of Winchester, 1894-1902.

W. J. Courthope was Professor of Poetry at Oxford, 1895-1900.

Both Bosanquet brothers became country clergymen.

Rutson will be mentioned at length later in the narrative.

Two of the surprising omissions are Walter Pater, who was at Queen's from 1858 to 1862; and, even more surprising, A. C. Swinburne, who was at Balliol in 1858.

† The Hon. L. A. Tollemache went on to become a barrister and was later much given to reminiscences of his Oxford years.

Albert Dicey became a noted jurist. He was appointed Vinerian Professor of English Law at Oxford in 1882.

Cholmeley Puller was reported as a student at Lincoln's Inn in 1872 but then fades into oblivion.

Among such companions he gradually discarded his protective shyness and slowly began to develop an easy manner in society. He was quiet but, when he spoke, he did not utter nonsense; and, as word got about that he was a rather remarkable young man, he found himself being invited to meet some of the more outstanding older members of the University. In May 1859 he attended a reception at the Vice-Chancellor's in honour of the Prince of Wales who had recently come up to Oxford, an event made even more splendid by the presence of Gladstone and his wife. 'All the Heads of College were there, & the . . . entertainment was big & grand. Mr. G. looked much older than I had expected. . . . Mrs. G. was said to be handsome: she was "splendidly attired" in a robe of deep & rich green velvet, trimmed with old point lace: the honourable lady also wore a bertha of superb point lace which is said to have been purchased at a great cost in the Ionian Islands.'[9]

It was at this gathering that he met John Conington, who had been elected to fill the newly-founded Corpus chair of Latin Language and Literature in 1854, a man destined to become one of the major influences on Symonds at Oxford. Conington's conversation was an education in itself for a young man with pronounced literary tastes. Homely, with gleaming spectacles and quivering protruding lips, he delighted his audience with his puckish humour and flow of talk. He took an immediate liking to Symonds and they were soon making a habit of drinking strong tea and talking far into the night in Conington's rooms. For a time Conington encouraged Symonds to try for a scholarship to Corpus. In later years Symonds looked back on Conington's influence as almost wholly good, although he was critical of the older man's insensitivity to any of the arts except literature. While expecting Conington to tea one afternoon, he dashed off a letter to Charlotte: 'I see a great deal of him, & like him even better than I did at first. Though pompous rather & conceited (I fancy) a good deal, he is yet very kind; & of course it is an immense advantage for me to see so much of such a man.'[10]

Symonds became one of the few intimates who was allowed to share Conington's daily walk. Conington had such a passion for intellectual discussion that he often said he wished he could confine his walks to a lane between two high walls so that he could shut out any distracting irrelevancies like natural beauty. His famous reading-parties brought together groups of promising young men, who would tramp along the high road beside Conington who continued to stare stolidly ahead as the words poured out, while his companions tried unsuccessfully to draw his attention to the beauties of their surroundings. When Donati's wonderful comet appeared in 1858, it was characteristic of him to remark that he did not think '*that* phenomenon ought to be encouraged'.

Conington, as we have seen, insisted on Symonds revealing to his father the facts of Dr Vaughan's activities. Nevertheless, in a subtle way which he could not foresee, Conington also encouraged Symonds's homosexual tendencies. While scrupulously correct in his own conduct, he was sympathetic towards the infatuations of young men as long as any physical element was suppressed. He gave Symonds a copy of William Johnson Cory's *Ionica*, a series of romantic poems addressed by an Eton master to one of his charges, Charles Wood, later Viscount Halifax. 'I suppose you have not any of you read poems called *Ionica*', Symonds wrote Charlotte; 'they are making a stir in Oxford, both on account of their true poetry & the curious personal history involved. The author is an Eton master, & I had all the enigmatical facts expounded to me.'[11] He was so stirred by the volume that he wrote to Cory, admitting his own bias and asking for advice; he begged Mr Cory to write to him as O.D.X. at the Oxford Union. In due course he received from Cory a long and passionate defence of pederasty. Symonds, in his Memoirs, remarks that this letter was threaded with a wistful yearning, a note which he had never found absent from any homosexual relationships.*

Another striking figure who impressed him early in his Oxford career was Thomas Hill Green, a Fellow and tutor at Balliol, who was appointed lecturer in Ancient and Modern History in 1860. A remarkably handsome man with thick black hair, dark eyebrows, and fine brown eyes, Green's presence created an immediate effect of solidity and moral strength, unusual in a man of only twenty-two. His mother was a sister of Dr Vaughan's and he too had been educated at Rugby. A pupil of Jowett's, he had become highly enthusiastic about a German philosopher, Hegel, whom his tutor was introducing to Oxford. His interests were all

---

* In 1892, when his daughter Madge was reading *Ionica*, Symonds wrote to her: 'I used to dote on that book when I was a lad at Oxford. But the best things in it (those written at Eton) are morbidly sentimental' (MS. letter, Davos, 1892, University of Bristol).

profoundly serious and his early ripeness reminded people of Arthur Hugh Clough, who had been at Balliol only a few years before, although the engaging Clough could be flippantly gay upon occasion.* Green was four years Symonds's senior and while their association became very close during the years Symonds spent at Oxford, Green treated him with a good-natured, elder-brotherly contempt which irritated Symonds at times. 'Unsusceptible himself', one of Green's contemporaries, Albert Venn Dicey, wrote in his diary, 'he pays little heed to other persons' minor susceptibilities.'[12] Symonds shared the general admiration for Green's formidable character, but their interests were widely divergent and Symonds was never able to share his passion for politics and philosophy. When Symonds first met him he was already deeply absorbed in Hegel, but he had difficulty in clearly stating the ideas which were agitating him so profoundly; indeed, Symonds always doubted if he ever successfully mastered a lucid formulation of his beliefs. Such a suspicion was beginning to develop as early as 1860 when he wrote to W. R. W. Stephens from Conington's reading-party at Coniston: 'Green is coaching me in Plato. He does it well, for he knows an immense deal about the Platonic and Aristotelian philosophy, as well as about modern systems. On the other hand, because he is a very original thinker, he does not express himself quite as clearly and fluently as such beginners as myself would like.'[13] Years later Symonds could never make head or tail of the *Prolegomena to Ethics*.

If these new friends and interests failed to absorb him completely, his obsession for Willie prevented him from becoming more than a detached observer of the Oxford scene. This suppressed emotional life checked his enthusiasm for his work and he felt only a mild regret that he had let his father down when he failed to gain a scholarship in November 1858. The following spring he was plucked for Smalls in Greek grammar. The examiner made him conjugate the Greek εἰμί (to be) and εἶμι (to go) tense by tense, and Symonds, with his highly nervous temperament, was completely thrown off balance. '*It was atrocious*', he told Charlotte. 'I never could decline or conjugate at any time or by any process, far less on paper in a nervous flurry.'[14] The news made so little impact on him that

* Green served as the model for Mr Grey in Mrs Humphry Ward's *Robert Elsmere*. 'I tried', she wrote, 'to reproduce a few of those traits – traits of a great thinker and teacher, who was also one of the simplest, sincerest, and most practical of men' (*A Writer's Recollections*, W. Collins & Sons, 1918, p. 132).

he was left with a far more vivid memory of gathering fritillaries in Magdalen meadows all that afternoon, and of enjoying the sunset from the top of Magdalen Tower. However, if he had failed to measure up to his father's standards at the outset, later, in June, he appeased him when he was elected to an open exhibition at Balliol.

As early as the end of his first week at Oxford, he described the lectures as 'very elementary, but the subjects are good standard ones' which included Euclid, Logic, the Gospel of St John, the *Aeneid,* and Herodotus. He had the opportunity of listening to many eminent figures. 'A good lecture', he noted in his diary of Matthew Arnold's talk 'On Translating Homer',* 'and full of impudence'[15] – although his enthusiasm for Arnold was short-lived. He attended a course of lectures by the Linacre Professor of Anatomy and Physiology, George Rolleston, an advanced thinker and admirer of Herbert Spencer. Symonds informed 'Auntie' proudly that he now felt 'Pretty confident to differentiate a monkey's from a man's "cerebral hemi-spheres". . . . I had a pet notion that a new psychology might be constructed on a purely anatomical & physiological basis, but Rollestone [*sic*] has upset that by answering me that the more he studies the less connection he sees between the mind & the nerves.'[16] In June 1859 he heard 'a splendid Lecture of Goldwin Smith's in the Theatre:† it was an Inaugural Lecture, showing that History is a Philosophy not a Science'.[17] The controversial Max Müller, the expert on comparative philology, stimulated Symonds's interest in myths to some degree. But none of these figures made any decisive impact on him, nor did he take any interest in politics or the Union debates even though it was the momentous period of the great American Civil War and the Lancashire cotton famine.

Several influences coalesced to stir his ambition. Foremost among these was Benjamin Jowett, although their initial meeting proved unpropitious. During his first week in Oxford Symonds was disappointed to learn that he would not be in any of Jowett's classes, but eagerly seized the opportunity of calling on him when Dr Symonds gave him a letter of introduction after sitting beside Jowett at a Magdalen Gaudy. The young

---

* This lecture was an attack on Francis Newman, a recent translator of Homer, and a friend of Dr Symonds. It is impossible to determine which particular lecture he attended of the group which were later published under the title *On Translating Homer.*

† Goldwin Smith was Regius Professor of Modern History, 1858-66.

man timidly entered the panelled rooms of the distinguished man who, at forty-one, was already becoming something of a myth. Finding him dozing over a fire, Symonds shyly handed him the letter of introduction. Jowett glanced at it, turned his languid gaze on Symonds, and finally drawled: 'I do not think I know your father.' An awkward pause ensued; after an interminable silence, Jowett rose abruptly, held out his hand, and said: 'Good-bye, Mr Symonds.' The sensitive young man was completely rebuffed.

After this inauspicious meeting, he did not see Jowett again for more than a year. Just before he was to take his Moderations, Jowett inexplicably began to take a serious interest in his work and sent a message to him to bring some Greek and Latin verses to his rooms. 'The few evenings in which he coached me made me feel, for the first time', Symonds recalled, 'what it was to be taught. He said very little, gave me no "tips". But somehow he made me comprehend what I had to aim at, and how I had to go about it. In some new to me unapprehended way, he showed me how to use my reading in Greek for the purpose of writing. I am sure that the iambics I produced for those few lessons were better than the thousands laboured at before.'[18]

Jowett exerted a mysterious attraction over almost all those who had any contact with him. After one of his breakfast-parties, Symonds sat down, still mesmerized, and enthused to Charlotte: 'Half an hour of Jowett's society makes one feel a better man.'[19] Whether his recollection was of drinking the lukewarm tea which Jowett served in clumsy cups or of one of his excruciatingly stilted breakfast-parties, or of one of those walks with the Master* which he (among the favoured few) was privileged to take, Symonds cherished every one of the laconic utterances that fell from Jowett's lips. One evening Jowett roused himself from a long reverie by the fire to announce: 'When I don't say anything, people fancy I am thinking about something. Generally I am thinking about nothing at all. Good night.'[20] Such words would not be taken seriously by an inveterate hero-worshipper like Symonds.

In later life Symonds shared Sir Leslie Stephen's view that Jowett did not accept any articulated doctrine to which his admirers could adhere.[21] His comments in his Memoirs also bear out Goldwin Smith's opinion

* Jowett did not actually become Master of Balliol until 1870.

that there was 'no clinch in his mind. He would have doubted and kept other people doubting forever.'[22] Jowett did nothing to dispel the religious perplexities which had begun to disturb Symonds during his last year at Harrow. From Hegel Jowett had derived the notion that it was impossible to define any idea without bringing in its opposite. As far as Symonds was concerned, the positive value of such an outlook was to confirm in him a determination against dogmatism, an approach characteristic of all his later writing; but Jowett's influence was negative to the extent that it reinforced an already latent scepticism. A religion based on rational foundations might have appealed to the intellectual in Symonds, but it was insufficient to satisfy his overwhelming emotional needs.

Common sense applied to daily life and honest labour in the service in which one found oneself – these were Jowett's simple tenets. With this austere equipment, he managed to instil in his adoring young enthusiasts a recognition of the value of success, of achievement which could be attained only through hard work. Work was invested with a Carlylean badge of honour; work could not fail to produce some sort of success, if only to clarify the confusing disorder of life. Jowett's attitude to work was never more clearly expressed than by the contemporary whom he admired most, Arthur Hugh Clough: 'All things become clear to me by work', said Clough in words which might have been spoken by Jowett, 'more than by anything else. Any kind of drudgery will help one out of the most uncommon either sentimental or speculative perplexity; the attitude of work is the only one in which one can see things properly.'[23] On 16 March 1869 Symonds wrote lyrically to Charlotte: 'Such a man was never found, so great to inspire confidence & rouse to efforts. Other people may prate for hours, & set the pros & cons before you, yet never stir your lethargy. By a single word, with no argument, but a slight appeal to the natural power of most men, or a plea for work as work, *he* makes me feel that to be successful is the only thing short of dishonour.'[24]

Under pressure from Jowett Symonds began to win academic distinction. Before he sat for his Moderations,* he told Charlotte: 'Jowett

* An examination between Responsions and the Final Schools, first introduced in 1850, and known technically as the First Public Examination. The subjects were the 'Holy Gospels in Greek, polite literature and mathematics: but a test of classical scholarship was the chief aim in view' (C. E. Mallet, *A History of the University of Oxford*, III, Methuen & Co., 1927, p. 297).

says that my only thought till Mods. must be my work . . . the rules I laid down for reading must be steadily adhered to, and herein help me; all byways of literature must be carefully eschewed, hard. Such are the resolutions roused by Jowett's trumpet, how long to last?'[25] In June, just before the examinations, he wrote to his sister again, this time in a mood of dejection: 'I am so tired, and so lamentably dismal about my work for Moderations that I do not know what will become of me. I forget everything that I read and have read, and am now unable even to read with understanding, so that I am beginning to dread that my Mods. will have to be put off till the autumn.'[26] However, against all the portents, he pulled himself together and obtained a First Class.

He then started work on the Final Schools in Litterae Humaniores – philosophy, logic, and history – which meant that he came into closer contact with Jowett as he now had to read an essay to him each week. During this period his diary is filled with references to Jowett, and a typical entry reads: 'Tait* and I met at 8 to read an essay on the Eleatics to Jowett. Tait read first, while Jowett gave me tea. Jowett was pleased with his essay. Then I read mine, which was elaborate. He interrupted me several times to talk, but at the end seemed pleased; he said: "That is very good, Mr. Symonds, a good essay"; nor did he make any strictures on the style or mannerism, with the exception of the use of "Generally" in opening the subject. . . . Then he gave me a lecture on Hegel. He thinks him marvellous in metaphysical distinction, practical acumen, and poetry. His theory, one in which the existence of a universal God is to be seen in all things and thought. Distinct personalities are allowed by this God to exist under and independent of Him. This I had not understood from Hegel.'[27] In later life Symonds believed that the greatest debt he owed Jowett was the fact that he impressed upon him the importance of possessing a firm grasp of one's subject and writing about it as clearly and as simply as possible.

Needless to say, Symonds was one of the most partisan of Jowett's supporters in the various battles in which he became embroiled during this period. On 27 January 1861 Symonds records in his diary a discussion with a large group of friends about 'the storm brewing' over *Essays and*

---

* Walter James Tait was a lecturer in Modern History at Worcester College, 1864-71, and became Rector of St Edmund's, Salisbury, in 1883.

Reviews.[28] These were a series of historical studies of the Scriptures by a group of Oxford dons and Jowett's contribution, 'On the Interpretation of Scripture', was a plea for the application of reason to the study of the Bible. A vehement attack against the essayists appeared in the January issue of *The Quarterly Review* in which the writer declared that 'the attempt of the Essayists to combine their advocacy of such doctrines with the retention of the status and emolument of Church of England clergymen is simply moral dishonesty'.[29] Although the article was unsigned everyone rightly suspected that it had been written by the Bishop of Oxford, Samuel Wilberforce. Symonds and Green attended service at St Mary's on the Sunday following the attack. 'Full to overflowing', he writes in his diary. '[Wilberforce] preached from the text, "For all that He did so many miracles, yet they believed not on Him." I knew he would level at the Essayists, and, from the text, expected more than came. It was a general harangue against neglect of Revelation, considered in four lights – kinds, causes, consequences, cures thereof. The kinds were three, as resulting from pride of the world, pride of the flesh, pride of intellect. And each of these three kinds he treated with regard to the last three divisions of his subject. Therefore the Essayists only came in for the third part of the abuse; but he gave it them strong. His peroration to the consequences was fine. He spoke of men who, trusting to their own reason, thought they could elevate themselves into a purer atmosphere, leave behind for the vulgar a belief in the Crucified, and hold direct communion with the unapproachable God.

'More oratory than argument.'[30]

On 1 February the Bishops held a meeting at Lambeth. While what passed was not disclosed to the public, everyone assumed that they had met to discuss what course they should follow to deal with the writers of the *Essays*. Public interest was excited and wild rumours circulated. On 16 February Symonds wrote an indignant letter to Charlotte asking her what their father thought of 'these foolish Bishops'.[31] In June two of the writers were suspended by the Court of Arches, although the decision was later set aside. The following year when Dr E. B. Pusey made an unsuccessful attempt to have Jowett prosecuted, Symonds was typical of the majority of liberal undergraduates who invested Jowett with the crown of heroic martyr, and crowded into the Vice-Chancellor's Court to watch the

Dr Vaughan

Professor John Conington

J. A. Symonds at Oxford

Catherine Symonds, c. 1864

Dr Symonds with his son and Charlotte

The wedding photograph of J. A. Symonds and Catherine North, 1864

abortive proceedings. 'Theology penetrated our intellectual and social atmosphere', Symonds wrote of the Oxford of his day. 'We talked theology at Breakfast parties and at wine parties, out riding and walking, in College gardens, on the river, wherever young men and their elders met together.'[32]

Symonds also felt passionately concerned about the long struggle for an increase in Jowett's meagre salary of £40 a year as Regius Professor of Greek, and his letters until 1864 when it was finally augmented, are filled with acid comments about Jowett's opponents who were 'behaving in such an impotently spiteful manner'.[33] He and Jowett were intimate enough by the autumn of 1861 for Symonds to be able to tell him frankly about a meeting he had attended of Convocation over the question of Jowett's salary. 'He was interested & amused, & betrayed more anxiety than I had ever seen in him about such matters.'[34] Despite Jowett's taciturnity, a friendship gradually developed between them in which the barrier of age was almost overcome. Jowett began to make frequent visits to Clifton Hill House where he found a congenial spirit in Dr Symonds, and many years later he recalled to Symonds the pleasure he had found in his company: 'I can never forget your Father's regard for me & the hours we used to spend talking at night in the Study.'[35] But the speed with which the friendship developed appears curious for a man of Jowett's reserve. The explanation may lie in Geoffrey Faber's surmise that Jowett was courting the daughter of the Dean of Bristol and was eager to make as many visits to Bristol as possible.[36]

One surprising mystery is why Jowett never invited Symonds to any of his annual reading-parties. No one felt more dismayed or perplexed about this oversight than Symonds himself. In the spring of 1861 he was very disturbed by the news that Jowett contemplated retiring from the battle over *Essays and Reviews* to spend a term working on his translation of *The Republic*. And, unkindest cut of all, he had invited another man to spend the Easter Vacation with him. 'Before I go down', Symonds confided to Charlotte, 'I must try to speak to him alone and intimate that I have no one to read with in the Long. More than that I cannot do. If he w^d only take the hint and ask me to come & stay with him, I should be so happy. If he does not, I think I must retire for a few weeks with my friend Stephens alone to some quiet village in Wales. . . .'[37] But Jowett did not take the hint.

There were other influences besides Jowett which contributed to Symonds's renewed vigour. One was a tendency in his own character, which manifested itself a number of times during his life: namely, a stubborn desire to prove himself when aroused by other people's slighting opinions of his powers. During a reading-party organized by Conington in the summer of 1860, Symonds was sitting reading in a little room in the farmhouse they were occupying at Coniston. In the kitchen on the other side of the wall Conington and Green were talking, unaware of Symonds's presence in the next room. Presently he heard himself spoken of by his nickname. 'Barnes will not get his first,' said Conington. 'No,' Green replied. 'I do not think he has any chance of doing so.' They then began to analyse his languorous temperament and his aesthetic leanings which had always distressed Conington. Symonds scraped his chair on the floor and the conversation broke off abruptly. 'The sting of it remained in me', Symonds recorded in his Memoirs, 'and though I cared little enough for first-classes, I then and there resolved that I would win the best first of my year.'[38] And he did.

Work also served as an opiate from his pressing emotional problems. In his attempts to break off the friendship with Willie, he turned to work as the solution Clough had recommended for 'sentimental' perplexities. This was not the drudgery which had dulled the sordid realities of Harrow but congenial literary studies which could serve as a partial substitute for his repressed instincts.

He began to be regarded as one of the abler men at the University and he was hurt when he failed to be elected to the Old Mortality, a short-lived essay society organized by John Nichol* in 1856. To belong to the Old Mortality was considered an honour and its distinguished members included Swinburne, Pater, Green, Dicey, and Birkbeck Hill. Symonds later learned that his admission had been blocked by the vote of Lyulph Stanley. In October 1859 Symonds tried to persuade Puller to help him form a club of '50 other intellectually pursuited men, & making ourselves more or less exclusive of the usual vast fluctuating society: we ought to take each one day in the week to receive the rest at wine'.[39] He was obviously planning to organize his society on the lines of the Old Mortality which met once a week in the various members' rooms after

* Professor of English Language and Literature at Glasgow, 1862-89.

dinner to read essays or selected passages chosen by the host. Conington formed another such society and Symonds proceeded to take an active part in its activities. He became President of it in his last year, and read a number of essays, including one on *Tannhäuser* 'to a numerous & delighted audience'.*[40] Very conscious of the fact that he had 'no oratorical powers', he was delighted on one occasion when Conington praised him for his delivery. 'My nervousness takes the form of a constant fear', he confessed to Charlotte, 'that I shall not be able to pronounce certain consonants . . . the very smallest quantity of wine increases the tendency to stick at particular words.'[41] He listened critically to eminent public speakers and had a qualified reaction to a speech of Gladstone's on Lancing College: 'It was the speech of an able & accustomed speaker, not of a great orator. The oratorical defects of false emphasis & constant repetition of ideas was glaring. The subject, however,' he added charitably, 'was not one to w^h a man c^d warm.'[42]

In his last year at Balliol Symonds resigned from Conington's essay society and the same year was finally elected to the Old Mortality. But subsequent events destroyed all his interest in University activities.

His most outstanding success occurred during his final term in 1862 when he won the Newdigate Prize for a poem on the Escorial. Conington, who had twice been an unsuccessful candidate, was astounded. Symonds recited the poem in the Sheldonian before the Prince and Princess of Wales, and when he had finished, 'Matthew Arnold, then our Professor of Poetry, informed me very kindly, and in the spirit of sound criticism, that he had voted for me, not because of my stylistic qualities, but because I intellectually grasped the subject, and used its motives better and more rationally than my competitors. This sincere expression of a distinctive judgment was very helpful to me. It gave me insight into my own faculty, and preserved me from self-delusion as to its extent.'[43]

Despite all these external successes, his inner life was always threatening to explode and required an exhausting effort to control. His exaggerated response to artistic beauty is more than proof of this tension,

* According to L. A. Tollemache, *Old and Odd Memories* (Edward Arnold, 1908; p. 135): 'We were both members of a society which was variously designated as the Essay Society, the Mutual Improvement Society, (less modestly) the Wise and Good, and (with specific reference to two or three of its members) the Jolly Pantheists – a society of which Conington, himself anything but a Pantheist, was founder and patron.'

whether the stimulus was a stained glass window or a Handel oratorio. He proved even more susceptible when the stimulus was provided by a short, rotund undergraduate with long curling yellow hair called G. H. Shorting, who came up to Oxford from Rugby in the autumn of 1859. Shorting shared Symonds's 'Arcadian' tastes, as he called them at the time, and the latent possibilities of their relationship were tacitly recognized by both. Shorting was vain, possessive, and strong-willed, and they had endless bitter scenes of jealousy and recrimination. Symonds was torn between a desire to break with a man he did not admire, and a strong physical pull towards him. He also felt a call to save Shorting from the ruinous eventuality towards which his desires were leading him.

Salvation presented itself in the form of another handsome Bristol choir-boy. This one's name was Alfred Brooke. Where Symonds's feeling for Willie Dyer had been romantically etherialized, now he was devoured by an irrational passion. Alfred satisfied him aesthetically and physically: his face and voice were more beautiful than any he had ever known, and he was consumed with a desire to possess him, not just to gaze romantically into his eyes as he had done with Willie. The torment was intensified by his belief that his feeling was sinful and by his knowledge that his father would be deeply troubled if he learned that he had not yet been able to suppress his cravings. At night he tossed in bed driven by erotic fantasies, by day he appeared bland and courteous to Dr Symonds's friends, some of whom he began to describe as 'bores'. Their self-importance, which had once impressed him, now seemed dull and pompous in comparison with the voluptuousness of Alfred Brooke.

His intellectual life took on a feverishness to match his emotional agitation. He was studying for his Final Schools and at Oxford threw himself into writing essays; at home in Clifton he worked even harder on the books he had to prepare for the examinations. One October morning, while bent over Plato on the desk in the 'Gothic' study at Clifton Hill House, he happened to glance out of the window and see Alfred in the street above. The boy nodded, smiled, and passed on. Symonds held his breath for a minute, stumbled to the window, and when he could no longer see him, rushed out to the empty street. In a state of misery he ran into the garden, and flinging himself on the dead leaves, writhed and groaned with frustration. One evening, Alfred, who was constantly making suggestive overtures, came to his bedroom. Symonds stood in his dressing-gown, overwhelmingly attracted to the boy sitting provocatively on the bed in the corner. Tension lay between them, and brusquely Symonds sent him away. He became almost manic as soon as he had left, throwing himself on the floor and kissing the spot on the bed where Alfred had sat, sobbing and cursing and praying all through the long night. In the morning Dr Symonds was concerned to find that he had developed a fever. Symonds fled abruptly to Oxford, resolved to stay away as long as he could. In his diary, the entry for 29 September 1861 reads: 'I have ceased to care about the Schools. My ship has sailed into a magic sea with tempests of its own.'[44]

A few weeks later he was driven to come back, and went directly to Alfred's house where he found the boy copying out attorney's parchments. They passed a strange evening walking about the dark gusty streets and stopping at street corners to look at each other in the flickering flame of the gas-lights. Finally they climbed into a carriage and drove about aimlessly. When they parted at midnight, Symonds handed the boy some money, which he took readily, but there was also an expression of disappointment on his face.

Symonds's love brought him nothing but torment. Jealousy was added to frustration when he saw Alfred and another boy sauntering across the College Green with their arms lovingly encircling each other. As with Willie Dyer, Symonds poured out the record of his passion in verse. Two sonnets in *Vagabunduli Libellus*, entitled 'Renunciation', were inspired by Alfred; the first obviously refers to the incident when Alfred passed before his window:

> Ah, what pain is here! All through the night
> I yearned for power, and nursed rebellious scorn,
> Striving against high heaven in hot despite
> Of wavering nerves and will by passion torn.
> I dreamed; and on the curtain of the gloom
> False memory drew an idyll of old hope,
> Singing a lullaby to mock my doom
> With love far off and joy beyond my scope.
> I woke; the present seemed more sad than hell;
> On daily tasks my sullen soul I cast;
> But, as I worked, a deeper sorrow fell;

Like thunder on my spirit; for she past
Before the house with wondering wide blue eye
That said, 'I wait! why will you not reply?'

Headaches, feverishness, sleepless nights, aching eyes – the inner maelstrom had to express itself in some way. People said that he was suffering from overwork and from the religious doubts that were perplexing young men of the time. His anxious father decided that a change of scene might be beneficial and, after the news of his double first – achieved at the cost of broken health – took him off on a European tour. They travelled by way of Munich and Innsbruck to 'the city of the lagoons' where they stayed in the Hotel Europa overlooking the Grand Canal. He later said of his first impression of Venice: 'The magic of the place enthralled me and it has never wholly lost that early fascination.'[45]

Symonds was thrown into excited agitation by Venetian painting, and his diaries and letters are filled with copious descriptions of the Venetian masters. With the living, breathing reality of Alfred Brooke always in the back of his mind, it was not artistry he was looking for in Venetian painting, but vivid pulsating life. In a letter written to A. O. Rutson the following year he is still harping on the qualities which appealed to him in that first trip to Venice: 'Notice how large a space of their pictures is given to accurate landscape & architecture. This again marks the early germs of true Venetian love of life & fact. . . . Splendour & nature & the ideal of Passion rather than of intellect, of Life more than Form; sensuous love of colour, & feeling for the beauty of mere breathing flesh; sympathy with the breadth of landscape & the sea with storm & blinding summer suns; the pomp & pride of festivals & palaces & war & merchandize fill all their pictures from the earliest to the latest, & even inspire their devotion with a kind of earthly heat. The Venetians were the giants of the World of Art, children of God's Sons & earth's fairest daughters: not angelic like the fancy fostered Florentines, not merely human like the sober Flemish, not abstractedly intellectual like Dürer. To them I give the throne of Art, for they achieved what Art aspires to – they breathed into the world the breath of Heaven & made the ideal live instead of abstracting it to unreality.'[46]

When Symonds was travelling in Germany and northern Italy the previous autumn on his first European tour, his father had encouraged him to keep a diary in which he began to write voluminous descriptions of all he saw. These travel-sketches which were now resumed in Venice, he continued writing throughout his life, and they subsequently formed the basis of many of the published essays. When Symonds came to write his Memoirs, the diaries proved invaluable as a means of re-living the emotions of long ago and many passages were inserted verbatim into the autobiography. Horatio Brown included some of the discarded sections in his biography but seems to have destroyed the diaries after he had finished the book.

His father industriously rushed him about to art galleries and ancient monuments but the novelty of foreign places did not dispel the anxieties of Symonds's subconscious. Always subject to bad dreams, he had one in Hospenthal just before they returned to England, which was curious in its Freudian implications – and, even more, for Symonds's realization of these:

I thought that papa and I were travelling [he recorded] and were sleeping in adjoining rooms. We were in some hot country, and I had just come to the end of a night spent in great pain. Toward the morning I slept fairly, and when I woke the sun was shining hot upon my darkened room. For some reason or other papa had left his room, and I was alone. As I rose a horrid sense of impending evil oppressed me. I could hardly stand, and in great weakness I tottered to a chair that stood before a tall looking-glass. There I saw myself a hideous sight. My skin was leprous white, like parchment, and all shrivelled. From every pore burst a river of perspiration, and ran to my feet. My feet were cramped and blanched and cockled up with pain. But the face was the most awful sight. It was all white – the lips white and parted – the eyes pale, and presenting a perfectly flat surface. They were dilated, and shone with a cold blue eerie light. I heard a noise in Papa's room, and knocked. He said 'Come in' in his usual tone, and I crept up to him. He was shaving and did not see me, till I roused him by touching him and saying slowly, 'Papa'. Then he turned round and looked intently at me and inquiringly. I shrieked, 'Papa, don't you know me?' but even while I cried the vision of my own distorted features came across me, and filled me with my utter loneliness. At last he cried, 'My son,' and, burying his face in his hands, he added, 'All in one night.' In an ecstasy of deliverance I clasped his neck, and felt that now I need not go back into that twilight room with its bed and the mystery behind its curtains. But he went on in a hesitating voice, 'My poor boy! what fiend – or demon?' I stopped the question with a yell. Something seemed to tear me, and I awoke struggling. Such was my dream – more horrible than it seems, for the terror of dreams bears no relation to the hideousness of their incidents, but to some hidden emotion.[47]

II. MAGDALEN

By the time Symonds returned to Oxford in the autumn of 1862 he had been able to control the excesses of his feeling for Alfred Brooke. The future looked bright. He was asked by the Librarian of the Union to be a member of the Library committee: 'I have gladly accepted as I shall thus put a foot on Union ground & prepare myself for making that debut w^h seems inevitable after my degree. . . .'[48] On his birthday, 5 October, he wrote confidently to Charlotte: '22 years is a good age, – an age certainly at which I ought to be better, stronger, more fixed in character, & more developed in organization than I am. If birthdays are of any use, they serve at least to remind us of such truths as this; & so little by little we become accustomed to take our lowly places in life, & not to fret onwards for what is not to be. I do not see any reason why I should expect unhappiness in the future. Every year lessens our discontent, hardens us to the chances of the world, dries up some spring of yearning or vain fancy, & so makes us more equable & more ready for the future. It is not in what we have to bear, but in the way that we can bear it, that our happiness or misery consists. . . .'[49]

Symonds would have liked to have become a Fellow of Balliol but was discouraged by Conington who felt that he had little chance against G. A. Simcox, widely considered to be dazzlingly brilliant, an opinion not entirely shared by Symonds: 'Simcox is a most absurd man. I do not wonder at your wavering between thinking him an idiot or a genius', he told Charlotte. 'He is really very clever, though not practical enough to be successful in the ordinary affairs of life I s^h judge.'*[50] Conington urged him to try at Magdalen for one of the Fellowships which had been thrown open by the Act of 1854. Jowett, of course, was also consulted. He recommended that Symonds stand for each of the three Fellowships which were open to competition during the autumn term. The examinations for Queen's came first, on 3 October, and he lost out to Charles Elton.

* Symonds's forecast proved correct. At Corpus Christi, Simcox had distinguished himself as a brilliant classical scholar. He became a Fellow of Queen's in 1863, and subsequently edited Greek and Latin texts, wrote *A History of Latin Literature*, and a volume of essays, *Recollections of a Rambler*. He achieved fame, however, not from his scholarship but from his eccentricities. A dishevelled character, he failed to keep appointments, he once gave a tutorial in his nightshirt, and he would burst into maniacal laughter in church. In 1905 he disappeared mysteriously on a walking-tour in Ireland and his body was never found.

In his diary he recorded a conversation with Jowett following his defeat: 'He talked about fellowships, and about staying up at Oxford. That he does not wholly approve of. He calls it living in a hothouse, and says men get braced in London. About health, he thinks young men of my age are apt to pule. To read conscientiously for years on one subject requires peculiar gifts. Great perseverance and freshness are needed; for after a time the acquisition of knowledge becomes tedious, and its reconstruction ceases to be anything but restitution.'[51]

The defeat at Queen's seems to have made little impact on him because he was still attracted to the idea of the medieval beauty of Magdalen and its lovely chapel, but the strain of collecting testimonials told heavily on his nerves. He even began to suspect that Jowett, who had informed him that he was going to remain entirely neutral, might be playing a double game. Uncle Fred increased his anxiety by gloomily forecasting that Lyulph Stanley's rank would weigh heavily with the Magdalen examiners. He wrote an aggrieved letter to Charlotte: 'The intolerable injustice, the indignities, & the necessity of seeking people's grace or waiting for their leisure, connected with Fellowship Examinations, make them the most odious kind of ordeal. To do work & be paid for it as a carpenter or as a professional man, or to receive orders & dance attendance on an attorney involves no personal disgrace. But this exposure to scrutiny, this arbitrary gaining or losing of character, & the minor nuisance of playing like blind Samson in vivâ voce before the Philistines, I only endure with the hope of gaining a position & the power of future redress or retaliation.'[52]

In October he sat for the examination in the hall next to the chapel where he could hear the voices of the choristers while he bent over his papers on philosophy and history. A greenfinch flew into the room as he worked and its feet became entangled in the cobwebs hanging from the ceiling above the oriel window. Symonds reached up to release the bird, and watched enviously as it fluttered away to freedom.

All his anxiety was dispelled when he finally heard that he had been unanimously elected Fellow, and on 25 October dined at high table as stranger and visitor to A. O. Rutson, who had become a Fellow in 1861. His victory fell on the festival of the Restoration of the Fellows, and after Hall the whole College gathered to drink out of the great cup, intoning

Jus suum cuique. Later, in the Common Room, the vice-president, J. W. Knight, made a short speech, to which Symonds replied in a few words. The bells chimed jubilantly to announce his victory and he gave the ringers a guinea. There was a double pleasure in the occasion: aesthetic response to the beauty of the ceremony, and the gratification of surpassing so formidable a rival as Lyulph Stanley and twenty other competitors.

On 27 October he was admitted Probationary Fellow, after taking the traditional oaths to the House of Hanover, and on 1 November he moved from his lodgings at Nalder's, 56 St Giles's, to rooms in the College cloisters nearly opposite the State apartments. The following day he wrote to Charlotte: 'I have just passed a strange night in learning my new position & the new noises that surround me in a College. My rooms are good; one large sitting room looking out into the tree of the Walks, with a smaller one on the cloister green opposite the old square tower of the Royal lodgings, & an atom of a bedroom.'[53] He planned to give Jowett a print of San Sisto 'as a kind of parting present' and 'I hope I may begin to do something for the College too.'[54] The new life was anticipated with pleasure: 'To have time for my own reading, to be able to think of the Elizabethans and Music, with a good library & no thoughts of Examinations, is a blessing for which I cannot be enough thankful.'[55] He also began to take Italian lessons from a Mr da Tiroli.

Shortly after he moved into Magdalen he was offered the post of tutor to the fifteen-year-old Lord Pembroke, then at Eton. Knowing the dangers of close contact with a boy, he prudently refused, but the offer made him face up to the fact that he must decide upon a career. He journeyed down to Clifton to talk the matter over with Dr Symonds. Father and son had grown very close and they sat far into the night smoking and talking over a fire in the doctor's study. John told him that he had 'ambition rather for literature than for anything else, and carelessness for politics and Parliament'.[56] No precise plan was established, but they decided that he should try to find some tutorial work which might eventually lead to an academic life.

Such a future appealed to him although he would have preferred the more intellectual atmosphere of Balliol. 'The Magdalen people are amusing', he wrote to Charlotte a month after he had been admitted. 'Their clerical society is of a toping sort. To drink sherry argues Radicalism with them, & they nickname each other jovially like boys. At night they often take their pipes comfortably together with beer & spirits, & last evening I formed part of such a reunion – excellent for mirth & good humour but not remarkable for wits . . . there is no harm here, & no leaven of bitterness, as in the Balliol Commonroom.'[57] He never fully entered into the levity of the other members of the College on occasions like the 'Pippin Audit': 'If the College business is treated with no more lucidity than the steward evinced in his speech last night, I am afraid that many incomprehensible questions about our finances might easily be answered. Such a meeting is pleasant in its way. It makes one feel the magnitude, & I wish it made everybody feel the responsibility, of such a body. Thirty thousand pounds had been reviewed by them for good or ill as their annual revenue in the daytime, & in the evening they celebrate their society by a sumptuous festivity. Nothing of the sort takes place in poor intellectual colleges like Balliol. . . . You must not fancy that our long heavy dinner was enlivened with much wit. I was glad enough to escape a little before ten & to walk with Bromely round the walks in the moonlight.'[58] But this lack of *rapport* was offset by his aesthetic response to the music and the physical surroundings of Magdalen, particularly the beauty of the College by night. Before going to bed he would gaze out of his window at the figures of the Virtues standing in clear relief against the shadows. He wished that the great gates were not locked at night because he longed to make a practice of a nightly walk to look at 'the broad meadow, & the cloister trees chequering the path with moonlight, the sparkle of the water, the dim rows of elms in the Park & shadowy deer beneath them, the tower rising alone against the clear grey sky. . . .'*[59]

The satisfaction of his achievement was not to last long. Disaster materialized in the form of the volatile Shorting whom he had promised to coach in philosophy. Symonds felt nervous about allowing him to

* Symonds was particularly attracted to night scenes. From Nürnberg he wrote 'Auntie' on 9 September 1863: 'I always try to see such a town first at night. Its buildings then derive an ideal unity from their subdued colour & loss of detail. Our modern gas lamps too produce splendid effects by shooting up their light through some dark cranny on a sculptured crucifix or a projecting window throwing masses of strangely shaped shadow over housefronts w^h in daytime are uninteresting and generally revealing & concealing with a picturesque wilfulness that stimulates curiosity & adds the sense of mystery to all one sees. Water too among buildings looks more terrible & infinite at night, whether swirling under bridges with the fitful long lights flickering over it, or sleeping sullenly beneath dead walls & sombre poplar trees' (University of Bristol Collection).

come to his rooms as Shorting was already in bad odour with the dons at Magdalen because of his persistent siege of one of the choristers. Anxious to acquit himself well at Magdalen and determined not to court trouble, Symonds suggested that the coaching sessions should be held in Shorting's rooms. Furious at having his designs for easy access to the choristers frustrated, Shorting fired off an indignant letter to him.

On 20 November Symonds heard disturbing news from a friend, Claude Cobham, an undergraduate at University College. Shorting had been dining at University College with Cobham and had made hysterical threats about how he was going to revenge himself on Symonds. Deeply distressed, Symonds rushed off for advice to Conington who assured him that he had nothing to worry about. Before he went to bed that night he turned for help to a divine source whose efficacy he had often questioned in the past few years. Taking out a book of texts which had belonged to his mother, he read the verses for that day: 'As one whom his mother comforteth, so will I comfort you' and 'Blessed be God who comforteth us in all our tribulation.'

Shorting did not wait long. On 24 November Symonds was staying in London with Rutson, who had begun to read for the Bar, when he received word from Cobham that Shorting had sent to six of the Magdalen Fellows poems and extracts of letters which Symonds had written to him. These, Symonds later learned, had been patched together so skilfully that Symonds was made to appear to share Shorting's habits and to have aided him in the pursuit of the chorister. In actual fact, Symonds had done everything he could to dissuade Shorting from his foolhardy actions. Although his conscience was clear, he shuddered at the prospect of the ensuing investigation. He was nervous too, as a Balliol man – 'Everyone detests Balliol'[60] – of being judged by Magdalen Fellows. Magdalen was still antagonistic to open Fellowships and highly distrustful of Jowett and the liberal ideas of his clever young followers. Blow followed upon blow. Lyulph Stanley was elected Fellow of Balliol and the formidable G. A. Simcox proved a delusion. If he had beaten Stanley in the examinations for Magdalen, Symonds realized bitterly, he could just as easily have taken the Balliol Fellowship from him. Moreover, if Shorting had made his charges at Balliol, they would have been swept aside contemptuously. A feverish fortnight was spent in collecting letters of support from his

Oxford friends as well as from many of his father's distinguished acquaintances. Little had he known that it would be such a short time before he was again faced with the unpleasant task of gathering testimonials. Weighed down by anxiety and weakness, he also had to write out a letter in his own defence.

On 28 December Symonds was acquitted by a General Meeting of the College of Magdalen. While, in effect, he had been completely exonerated, a certain ambiguity remained, and Dr Symonds was highly disturbed by the verdict. Two of Symonds's letters were strongly censured and Symonds himself admitted that one of these was in execrable taste. The ordeal was not yet over. As a Probationary Fellow he was bound to stay in Magdalen for a full year. But there was now no possibility of forming friendships which might have developed had the scandal not arisen. 'Everything annoys me,' he complained to Charlotte, 'even the conversation of people I used to like.'[61] The members of the College were courteous but decidedly cool and he was painfully aware that suspicion lurked behind the bland demeanour of his colleagues.

Symonds's attitude towards the affair in his Memoirs, written in 1889, is worth examination. It had been such a traumatic experience that he obviously relived the emotions and attitudes of nearly thirty years before. He proudly claims that he bore up very bravely throughout the episode. Dr Bulley, the President of Magdalen, and the various Fellows are described in the most contemptuous terms as his moral and intellectual inferiors. He is scornfully amused at the thought of Dr Bulley reading aloud to the entire assembly a poem addressed to the Shepherd Hymenaeus by Hesperus. In a gesture of defiance, as late as 1880, he included this in the collection *New and Old*. In retrospect he claimed that he would never have got along well with his Magdalen colleagues, yet he was eager enough to enter Magdalen. A little rationalization had served to cushion the blow.

His proud aloofness enabled him to get through most of the year. He took a short trip to Belgium with W. R. W. Stephens during the Easter vacation and on 23 March Jowett wrote his father: 'I took a walk with John before he left. I thought him very able, and much improved in ability since he went into the schools. I do not think his health has been any disadvantage to him mentally, but rather the reverse, although this seems strange.'[62] On Symonds's return he entered the spring term with six pupils in philosophy but within three weeks his health collapsed. 'My illness declared itself one night', he wrote in his autobiography, 'in the form of a horrible dream, the motive of which was that I saw a weak old man being gradually bruised to death with clubs. Next morning I rose with certainty that something serious had happened to my brain. Nor was I mistaken. During the next three years I hardly used my head or eyes at all for intellectual work, and it was fully ten years before they re-covered anything like their natural vigour; while in the interval I began to be consumptive. I do not doubt that the larger part of this physical distress was the result of what I suffered at Magdalen, coming after the labour of reading for my degree. . . .'[63] In his biography of Symonds, H. F. Brown omits the passage in the Memoirs in which Symonds attributes the basic cause of his breakdown to his unfulfilled passion for Alfred Brooke. Walking on the edge of a precipice, the experience at Magdalen was all that was needed to push him over into the abyss.

Charlotte took him off to Malvern. Here he was supposed to have a complete rest but in his nervous, highly-charged state relaxation proved impossible. He had already started a study of the Renaissance which he planned to submit for the Chancellor's Essay Prize, and Jowett's pupils seldom left things undone. Determined to make amends to his father for all that he had suffered during the Shorting affair, with eyes smarting and inflamed under blue spectacles and a green eyeshade, he drove him-self to finish the essay.

In later life he was highly critical of the finished product which he describes as a crude and superficial rehash of Michelet, but he admits that it had the merits of freshness and breadth of survey. It is a remarkable production for so young a man. In his diary of 24 June 1863 appears this laconic entry: 'Since I wrote last in this book I have got the English Essay Prize. Papa and Charlotte heard me recite it before the Prince and Princess of Wales. I have made a new and pleasant acquaintance, L. G. Mylne.'*[64] His life at Oxford ended on this unenthusiastic note.

* The friendship never developed. Mylne was appointed Bishop of Bombay in 1876.

CHAPTER IV

The Young Bachelor

THE full effects of the Shorting affair did not manifest themselves immediately. While never robust, Symonds had been able to lead a comparatively normal life as an undergraduate and seldom complained of fatigue after long walks or rides, but when he left Magdalen he was destined to spend the rest of his life as a semi-invalid. Whether he had a nervous breakdown in the technical sense is open to question. His emotional equilibrium had been shattered and he was to be plagued by a series of nervous ailments which aggravated his latent pulmonary condition.

Three years later he was still brooding about the Magdalen scandal when he wrote disconsolately to Graham Dakyns: 'It was on the 7th of April 1857 that I first began to live about the hour of 3.30 p.m. It was on the 22nd of November 1862 that the life born in April sunlight began to die. It is now quite dead & I have another kind of life.'[1] In modern parlance, he was probably suffering from an acute anxiety neurosis. He had been stunned by Shorting's attack and by the reaction of the Magdalen authorities. Real danger had never actually touched him in his relationships with Willie Dyer and Alfred Brooke, but he now realized that disaster could have overwhelmed him to the ruination of his entire career through his association with Shorting. Long before the exposure, he had known that he must try to become what he called a 'natural man'. His father made him see this when he persuaded him to break off his liaison with Willie, and yet his subsequent hopeless entanglement with Alfred might have been a warning that his whole nature would rebel against the pressures towards conformity. With renewed desperation, he set out to force himself to respond to the charms of women.

There was one woman with whom he already had an unusually intense relationship, but Charlotte was a very special case and other girls seemed frivolous and superficial in comparison with his sister. As young

children they had shared a passionate attachment to their governess
Sophie Girard, and after John went away to Harrow he never failed to
write his sister at least once a week begging for news of home. As brother
and sister matured, their mutual love of the arts, particularly of music,
deepened the pleasure they found in being together. Charlotte often
played to him and he believed that she had a natural gift for music.*
Music apart, he took an elder brother's interest in her reading (he
recommended Ruskin to her but warned her that sometimes he 'twaddles');
they read Tennyson together and worried about the implications of *In
Memoriam*. Symonds proudly introduced all his Oxford friends to his
talented, intelligent sister, and he assured her that he would trade none
of them for her. 'Mind, what I say about wishing for Oxford friends at
Clifton does in no way diminish the full perfection of home. I need some
attendant in those places only where my dear sister cannot go. As it is, if I
had my choice between the two, I would rather live at home, with solitude
and cherub contemplation, when I walk about, than stay at Oxford with
fifty devoted friends.'² They adored their home and Symonds wrote to
her ecstatically about a picture of Clifton he had seen at Christie's,
confident that she would try to persuade their father to buy it – 'perhaps
a little faded', he admitted, 'but by far the most poetical view of our downs
that I have seen. . . .'³ Charlotte, his father, and Clifton formed a much-
loved triumvirate, and when the older girls married and moved away from
home, the relationship among the three grew even more intimate. After
Edith's marriage in the spring of 1859, Symonds wrote to Charlotte from
Oxford: 'How we shall comfort ourselves without her, I know not: but
we must bravely

> Make an oath, & keep it with equal mind
> In the hollow Lotos land to live together
> Careless of mankind——

* He confessed to her how much he regretted that he had never been taught to play the piano,
and when he wrote an analysis of his favourite musical composition, Handel's *Messiah*, she alone
was told of his short-lived ambition to be a music critic: 'If I could play, how much in this
comparatively new line of criticism I should be able to effect. By dwelling long on the structure of
one of Beethoven's sonatas, by playing it to myself as at this time, & by forcing the thoughts of
solitude into harmony with it, I feel that I c^d produce something more definitely a work of art
than any criticism or analysis of painting can be. I feel sorely tempted at times to make the sacrifice
of time w^h the mastery of music w^d involve' (MS. letter, Oxford, 11 May 1863, University of
Bristol).

which though it is not quite Tennyson's idea or expression will serve at present to indicate the life tranquility [*sic*] you & I intend to live together, when you are an old Blue & I an old Pedant in Minerva cottage stuffed with books.'[4] In reply to her annual loving birthday letter in 1862, Symonds declared: '. . . if I am much to you you know that you are much to me . . . how much we neither can calculate.'[5] But the warmth of Minerva Cottage had to be abandoned reluctantly for the more pressing and less attractive demands of the outside world.

With the same resigned acceptance which had reconciled Symonds as a boy to the grim reality of Harrow, he now began to cast about for a suitable woman. In the spring of 1863, he first encountered Letitia Malthus, the daughter of some neighbours in Clifton. She was a rather boyish young woman and he told himself that she was probably the sort of girl with whom he could fall in love. Both her parents and Dr Symonds encouraged the incipient romance and the young people seem to have been thrown together a number of times, but the relationship did not progress beyond small gallantries. Uncertain about how he should approach a young lady, he consulted Charlotte as to whether she thought he would appear too pressing if he sent Letitia a bouquet. For four weeks in his diary he coolly noted the symptoms of a simulated passion very different from the torrential outbursts Willie Dyer or Alfred Brooke had driven him to pour out on paper. Not a single poem was inspired by her. And then, at the beginning of May, Letitia abruptly disappeared from the pages of his diary as he and Cecil Bosanquet began to make plans for a visit to Switzerland.

Ill health was still troubling him and Dr Symonds insisted on his making another trip to the Alps in the hope that the mountain air would revive him. Before they set out, Symonds confessed to Charlotte that he regretted Cecil was not 'stronger in character & more intellectual',[6] yet he soon discovered that Cecil could not have been a more ideal companion – gently sympathetic with his misery, sensitive to his changes of mood, and capable of diverting him with his gay spirits.

Symonds had been reading G. H. Lewes's *Life of Goethe* and looked for reminders of Goethe at every stage of their journey. At Strasbourg, inspired by Goethe's example, he was determined to ascend the spire of the cathedral. Cecil gave up before they reached the top, but Symonds pressed on at the expense of a blinding headache. From Strasbourg they travelled on to Basle, Lucerne, and Interlaken. Symonds wrote to Charlotte: 'Generally I avoid writing about mountains. Clear uniform sunlight fatigues me. It has a topographical utility, for it enables one to discriminate all the members of a range or network of valleys. But it makes nature dead. And for this reason I believe that a common English landscape contains all the elements of the sublime and beautiful. No Alpine views have touched my soul or elevated my feelings more than certain aerial effects of coming and departing storms which I have watched at Shotover. None have so thrilled me as the beauty of the morning and of evening in the skies and vapouring distances of Clifton.

'I wish so much that there were some chance of your coming abroad with papa. When several of us are away together the unhomeliness of travelling is not so felt as it must be when one is alone, and has so many absent ones to think of. I believe that nothing will induce me to leave England again for Italy, when once I have got home.'[7] Clearly, he had not yet succumbed completely to the power of the Alps, but he could not fail to be utterly enraptured by his first sight of the mountains covered in spring flowers, many of which he was to learn so intimately by name in the years to come.

Exhausted by the long journey, the young men decided to stop at Mürren in a quaint, unassuming inn run by a Herr Sterchi and his family. Within days it was apparent that Symonds was responding to the Alpine air. He spent hours clambering about the mountains, an umbrella grasped firmly in one hand, an alpenstock in the other. The only discomfort he suffered was sore feet, and he spent his evenings soaking them in cold water and rubbing them vigorously with arnica. He tried to make a conventional sketch or two but the results were dismal: 'My appreciation of the details of scenery is so far more perfect than anything I can possibly put down on paper that it distresses me to draw.'[8]

One July afternoon Symonds looked out of his window and was annoyed to see that an English family had arrived to disturb their idyllic isolation. He had no idea then of how important this casual encounter was eventually to become, but a few days after they had left, he noted in his diary: 'They were Mr. Frederick North, M.P. for Hastings, and his two daughters. Both the young ladies were devoted to sketching. The elder was blonde, tall, stout, good-humoured, and a little satirical. The second was dark and thin and slight, nervous and full of fun and intellectual acumen. The one seemed manager and mother, the other dreamer and thinker. Neither was remarkable for beauty, but the earnest vivacity of the younger grew upon me, and I could soon have fallen in love with her. Her name was Catherine. Mr. North is kind and easy-going. They seemed to have travelled in most parts of Europe.'*⁹

Whether he could have fallen in love or not, he did not have time to discover, for the Norths stayed only a week and Catherine was soon dismissed from his thoughts by an attractive substitute. During the summer the Sterchis' fifteen-year-old niece from Thun helped them to run the inn. Tall, fair Rosa Engel, in her quaint Bernese costume with its heavy silver chains, reminded Symonds of Faust's Margaret, and when her housework was finished, she and the young Englishman fell into the habit of meeting on the balcony in the evenings to talk shyly in French.

However, before the relationship had any chance to develop beyond the exploratory stage, Symonds was forced to leave Mürren as he had arranged to meet T. H. Green in Zürich on 10 August. In the meantime, Bosanquet, whose money was running out, had departed after declining Symonds's offer to pay his expenses. The night before Symonds left, he gave Rosa some wild flowers he had picked for her and with a sudden audacious impulse, kissed a woman for the first time in his life. Blushing furiously, she rushed away from him to hide among the other maids. Unfortunately, Symonds's reaction to the experience is not recorded.

In Zürich he had to comb all the hotels before he found Green, who had just come from Heidelberg and was full of German philosophy, politics, and the higher poetry. He could talk of little else but a scheme to translate F. C. Baur's *Geschichte der Christlichen Kirche* which he did start later in the year but never finished. They spent a quiet week at an inn just above Zürich where they worked during the day on wooden beer-tables under the thick beech-trees and in the evenings took long walks among the glow-worms. In his present mood, Symonds was

---

* The Norths were great travellers, as Symonds suggests, and the young ladies were among the first to discard the crinoline in travelling. The elder sister, Marianne, published an account of her travels in *Recollections of a Happy Life* in 1892; and after her death, her sister edited a further series, *Some Further Recollections of a Happy Life* (1893). Marianne North bequeathed her botanical paintings to the nation and the collection is housed in Kew Gardens.

receptive to anything connected with Goethe, and when Green introduced him to the proemium to *Gott und Welt*, he reacted fervently to it. He later described it as 'a poem which took deep hold upon me, and began to build my creed'.[10]

The memory of Rosa, he found, kept pushing out other interests, as a letter to Charlotte indicates: 'It is your birthday. . . . I wish I could send you some souvenir from Switzerland, but things cut in wood I hate. Would you care to have one of the Bernese costumes? I thought of getting that for you. It is to me a most lovely costume.

'At Mürren there was a young girl of the better class from Thun, who had come as a friend of the landlord for a change of air, and who helped his people in the waiting on their guests. She always wore this dress when she dressed for Sunday or for dinner-time, and it suited her well. . . .'[11] Suddenly, while still in Zürich, he decided there was no reason to resist his longing to see Rosa and the Alps once more. Green wanted to visit Gais but Symonds prevailed upon him to return to Mürren. By now 'very sulky at having come so far',[12] Green finally agreed reluctantly, although he remained adamant about leaving when it suited him. Symonds, with his usual impetuosity, set off immediately to call on Rosa's family in Thun, but when he presented himself to her mother, the startled woman appeared highly suspicious of the Englishman's motives for seeing her daughter again.

On 18 August, he battled his way through a sleet storm to reach Mürren. The following day the sun came through again, but it was clear that Rosa was now avoiding him for some reason. In the afternoon he caught sight of her in a window writing. As he passed slowly, stooping self-consciously to pat the landlord's great white dog, she bent even more intently over her letter. The second time, as she sat in her window sewing, she could not avoid his eye. He smiled at her but she returned a cold stare. Throwing discretion to the winds, he handed a maid a poem to give her, which started 'ich liebe'. On the 21st Green arrived, and as they were sitting on the rocks above the inn, Symonds's eye was caught by Frau Sterchi and Rosa sorting linen on a table under the projecting eaves of a chalet opposite. Leaving Green engrossed in his Baur, he approached hesitantly and this time was greeted by a warm smile. The young people were soon engaged in an animated conversation, all the time watched anxiously by

Frau Sterchi who did not understand a word of French. The diary goes on
to record every minute step of the romance – attempts to hold Rosa's
hand in the darkness of the balcony, the shy offering of a spray of oleander
blossoms, the careful choosing of a ring with a deep red stone. When he
pressed her to take the ring, she replied 'Je suis trop jeune' and around
these words he wove a sonnet which he later included in *Vagabunduli
Libellus*:

> Leave me awhile; I am too young to love:
> My maiden fancies are enough for me:
> Leave me awhile; too soon will passion move
> The silent springs of my virginity. . . .

A stout, self-important acquaintance of his father's from Clifton, who
was staying at the inn, witnessed the incipient romance with unconcealed
curiosity and made a coarse jest to Symonds about his conquest. Symonds
felt a secret thrill of pleasure. Was he indeed finally becoming a 'natural'
man? Just before he left, one of the guides asked him to stand with Rosa
as godparents to his baby. At the gay party after the christening, which
was his first happy encounter with the home life of the Swiss peasants, he
sat close beside Rosa with his arm around her waist and, flushed with wine
and confidence, boldly whispered into her ear until she flung herself off
in consternation.

Unfortunately, the romantic idyll came to an abrupt end the following
day when Symonds was finally dragged away by Green to fulfil the
previously-arranged commitments of their tour. After he left, he never
met Rosa again until 1887 when she paid him a visit in Davos Platz. By
then a white-haired lady of immense dignity, she told him that she had
returned his affection but did not encourage his attentions because she
knew that no good could come of a romance between a simple Swiss girl
and a well-born English gentleman. Symonds himself says in his Memoirs
that he did not love her with sufficient passion to want either to seduce
or to marry her. But the fact remains that he felt more sexually drawn to
her than to any other woman in his entire life and Green had to wrench
him away from Mürren.

As soon as he left, all the old nervous disorders returned – headaches,
sore eyes, and sleeplessness, aggravated by painful or erotic dreams. His
misery is reflected in a letter to Charlotte on 3 September, although he

does not admit its true cause: 'I tore myself away from Mürren . . . not without a spasm. Certainly I must in some sense be slow to take up impressions; for last year I could never have believed it possible to grow so deeply attached to mountains or to feel their spirit and their strength as I have done this summer. Everything seems cold and tame and lowering now. Munich and its art is bare and vulgar. I cannot return into my old self. . . .'[13] Before they reached Munich, he forced the long-suffering Green to make a detour to Thun where he desperately ransacked the shops in the impossible hope of finding a photograph of Rosa. Green finally managed to get him to Munich where they were joined by A. O. Rutson. From Munich they pressed on to Dresden where they moved into a pension filled with Cambridge men 'who, one & all, play the piano & spend their time in nothing but learning German & talking about music. This is somewhat of an affliction . . . there is something sad in coming back to old ways of going on, old gossip, old college talk, old associations of foregone life, much of w[h] I s[h] be glad to spurn for good, after the fresh divine existence w[h] I led among the mountains. There I did nothing common or mean, but everything was new & had a definite import. Here there are the thousand indifferences and little interests that vulgar life brings with it. . . .'[14] The Cambridge men included J. R. Mozley,* Oscar Browning,† and Henry and Arthur Sidgwick; of these Symonds was most attracted to Arthur Sidgwick's grace and intelligence, and a lifelong friendship was initiated which once more, in its early stages, had strong erotic overtones.

Again Green and Symonds set off together, this time for Leipzig to visit the book fair. Here they had a rather comical adventure. In the next bedroom two drunken Jews were shouting from bed to bed in a violent argument on the immortality of the soul. Finally Green could stand the

---

* J. R. Mozley was an assistant master at Clifton College, 1864-5.

† Oscar Browning, historian and purveyor of light gossip about European capitals. Symonds and Browning knew each other for the rest of their lives, corresponded, and sometimes stayed together, but no particularly close bond seems to have developed between them. At Eton Browning's tutor had been William Johnson Cory. After leaving Cambridge he returned to Eton as an assistant master but was dismissed in 1875 because of his intimacy with some of the boys. The charges were never specified but the case aroused so much interest that it was even debated in the House of Commons. Hornby, the Headmaster, was a Balliol man and Browning wrote to ask Symonds if Jowett had heard anything libellous about him; Symonds replied that he had not but his sympathies lay with Browning. Browning was also a close friend of Henry Sidgwick's.

racket no longer; he jumped up and knocked at the partition begging *die Herren*, as politely as he could in the circumstances, to remember their suffering neighbours. Thereupon, the Jews leapt from their beds and directed their passion to trying to batter the door down, shrieking obscene curses in incongruous contrast to the metaphysical discussions in which they had just been absorbed. Luckily the bolts held.

For the last lap of this piecemeal holiday, Symonds travelled alone from Leipzig to Cologne in the same carriage with G. J. Goschen,* whom he had known at Oxford. Goschen was reading a new book – Renan's *Vie de Jésus*. At Cologne Symonds met Arthur Sidgwick and the two returned to England together.

Symonds spent a miserable autumn in Clifton. The only events of any importance were the ironical but futile gesture of being admitted to Magdalen as a full Fellow and his meeting with H. G. Dakyns, a new classics master at the recently-founded Clifton College. Dakyns, two years Symonds's senior, was a Rugby and Cambridge man, who had been tutor to the sons of Tennyson to whom he had been recommended as the most popular man in Cambridge. Although extremely short, he was handsome and physically vigorous; sympathetic and emotional as well, he appealed to Symonds immediately. Their interests and temperaments were remarkably similar: both responded ardently to beauty, each possessed a gentleness and sensitivity which at times could sharpen into nervous irritability, and they shared a profound interest in philosophical speculation. This in Dakyns was supported by Comtism, while Symonds at the time was floundering among various perplexities. They soon got into the habit of meeting daily when Symonds was in Clifton, and if they were separated, long letters would be exchanged, faithfully recording the minutiae of their lives, particularly the record of their emotional tribulations. On 29 March 1864 Symonds wrote to his friend: 'You know now that to be loved is what I desire more than anything on earth. But I rarely can hope to find one so unselfish, so true, so pure as you to love me.'[15] They continued to write until Symonds's death, although in later years longer periods separated the letters, and H. F. Brown eventually replaced Dakyns as the repository of his introspective outpourings.

* 1st Viscount Goschen (*cr.* 1900), Chancellor of the Exchequer in Lord Salisbury's second administration, 1887.

Dr Symonds, convinced that the climate of Clifton did not agree with Symonds – or perhaps wanting to keep him as far away from Alfred Brooke as possible* – in December sent him off on yet another European tour. Symonds tried to persuade Arthur Sidgwick to join him but Sidgwick was unable to leave his duties as assistant master at Rugby. In his letter of invitation to Sidgwick, he wrote: 'I have today a desire to embrace at once all that is beautiful and deeply thought in Art, Philosophy, and Nature. . . . Thus I am caught in a whirl, and I do nothing but feel intensely a various and changing life.'[16] A. O. Rutson took Sidgwick's place, but Rutson was not the best of travelling companions: argumentative, exhaustingly analytical, he subjected the most trivial of statements to close scrutiny; it was impossible to relax mentally in his company. To add to Symonds's troubles, his father insisted on his being accompanied by a courier whose close attention became an intolerable nuisance until, in a rare gesture of defiance towards his father, Symonds dismissed him at Genoa. He kept Dakyns posted on what he called 'our india rubber travelling map'.[17] From Turin he wrote: 'I have had a long and stupid journey. My eyes got worse when I was at Oxford, owing probably to our habit of sitting round a blazing fire after dinner; they were again weakened by a stormy passage, and when I got to Paris I could hardly see. Of course I can neither read nor look out of the window when I am in a train, nor can I read or write during the evenings at hotels, so you may fancy how much time I have for reflection.'[18] In Florence they ran into Richard Congreve, the Positivist priest whom Symonds had already met at Oxford.† They took long walks with him but Symonds remained unconvinced by his arguments: 'I have asked for bread, & he has given me a stone', he wrote to Dakyns. 'Why not deny me bread & say "I have none: science has petrified my store?" I should be more content. But to offer me religion, prayer, a Church, a liturgy, a stool to kneel on, a pulpit to hear sermons from, & to bid me fix my hopes upon a

---

* This is probably what Symonds had in mind when he told Dakyns, 'Remember that Clifton is a terrible enchantress, & her secret things are poisonous' (MS. letter, dated Union Club, 24 May 1865, Dakyns Collection).

† Congreve had met Comte in Paris during the 1848 Revolution and had been so impressed by his philosophy that he resigned from Wadham where he was a tutor, to spread the doctrine of Scientific Positivism.

summum genus which I help to make – it is too absurd. If I ever become a positivist, it will be of the Mill kind.'[19]

In Rome, Rutson, in an embarrassing burst of confidence, divulged that he was in love with Charlotte, but he hedged his sentiments with so many qualifications that Symonds did not take him very seriously, particularly as many of his friends, including Dakyns, seemed to make a habit of falling in love with his sister. Then, to Symonds's vast relief, Rutson decided to return home. He was replaced by another of the endless succession of travelling companions, this one the sweet-natured W. R. W. Stephens, who, if not as intellectually alert as Rutson, at least did not rub abrasively against Symonds's sensitive nerves. As a result of this change Symonds felt better than he had done since he left England. With Ruskin in hand, he 'drank in buildings, statues, pictures, nature – the whole of the wonderful Italian past presented in its monuments and landscape. I learned a great deal undoubtedly, which proved of use to me in after years. And the life was simple, reserved, free from emotional disturbances.'[20] Juvenal and Tacitus enabled him to rebuild the Forum, and the Raphaels in the Vatican were 'like the Bible', for he had copied many of the artist's designs even before he went to Harrow. Yet he failed to be deeply moved by the experience. His long descriptive letters to Dakyns and his family are like set pieces, and his stock responses very different from the rapture of his first encounter with Venice.

Even a delicate young man of cultivated tastes and comfortable means could not tour around Europe indefinitely, gazing at statues and picturesque vistas. After the *débâcle* at Magdalen he had no wish to return to Oxford, and Dr Symonds saw the law as the only alternative open to him. Knowing his son's moody disposition and lack of physical stamina, he was disinclined to encourage him in a career of letters lest he drift into dilettantism. Far better to have a respectable profession such as his own in which literature served as a delightful pastime. Symonds unenthusiastically agreed, and in April 1864 took furnished rooms at a hundred guineas a year on the first floor of a house at 7 Half Moon Street, London, in which Rutson was already installed on the second floor. It would be interesting to know whether Symonds was aware that Shelley had once lived in Half Moon Street. It would have struck him as appropriate that he should live in the shade of the poet during a period when he was frequently comparing himself to Alastor; he told Charlotte that he had begun 'to think that something must be wrong with my intelligence because I find "Alastor" and "Epipsychidion" explicable'.[21]

He ate his dinners at Lincoln's Inn and made a feeble gesture of studying the law, which seemed to him to be composed of 'endless divisions, & the most tortuous ingenuities of interpretation hypothesis & provision'.[22] Most of his time he spent at the Union Club in Trafalgar Square, whose stolid unacademic atmosphere he found much to his taste. Here he wrote long introspective letters to Dakyns, or read, or composed unsigned articles for *The Saturday Review*. He turned out nineteen of these between December 1862 and June 1864, mostly written in less than three hours and paid for at the rate of £12 each.* They encompassed a wide range of subject, from the nature of genius to Icelandic sagas, and the Editor, Cook, was impressed with their fluency and confident air of profound knowledge. Symonds himself knew that they were marred by what Dr Vaughan once described as his 'fatal facility'. The style of these reviews is wordy, the views priggish and unadventurous, and the attitudes those of a superior young man just down from Oxford. 'The Novel and the Drama', which appeared in the March issue of 1864 bears a startling resemblance to T. H. Green's essay, 'An Estimate of the Value and Influence of Works of Fiction in Modern Times', which had won the Chancellor's Prize in 1862. Both take the traditional Aristotelian view that we cannot help enjoying novels because their characters are so much like ourselves, but hold that such self-indulgence cannot be compared with the ennobling effect of a great play. Neither Green nor Symonds had read many novels.

He covered reams of paper with poems, including an eight-hundred-line lyric entitled 'Theodore'. 'But I find it wholly impossible to say anything that is not grossly autobiographical', he told Dakyns.[23] When Dakyns asked him to send him some of his poetry he replied: 'Why, when you have Shelley & Tennyson, do you want to hear my pitiful ravings? If

---

* Two years before Symonds's death, when young Arthur Galton asked him for an introduction to *The Pall Mall Gazette*, for which he started writing in 1865, he replied: 'Unless you want to earn the few pounds of the reviewer, I do not see much use in writing for a newspaper. I threw away much time and many thoughts on work of this kind, w^h I began while I was still an undergraduate at Oxford. I think it did me harm as a writer' (MS. letter, dated Davos Platz, 8 March 1891, University of Texas Collection).

you read my verses, I could not fail to talk about them, & to tell you of a time (now, thank God, past & gone) than w^h I could not imagine, any time more terrible. . . . I had better not send them. Reading them myself has made me miserable. I am ashamed to know how helpless I have been, & I c^d cry with pity for my past sorrow. . . . Please be content to know me now in my autumn & do not rake up old embers – I am not a poet: this I know emphatically: so you suffer no literary loss: You are duly spared a long & sickening recital of disease & disappointment & delusion & suffering.'[24]

'Externally graceful', he described himself to Rutson, 'I am inwardly at war – the sport of a hundred wild desires which you probably have never felt.'[25] In the external social world he appeared to lead the same sort of life as many other well-connected young bachelors in London. He visited art galleries and attended innumerable concerts where he listened to the piano of Rubinstein, the violin of Joachim, and the voices of Trebelli, Patti, and Pauline Lucca. Personable, amusing and attractive, he frequently received invitations to evening parties and he described to Charlotte one entertaining *soirée* at the home of the historian George Grote:

First of all Mrs Grote herself is like a Grenadier in petticoats: she stands at least six feet in her shoes, wears no crinoline, mounts a huge plume of ostrich feathers above an auburn wig, and rolls fierce ogreish eyes while she devolves her periods in a deep bass voice. Mr. Grote is a calm gentlemanly man, very kind and agreeable, but not in appearance, or in the few words which he was so good as to speak to me, striking. He used one Greek word, $\phi\theta o\rho a\grave{\iota}$ [destination], in his conversation, and technically, which proved that he had recently been studying Aristotle.* We had good music . . . . Mme Goldschmidt† sang an air from the Flauto Magico, 'Oft on a plot of rising ground,' . . . They (i.e. the Goldschmidts) sent their carriage for me and sent me home in it, which was most kind, for a furious thunderstorm was raging all the evening. It sounded very strange above the Music. . . . Mrs Grote turned me eventually out of the house; for Mme Goldschmidt had asked me to stay until the end and then settle about driving

* Apparently Symonds was unaware that when Grote finished his *History* in 1856, he began putting his papers in order for a work on Plato and Aristotle, which he regarded as its necessary complement. For some years he spoke of the coming work as 'on Plato and Aristotle' but by 1862 Aristotle had dropped into the background. (G.C.R., *D.N.B.*)

† Jenny Lind.

down to-day; which I did; until Mrs Grote, wanting, I suppose, to be alone with her, came up and gave me a Gorgonish good-bye.[26]

Another letter written during this period to Dakyns describes 'two days of rare enjoyment' spent at Cambridge:

I say 'rare' because, though of course I did not enjoy myself continuously, or at any time so much as I have done in the Vatican, yet there is a charm about the place & an exceeding pleasantness in Arthur Sidgwick wʰ made me happy. It is long since I was at Oxford, & you know how painful Magdalen is to me still. Therefore, though I longed once more to be in a college, to hear the tumult of the halls, to see the Chapels filled with insolent curlheaded youth, to talk the quiet talk at midnight, in old square low rooms, to listen to the chimes & winds & watery noises through half dreaming wakefulness at night, I could not do this in Oxford. Cambridge gave it me without recalling too much of myself. All was there, so different in detail, & yet essentially so much the same.

Henry Sidgwick took me in to dinner in Hall on Sunday. I like him better than I did, but I do not get on with him. We are quite different from one another yet we do not dovetail. I should like to see much of him. He would tell me many things I do not know, & give me many a new point of view. I can hardly measure the extent to wʰ I think he is happy in his strength & clearness of mind & straightforwardness of purpose. Arthur of course I get on with better. He has many of his brother's good points, & though I do not think his mind is of so high an order, it possesses gifts of delicacy & subtlety of feeling wʰ I expect Henry misses. Arthur will develop greatly in the aesthetical part of his nature. I doubt whether he will ever be remarkable as a connoisseur or historian, or as a practical artist but he will steadily increase in the power of fresh & vigorous enjoyment. He enjoys all things fully, so purely & so spontaneously that I love him for that alone. God has been very kind to him, & he has used the world well. I like all his friends. There is no fever about them. So tranquil an atmosphere does not probably exist in Oxford, where party strife, metaphysical speculation, & personal passions of all sorts make every kind of man irritable.

It was pleasant strolling about the bridges & lying on the river bank, talking of art religion love & people, Arthur definitely & logically, I dreamily – for we do not argue, both listening & 'dovetailing'. But it is no use being sentimental about those two days. They were pleasant – voilà tout.[27]

During this period Jenny Lind often invited him down to her home in Wimbledon. She was a deeply religious woman and it was said that Bishop Stanley had persuaded her to give up the stage; in any event, since 1849 she had lived in semi-retirement except for a rare appearance at concerts or to sing at the wedding of the Prince of Wales to Princess Alexandra of Denmark in 1863. Symonds venerated her as the ideal woman, a noble creature who had come through worldly existence completely unsullied. She told him that when she stood before vast audiences she always addressed her song to God. Returning from one of his many visits to Wimbledon, he sat down and wrote to Charlotte: 'She grows upon one each time one sees her: but she is tiring – she requires sympathy to be wholly understood & it is a strain to raise one's feelings to her pitch.'[28] Mme Goldschmidt foresaw a brilliant future for him and, according to his daughter Margaret, was keenly disappointed when he made an early marriage.[29]

A more disturbing influence on his life at this time was Mrs Josephine Butler. Symonds had met the Butlers in 1856 when they spent a brief year in Clifton; and George Butler had suggested many books on the Renaissance to him when he was preparing his essay for the Chancellor's Prize. During 1864 Symonds paid them at least two visits in Cheltenham where Butler had been appointed Vice-Principal of Cheltenham College. At the time Mrs Butler was in a state of suppressed hysteria because, earlier in the year, her small daughter, falling through a balustrade as she rushed out to greet her parents, had been killed at their feet. 'I was possessed', Mrs Butler wrote, 'with an irresistible desire to go forth and find some pain keener than my own, to meet some people more unhappy than myself – my sole wish was to plunge into the heart of some human misery, and to say (as I now know I can) to afflicted people – "I understand; I too have suffered."'[30] Her first call was not directed towards fallen women but to reviving the flagging faith of sceptical young men. At thirty-six she was still a beautiful woman, but while Symonds was disturbed by the agitation into which she threw him by her curious combination of religious fervour and flirtation, he remained unmoved sexually.

She talked vehemently of how she suffered in her mind. As she lay there exquisitely slender and mobile, full length on the sofa, she did look torn by demons. She told me the torture of her thought, how religious, social, political doubt weighed on her. She never lost her feeling for God, but could not help thinking of Him as a tyrant. Sympathised with me, when I said such thoughts goaded one on to suicide as a means of finding out the truth.[31]

Mrs Butler had a curiously narcissistic method of seeking God: she would kneel before her looking-glass and then call in Symonds or Arthur Sidgwick or some other young man, who happened to be visiting her at the time, to witness her exhortation to God through her own image. On 17 April Symonds wrote to Dakyns: 'My conversation with Mrs Butler was very pleasant, far more peaceful than the feverish interview I had with her on Friday afternoon, more satisfactory to my taste, and one that made me understand myself better. Θήρ, παῖς and Θεός [wild beast, boy and god]. I was no longer one in all & all in one but simply a sentient & receptive being upon whom light and sunshine descended.'[32] Mrs Butler's fervour reminded him of St Catherine, and as he wrote his essay, 'Sienna and St Catherine', her face constantly interposed itself between him and the page. 'We see in her', he wrote of both women, 'the ecstatic, the philanthropist, and the politician combined to a remarkable degree.'[33] He regarded her as a very 'great lady' for a number of years until her campaigning zeal for wayward women disillusioned him with his former ideal.

The constant trips, the social life, the new friends, male and female, did not allay his persistent listlessness, and his health showed no sign of improvement. His inner life as revealed by his diary and in his letters was in a ferment of neurotic disturbance. Inflamed eyes and a feeling of great pressure weighing down upon his head made it necessary for him to hire readers. He paid Sir William Bowman, the ophthalmic surgeon, a guinea a day to drop deleterious caustic under his lower eyelids. 'I am very much alone', he told Dakyns, 'I cannot read at all by candlelight & only a little in the daytime. Therefore there are wildernesses of unemployed solitude when the over-taxed brain does not enjoy itself.'[34] By June his condition was worse. 'Every nerve seems as if it had been stripped of its integument & opened to the influences of the world,' he complained. 'My being might have been an eye from wh a cataract & [sic] has been removed amid the blaze of day.'[35] Even music proved no solace. 'Yesterday I went out in a cab', he says in the same letter, '& heard Beethoven's Symphony in C. Minor. It is no exaggeration when I say that every note found a place here in my heart. I was so weak & sensitive that he played upon me as upon an instrument. I never so heard music before & I was obliged to leave the concert.' He longed to get out of London and back to Clifton.

'In this stifling city of bricks & dust & iron', he wrote Dakyns, 'I have often seen you knee-deep in the bluebells & anemones of Leigh Woods, under the tender screen of fresh green beech & hazel leaves, or in the solemn shadows of the rocks at night, looking across to those deep cloven dells. Longing so intense that it supplies the sight it craves for, has filled me for the valleys of Switzerland & the sweet strange languid spirit of Clifton.'[36] The law was abandoned temporarily and in order to rest 'the overtaxed brain' he had a Surbiton waterman row him on the Thames. Not unexpectedly, he began to fall in love with him.

Yet still he did not get to grips with the root of the trouble. 'Woe to those who waste the best years of their virginity', he lamented to Dakyns, 'in vain yearnings after exhausting sources of delight. The spring comes to them but can call forth no new buds & stir no strong sap.'[37] His reproductive organs began to swell and irritate him and another doctor cauterized him through the urethra. As a last resort, Dr Symonds sent him to Dr Spencer Wells, the surgeon to the Queen's household. Dr Wells prescribed a simple remedy for his eyes – a lotion of vinegar and water. Then, turning to the cause of his other disorders, he diagnosed these as fundamentally the result of his repressed sexual instincts, and he advised him that he must either take a hired mistress or a wife. Dr Wells appears to have formed a fairly shrewd estimate of Symonds, for he talked to him bluntly about marriage, warning him not to regard it as a romantic ideal but simply as an arrangement to satisfy mutual sexual needs and as a social and domestic partnership.

In a letter to Rutson it is obvious that he had been deeply impressed by Dr Wells's views and had begun to reflect on what he expected from marriage.

What a man and woman seek in wedlock is mutual support in respect of feeling more than of intellect. Each represents a different type of moral excellence. They invigorate & supplement one another; & I am convinced that if both be made of true stuff, some conflict with the material difficulties of the world will aid their development & make them nobler creatures. They will learn themselves better, & have more play for the exercise of those active sympathies w^h in marriage complete men & women. What after all is the object of life? Is it not to live as much as possible; & if it may be at the close of life to feel that every year has passed almost unheeded from its fullness of occupation? . . . I do not mean to advocate poor marriages as superior to those w^h are made with plenty of money, for I am sure that mere material comfort is half of virtue in this world. . . . I think that people who have never felt discomfort & pain, are either apathetic or ennuyé, unless they have a wellspring of intellectual vitality within them; & that is what 499 women out of every 500 lack – . . . I should always be seeking intellectual sympathy, stimulating her interests, & living in a fever of mixed feeling & speculation. And there are ten chances to one that such a woman would at times fly off at a tangent from her husband, open new veins of interest where he would be unwilling to follow her, & irritate him by that bad taste w^h intellectual women are almost doomed to suffer from. – I . . . feel sure that strong well tested personal feeling on one side is the true basis of marriage & that other things may be left to themselves. There is an instinct in these matters w^h [we] are justified in obeying, & if two natures meet sympathetically upon that common ground, I do not think that they will often find obstacles in other regions of the character. . . .[38]

As for Dr Wells's advice, Symonds was quite certain that the only illicit connection he could form would be with another male. Marriage, however, presented an immediate solution to his difficulties and he began to think seriously of it for the first time. Such a decision could not be taken without a serious discussion with his father and he found that Dr Symonds welcomed the idea with extraordinary enthusiasm.

He still yearned after Rosa but marriage with her was completely out of the question. Suddenly he remembered the girl he had met the previous summer at Mürren, Catherine North. With characteristic impetuosity, he immediately sought her out at 3 Victoria Street, where he knew that her father had taken a flat. He received a pleasant welcome and for the next six weeks made every effort to arrange to have himself invited to all the social functions which he knew the Norths would be attending. There were many of these while they were in London because, as a branch of the distinguished North family, they had a wide circle of social acquaintances. On one occasion Catherine asked him teasingly if he had a broomstick since he was always crossing their path. Unabashed, he determinedly set about making himself agreeable to her at operas and concerts, and the more he saw of her, the more determined he became to marry her.

He ignored the difficulties that might arise in a union which had been pursued so coolly and with such calculation; yet his letters to Dakyns over that summer reveal that his state of mind was far from untroubled. In early June they made some vague plans to travel to Switzerland together.

For some reason Dr Symonds vetoed the idea and on 2 July Symonds suggested that they spend August on the north-east coast with Green. On 15 July, knowing that the Norths were planning to leave for Pontresina at the end of the month, he again wrote to Dakyns: 'W^d you under any circumstances be willing to travel with me to the Tyrol & to leave me alone when I requested you to do so? This is a strange request. But if you are going off on solitary wanderings, you *might* under peculiar conditions into w^h I cannot now enter, greatly aid me without disturbing y^r own plans?'[39] The next communication Dakyns received was a frantic letter written on 19 July: 'I am in *deep trouble*. And I cannot yet settle to do anything this summer.'[40] On 23 July he again impressed upon Dakyns that 'The circumstances w^h are controlling me are as likely as not to make it impossible for me to go with you abroad.'[41] Less than a week later he informed him that he planned to leave for a short stay in Buxton the following day, 'having seen one fair face for the last time'.[42] The following day he finally admitted the cause of his vacillation: 'The business I have been about lately is paying my addresses to a young lady whom I met last year & who won my admiration. But, though every-thing else is favourable, there is one point w^h cannot be got over – the most important of all perhaps – the health of her family. I had thought of joining her in the Engadine & travelling with her party for a short time. But everything has now been broken up. I am able to retreat with a weary heart & heavy head before it is too late.'[43] Apparently Dakyns had had enough of this vacillation and decided to set off for Switzerland on his own with Arthur Sidgwick. Symonds was disappointed at having lost the chance of being with Arthur, for Sidgwick, as he told Charlotte in an unwittingly revealing letter, 'among my newer friends, is one whom I most truly like & from whom I derive most enjoyment on the subjects of Art etc. w^h interest us both. But it seems necessary to blunt all my sensi-bilities at present, & therefore the more I like a companion the less he is esteemed a healthy one.'[44] Just before they left, Symonds sent Dakyns a final letter: 'I may go after all to the Tyrol. This affair I told you of has some chance of coming on again. I at least return about it tomorrow to Clifton.' But he also enclosed a letter which he asked Dakyns to give to Rosa if he went to Thun, as well as a Napoleon for his small godchild. Then, in a postscript, he added: 'My whole soul yearns at the thought of

Mürren . . . remember when you see Rosa that I loved her more than I loved any woman & that she taught me what Mürren is.'[45]

His reaction to an experience to which he refers briefly in his Memoirs reveals disquieting symptoms. Between the time the Norths left England and his own departure he paid a visit to a clergyman in Norwich whose name he does not reveal. The young wife made it only too obvious that she was attracted to Symonds. But though her voluptuous incitements aggravated his already agitated state of nerves, she herself got from him nothing but a violent physical recoil.

Before the Norths left England, Symonds had asked Miss North if he might follow them to Pontresina, making it quite clear that it was for Catherine's sake. While Marianne did not press him with a warm invitation, she agreed noncommittally, but decided against telling Catherine about his plans. The sisters had never been close and the family as a whole were undemonstrative and uncommunicative. Since their mother's death ten years before, Catherine had never received much affection from her sister. As a result, she had become somewhat withdrawn, and struck people as reserved and serious although at times she could break into a wild gaiety. She was generally considered a handsome girl and artists liked to paint what they described as her Dantesque beauty – dark southern colouring, a bold Roman nose, and black hair drawn severely back from her forehead. Left to her own devices a great deal of the time, she had become such a voracious reader that Symonds discovered he could expect a familiarity with many of the things he talked about. Moreover, unlike the rattles most girls he met appeared to be, she had no small talk, was often comfortably silent, and he approved a dignity about her unusual in so young a woman.

The last night they were in London, Symonds and Catherine, after attending service together at Westminster Abbey, walked silently back to the flat, each ignorant of the other's feelings. Catherine had already fallen in love with him, but when they said good-bye, she resigned herself to not seeing him again for many months. Furthermore, she feared that she could never live up to his high ideal of womanhood which he had expounded to her – a difficulty complicated by the fact that she was three years his senior. A day or so after they arrived in Pontresina, Marianne mentioned casually that she had seen two letters waiting for Mr Symonds in the Post Office. Catherine hardly dared to hope, but when she came downstairs the following day she found Symonds standing talking to her sister.

Early in August he had set off to overtake them on what he described as 'this voyage of discovery'.[46] He was so uncertain of the issue that he brought with him a large pile of books, mainly the Elizabethan dramatists, to work on in some corner of Switzerland if his mission were unsuccessful. During the first few weeks at Pontresina Symonds followed Catherine about when she went out on her sketching expeditions, talking sometimes, more often silent. He developed neuralgia from sitting beside an icy mountain stream as she sedulously recorded the local flora and fauna. Catherine was bewildered by the calm way in which he told her that he knew the dangers of his exposure but balanced the pleasure against the pain. However, he went up to his room and expressed himself somewhat differently to Charlotte: 'She is so fond of fresh air that paying one's addresses to her entails one sitting about in draughts or more imperviousness to cold of all sorts than I think desirable. . . .'[47]

Mr North and Marianne behaved as though nothing untoward were happening and the young people were in an agony of nervousness, neither certain of the end towards which they were drifting. On 4 August Symonds wrote to Dakyns: 'My life is strange. I do not read or write. I do not walk much. I think only of one person, & when she is away my mind seems empty. Yet I am not passionately in love. What it will come to depends on her.' And in the same letter, he exclaimed: 'Why did you not give me some news of Rosa Engel when you & Sidgwick wrote?'[48]

Charlotte was informed of every step in the campaign. 'I wish you were here', he wrote to her on 14 August. 'Perhaps you c^d enlighten me with female instinct as to the state of Catherine's mind. I cannot make out *how* she cares for me. That she does like me & likes to have me near her is very certain. But I know no more. She does not despise me as a boy. On the contrary she seems to have thought me at Mürren rather unapproachably clever, & she wonders now that we should have become such friends. I am to continue travelling with them. So there is no need yet to come to an abrupt decision. . . .'[49] Here he broke off and the letter was continued later in the day.

That very afternoon as Catherine and Symonds leaned over a bridge, watching the swirling waters of a mountain stream, he began to tell her of how miserable he had been before he had gone to Mürren and how it had restored him to life. Then he added: 'If it had not been for Pontresina I should have gone to Mürren.'

'Why do you not go to Mürren?' Catherine asked in a low voice.

'Shall I go now?'

'Oh no! This place would be very miserable.'

'You must know *why* I came to Pontresina.' Then, as though speaking in a dream, he asked, 'Could you manage to be content with me all through life?'

'It is odd, very odd', Symonds wrote to his sister that night. 'Often as I have thought what a declaration of affection might be, I c^d never have pictured it to myself as it really was.'[50]

When they returned to the inn, and Catherine told her sister of their engagement, Marianne replied that she was delighted that Catherine was going to marry a good man, not some frivolous dancing partner as she had always feared. At tea they were quiet and self-conscious, but when they were left alone Symonds assured Catherine that he had never cared for any other woman before he met her (he was being strictly accurate because he had met Rosa at the same time!) and that if he had seemed cold it was because he had a Greek contempt for women.

Two days later they climbed to the top of the Pinz Languard and there on the Alpine heights, they exchanged rings. Symonds gave Catherine his signet ring, she gave him a lapis lazuli, inscribed JCN. There they sat holding hands and gazing down at the magnificent panorama until a horde of German tourists drove them from their eyrie. The setting could not have been more romantic and yet Symonds was perturbed by grave doubts. He was convinced that he loved Catherine ardently, yet he knew that it was a feeling devoid of all passion or desire. He knew that she would never be able to create the sort of holocaust within him that had been stirred by Willie Dyer and Alfred Brooke. His doubts were reinforced by the words of an artist, Charles Knight, who was staying at the inn. 'No man', Knight told him very seriously, 'has the right to marry a woman unless he loves her passionately.' Symonds managed to quell his doubts temporarily by remembering Dante's love for Beatrice. His would be such a love: pure, spiritual, ennobling.

Dakyns was, of course, informed of the engagement:

Pontresina, Aug: 20. 1864.

My dear Dakyns

I write again a hasty note to tell you that I am engaged to be married to Catherine North. She is the second d^r of the Member for Hastings. My happiness is very great. I need not dwell on that. One point, however, gives me great satisfaction. And that is that I have won her for myself, without offering any advantages of birth or fortune, without even my own kindred being known to hers. It is not what I wish to do to write a long account of her or of the perfect days w^h have made this valley the dearest spot in Europe after Clifton. And as I have nothing else in my head, I may as well say good-bye to you, telling you that my friends are Catherine's.

Write to me soon to Botzen in the Tyrol.

I am y^r ever aff

J. A. SYMONDS[51]

During the last weeks of August and early September the inn was crowded with English tourists, among them Mrs Gaskell, already showing signs of her fatal illness, and working on her last, unfinished novel, *Wives and Daughters*. Symonds continued to join Catherine on her sketching excursions, reading aloud to her from his old diaries or from Tennyson and Browning. It was decided that he should accompany the Norths as far as Venice on their way home, and on 12 September he wrote to Dakyns: 'Miss Catherine & I will have had six weeks of each other's society, not a bad specimen of life.'[52] Mr North warned him several times that Catherine had a terrible temper but he was not unduly disturbed, being only too aware of his own deficiencies. They were gentle and formal with each other, Catherine mutely adoring, Symonds often quiet and thoughtful. On one occasion, attempting to be playful, she threw a snowball at him and was reduced to tears when he lost his temper as it trickled icily down his back.

They spent three days in Venice and on 6 September, Symonds wrote to Charlotte: 'Mr. North lounges about by himself, Miss North sketches industriously, while Catherine & I row in a gondola eating figs, peaches & grapes, & looking into churches now & then. They leave us alone to our own devices. Catherine has no love for old art, & I cannot get her to take sufficient interest in Vivarini & Conegliano though I never knew any one so thoroughly enjoy the gorgeous sunsets or splendid views of every sort which we have seen together.'[53] This letter also contains a significant reassurance: '. . . whatever happens, I do not lose a bit of my desire to be with you again. I long as much to come home as I ever did.' On their last evening they rowed back from Torcello through the lagoons shimmering with the reflected light of the sun setting behind the black shapes of distant Venice, while the stars came out one by one.

Leaving Venice, they travelled by night over the Mont Cenis pass, Symonds and Catherine sitting together in the cold on the courier's box, where she listened patiently as he analysed her character and pointed out her faults. At Dover they parted. Symonds was back in Clifton on 22 September where, as they did not want to have a long engagement, he was immediately plunged into plans for the wedding, including a visit by Mr North to his father. He and Charlotte also made a trip to Hastings, fraught with anxiety for what his sister would think of Catherine, and on the return journey in the train he badgered her to be ruthlessly truthful about his future bride. 'I fear you must have thought I lectured you dreadfully going up to London', he later wrote apologetically, 'but I feel this separation from my home w^h marriage entails very much, more perhaps than I ought to do, & I want you to occupy at home my place as well as your own – to be to our father more than you have been & as much as you can be & as he could wish you to be.

'I hope too, dearest Charlotte, that you will be able to love Catherine, both as a sister & as a friend. If you do I shall not be really separated from you all, but we shall grow even more & more united among ourselves. It made me very anxious at Hastings to see how you would get on together. . . .'[54]

Only a month before his marriage he wrote a brief note to Dakyns on the subject of passion. 'For me it', and here he crossed out 'is' and substituted 'has long been over. I am quite calm, ready to bear the loss of what I sacrificed in the past, content to believe that I was bound to dwindle & be thankful for it, & finally expectant of a happier & loftier future purged from the pangs of passion though drawing sweetness from its beauty. Do you also look forward. Jacob served 14 years for Rachel, & I do not think she was his first love. I am y^r aff J. A. Symonds. You may, perhaps, not see me for some time.'[55] On 10 November 1864 he married Catherine in a large fashionable wedding in St Clement's Church, Hastings, which was attended by all the local notables, including the Duke of Cleveland.

His romantic experiences with women had been confined to little more than one brief year.

CHAPTER V

The Restless Years

I

In October 1861 when Symonds informed Jowett that he had just reached the age of twenty-one, his tutor's sober rejoinder was that 'the most important era in a man's life is when he leaves college'.[1] Convinced by Jowett that there were great things to be done if only he could discover them, he passed a despondent year before his marriage, troubled by wretched health and by the drifting restlessness resulting from his inability to find any purpose to direct his life. Fully aware that practical concerns could not be dealt with effectively until he had stabilized his turbulent emotions, he expected great things of marriage. He entered it not only in the naïve belief that it would redirect his sexual proclivities, but also in the vague hope that its responsibilities would renew his enthusiasm for a career which had so far failed to attract him in any way.

Almost immediately he was to be disappointed. The first few days of the honeymoon were passed in Brighton, where the young people fumbled and blushed and irritated each other. Since Symonds lacked the faintest knowledge of female anatomy, it was several nights before they were able to consummate the marriage. He found, to his relief, that contact with his wife could rouse him to potency, but the experience, instead of transporting him as he had romantically imagined it would, left him depressed and curiously empty. The miracle which was to transform him did not occur.

The first letter of his married life was written to 'my own dearest Charlotte' on the morning after the wedding. All the previous day he had longed to have a minute alone with her; and now, the initial, unspoken disillusionment crept into the flat tone of his letter

There were many things I should have liked to say to you, not worth recording now, but of interest had we been able to sit alone together for an hour. Such a

94

great event as yesterday, however long anticipated, well prepared for, & leading to however thoroughly foreknown a termination, always at last falls suddenly upon one. I felt all through the day that I was acting a part, & this helped me. When men have to do things, there rises up between their self & the deed a screen of unreality. So action is always less essential than contemplation. But after it is done, a sense of inadequacy & incompleteness, proceeding from the contrast between the deed meditated & the deed accomplished, springs up.

We reached Brighton safely in time for a comfortable dinner. Our windows face the sea, foggy enough to-day. I am happy & calm, as I wish to be. I hope Catherine too is happy, though it would not be her way to say she never knew till now what happiness was! – a very foolish or a very fresh & simple remark. Most people are in the state of Faust, saying to no moment 'Stay: thou art fair.' Yet if I ever felt inclined to say that magic sentence it would be now. I believe, however, in continuance of affection being more really good than its first blush. . . .

Give . . . my best love to Pop* & Mr North & tell them how happy I am with Catherine. I hope I may be able to make her happy: if loving her more & more will do so, I do not fear. . . .[2]

The adventure of early married life did not stave off the inevitable physico-nervous symptoms. 'My eyes & other physical maladies have not been scared away by even so bright a vision', he wrote to Dakyns from the Isle of Wight where they were spending the latter part of their honeymoon. 'This is not Love's fault, it is my cross. And I will learn to wait. Meantime Love is very precious to me, & I of him am unworthy.'[3]

Symonds had long been anxious to visit Tennyson, and, finding himself in the neighbourhood of Farringford, he took the opportunity to present a letter of introduction written for him by Jowett. Everything seemed propitious to produce a most memorable occasion, but unfortunately Tennyson was in London. However, there were other compensations – '. . . as the Play of Hamlet even if given without Hamlet's part, leaves Ophelia, Polonius & Laertes, the terrace at Elsinore & the Ghost, – so of Farringford, – ' a description he was obviously proud of as he repeats it in letters to Charlotte and Dakyns, who both received long accounts of the visit. Charlotte's letter is filled with the kind of detail which he thought would interest her. There is a description of the old country house with its dark passages, its Gothic rooms sparsely furnished

* Marianne's nickname.

except for plaster casts from Michelangelo and masses of prints and photographs of famous works of art.*

He tried to convey to Charlotte his impression of Mrs Tennyson's wistful sweetness in her cloud of grey drapery. But the longest section is devoted to the appearance of Tennyson's sons, Lionel and Hallam, who were then ten and twelve:

. . . Lionel, whom we saw first, a splendid creature, tall & lithe, with long curls & a pear shaped face extremely beautiful. He was curled up in an oak arm chair having his red legs over its side. Some hurt had kept him in the house. . . . While we were discussing Mr. Jowett's salary, the other boy, Hallam, came in, also mediaeval, but not so handsome as his brother. These are remarkable children. They will be great some day, if they are not spoiled, & if their obviously over irritable nerves & delicate sensibilities allow them to expand & harden in the world. Now they are growing up in a hothouse, & are pale, feminine, & full of upward striving, accordingly.[4]

The letter to Dakyns, written the previous day, is more significant. Familiar as he was with the house and its inhabitants, Dakyns required no extended descriptions. To him Symonds reveals far more of the deep emotional impact which the boys made upon him:

But these boys: when I saw them, & thought (with Mephistophele) of each:

> *Staub muss er essen und mit Lüst*
> *Wie meine Muhme, die berühmte Schlange:*

My heart bled & my soul yearned to them. They filled me with a love sadly deep even at first sight. It seems folly to say so. Yet I am not in a vein of sentimentality. I felt as if I knew them. And I knew that if I saw them daily they would find in me strong sympathy. I touched their hands & I looked at them & I spoke three or four words. That was all. But there was something in the light that ran over Hallam's face, in Lionel's grace, & in the delightful fibre of both felt through their fingertips, wh revealed them to me. You say they have 'la maladie du siècle' already. But good God! do you know what form this will take with one or both of them? I see it. In this I am not apt to be mistaken. But the bitterest cup may be kept from them. Would I could die for you, my brothers. . . . There is such waste of sorrow in the world. A worm like me lives through one misery:

* His attention was particularly drawn to Kirkup's mask of Dante hanging on a bookcase; when his own *Introduction to the Study of Dante* was published in 1872, he used as the frontispiece a photograph of this mask, the replica of which Kirkup had given him in Florence.

and after he is safe he sees angels beginning the same life & cannot save them. . . .
Tell me about these boys. I will never forget them.[5]

This letter was written when he had been married only a little more than
a fortnight. The old susceptibilities were not to be quelled so easily after
all.

II

Early in the New Year Symonds and his bride returned to London and
settled down to commonplace married domesticity. They took temporary
lodgings at 13 Albion Street near Hyde Park, but Catherine was already
pregnant and Symonds spent the grey January days looking for a larger,
more suitable house. 'Do not marry a man', he warned Charlotte, 'unless
he is very rich. As long as you are single you will be better off. I see that
the world is not designed for genteel young couples with moderate
means. They fall between splendour & squalor, for neither of w^h are they
adapted.'[6] They eventually settled upon a large, shadowy house at 47
Norfolk Square in the dreary Paddington area, to which they moved at
the end of the month. As Catherine was feeling unwell Symonds found
himself left to cope with the practical details, even down to the puzzling
problem of what sort of bacon to buy: 'The man showed me several kinds
of different shapes. I selected what I thought the most appropriate form
& the most delicate substance. He endorsed my good taste by saying it was
very good bacon, 11 pence a lb I believe. Does Auntie consider that dear.
Is 4s a lb. dear for tea. . . . For our dinner we ordered in a leg of mutton –
only that, forgetting vegetables & sweets. But I think we shall send up
Lewis early to buy potatoes & tapioca. Milk, butter, eggs, bread, mustard,
candles, pepper, sugar, I did not forget, nor soap.'[7]

Another attempt to make Symonds into a lawyer was now launched.
He entered a lawyer's chambers in 5 Paper Buildings, The Temple, but
was given little to do – or so he informed his friends – and most mornings
he spent in writing, principally essays on the Elizabethan dramatists. In
the afternoons he and Catherine made calls and visited art galleries. In
the evenings they sometimes went to parties; more frequently, they
would sit at home and read aloud from Villari's *Savonarola* or Grimm's
Life of Michel Angelo. This innocuous round left him vaguely dissatisfied as he confided in a letter to Dakyns:

I am in a state of suspense about law and literature. Am I to serve God or Mammon? Am I to study and write or to pursue this profession? Am I to be poor with letters, or to run the chance of being rich with the law? Then, again, am I justified in assuming myself to be of the priesthood of art?... You see I am settling the question of life; and if you can give me any definite ideas on these vague problems, thanks be to you. It is a terrible and consuming problem. I feel so weak, so unable to do anything, or to take hold of any subject. In the room with me at this minute, are five men, all provided with clear brains for business, all talking slang, and all wondering what strange incapable animal I am who have come among them. They can move stones with their little finger which my whole strength will not stir. But is it likely that they can touch the subjects which thrill my soul?[8]

Symonds was convinced that no event occurred purely by chance and in later life often spoke of how apparently trivial episodes could serve as turning-points for our future lives. Such an incident happened to him in the spring of 1865. About midnight, after spending the evening in the Century Club, he turned down a little passage leading from Trafalgar Square into Leicester Square. As he passed a barracks, a young grenadier in a scarlet uniform approached the slight young man in the evening cape. Symonds was too innocent to grasp the import of his words immediately, but he felt himself drawn to the strapping fellow. When the latter mentioned a house they could go to, Symonds quickened his steps in horror, followed by the imploring grenadier. The incident left him deeply disturbed and he reflected upon it for a long time afterwards. It lay like a shadow on the edge of his mind, and a letter to Dakyns reveals that the experience had influenced his attitude towards his sexual problems. He never hesitated to analyse and probe the state of his feelings in long outpourings to Dakyns, and these letters are far more introspective than those written to his other chief correspondent, Charlotte. This one letter in particular expresses the rationalizations by which he deceived himself that if he indulged his instincts he could prove how illusory they really were. Dakyns's discontent in his life as a schoolmaster served to heighten his own preoccupations:

You at present are ill fitted for the Damascus that you used to talk about, & are an illustration of the tendency in men to hanker after what is really alien from their nature. I know this in my own case to be the truth. And hence I am always willing that men should buy experience by indulging their strong predilections. A small trial will often show them the unreality and inadaptability of desires w^h, if checked, may poison a whole lifetime. This is the truth of Wilhelm Meister. But the learning of the lesson takes time, & it sometimes happens that instead of wise satiety the morbid nature gains new needs. Wherefore Goethe devised in his moral the protective family to secure the interests of Wilhelm. These reflections grew from the mental comparison I make between your proposed want of solitude, & y^r practical intolerance of loneliness — It might seem as if the reflection militated against advice w^h I have given Sidgwick & w^h I have detailed to you. But here new elements are introduced — duty to society *imprimis* w^h should check any tendency to its disintegration & foster respect for its wise customs; secondly regard for our own character; thirdly a strong conviction of my own that he is open to degeneracy of sentiment similar to that observed by me in others. All these reasons induce me to advise him not to indulge a strong predilection even at the risk of shutting up inside himself a wolf. . . .[9]

Apparently Arthur Sidgwick could not be trusted to emerge from the destructive element unscathed, because he was not protected with the same safeguards as Wilhelm Meister — or Symonds.

In August the young couple escaped to Clifton from the heat of London. At the time the sculptor, Thomas Woolner, who had been associated with the Pre-Raphaelites, was doing a bust of Dr Symonds. Short and stocky, bumptious and outspoken, he talked confidently to the young man by the hour about his ambitions and his intimate friends, Browning and Tennyson. 'Men like Woolner and my father make me blush', Symonds wrote in his diary. 'They will, they do, they enjoy. They have a work in life. They have brains, clear and strong. . . .'[10]

Unless he had very special talents or interests, the choice of a career for a young man of good family in the mid-nineteenth century was appallingly limited. Convinced by now that literature was the only congenial course open to him, he hesitated to make a definite break with the law, knowing how much his father would disapprove of such a step. It occurred to him that perhaps Dr Symonds might be more open to persuasion if he could obtain Jowett's concurrence in his wishes. Accordingly, he decided to write to Jowett to ask if he might come up to Oxford to talk the matter over with him:

I do not think that any one could give me better advice upon this point than you. What weighs with me in favour of literature is — first, my health, which could be more humoured in a life of study than at the bar; secondly, my inclinations which are most decided in favour of study; thirdly, my capacities, which seem to me ill-adapted for the bar. Still literature is a service not lightly to be undertaken. And the strong assurance, from one who knows me so well as you do, and knows all the difficulties of a student's life, that I am unfitted for it, would weigh greatly with me.[11]

Jowett did not give him the unqualified support he expected. He told Symonds that he did not think he should desert the law until he had been called to the Bar, suggested that he devote himself to some hospital work in London, and advised him to consider a possible future in politics; as for his literary interests, they could be satisfied by translating some work like Zeller's *Aristotle*. Such advice could not have been less congenial to Symonds, and the fact that Jowett recommended these pursuits to a man whom he had known well for three years indicates an astonishing imperceptiveness. On the other hand, Jowett had formed a shrewd idea of his abilities, if not his temperament, when he told him: 'You have a very good memory, remarkable facility, and considerable powers of thinking. It depends on yourself to bring these to perfection.'[12] Symonds headed back for London – 'full of thoughts, with hope and a purpose in me',[13] he wrote in his diary – despite the fact that Jowett had characteristically said little, and that little had been antithetical to Symonds's wishes – a remarkable commentary on the power of Jowett's personality.

Marriage into the North family made him see more clearly than ever that the practical concerns of law and politics were completely alien to him. 'I do not care for this kind of society', he wrote to Charlotte from the midst of a house-party at Hastings at Easter, 1865:

It bores me. Yet I am not blasé. Nor am I contemptuous. The ability of such people I cannot aspire to. But the conversation, frivolous, dealing with everything that is transient, dwelling upon nothing beautiful, serious only about political trumpery, & amusing only about scandal, wearies me. Mrs. May,* a thorough woman of the world, pronounced me charming & took me into her confidences. So if I try I can succeed in these circles. But to go on trying would be slow death moral if not intellectual, for repose if not for energy, for dignity & honour if not for wealth & reputation. 'Who will show us any good?' 'What is life made for?' I cannot rid myself of the questions. I do not see *mon but*.[14]

* Wife of the Clerk of the House of Commons.

However, his literary endeavours had not yet progressed beyond articles for the periodicals and he was stung when a friend of Mr North's referred condescendingly to his 'writing for the magazines'. The first article to bring him any recognition was a piece on Orvieto which appeared in *The Cornhill* in February 1865. 'I have had several congratulatory addresses upon Orvieto', he proudly informed Charlotte. 'Mr. and Miss North say that it redeemed the last Cornhill from dullness but wonder whether my style does not need pruning.'[15] They did not require very remarkable critical powers to perceive how stiffly ornate the essay was nor how its conventional attitudes were permeated by Ruskinism, particularly in the close connection he drew between ethics and art. 'If Italy is to live again', he pontificated, 'she must quit her ruined palace-towers to build fresh dwellings elsewhere. Filth, lust, rapacity, treason, godlessness and violence have made their habitation here; ghosts haunt these ruins, these streets still smell of blood, and echo to the cries of injured innocence; life cannot be pure, or calm, or healthy, where this curse has settled.'*[16]

During 1865 he began to turn some of his enthusiasm for the Elizabethan dramatists into articles for *The Cornhill*, and wrote a further series for *The Pall Mall Gazette* in 1867. He had been introduced to these early playwrights in 1862 when he and Stephens were at Malvern studying for their Final Schools. At the end of a hard day's work, he would thumb through Charles Lamb's *Specimens of English Dramatic Poets Who Lived About the Time of Shakespeare*. 'Elizabethan literature, if I had time, wᵈ be now my rage', he enthused to Charlotte.[17] His faith in Conington's taste was disturbed when he discovered that he failed to respond to the Elizabethans. Symonds read right through the 1854 Bohn edition of Lamb, underlined many passages, and on the blue interleaves separating each page jotted down copious notes, many of which were later incorporated into his published work. He was so captivated by these selections in Lamb that he went on to cover the entire field of late sixteenth- and early seventeenth-century drama. The Elizabethans appealed to him because in the conventional mode of the day they seemed vital

---

* Although he was later to discard most of the Ruskin equipage, it is rather curious that as late as 1891 he had the same emotional reaction to Orvieto when he revisited it. '... Orvieto, as usual, left on my mind a sinister impression of ancient guilt', he wrote from Rome to Mrs Janet Ross (Janet Ross, *The Fourth Generation*, Constable & Co., 1912, p. 307).

creatures, men who were able to express themselves freely, unhampered by Victorian taboos. Many of the vacant hours of 1865 were filled by writing a full-scale history of the Elizabethan drama – written, as he told Dakyns, 'merely as a test of my tenacity in literary work'[18] – but he laid it aside impatiently and did not undertake another major study until 1883 when he started work on *Shakspere's Predecessors in the English Drama*. These periods of relaxation from the law were not wasted, for he began to be recognized as something of an Elizabethan expert and after *The Academy* was founded in 1869, the Editor, Dr C. E. Appleton, frequently sent him various editions of the Elizabethan dramatists to review.

During this period he also became deeply interested in De Musset whom he saw as a fragmented creature like himself, one whose most congenial emotional milieu would have been among the Greeks. 'I have been making a study of your old friend de Musset', he wrote to Dakyns in June. 'He is worth it. I have read *Elle et Lui* and *Lui et Elle* and all the poems & some of his stories and his life. I hope to go further – &, if I only can, to say something in print apropos of him about the Scepticism of the period. But it is terribly hard to write Essays upon the matter of your own heart.'[19] He eventually wrote an essay on the French poet which was turned down by *The Cornhill* – 'It is too long (also, I suspect, too *langweilig*) for them.'[20] It was eventually accepted and published anonymously by *The North British Review* in 1868.[21] Symonds clearly had himself in mind as much as De Musset when he wrote:

Had he been born at a proper age in the world's history he might have been an Athenian. As it was, he resembled a man trying to lead a Greek life in modern times, and striking against the stumbling-blocks of education and society. Had he really been an ancient Greek, the unaffected sensuousness of his nature would not have been tortured by the unsolved doubts of religious scepticism. His nerves would have been calmed by exercise and soothed by the continual sight of beauty.[22]

But Symonds was not an Athenian. He was the son of an eminent Victorian physician and, as such, was invited by Woolner to drop in one evening after dinner to sit in the background and listen while Gladstone, Tennyson, Francis Palgrave, and his father exchanged ideas on the Eyre case, Greek translations, and moral values in art. That same correct young Victorian gentleman, only a few weeks before, had been thrown into a state of shaking consternation by suddenly confronting some obscene graffiti scrawled on a slate at a street corner. Still tenaciously clutching the hope that marriage was 'curing' him, he was seized by despair at the discovery that he was fighting a losing battle with an enemy that would not be denied. 'How I loathe myself', he exclaimed. 'At a great London dinner party last night I was among Marshalls Monteagles Myerses & Spring Rices, & they all talked & seemed to think that I had something to say too. It was all I c^d do to withhold myself from falling flat upon the floor & crying out to them: Behold I am a scare crow a thread paper a hypocrite, I am not what I look, tear off the clothes & flesh & find the death & hell inside: if anyone of you have got a God let him first search me, let him scatter me to the winds & discover my emptiness.'[23]

Feverishly he tried to throw himself into activities which helped to muffle the truth. He planned to join Rutson in distributing charity to some of the distressed areas of London, but the scheme never came to anything. He became enthusiastic about decorating his home, making it as much like the interior of Clifton Hill House as possible. The walls of the drawing-room were 'studded' with pictures – family photographs, Luini's 'Marriage of the Virgin', a Correggio drawing, views of the Grand Canal – which he spent a great deal of time rearranging. Catherine installed a piano, but she lacked Charlotte's ear, and the music irritated his nerves. At night, before falling asleep, following a classic Freudian pattern, he would imagine himself a bird flying over the roofs of the houses to Clifton or released among the cool Swiss mountains.

Catherine tried to comfort him in his moods of depression but the baby was almost due and in her edgy, apprehensive state she felt she needed a little comfort herself. Charlotte was still the very tender, the always understanding sister. As usual on Symonds's birthday, loving letters passed between them. 'I think', he told her, 'we ought both of us each year to become more to one another: the strengthening of old bonds seems to me one of the most important parts of growth. Severance from the Past or any relinquishment of affection causes me the deepest anguish & spreads itself out over my whole life like a paralyzing influence.'[24]

Letters written on blue paper flowed out to all his friends, urging them to scrutinize their beliefs, share their sorrows, rhapsodize over their enthusiasms. These were the earnest young intellectuals of the mid-century, the Robert Elsmeres, with their intense friendships, their religious doubts, and their interminable questions. Most of them had brilliant academic records behind them.* Their keynote was 'sincerity' and they venerated Arthur Hugh Clough for his 'honest scepticism'.

In 1869, after a lengthy period of profound self-analysis to which all his friends contributed, Henry Sidgwick felt forced to resign his Fellowship at Trinity College, Cambridge, rather than sign the Thirty-nine Articles. When T. H. Green finally signed, he had to justify his action with the rationalization that 'one kiss does not make a marriage'. They read Renan and Strauss and Baur – and pondered. They listened to Darwin and Huxley and Spencer – and worried. Sidgwick eventually found his peace in the rationalism of Mill, Green in the idealism of Hegel, and F. W. H. Myers in the spiritualism of Madame Blavatsky. Their idols were not those of the older generation: Carlyle's raucous yawp might have been lost on the wind for all the attention they paid him; Charlotte was warned that Ruskin 'twaddles';[25] Matthew Arnold's tone of condescending assurance drove Symonds to describe him as 'the egotistical Mat';[26] Sidgwick irreverently thumbed his nose at him in 'The Prophet of Culture';[27] and Symonds rejoiced to see the movement which was gaining momentum against 'the nightmare of Tennyson'.[28]

Curiously, Symonds was the only non-Rugby man among the group, most of whom had also gone on to Cambridge. Rugby appeared to him infinitely better than Harrow and he resented the fact that he remained somewhat of an outsider; but none of the others could resist his obsessive capacity for friendship. When the decision was finally taken to devote his life to literature, he wrote to Dakyns: 'Help me, my friends, with counsel, with exhortation; lift up my feeble knees; comfort my failing spirits; goad me when I flag; & tell me truly what I need. I depend on you greatly, on Graham for his love & for his soul, on Arthur for his sympathy & for his youth, on Green for his vigour, on others too who need not here be mentioned. A man is nothing by himself: I live by exhortation & encouragement, I die when left alone.'[29] The Sidgwicks

---

* Henry Sidgwick had been Senior Classic at Cambridge. The intellectual bent of the whole Sidgwick clan was so marked that Francis Galton declared that it was one of the most remarkable cases of kindred aptitude that ever came to his notice. He included Henry, as Senior Classic, in *Hereditary Genius* (1869).

he admired enormously, and with them he was beginning to form the basis of a profound friendship. Henry's impressive gifts were a little overpowering – 'I think he is the greatest man of my generation', he told Dakyns.[30] He romanticized the handsome Arthur and asked Dakyns plaintively: 'Tell me: do you think Arthur cares for me? W[d] he value my friendship really if I never grew more strong?'[31]

Perhaps the intensity of his friendships could be traced in part to his uneasiness over violating Pretor's confidence and his sense of betrayal by Shorting. Among his papers is a sheet entitled 'Loyalty to Friends'.

The truly loyal friend, is not merely staunch in his adherence – for this he might be from a sense of duty – nor devoted in his love – for this he might be through passion: he is both staunch & devoted; but he is also true in every corner of his soul to his friend, honouring & respecting him, incapable of believing evil in him, betraying his secrets to none, criticizing him to none, never complaining of him, waiting if wronged by him in the hope of explanation; & if such a friend has to break from his friend at last he still honours the past & is silent preferring to suffer before the world rather than to throw blame on one whom he once greatly loved.[32]

Never was the Platonic concept of friendship stated more romantically.

His relationship with Albert Rutson forced him to draw on all his reserves of forebearance and sympathy, and only occasionally did he let out the sigh of impatience which escaped him in a brief dinner invitation to Dakyns: 'Hosanna in the Highest, there will be no Rutson.'[33] In 1864 Rutson again brought up the subject of his love for Charlotte and asked Symonds to sound out his father's reaction. Dr Symonds was fond of Rutson but felt uneasy about allowing him to marry Charlotte because he knew there was insanity in his family. He consulted a number of London doctors who agreed with him, and Rutson gave vent to his disappointment in violent outbursts of bitterness against Dr Symonds.

After Symonds and Catherine were married, Rutson suddenly revealed that he had always been in love with Catherine, and the feelings he had professed for Charlotte were nothing but pure artifice. He began to berate Symonds because he did not sufficiently appreciate the extent of the sacrifice he had made on his behalf. Rutson took to lying in wait for him on his way home from the Temple, and for hours would hold him captive on park benches while he poured out an incoherent recital of his grievances. Symonds was completely bewildered by the bizarre situation and seriously worried about Rutson's mental health. He got in touch with his family to tell them of his misgivings – a step which goaded Rutson to a state of hysterical fury. 'Paranoia . . .', Freud declared, 'invariably arises from any attempt to subdue unduly powerful homosexual tendencies';[34] and there can be little doubt that Rutson's obsession with Symonds was due to a very compelling homosexual attraction.

Among Symonds's papers is a letter from Rutson analysing his feeling for Symonds:

It was the instinctive sense of your *discontent with the present* & of your (then unconscious) tendency always to rise higher that made me your friend at first, & has since made me continue to love you more than any one else in the world, at great cost in the reckoning of men, & with a disparagement of other friends, not really to be named with you, whom most men w^d think worthier.

The differences between us are certainly great. Your griefs are all subjective, mine are all objective. You have always suffered & despaired. I have always enjoyed & hoped. You have sought to rise by understanding yourself, God & life. I have always wished to understand what is best in the world around me, to understand, & to influence men, to feel in its highest & purest form what is beautiful in the world. You, in a certain sense, enjoy suffering. It helps you to realise the idea of your being. It makes you see some of the secrets of life. It satisfies the Artist in you. To me suffering is absolutely alien. Therefore I shriek as I do. I have absolutely no satisfaction in suffering.[35]

And shriek Rutson continued to do on park benches and in letters which were now addressed to Catherine as well. Receiving one of these, Symonds replied:

We have both read what you wrote last night & although if you wish to come & talk to us we shall be ready to hear what you have to say, we do not think it can possibly do much good to discuss such matters. We are both of us anxious to keep up our old friendship with you; yet each time a question of this sort is reopened it makes it doubly difficult to be upon a frank & easy footing.[36]

Symonds became emotionally and physically exhausted by the strain of trying to placate Rutson, who could not have been a worse influence during this troubled period of his life.*

* After 1866 Symonds broke off all contact with Rutson for a number of years. Rutson became a barrister and held the post of private secretary to Lord Aberdare, the Home Secretary in Gladstone's Cabinet. They later resumed the friendship and Symonds followed Rutson's campaign for the Northallerton seat in 1881 with great interest. Rutson died in 1890.

In 1866 he wrote an essay, 'The Love of the Alps', in which Rutson's emotional demands, his own conflict about the law, and his anxiety to make his father proud of him, all coalesce in a longing to escape to the peace of the Alps: 'Society is there reduced to a vanishing point', he wrote wistfully, ' – no claims are made on human sympathies, – there is no need to toil in yoke-service with our fellows. We may be alone, dream our own dreams, and sound the depths of personality without the reproach of selfishness, without a restless wish to join in action or money-making, or the pursuit of fame.'[37]

He found compensation for the difficulties with Rutson in the loyalty and devotion of Graham Dakyns. 'You are together with two or three in all the world my best & dearest friend', Symonds assured him.[38] To Dakyns he could release all his anguish as he could to no one else. 'Write me more about the deep things of thy soul', Symonds begged him. 'Cry unto me as one deep crieth unto another deep.'[39] They still confided in each other completely, they read the same books, they took long walks together, and sometimes they were joined by another master at Clifton College, the Manx poet, T. E. Brown, for an evening of whisky and poetry readings. Whenever Symonds stayed at Clifton Dakyns gave him a latch key so that he could let himself into his lodgings as he liked, and Dakyns often travelled up to London to attend a concert with him.

Symonds needed Dakyns desperately during these years of early manhood which he described to his friend as 'a sad period for me of weakness & decline, blear eyes, shaken limbs, terrible dreams at night, & a disordered brain by day. Catherine stays by me like Electra: but alas! even the consolations of tragedy are gone out of my life. The blank prose of debility & suffering & unaccomplished hope is all I have. . . . I read the pelican of de Musset & long that to some young still to be established soul I could pour out all that in me is vital & godgiven & then die having reinforced his youth by the sacrifice of what in me is worthless.'[40] On another occasion he told him: 'You are never burdensome to me. Rather let me say that I find great sweetness in you, a perfection of love w^h makes my selfishness blush.'[41] Dakyns hastened to rendezvous 'on the observatory' or under Brunel's new suspension bridge or in various churches where they sat and listened to Willie Dyer playing the organ.

Time and again he was ordered to burn or destroy poems. The friendship was by no means one-sided, for if Symonds demanded much, he was prepared to give as much in return. He was always ready with praise for Dakyns and sympathy with his problems. Dakyns did not get on well with the Headmaster of Clifton, Dr Percival, and he felt himself spiritually inhibited within the narrow confines of a boys' school. He had begun a translation of Xenophon, in which – though the work dragged on for years – Symonds never failed to show unflagging interest. He had also become deeply attached to one of his pupils, a boy called Cecil Boyle, and Symonds's letters are full of concern and advice and exhortation about 'Cecy'. There is no hint of any homosexual relationship between the two men, although their mutual proclivity created a strong bond of sympathy. However, Symonds's determination to avoid temptation is often apparent in his letters to Dakyns. His position is clearly stated in a letter about a liaison between Arthur Sidgwick and a boy at Rugby:

I do not intend to discuss his conduct much more. I shall long to hear of him, every new thing; & I believe in his goodness. But that he is in a dangerous position cannot be denied; when I think of him I range the matter somehow in questions & answers like the following –

Is this ἔρως [love] Greek? No.

If it were Greek, is it what Plato w^d allow? No.

Is it established in modern Society? No.

Is it what the world at large w^d call romantic, sentimental, effeminate, on the verge of vice? Yes.

Supposing the world wrong in a special instance, may not its general verdict be right? I think so.

What is the source of Arthur's love? Is it intellectual sympathy? No.

Is it moral good? No.

Is it consentaneity of tastes? No.

Is it chiefly aesthetical enjoyment & the pleasure of highly refined sensuousness? Yes.

Are these likely to produce moral & intellectual strengths? No.

Are they capable of producing moral or intellectual debility? Yes, *capable*.

What has y^r experience been of this ἔρως [love]? That if uncontrolled it is evil.

In all cases of possible harm, what does Duty say? Avoid all appearance of evil.

In case moral injury were to accrue, where w^d the evil fall most heavily? On the boy, & if on him then through him on his fellow boys.

Does Arthur expose himself to external danger? Yes, to a very g^t extent. These questions by no means settle or exhaust the matter. It is a case of absolutely new casuistry. There is no rule by w^h to measure it as yet.[42]

On 22 October, Dakyns received word that Catherine's child had been born:

47 Norfolk Square
Oct: 22 1865.

My dear Graham

This is not about myself, but to tell you among the earliest that a little daughter was born to us this morning at 8.30 & that my dearest Catherine & her child are doing well. I am very thankful & seem to see a wonderful beauty in the world.

Ever y^r aff

J. A. SYMONDS[43]

For the moment anguished introspection was abandoned. It had been a difficult birth, but each day Catherine and baby Janet grew stronger. 'I am well too,' Symonds wrote, 'we are always well when wholly altruistic & I have not had a moment to sit down & think of self.'[44] Again: 'My hours are now divided between the cobweb of the Law and my dear wife's room.'[45]

Shortly afterwards the rosy picture faded. Catherine suddenly went into a nervous collapse and Symonds was frantic with worry. The note in his letters changes completely. 'Morning & noon & night are all one weariness to her', Symonds now confided to Dakyns, 'and I have much to do. It wrings my heart, for it is so like my own pains – I know the least quiver of her nerves.'[46] Catherine was touched by his gentle consideration when he sat on the side of her bed and talked of the trip they would take to the Alps as soon as she was stronger. Her face lit up with joy and in a rush of emotion she buried her head in his arms. The new responsibility of the child weighed on her, she disliked housekeeping, and she longed to get out of the dark, cavernous house.

By the end of the month she seemed to be making some progress and Symonds was able to write: 'Catherine is slowly getting better – she is dearer to me inexpressibly day after day. We see my future a little more clearly now & the cloud of Law has shrivelled to the size of a man's hand – but that is not yet acknowledged to the world, so be you wary.'[47]

Catherine was well enough to travel down to Clifton for Christmas. Early in the autumn Symonds had caught a cold which he believed was the result of sitting shivering on park benches with Rutson, and the baby's wet nurse cheerfully told him he had a 'churchyard cough'. His father examined him shortly after he arrived home and was disturbed to find that, far beyond the threat of a mere cold, the left lung had been seriously damaged. Constantly Dr Symonds remembered that consumption was a hereditary disease in his wife's family and that his daughter, Lady Strachey, now had to spend every winter on the Riviera. He became medically autocratic, and the only exercise he would allow Symonds to take was an occasional drive in the carriage. Jowett and Conington came down for the holidays but Symonds's part in the festivities was severely curtailed. 'Tonight they have been at the Messiah', he wrote wistfully to Dakyns, '& I have had to stay home. I longed to pour out my soul to God in that gigantic poem, to weep inwardly & be comforted.'[48]

When they returned to Norfolk Square in January 1866, Symonds was by no means recovered and Catherine's nerves became so bad that she was ordered to take a complete rest. 'Marriage reduplicates our happiness & pain & makes Life altogether a more solemn thing', Symonds wrote anxiously to Dakyns. 'Therefore I am glad to bear her weakness with her, & my only regret is for her sense of loss & deprivation. You must not think she is really ill: but only likely to be out of tune for active life & exertion.'[49] Both of them hated to return to their gloomy house and Clifton seemed even lovelier in comparison. 'No one who has not tried it knows the sweetness of our home at Clifton', Symonds told his friend. 'I cannot express it to you. You can divine it better than anyone I know. It is sacred, it is perfect, it is more a realized ideal than anything I ever saw. Leaving it is very hard.'[50]

III

The state of Symonds's health finally resolved the uneasy question of becoming a lawyer. He had been proved prophetic the previous summer when he wrote to Dakyns: 'You spoke about y^r father settling your destiny. My father & I have been trying to do something of the sort for mine. But, like all destinies, it won't be settled – it insists on settling itself. The fates

refuse to show their hands & I go.'[51] The fates had expressed themselves
in a diseased lung and there was no alternative except to escape to a warm
climate. On 24 February he and Catherine started off for the Riviera.
At Mentone, where they joined Lady Strachey, his restlessness found
vent in an ambitious intellectual programme, spurred on by a letter
from Jowett. 'I think that you may look forward to a literary life
with good hope and prospect of success', Jowett wrote. 'To have nothing
to do is the best of all lives, if you only make something real to do. You
escape the narrowing influence of a profession, and what you do for others
is far more deeply felt. The point is, I think, to get a position and
occupation, and each year to look as anxiously to one's own progress as
you would to the coming in of briefs at the bar.'[52]

He hired a teacher and resumed his study of Italian which he had taken
up briefly while he was at Magdalen. In short order he read through the
Decameron and a great deal of the poetry of Ariosto and Dante. His
feverish energy also expressed itself in a translation of Empedocles which
he did for Jowett and an article on the Greek philosopher which was
published anonymously in *The North British Review* in December. The
despairing mood of Empedocles is echoed in a dithyrambic letter written
on Good Friday to Dakyns: 'There is no voice neither any that answers
me. My spirit is even as a bird shut up within a cage of glass. She breaks
her wings against these mocking & transparent barriers. She strains
heavenward & falls down to earth. She dives into the earth to hide herself
& finds the dull dead imperturbability of resisting clay. Then she lies
panting quivering & horrorstruck — & the whole vast Universe around
the walls of her translucent prison, blazes, whirls, grows up & dies,
changes, throws out its galaxy of stars & million waves of dancing waters
& infinite variety of coloured flowers.'[53] Empedocles had ascended Etna
to fling himself into the crater. Symonds climbed a hill to a Roman
Catholic church to attend Mass, and he found not peace but the deafening
sound of rattles and clappers. 'And I went forth sick unto death. Then said
I to myself: They have forgotten the reality & kept the semblance.'[54]

Symonds's letters during this period are filled with accounts of his
attempts to stand 'face to face with the Eternal'.[55] Marriage had failed
to give him a *point d'appui*, he would never find it in the law, and he had
serious doubts whether literature would provide his life with an over-

whelming preoccupation to compensate for its other inadequacies. He was still trying to evade the same old fundamental problem, and temporarily all his anxieties were channelled into an unwilling agnosticism. H. F. Brown's interpretation of Symonds's character was that 'the central, the architechtonic quality of his nature was religious'.[56] Perhaps as the result of Brown's emphasis, W. E. Houghton in his admirable *The Victorian Frame of Mind*, has come to the conclusion that no Victorian suffered more from the atmosphere of general anxiety than Symonds. His scepticism, however, stemmed from a series of highly personal influences. His father inclined towards agnosticism; his grandmother and her Plymouth Brethren were repellent to him; during the period of confirmation he experienced a brief devotional phase which was arrested by his shocked discoveries about Dr Vaughan; at Oxford a general feeling of scepticism prevailed among his friends, which was not dissipated by the ambiguous attitudes of his adored Jowett. Granted that all these influences unsettled him and that he longed for something in which to believe, nevertheless this desire was secondary to the initial, fundamental, undeniable problem of sex. If the answers to the first could be found, he wistfully hoped that they would provide a solution to his more pressing anxiety.

The truth of the matter is that the religious and the sexual problem were inextricably connected in his restless search for the means whereby he could achieve what he called 'self-effectuation': but he was eventually forced to face the fact that he could unleash his capacities only through the frank acknowledgment of his sexual nature. With this accomplished, he could claim that he had finally reached the point where he felt in harmony with all the forces of the universe, and to this sense of spiritual communion, he applied the word 'religion'. Such a development lay many years ahead, and in 1866 he was still groping for a solution. A book like Seeley's *Ecce Homo* moved him as it did so many others that year, but Symonds had to work out his own faith in actual experience.

In April he and Catherine moved from Cannes to San Remo to stay with her half-sister, Lady Kay Shuttleworth.* Paradoxically, the beauty

* Her mother's daughter by a previous marriage to Mr Shuttleworth of Gawthorpe Hall, Lancashire. Miss Shuttleworth married Dr Kay, who took her name and became Sir James Kay Shuttleworth.

of the coast exacerbated Symonds's nerves. 'I long for some repose, for such dignity of daily life as I find in our Clifton home.'[57] As summer approached, he moved on through Genoa, Pisa, Florence, Siena, Bologna, Ravenna, Parma, and Pavia to Milan. Everywhere they went they saw signs of the Risorgimento. This time he was more emotionally stirred than he had been four years before when he witnessed a Milan mob incited by a speech of Garibaldi's, and reacted predominantly to the visual aspects of the scene. 'I often wondered what a demonstration meant', he wrote in his diary, 'this is a pretty and picturesque specimen.'[58] Now his pen raced along the page as he described the scene to Dakyns:

It is no small thing seeing the tumult of a nation, high & low, rich & poor, men & women. They have swelled themselves up like a huge wave w^h is now ready to burst upon the quadrilateral – all along the valley of the Po we have seen it chafing surging foaming piling itself up – now it is ready, the crest stands poised, balanced for a moment in suspense – we shall soon hear the crash reverberating throughout Europe, & then, daring to lift up our eyes, shall see – either the billow triumphing upon the broken barrier, or the white foam flakes torn & muddy eddying round unshaken rocks & drifting helplessly. So it seems to me at this moment. From Siena Northwards we have journied with the assembling together of these armies. We have seen the towns crowded with their people singing hymns of war as the troops filed by the passes of the Apennine alive with artillery, the railways converging laden with soldiers, the piazzas turned into camps, theatres rising like a man to greet a general or to sing a strophe of a battle ode. Meanwhile we of course have gone about our churches & our pictures, have eaten & slept as of old.[59]

Enthusiasm and excitement were soon driven away by the old languor, ennui, and frustration.

The word w^h tells in my ears, night & day, is 'waste'. When I wake from sleep I cry like the wretch in Persius 'Imus, minus, proecipites.' My soul is stagnant, & I see no God, no reason for the world, no vigour in myself, no content in the things around me – nothing but slow sliding barren years; when I think, no new thoughts come, but old ones long used up & lacking life; when I write or speak it is as though a man should spit against the wind & have his own filth cast against his face.[60]

As he moved on into the Alps, the mountains began to exert the serene influence which had soothed him in the past. Despite his genuine love of the mountains, there is something very self-conscious in his descriptions of the Alps, a straining after fine effects which marred too much of his writing. Symonds often used his letters as drafts for travel pieces – 'save this letter' he would frequently advise its recipient – and his letters from Switzerland obviously served as the basis for the article, 'The Love of the Alps', which was published in *The Cornhill* in July 1867. Again he was enchanted by the effect of their slopes blanketed in spring flowers. Those which appealed to him most were the saxifrages and he strikes a much more sincere note when he tells Dakyns that 'the other day at Varallo we cut an armful by the torrent, & then felt like murderers – it was so sad to hold in our hands the triumph, of those long patient months, the full expansive life of the flower, the creature w^h so loved its freedom & its savage loneliness, the splendour visible from valley & hillside, the defenceless plant w^h had done its best to make the gloomy places of the Alps most beautiful'.[61]

His temporary respite was destroyed by a letter from Dakyns, now deeply involved with 'Cecy' to the point where gossip had begun to circulate. Symonds took pen and paper into the beechwoods and poured out advice and sympathy. 'Harrow & Magdalen: these two measure the extent of my sympathy – the first for him, the second for you. But thank heaven that, as far as I understand you, the worst brand has not yet burned into y^r soul.'[62] He felt so passionately on the subject of pederasty that he had begun preaching to anyone he might influence, including Dr Percival, on his return to Clifton. Once when they were out riding together, he talked to him about the homosexuality he had encountered at Harrow and Oxford.

He seemed very ready to discuss & anxious to be informed. I was surprised to find him so ignorant of the real evil w^h is going on. He was just alive to the fact that boys by herding together acquire coarse & vicious habits among themselves. But he conceived that the more intellectual would, by the energy of their minds, be protected & diverted. Whereas I have always held that, admitting the sensuality of the coarser natures, & quite independently of it, the most sensitive delicate and nervous organizations are exposed to corruption less offensive in itself but more awful in its consequences. You know what I mean. You know that I consider the tone of F. Myers to be radically wrong in matters of passion, & that I regret the peculiar colour of A. S.'s erotics, not to speak of the misery w^h I have myself suffered. There, salvâ modestiâ, are at once three of not the least intellectually constituted members of our Universities assailed by the same disease. But I found it difficult to express to Percival the exact nuance of the evil in this its most subtle manifestation. The grossness of boys is palpable & when observed is easily dealt with. But a man who regards Swinburne as a clear case of lunacy *because* he treats of Sappho* cannot readily understand how there is much danger of the best & purest of his pupils idealizing the passion of the Phaedrus. If you ever talk to him about these matters, please be careful. I of course spoke to him only of what I have observed not of what I have personally *experienced*. I was glad to get the ear of a Head Master on a topic w^h I consider to be the most vital.[63]

And yet – with what voice is he speaking when he describes a visit in November to Arthur Sidgwick in Rugby? Arthur let him sit in his class while he conducted a Latin lesson; and all the time Symonds was aware of Arthur's favourite sitting beside him: 'a face & form of unimaginable beauty, haunted by thoughts & passions w^h as yet are undeveloped. Fancy a form of loveliness over w^h its own predestinated soul of power & passion hovers; not as poets have dreamed, the dead clay haunted by its ancient spirit, but the just dawning life environed by cloud shadows of the youth & strength to be.'[64] The wolf would not be stilled.

During the European trip he had worked unceasingly at essays, poetry – and the interminable Zeller, spurred on by the fact that Jowett had spoken to William Longman about its eventual publication. Most of his early prose was written off the top of his head, and produced, as he put it, 'for bread'. When he tried to put a little of himself into his articles for *The Saturday Review*, the Editor deleted all the personal passages.

Poetry was a different matter: he soon discovered that in this medium alone he could express his real feelings. The possibility of becoming a poet like Tennyson or Browning was never entertained, but writing poetry became a safety-valve for the release of painful emotions, a very private affair, which would satisfy a hostile audience only if the true facts were distorted. His friends were bombarded with poems and begged to give a candid opinion. 'I expect from you a frank judgment', he told Dakyns. 'Are these verse compositions i valueless or ii harmful or iii of

---

* Swinburne had made a loose translation of Sappho's 'Ode to Anactoria' in 'Anactoria', included in *Poems and Ballads* (1866).

some possible utility? . . . My subjects so possess me, that I know *them* & not my presentation of them. Therefore I cannot judge & fear to make myself a fool.'[65] The subject of one long poem, 'John Mordan', was a newsboy he admired at Piccadilly Circus. Henry Sidgwick made it quite clear that he was scandalized by what he read, and a frantic message went out from Symonds: 'Please do not disobey me but *destroy* "J. M." "The Cretan Idyll" . . . wild fire is abroad in the world & who am I that I should offend against God's elect.'[66] When Graham Dakyns attempted to remonstrate with him over 'the sacrifice to Moloch', he replied that in this instance Moloch was 'a very mixed god – a god of Canaan & not of Israel, but yet a god whose name none of us may wholly neglect'.[67]

Still, a son of Dr Symonds had to produce something substantial, something above the 'floundering & sprawling & Sybaritical lying in roseleaves & eating of dew & honey'.[68] Constant introspection forced him to recognize that he could not completely blame misfortune for not having been born with the balanced sanity of Henry Sidgwick. At the time his life seemed 'one long monotony', but in retrospect this period appeared to have been less ineffectual and more productive than the mere 'satisfied inaction'[69] that he had thought it, at the time, to be. Looking back on the winter of 1865-6, he realized that the various essays he wrote for periodicals helped to form his style and provided excellent preparation for more serious extended work in the future.

How seriously could one take Symonds when he complained that he was 'broken in health & hopes with the sore smarts of wounded pride, with the despair of utter Godlessness, & with the thread of my whole life broken'?[70] Such a letter was just as likely to be followed by one in which he could state quite calmly that he was not looking forward to spending Christmas at Hastings with the Norths because 'I have never been more sane in every way than during the last four months; & can I transport my powers of work & happiness & head healthiness with my box of books?'[71] The mood of comparative serenity was easily destroyed by hearing that Dakyns had decided to take 'Cecy'* to Mentone rather than stay near Symonds in Hastings as he had hoped. Graham was encouraged to

* Cecil Boyle, after a brilliant career at Clifton and Oxford, went into business for a short time. His death in the Boer War distressed Dakyns deeply. Symonds also took a great interest in his early career and wrote him many letters of advice.

indulge his Arcadian tastes as long as these did not interfere with his devotion to Symonds. Jealousy and pique are poured out in a wail of self-pity: 'I meanwhile have my wife, my child, my books, my blue paper, my quill pens, my cough, my head throbbings, my yawnings at dawn & noontide & dusk, my solitary pacings upon grey seabeaches, my languors, my aspirations, my no martyrdoms, my sickness unto death, my nightmare, & my failings of weakness & unstrengthened eyelids.'[72] 'Cecy' and Graham would be enjoying the beauty of Mentone while Symonds was deserted by his dearest friend. 'It is very very weary this head of mine. I want to lean it on your shoulder.'[73] The moods alternated so wildly between paralysing self-pity and gay confidence that one cannot escape the suspicion that self-dramatization formed an intrinsic concomitant of his neurosis.

IV

1867 opened inauspiciously. The Norths entertained a large house-party over Christmas at Hastings and the hubbub made it impossible for Symonds to work. The only place to which he could retire was his bedroom where he had a fine view of the harbour, but here he was so cold that he had to wrap himself in cloaks in order to write. Sometimes he escaped from the uncongenial group to march gloomily along the red shingle beach, to brood about 'Cecy' and Graham among the olive trees by a sea sparkling in the sunshine. On Christmas Eve, while the others were enjoying the festivities downstairs, he wrote to Dakyns: 'The great fact of my life is that the spiritual cannot emerge from the material: I am thwarted in every way by mere physical weakness; *and no one here understands the desirability of leading a spiritual life*: they think study at best an amiable weakness & keep suggesting the higher charms of open air & idleness.'[74] To Charlotte he wrote gloomily: 'I am in need of companions. The constant attempt to arrive at the meaning of books without intercourse with congenial minds is very exhausting.'[75] The only ray of sunshine was little Janet who prattled 'Papa' continuously.

Despite the cold and the dull company and the regret for Dakyns, Symonds managed to write 'solid stuff (I said not sense) incessantly, two Lectures on the Biographies of Musicians, an essay on the Theology of Clough, a long article on the Gk. Gnomic poets, a short Review of

Wright's Golden Gk. Treasury* . . . why have I not one ray of your lune de miel wrapped up & sent by post to glimmer in my twilight?'[76] When Dakyns returned, the radiance of his happiness was a knife in Symonds's heart. 'I think you live an inner life absorbed in your own feelings too much', Symonds told him bluntly.[77] Apparently Dakyns was offended because on 29 January, from Hastings, Symonds complained, 'You never write . . .';[78] but the estrangement was quickly healed and Symonds presently began writing ecstatically to him about his new discovery, Walt Whitman.

At Hastings he caught a troublesome cold which settled in the diseased lung, and Dr Symonds thought a period away from the damp English air might be beneficial. Catherine was pregnant once more, and when he set off on yet another trip to northern France it was Charlotte who accompanied him. Brother and sister thoroughly enjoyed each other's company, but even in June he complained that he could never feel warm, and he always had to apply a mustard plaster and liniments to his chest before going to bed. Within a few weeks this tour came to a close as he headed back for England in worse shape than when he set out.

The second child, Lotta, was born on 30 July. The pregnancy had been a very difficult period for both man and wife. Catherine's moods became black strangulating depressions and Symonds, driven into himself by his own anxieties which he could not confide to her, was unable to give her the love she was too proud to seek. Inevitably a detachment, each withdrawing deeper into his own misery, began to separate them. The strains were so difficult that they agreed soberly that she must never become pregnant again; and according to Symonds's Memoirs the other children were conceived out of the desperation of prolonged frustration. He was beginning to realize that his wife could not give him even the emotional satisfactions he received from Dakyns:

. . . she & I are for the broad calm onward purposes of life. These regurgitations & backward glances, & old burdens, & multitudinous eddyings of thoughts she has not felt – I cannot carry them to her. It is hard to say how much these some times isolate me, stifle me, drive me into a wilderness from wʰ I come back maddened. . . . This isolation, worse than being quite alone, I used to feel terribly when I

* The biographies seem not to have been published but the *Golden Treasury* review appeared in the *PMG*, 6 Feb. 1867; that on the Greek Gnomic Poets in *The North British Review*, Sept. 1868; the Clough article (*The Cornhill*, Oct. 1866) must have been written earlier.

went abroad with C. I would sometimes have given days of my life for you to come & take my burden & give yours, that I might have felt the full sweetness that two laden rain clouds must feel when they meet in heaven & their drops mingle & the earth & cornfields laugh with exceeding abundance of tears.[79]

But Symonds still was not ready to face the consequences of the sexual breakdown of his marriage. Frequently tempted to succumb to homosexuality by a practising invert, Roden Noel,* he could not bring himself to yield to his entreaties. Still parrying for time, his instincts sought other outlets, despite the fact that 'experience goes on teaching me that it is of no use trying to live for intellectual ends alone'.[80]

Early in the mornings he would wander across the park to the Serpentine to gaze at the nude bodies of the male bathers and turn away in an agony of frustration. Sometimes he would visit the Victoria Swimming Baths, torn by the same longings. As usual poetry served as a palliative for his frustrations. He wrote the poetry of this period† in conscious imitation of Walt Whitman, for Whitman was growing into one of the great obsessions of his life. He first discovered the poet on a visit to Frederic Myers at Cambridge in 1865 when Myers suddenly pulled down a volume from his shelves and began reading in his nasal voice: 'Long I thought that knowledge alone would content me.' This was a section in 'Calamus' omitted from later editions of *Leaves of Grass*, and Myers read on:

> – One who loves me is jealous of me, and withdraws me from all but love,
> With the rest I dispense – I sever from what I thought would suffice me, for
>   it does not – it is now empty and tasteless to me,
> I heed knowledge, and the grandeur of The States,
>   and the example of heroes, no more,
> I am indifferent to my own songs – I will go with him I love,
> It is enough for us that we are together – We never separate again.

* Noel, a son of the Earl of Gainsborough, had preceded Symonds at Harrow and probably met him through Henry Sidgwick. He was handsome, feminine in manner, and inordinately vain. His friends were amused by his faith in his own poetic genius but his volumes of verse like *Behind the Veil* do not testify to it, although *A Little Child's Monument* (1881), written after the death of one of his sons, is tenderly moving. 'I do not exactly think Noel a poet,' Sidgwick reported a friend as saying, 'but I think he is a poetical man.' Noel also wrote a great deal of literary criticism and dabbled in the Society for Psychical Research. A great admirer of Whitman, he embraced a philosophy of transcendental idealism of which Symonds wrote lyrically in an introduction to a selection of his poems in *The Poets and Poetry of the Century*. Symonds also dedicated *Many Moods* to him in 1878. Noel died suddenly in 1894.

† The second half of 'John Mordan', 'Diego', and 'Love and Music'.

Symonds sat transfixed. Here was the voice of his own heart, speaking of things he dared not say aloud. Here was a voice celebrating the beauty of a love which he could not confess.

He did not actually write to Whitman until 1871, but long before then he appealed to all his friends to read the American poet. Dakyns heard that it was his 'duty' to read *Leaves of Grass*. 'Leaves of Grass were published in 1860, when I was just two years old. Is it not strange I should have read them this last week & I am now 9 years old? Providence orders things so crookedly. If I had read them & *if* I had understood I should have been a braver better very different man now. It is quite indispensable that you should have this book. It is not a book; there are many better books; it is a man, miraculous in his vigour & love . . . & omniscience & animation & omnivorous humanity.'*[81] When William Rossetti sent him a specimen of the poet's handwriting, he rhapsodized to Dakyns that 'I would as soon have this as that of Shakspere or Plato or Dante.'[82]

In April 1867 Francis Newman gave him a letter of introduction to Moncure D. Conway, who had published an article on his meeting with Whitman in *The Fortnightly Review* in October 1866. 'From him I hope to learn something more about the innovator. I shall not omit to ask him questions about the substance of "Calamus" – as adroitly as I can with a view to hearing what nidus there is actually in America.'[83] Conway's impressive appearance reminded him of Tennyson, and they took an immediate liking to each other. Conway was a Unitarian minister who had been compelled to leave his church in Washington in 1856 because of his sermons against slavery. After the death of his father, a descendant of Washington and a large slave-owner, Conway colonized his father's slaves in Ohio and went about the Northern States preaching emancipation. Nevertheless, he had not won Whitman's complete admiration. 'He is the advocate, the debater,' Whitman told Horace Traubel, 'more anxious to have his case or his man proved true than to *be* true. There is in him a strong vein of the sensational – he likes to take odd views.'[84]

Conway presented Symonds with a copy of all Whitman's poetry, including a number of poems which he had not seen before. 'I am proud of

* This cryptic dating becomes clear if one remembers that he dated his 'birth' from his meeting with Willie Dyer in 1858.

having it: for it has been sent to Conway by W. W. himself to be given to some worthy proselyte.' He failed to persuade Conway to commit himself explicitly on the meaning of 'Calamus.' 'This, I think, means that "Calamus" is really very important & that Conway refuses to talk it over with a stranger. He cannot be oblivious of its plainer meanings.' He was determined, if he saw Conway again, to press him further, particularly as to the 'enigmatical warning' of the second part of 'Calamus'.[85]

At this stage of his life, although Whitman had caught his imagination and encouraged him to accept his own nature, Symonds could not yet put his creed into action. He was torn between desire and convention, and an article 'Mr. Swinburne's Poetry', published in the April 1867 *Westminster Review,* is an interesting revelation of his own moral dilemma. After the appearance of *Poems and Ballads* in 1866, Swinburne was regarded among the respectable as the *enfant terrible* of English letters, and became the object of a vicious anonymous attack by John Morley in *The Saturday Review.* Dr Symonds called him 'an impure windbag' and during the memorable evening at Woolner's raised the subject of 'morbid art' in connection with the poet. At dinner at Lincoln's Inn one night a stranger said to Symonds: 'Swinburne – faugh! I can listen to a fellow talking παιδεραστία [pederasty] – we understand that – but the Lesbian: – little beast!'[86]* Symonds himself was not much more sympathetic to Swinburne. On 19 August 1866 he wrote to Dakyns:

I wrote as severely as I possibly c^d a review of Swinburne's detestable, emasculate volume. . . . But the little wretch has withdrawn it from publication† – so my words are useless. I feel inclined to burn Arthur's copy: but I ought not to do so, since you lent it to me & it has now a money value. If he keeps it long enough some Ld Houghton‡ of the future may give him £5 for the facetious verses

* Symonds's dinner companion was referring to *Anactoria*, the translations from Sappho.

† Swinburne did not withdraw *Poems and Ballads.* After the attack by *The Saturday Review* on 4 August the report was spread abroad that *The Times* was preparing an attack which would include a demand for the criminal prosecution of the publisher. On 5 August J. Bertram Payne of Moxons informed Swinburne that *Poems and Ballads* had been withdrawn from sale. 'He did this, as Swinburne complained, without warning and without compensation, a victim to sudden and craven panic' (Edmund Gosse, *The Life of Algernon Charles Swinburne,* Macmillan & Co., 1917, p. 152).

‡ Richard Monckton Milnes, first Lord Houghton (1809-85). An admirer of Swinburne, he drew the public's attention to *Atalanta in Calydon* in *The Edinburgh Review.* He had literary ambitions, but he was essentially a dilettante and a friend of writers.

containing poems on some of the most highly flavoured myths of Greece & Rome, with much curious information on the amours of the ancients. Withdrawn from publication by its author, only a few copies having been sold to devotees [?] of the gay science. So I have seen like garbage hawked by salesmen.[87]

However, he began to concede Swinburne a grudging admiration for the courage with which he seemed to be defying Victorian prudery and, despite its cautious ambivalence, the fact that Symonds was beginning to form an attitude of his own towards the poet is apparent in *The Westminster* article. Basing his argument on Arnold's insistence on the choice of a noble subject in the Preface to the Poems of 1853, Symonds deplores the fact that 'Laus Veneris' and 'The Leper' are 'repulsive in subject', but defends 'Chastelard' because it is such a realistic portrayal of life, 'although not quite in accord with the prudery of this age of periphrasis'.[88] Fearing that he may have gone too far, he hastens to assure his readers that he has found a disturbing 'moral incompleteness' in Swinburne, and concludes: 'It would be premature to attempt an estimate of the influence which Mr. Swinburne will exercise upon the popular mind and the literature of his country. Whether that influence shall be deep, wholesome, abiding, or superficial, evanescent, and perhaps hurtful, will depend upon Mr. Swinburne's personal strength of character.'[89] That he was succumbing to Swinburne is clear in a letter written to Mrs Arthur Hugh Clough on 9 November 1867, in which he says of the poet: 'What a charm there is about poetical fullness, verve, & self-intoxication: even when turbid with bad taste I like such a torrent as that little man's enthusiasm.'[90]

An amorphous, unsettled creature, Symonds at this period admired colourful people like Swinburne who were not afraid to assert their personalities. To a much greater degree, he admired men like Jowett and his father and Whitman, but basically the attraction was the same: the impression of strength with which they faced the world. Both Dr Symonds and Jowett gave a reassuring sense of integrated personality, what Newman would call 'a moral centre', strong oaks beside the unformed young sapling in whom every passing contact set up tremors. Just to be with Jowett gave Symonds a sense of security and well-being, and Jowett once again had this effect upon him when he came up to London to stay with the young people before the birth of their second child, who was to be his godchild.

During this visit Jowett was particularly kind to Catherine, and showed a warm, responsive side of his nature Symonds had never known before. 'All that painful inscrutability, wʰ makes one feel him to be living a separate life & criticizing the lives with wʰ he comes in contact, was laid aside. He spoke freely of his likes & dislikes & told us stories of his college squabbles. As far as my literary prospects go he was not only reassuring but flattering. He told Catherine, what I was very glad to hear, that I seem to have grown rapidly & continually since I left Oxford.'[91]

But, once Jowett had departed, Symonds began to torment himself again about his wasted life. Mrs Butler reproached him for his coldness and indifference to everyone he met. Repeatedly he apologized to his friends for his detachment and his fits of deep melancholy. He was greatly distressed if he thought that he had offended them when he could not break the gloom that encompassed him. 'If you were here you should see me very simple & sensitive to your least word', he pleaded with Dakyns on one occasion; 'not brittle, complicated, hard, vain-glorious, & callous as I often am with you.'[92] Despite all his good intentions, he quarrelled bitterly with Dakyns and later wrote from Cannes, where he and Catherine had travelled to spend Christmas, begging forgiveness: 'I am very miserable – self-convicted, self humiliated. The fear of hell & horror of damnation is a consciousness that dreads its own continuity.'[93]

V

They did not write for nearly seven months. Symonds always declared that this was the worst period of his entire life. During the previous year his repressed sexuality, his restlessness, and the vague resentment of his inability to produce anything except an occasional magazine article, were rubbing abrasively against each other and it was only a matter of time before the tinder exploded. To Henry Sidgwick, he wrote: 'There are four οἰκεῖα κακά [domestic ills] from which I habitually suffer in the flesh – overworn nerves, weak eyes, delicate lungs, and a peculiar derangement of the digestive organs, which affects more subtle parts of the economy. All these are in a bunch upon me now, so that rest and beauty have but little meaning, and like the happy man in Aristotle, my chance of noble action consists in maintaining serenity amid a crowd of evils.'[94]

Sunny Cannes might seem an incongruous setting for a breakdown.

Moreover, he was surrounded by congenial companions like Henry Sidgwick, who had joined him for a brief holiday, and a pleasant new acquisition, Edward Lear, also in Cannes for his health. Symonds was already familiar with Lear's pictures, and had written an article about them for *The Pall Mall Gazette* in 1867. Lear took a great fancy to little Janet for whom he composed and illustrated rhymes, and she was particularly enchanted with the one about 'The Owl and the pussy cat' who went to sea in 'a beautiful pea-green boat'. Symonds, too, could not help being charmed by Lear's unobtrusive friendliness, and Lear was able to coax him into a grumbling competition which eventually became the 'Growling Eclogue' of *Nonsense Songs and Stories*. The interlocutors are Lear, Catherine, and Symonds:

> Edwardus: What makes you look so black, so glum, so cross?
>   Is it neuralgia, headache, or remorse?
> Johannes: What makes you look so cross, or even more so?
>   Less like a man than is a broken Torso.
> Edwardus: What if my life is odious, should I grin?
>   If you are savage, need I care a pin?
> Johannes: And if I suffer, am I then an owl?
>   May I not frown and grind my teeth and growl?
>
> ————————
>
> See Catherine comes! to her, to her,
> Let each his several miseries refer;
> She shall decide whose woes are least or worst. . . .

Walking with Lear one day, Symonds stumbled and sprained his ankle. There was no doctor in Cannes who could treat it properly and, as a result, he was practically immobilized for the next seven months. But his real problem was not physical; nor could distractions like Lear's genial company stave off the inevitable collapse. 'Mr Segwick [*sic*] – a fellow of Trinity College, Cambridge, dines with me to-day,' Lear wrote Lady Waldegrave on 9 January, 'but I can't ask poor John Symonds.'[95]

One terrible night, late in January, which he shuddered to remember for the rest of his life, Symonds suffered the dark night of the soul. For hours he writhed in mental agony while Catherine clung anxiously to him, and all the time at his shoulder sat what he melodramatically described as 'the obscene vulture, Despair'. H. F. Brown interpreted this experience as essentially spiritual: the passages he quotes from the Memoirs give the impression that Symonds had reached the end of his tether in trying to resolve his religious doubts. It is true that he had left England laden with mystical literature, the Confessions of St Augustine, and 'a bundle of Mrs Butler's letters'. From them he had hopes of finding some answer to his difficulties. 'Blessed, thrice blessed, are they', he reflected to Dakyns, 'who have characters formed by philosophy or morals or souls strengthened by personal feeling for God. They need not fear to press these films & fall, for if they do press, the transitory indeed divides & falls away — the real basis subsists & trembles not.'[96] None the less, while Symonds had not yet found any firm basis of faith, the breakdown was not due essentially to religious perplexity but to the strain of suppressing his sexual cravings.*

For a time he thought of suicide, but, as he once told Dakyns when they discussed the question theoretically, 'it would be most wicked to those whose love has given me such exquisite delight'.[97] What he craved was to shake free from the confines of his present existence: 'More life & fuller — *that* I want.'[98]

Gradually the old habits reasserted themselves. Work was there to be done but it no longer served as an opiate and his head felt as though it were enclosed in tight iron bands. Grimly he plunged into the Zeller again; but it was such an uncongenial task that he confessed he felt like a truant when he was not bent over it. Matters were not helped when Henry Sidgwick pointed out the large number of mistakes he had made. For some time he had been gathering materials for an essay on Greek love and he managed to find a measure of cathartic relief in writing the first draft. He wanted chiefly to explain how *paiderastia* had been intricately connected with the Greek conception of beauty. Much of this material later went into the privately printed *A Problem in Greek Ethics* and a modified form of it appeared in the final chapter of *Studies of the Greek Poets* in 1876.

* F. W. H. Myers, a close friend of Symonds who suffered the same sexual problems as Symonds in early adulthood, and who knew about the terrible night in Cannes, says in an essay entitled 'Marcus Aurelius Antoninus': 'Many a living memory records some crisis when one who had rejected as unproved the traditional sanctions was forced to face the question whether his virtue had any sanction which could still stand; some night when the foundations of the soul's deep were broken up, and she asked herself why she still should cleave to the law of other men rather than to some kindlier monitor of her own' (*Essays Classical*, Macmillan & Co., 1883, p. 220).

Symonds's letters at this period sometimes give the impression that he wallowed in self-pity, but proof that he did not always turn a gloomy face to the world and that his wife was gravely concerned about his sufferings is contained in a letter written by Catherine to a friend in Hastings:

. . . Johnnie, who is anything but well again, does not perhaps show it to people who only see him superficially. It is very hard to be cut off at almost every point, as he is now for three months past, unable to walk, unable to write, or read anything beyond the lightest book, & yet sent out into the world & told to amuse himself! – Amusing one self when it has to be carried on for many consecutive months on compulsion, is about the hardest work on earth. – He is very good & patient & cheerful generally so that I believe that my father was inclined to think him quite well, but his life now is a very sad one. – Sometimes I lose all hope in the future, it is so long that these weaknesses have gone on accumulating.[99]

He tried to recover his shattered equilibrium in Monaco, his favourite spot on the Riviera, in a quiet hotel perched on a cliff high above the Mediterranean. Hobbling out to the garden each morning, he lay back and smoked, languidly watching the seagulls circling above. Here he pondered some unsettling news he had received from Clifton. William Sisson, the elder brother of the eccentric clan he used to visit as a child in Bristol, had died the previous November, and Symonds was startled to receive a copy of his will. Against Dr Symonds's advice, Sisson had made the younger Symonds the trustee of his large estate and guardian of his mad sister's interests. How the money was to be spent was left entirely in Symonds's hands. Symonds had no money sense and was filled with fears that he, by controlling this property, might be contravening the Mortmain Act.* Such problems could not be resolved until he talked them over with his father, but in the meantime the responsibility only increased the weight of his worries.

He soon grew restless under the enforced rest and by April insisted that he was well enough to tour Corsica. By the time they reached Ajaccio his strength gave out and he collapsed again. Lear was visiting the island at the time, and on 15 April he noted in his journal: 'At D. R.'s where I call to say good-bye to the J. S.'s, I find S. far from well, & leave them uneasily with a feeling that his inability to travel may detain them here longer than they anticipate.' Catherine was trying to capture the rugged

---

* Ensuring the perpetual or inalienable tenure of lands held by a corporation or estate.

Corsican scenery on her easel and Lear was much impressed with the high quality of her work.[100]

At the end of the month they returned to the mainland, and through the summer months travelled northwards in slow stages in order not to overtax Symonds's small reserves of strength. Zeller might be put aside temporarily for Italian poetry, but Symonds could not read without making elaborate notes. Inevitably, he also wrote poetry continuously, much of it describing passing strangers who attracted him. As he approached the Alps, serenity almost seemed within his grasp, and by the time he arrived in Mürren he believed that he had worked out his problem. The experience at Cannes had tellingly revealed to him that peace would elude him as long as he resisted his own nature.

His collapse at Cannes also meant a break with another part of his life – the house in Norfolk Square – 'This home w[h] has never been & never will be a home, though I love it after its kind & very much love many of the hours passed here & things done & all that I possess in it.'[101] If his health would not stand the strain of a legal career, there was no longer any necessity to remain in London. The house would be used only during an occasional visit to London – especially an important one in the spring of 1869 – and on 17 November Symonds settled his family at 7 Victoria Square, Clifton. Just before they moved into their new home, he wrote to Dakyns: 'What personally degrades & plagues me is fear of the future. I represent my own state to myself as that of a man who has tossed up a penny & is waiting to see it fall: my heads or tails are a sound or a sick brain.'[102] The coming month was to determine the fall of the coin.

CHAPTER VI

The Turning-Point

SYMONDS arrived back at Clifton in a restive, highly-charged state, receptive to any experience that might fill the vacuum. He did not have long to wait. Early in December, Graham Dakyns gave a small dinner-party to which he invited Symonds to meet some of the Sixth Form boys at Clifton College. Of these, Symonds was immediately attracted to Norman Moor, who stood out in the group as unusually intelligent, agreeable, and mature for his seventeen years. Moreover, he had the sort of face that should have been cast in bronze: finely-chiselled features with deep-set eyes surmounted by a mass of glossy black hair turning to a hint of gold at the tips – he could have made a fortune as a model, Symonds later told Henry Sidgwick enthusiastically. Eager to know the boy better, Symonds approached Dr Percival with the suggestion that he lecture to the Sixth Form on Greek literature. Percival agreed readily and Symonds plunged into the preparation of the lectures which were eventually to appear as *Studies of the Greek Poets* – a work which had its origin in the greatest passion of his life.

Late in December Symonds wrote a poem entitled 'Eudiades' on the theme of a Greek boy and his older lover. When Henry Sidgwick arrived for a fortnight's visit in the middle of January, Symonds showed him 'Eudiades' and a number of other poems of the same nature. Sidgwick read them with horror and warned him of the dangers he invited by pursuing his erotic interests. He persuaded him to lock up all his poetry in a black tin box (except the MS. of 'Eudiades' which Symonds had given to Dakyns and which Dakyns loyally refused to surrender) and on 23 January, Sidgwick stood on the bank of the Avon and dramatically flung the key into the water.

On the 27th, Norman came to dine alone with Symonds for the first time. Despite Sidgwick's warnings, Symonds deliberately set about

winning Norman's affection and from the outset he did not deceive himself about the possible consequences of such a course. All his previous
warnings to Arthur Sidgwick, all his exhortations to Graham Dakyns and
his fear of his father's reaction were completely disregarded as he eagerly
succumbed to the excitement of this new attraction.

The intimacy developed with tempestuous rapidity. Almost every
evening Norman arrived home from school to find bundles of books or
dinner invitations awaiting him. To Dakyns, of course, Symonds confided every step in the pursuit, and at the beginning of February, he told
him frankly: 'If I had any strength I would in one way or another make
him mine & be good to him . . .'[1] and he signed himself with a drawing of
a burning heart transfixed by daggers. After agonizing hesitations he
finally sent a love-letter to the boy, and Dakyns was again informed: 'As
far as that creature can be attached I think he is becoming attached. But
vanity plays too large a part in the game.'[2] He soon discovered a disquieting indolence in Norman and determinedly set out to enlarge and
stimulate his mind. He helped him with his essays and these occasions
became incalculably sweet to him when Norman grew familiar enough
to lean against his shoulder as he was being instructed.

The relationship on the whole brought Symonds far more torment than
happiness. Although Norman responded to his advances, he was in turn
attracted to younger boys, and Symonds suffered the agonies of the
damned if he thought he appeared bored or preoccupied or indifferent.
On the nights when Norman failed to turn up for his essay reading,
Symonds was thrown into despair: 'Norman never came to me, as he
promised to do last night: nor did he write to say why he hid from me his
countenance all yesterday. I have sinned, I suppose, somehow in dealing
with him'[3] '. . . Norman whom I saw for just 10 minutes last night –
into such shreds are the gifts of the spirit scattered'.[4] Yet, despite the
inevitable miseries of any relationship in which the emotions are deeply
involved, Symonds felt more excitedly, vividly alive than he had ever
done in his life before, and his excitement communicated itself to all his
other activities.

After the long period of stagnation, 1869 was rapidly developing into one of
the richest, most complex years he had experienced. While the relationship

with Norman formed an emotional counterpoint in the background, his outer life became an intricate mesh of varied interests and activities. Under his father's guidance he began to familiarize himself with his duties as the administrator of the Sisson estate, a task which began to appeal to him for its challenge to his tact and delicacy.* And on 15 December the birth of his third child, Margaret, threw his personal problems into even sharper relief. These were forgotten temporarily when Jowett came to spend a night – 'a nox socratica' – and had his usual transforming effect. 'He was excellent, & I, disregarding phosphates & snapping my fingers at ramollissement, poured forth my brain – such as it is – & held wassail.'[5]

Among the subjects they talked over was a project connected with Arthur Hugh Clough. Symonds had first heard of Clough one November evening in 1861 when he took an essay to read to Jowett. 'I cannot hear your essay this evening, Mr. Symonds,' Jowett announced in his sweet, piping voice. 'I have just heard that Clough is dead.' Jowett concluded the interview with the words: 'He was the only man of genius, whom I knew to be a man of genius, that I have seen among the younger men at Balliol.'[6] In August of the following year, while staying with W. J. Courthope in Malvern, Symonds wrote Charlotte his first reaction to Clough's poems:

I am reading Clough's poems. They are just come out in Macmillan's pretty green & neat text with a very inadequate memoir by Palgrave. They are wonderfully good in parts. I read through all the jolting lines of the Scotch 'Bothie', lured on by its intense savour & love of simple life. He is very barren & hard at times. There are some poems written at Venice w^h, though not remarkable as poems, seemed consecrated by the place. If papa has not got the book I s^h like to give it to him, & ask you to order it.[7]

Four years later, after reading Mrs Clough's privately printed collection of her husband's poetry, on Jowett's suggestion he wrote an essay on

* In the course of the years he seemed to handle the estate efficiently and the experience was an invaluable training in the management of money. The greatest responsibility, Miss Elizabeth, died in 1877. The old lady was deranged, and to this problem was added the suicides of two of her servants from the Clifton Suspension Bridge. By 1889 the estate amounted to £19,000, of which Symonds spent a small sum each year on charities of which he believed Mr Sisson would approve, all of which had to be done secretly: 'It is part of the anomaly of my position that I cannot tell everybody how I am circumstanced' (MS. letter, undated, to Charlotte, University of Bristol).

Clough which appeared in *The Cornhill* in October 1866. He obviously used the essay to work off some of his own frustrations, partly as an aggrieved outlet for the condescension he had been subjected to by Rugby men. He blamed Rugby for the fact that Clough never seemed to recover from its 'hotbed system'. 'One of the characteristics of the Rugbeans of that day', he declared, 'was the profound belief in the institution to which they belonged. They seemed never to forget that when other youths were boys they had been men; while others had picked up ideas and opinions here and there by chance, they had received the sharp and glittering coinage of Arnold's brain. This made them as all the members of a new and pushing body must be, somewhat insufferable. They formed themselves into "a high Arnold set", and sought the improvement of their college by extending to its members the advantage of possessing Rugby friends.'[8] Symonds also drew a connection between Clough's premature atrophy and his own. 'Clough was one of those men', he stated, 'who long for work, whose consciences oppress them if they rest a moment idle, but who cannot set their hands to anything which seems to them worth doing.'[9] Clough's despair he saw as closely akin to De Musset's.

The poet's widow – a first cousin of Florence Nightingale – wrote to tell him that she objected to the article because he had drawn certain conclusions without sufficient knowledge of the poet's life. Symonds immediately sent off a conciliatory letter. 'There are several of us at Cambridge and at Oxford', he told her, 'who look on Mr Clough's poems as the expression of their deepest convictions & seek in him a mirror of themselves, deriving strength & support from his example. To such as these the good w[h] he has done lives after him in these very poems & martyrdoms of the spirit, while his actual life lies hidden from them.'[10] Apparently the letter placated her because a lengthy correspondence was initiated and she extended an invitation to stay at Combe Hurst early in December. Symonds learned to admire Mrs Clough, but a conciliatory tone runs through almost all his many letters to her, and the hero-worship for her husband is applied with too heavy a brush. He told her that he was thinking of writing a palinode to Clough, and repeatedly emphasized the main source of his admiration: 'His virtue as a thinker', he said, 'seems to me to have consisted in a singular open mindedness.'[11] Mrs Clough was only twelve years older than Symonds and it was not long before

'Dear Mrs Clough' had become 'Dear Blanche'. He began to confide in her his own frustrations as a poet: 'I have the molten fluid in my soul, but the strength to fashion the mould is wanting.'[12]

In May 1868 Mrs Clough suggested, with Jowett's approval, that Symonds collaborate with her in bringing out a collection of her husband's work, which would include a prefatory memoir. Symonds was delighted with the idea, and in order to prepare the ground for its reception, he wrote another article on Clough which was rejected by J. A. Froude, the editor of *Fraser's*, but eventually appeared in *The Fortnightly Review* in December 1868. In the second article, all the derogatory remarks about Rugby were omitted. There was far more emphasis on Clough's work, including a long analysis of 'Dipsychus'.[13] In both articles, De Musset, to whom he compared Clough, is described as the inferior man, but in the second Symonds failed to mention that he considered De Musset 'a far greater artist'. Although the second article did not contain nearly as much biographical data, Symonds concentrated most of his attention on Clough's religious beliefs. Here was a man, he believed, who had the courage of his convictions, who resigned from Oriel rather than pay lip-service to the Thirty-nine Articles – in short, the sort of man Symonds would like to be. In the *Fortnightly* article he stressed that Clough's poems 'are no flashes on the surface, occasional pieces, or set compositions upon given themes; but the very pith and marrow of a deeply-thinking, deeply-feeling soul – the most heartfelt utterances of one who sought to speak out what was in him in the fewest and simplest words'.[14] He told Sidgwick that he hoped to persuade Mrs Clough 'to bring out clearly the value of his *faithful Scepticism*'.[15]

Symonds found great satisfaction in the work, more especially because Clough's temperament continued to exert even greater fascination for him. 'It interests me deeply', he told Dakyns, 'the more I get to know him – only too deeply & at times painfully. I hope some good will come of it. . . . I find it hard to form a just conception of him. I cannot but believe he must have had some peculiar awkwardness of expression & unconquerable impediment. His life in some sense must have been mutilated. Mrs. Clough of course does not give me this impression or suspect it. But I think it ought to be made to appear in his life.' The main problem in their joint editing was Mrs Clough's reluctance to publish a complete edition of the poems, and her wish to omit some of the details of the poet's life from the prefatory memoir: '. . . she is very timid & desirous of suppressing points here & there. I say either a truthful biography or none. But it is hard to maintain the dilemma; & so here as in other matters il faut se contenter d' à peu près.'[14]

To Mrs Clough herself, he wrote:

Of course you have always known, & I have, I think, always reminded you that you must in publishing be prepared to risk somewhat; to face the opinion of the world to a certain extent. But I am sure you will agree with me that it would be of no good to publish another incomplete book. Either do the whole thing or nothing. It is my firm belief that most of those who read the new Collection will be pleased with its frankness and fullness than there will be found carpers and complainers. The mass of the remains are already known – accepted: the additions will interest and gratify those who already like the old things, and will not, I sincerely believe, scandalize many whose opinion is at all worth having.[17]

By November 1868 the memoir, prepared at Hastings and Combe Hurst, was completed: 'The memoir is written – inadequately, but still written – by Mrs Clough, & we rest on our oars.'[18] In the middle of February 1869 Mrs Clough came down to stay in Clifton and they plunged into the final exhausting work of arranging the poetry, the difficulties complicated by the fact that they had considerable trouble deciphering many of the manuscripts. However, the two-volume edition was ready for the printer only a month later and proved immensely popular. The renewed interest it created in Clough was clearly shown by the fact that it went into fourteen reprints. Symonds assumed that theirs would be the final edition, yet while it included a number of poems which did not appear in the 1862 or 1865 editions, a number of textual changes and omissions can be found if one compares it with the complete edition issued by the Clarendon Press in 1951. The sardonic commentary on the British Empire, 'O land of Empire, art and love' is omitted as well as 'The American's Tale' in 'Mari Magno', and the restrained version of the Spirit's temptations in 'Dipsychus' is reprinted just as it appeared in Mrs Clough's earlier version.

Another event occurred to complicate the turbulence of his life at this time – his father-in-law's political difficulties. On 10 November 1868 Symonds wrote to Dakyns from Hastings Lodge where Mr North was contesting his Liberal seat: 'We have nothing to do or think about but Elections. Mr North is not safe, but the fight is a good & hopeful one. I am immersed in the waves but waist deep; since I catch cold in & out of season. But I find that sympathy upon the brink is almost more fatiguing than action in the water.'[19] After a close fight Mr North was re-elected to the seat which he had held almost continuously since 1830 and then, suddenly and unexpectedly, on 19 March the news broke that the Hastings Conservatives were filing a petition against North and the other Member, Tom Brassey, alleging improper election procedure.

A curious aspect of Symonds's character, fluctuating and indecisive in so many ways, was that when faced with a practical problem, he frequently reacted with vigour and decisiveness. On the other hand, if he discarded the anguished analysis with which he scrutinized his emotional problems, he also tended to act impulsively, and at times rashly. He rushed up to London to consult lawyers and family friends. From the Union Club, he wrote Dakyns: 'I have not fared ill here; have been busy seeing Barristers, Police Magistrates, Privy Councillors, Members of Parliament, Judges. I think I have a plan, but it still has to be put to the test. Mr North has to be protected against himself to some extent. . . .'[20] The tone of self-importance was due to the satisfaction of actually having something concrete to add to the defence, but Mr North made it quite clear that he resented his interference.

Undeterred by Mr North's attitude, in April Symonds transferred his nervous energy to Hastings for the trial which opened on the 12th, and for the next five days he sat listening to the examination of witnesses. On the 15th he wrote back to Clifton: 'Mr North has not been . . . *once in a single instance* personally attacked. His name has scarcely been mentioned. But there are one or two points of joint agency which make me uneasy. These we shall have tomorrow. Before any judge but Blackburn the case would have been over ere now. But he is a stickler for legal technicalities & may yet prove too many for us. . . .'[21] Two days later Mr Justice Blackburn dismissed the case with a warning to Mrs Brassey to control her extravagance as it had been responsible for the suspicion of bribery clinging to her husband. There was great rejoicing in Hastings Lodge, but while no charges had been laid against Mr North, the worry of the trial had been a severe strain on the old man who always prided himself on his integrity, and it hastened the collapse of his health later in the year.

To all appearances Symonds seemed involved in the practicalities of editing and elections, but the very degree to which Norman had taken possession of him intensified the energy of his every undertaking. As he sat in his study scribbling away at reviews, or preparing the lectures which he had promised to begin early in May, the sight, touch, odour of the boy engulfed him so much that memory was transformed into the immediacy of actual experience. When Arthur Sidgwick came for a visit at the end of March he could not fail to see the highly-charged state Symonds was in, and, like his brother, felt that he should give him some sober advice on his approach to his classes. As he warmed to his subject, Arthur pronounced that 'Eudiades' was degrading and ought to be destroyed. For the first time since he had known him, Symonds felt irritated with his friend for his sanctimonious attitude. Nevertheless, Arthur's words made a deep impression and, after he had gone, Symonds sat down and wrote Norman a letter making light of the old sentimentalities and indicating that he wished to change the basis of the friendship. Norman replied reassuringly in a similar vein and Symonds felt satisfied that the relationship could now continue on a less dangerous level.

His peace of mind did not last long. On 20 April he went up to Cambridge to stay with Henry Sidgwick. Always eager to share his innermost heart with his closest friends, he showed his diary to Henry. Once more Henry lectured him — 'as severely as *he* can' — impressing upon him that his intellectual gifts were being destroyed by his erotic preoccupations. 'I confess that what he said pricked my conscience', Symonds told Dakyns, '& I was made very sick & sorrowful. Indeed I cᵈ not enjoy Cambridge; for to the illness I brought with me I had the gravest uncertainties & searchings of heart added.'[22]

His uneasiness was increased by the fact that he had already invited Norman to meet him in London on the 24th to spend a week in the house in Norfolk Square. However, he managed to stifle his conscience in the pleasure of showing Norman the sights of London which he had never seen before. All shadows were banished before Norman's delight in everything — 'The School for Scandal' at the Prince of Wales, 'I Puritani' and 'Trovatore', the art galleries, the Crystal Palace, Westminster Abbey and St Paul's. And then on the night of the 30th, they

slept for the first time in each other's arms. 'I am satisfied', Symonds
wrote the following day. 'I think that my poems were not all untrue to
life. . . .'[23] At the end of the golden week they returned to Bristol, Norman to the home of his aunt, Symonds to Catherine and the children who
were staying with the Stracheys at Sutton Court. The only shadow to re-
emerge was the suspicion of Norman's aunt. 'But if I can see her & have
fair speech allowed me I shall conquer her', Symonds boasted confidently;
'I do not yet know the woman I c[d] not overcome in such a cause.'[24]

It was even more important to reassure Catherine. After the birth of
the third baby, Margaret, she sank into the same prostrating post-natal
depression which always assailed her, intensified by her awareness that
Symonds's preoccupation with Norman was creating an even greater
distance between them. Constantly Catherine met the boy in the hall or
on the stairs, and in her bitter consciousness that he was supplanting her
she began to refer to him acidly as 'the ugly boy'.[25] Obsessed though he
was by Norman, Symonds felt a very tender affection for Catherine, and
his guilty knowledge that he was neglecting her was not assuaged by his
more intense realization that he could not break the connection with
Norman unless he moved away from Clifton.

When Symonds arrived at Sutton Court, he and Catherine took a long
walk through the spring countryside while he put a proposition to her
which any woman might have found dismaying. If only she would agree
to let him satisfy his desires elsewhere, he promised her that she would
find him a much closer and gentler companion who would take the most
careful account of all her other needs. Surprisingly, she did not react with
shocked indignation. She responded to his mood and conceded that his
breakdown at Cannes was probably due to the terrible pent-up force of his
frustrations. And then at last, reluctantly but with astonishing grace, she
agreed to all his proposals. Symonds was overjoyed at having won her
over to his wishes, but occasionally in the months to come, for all her
restraint, Catherine could not contain her jealousy and one day flew into
a violent rage when she discovered letters to Norman written with a
passion Symonds had never shown to her. For a woman of deep feeling,
the gradual realization that she could never satisfy the man she loved
must have been a devastating truth to have to accept.

The classes with the Sixth Form started in May. Symonds seems to have had a natural gift for lecturing and years afterwards many of his pupils recalled how he mesmerized them with his dazzling display of learning and enthusiasm. The classroom sessions continued on hikes in Leigh Woods and in groups around the fire in his study. Considering that he lectured to them for only one hour a week, the effect he had on the boys was nothing short of extraordinary. He enjoyed the hero-worship and could not resist exploiting his unfortunate circumstances by cryptic allusions to the fact that his ambitions for a career at the Bar and in Parliament had been blighted by the cruelty of fate. Some of the boys such as the young Scot, Horatio Brown (his future biographer), T. H. Warren (later Warden of Magdalen), and A. R. Cluer worshipped him, but from Norman, alas, he could not obtain this complete submission.

The golden time in London was soon forgotten in fresh miseries over Norman. Symonds had decided to buy the house in Victoria Square, a decision governed by the fact that it was not far from Durdham Downs where Norman lived, but Norman was giving him far less of his time. Absorbed by the activities of the summer term, he had also become infatuated with a younger boy, and the new situation was described to Dakyns in a letter written on 17 May:

He has not come tonight, w^h was to have been one of our sacred nights. In fact I have to get him to come by definite engagements & formal fixing of hours.

I am afraid of becoming to him what Rutson was once (in our happier times) to me. For though I am sure he likes me, yet he does not by any means feel strongly toward me. It is I who *baise* and he who *tend la joue*. Moreover my novelty has worn off; & there are little signs w^h – after due allowance for suspiciousness & over caution – make me pretty nearly certain that he has found me not so delightful as he once thought that I might prove.

Yet him for this my love no whit disdaineth. It only teaches me to be humble & sober.

Only I have asked so much & so often & so passionately & have shown such intense desire that I feel I ought in self-respect to leave him not [*sic*] to give of his free will. If he will not give, I am the loser.

That is what I meant by saying I must once more pump my energies into literature. I have offered him all, & he may still take all or part. But I must let him put forth or hold back his hand according to his good will. Meanwhile I shall of course, pedagogically, do all I can for him through the Lectures & the answers. But the Letters, Book sending, invitations, must cease henceforth. . . .

I am not after all his ideal, great scholar, or in anything very strong. . . . My strong liking for him may have surfeited him: he has so much good taste.[26]

All the resolutions in the world did not obliterate the misery. A fortnight later, he wrote bitterly: 'Norman lives an odd fungoid life on some decaying branch of my soul.'[27] Norman was affectionate, responsive, and conscious of the charm he exerted, but he was also wavering and indolent, and this refusal to yield himself completely, to commit himself unequivocally to Symonds drove the latter to despair. Symonds's nature was too tempestuously idealistic to accept the real Norman. To add to his general disquiet, Dr Symonds's health had begun to fail. He had gone off on a European tour with Charlotte and her letters recounting his various illnesses caused grave concern in Clifton.* Symonds characteristically blotted out the external world in the preparation of an essay on Aristophanes which he later believed to be one of the best of the *Studies of the Greek Poets.*

Anxiety about Dr Symonds was dispelled momentarily when he appeared to be in better health on his return. But peace of mind still eluded Symonds, for he was finding it increasingly difficult to get close to Norman. 'I wish I could have him alone with me for some weeks to read him', he lamented. 'He half kills me: but it is an odoriferous decay.'[28] Hoping to recover the ardour of their early intimacy, in July he took Norman off on a tour through France and Switzerland. They slept together in the small wooden rooms of country inns, they took long walks on the mountains and through the fragrant valleys, and at times he felt that he had recaptured the atmosphere of the first months of their relationship; but Symonds could not blind himself to the fact that Norman did not really fulfil the ideal he had envisaged that first evening at Graham's. 'I have not exactly regretted taking Norman,' he wrote sadly to Dakyns; 'that is, I think, the nuance of truth. I *have* regretted not being with you. I *have* terribly regretted not being with Catherine. This completes the nuance of truth. Norman has not in him the tracts of undiscovered country I imagined. I have done him no good. I ought to have remained self involved & not to have gone out toward this object.'[29]

The regular routine of domesticity was resumed early in September.

---

* Symonds advised his sister not to let their father spend too much time on works of art – 'they are second-rate as refreshments after all, especially architecture' (MS. letter, Sutton Court, 16 February 1869, University of Bristol).

Again, he escaped from the unpleasantness of reality by hard driving preparation for his autumn lectures. In addition to those for the Clifton College boys, he had also been asked to deliver the series to the Society for the Higher Education of Women.

On the 23rd he was deeply distressed to hear that Conington had died suddenly of blood poisoning caused by a malignant pustule on his lip. More bad news followed. Within a week he received a telegram saying that Mr North was dying. Unknown to them all, he had been suffering from diabetes, and Symonds arrived an hour too late. In death the old man, whom he had been very fond of, reminded him of one of 'the old fathers of the church'.[30] Catherine was in a state of exhaustion from keeping vigil by her father's bedside, but they stayed for a week to help Marianne with the funeral and the settlement of the estate. The tense household was 'in that hideously tragic mouldering state that prompts hysterical laughter or insane jesting. . . . I do not condemn or feel the ennui of this funeral state of things: it is so ghastly: it only makes life seem phantasmal more than usual & myself a "scape in oblivion".'[31]

He returned to Clifton as soon as possible and began lecturing to the serious ladies enthusiastically imbibing the culture of the antique world. The room was 'sadly empty' the first day, but good reports must have been spread abroad because later he regularly lectured to a class of about eighty. 'Johnnie's lectures are a success', Catherine wrote proudly to Mrs Clough. 'I mean they are entertaining & not too difficult of comprehension, & then he looks so very nice! And some of the young ladies send him extremely good papers. One of the best he read out last time "pour encourager les autres" – & in the middle he was seized with an uncontrollable impulse to laugh, as the sudden thought of what Mr Courthope would do if he saw him on that platform, gracefully exercising his vocation as the ladies' lecturer!'[32] As for the boys, his uneasiness about Norman made him generally insecure, and he felt that his lectures at Clifton College were beginning to lose their grip. 'I wish I knew how to manage', he complained to Dakyns, 'or that someone cd tell me what I chiefly lack. I shoot above, below, & all round them; but I never hit.'[33]

On 22 November Norman heard the good news that he had been elected a scholar at Balliol, and it was decided that he should go up to Oxford at the beginning of the Lent term. The only means of facing the inevitable break was a busy round of activities: lecturing; visits from Roden Noel, Jowett, and Henry Sidgwick; concerts and dinner-parties; and as many evenings with Norman as the boy could be persuaded to give him. Concern for Dr Symonds's health helped to obliterate more dangerously empty hours. Dr Symonds was shrinking to a shadow of the imposing presence he had once been and was sent off to recuperate in Brighton where Symonds visited him a number of times during the autumn. Always proud of his vigour, the old man made it plain that he wanted as little talk as possible about his illness.

On 27 January Norman came to stay with Symonds for two nights before leaving for Oxford. The time of his visit coincided almost exactly with his first appearance in the house a year before. He arrived late in the evening and Symonds ordered James, his manservant, to prepare a bowl of warm milk and bread for him. They sat quietly before the fire and Symonds spoke gently and fervently of his love. Upstairs, safe in the assurance that the rest of the household were sound asleep, he gave full expression to his passion. When he finally fell asleep he dreamt that he was wandering through a lane formed by rows of cedars and cypress trees. Roses encircled the trunks and spilled like fire through the dusky verdure, and the air was scented with their perfume. When Norman had gone, Symonds smothered his pillow with kisses but he could not bear to stay in the cheerless room. For a long time he sat before the fire in his study, imagining the boy's first night at his new College, and he shuddered to think of him lying between chilly sheets in his narrow, unfamiliar bed.

Long before Norman left for Oxford, Symonds realized that the ideal and the reality did not correspond. Slowly over the years the torment of his love began to ease. The relationship was continuously marred by suspicion and tortured analysis, the inevitable concomitants of a passion which demanded so much and met only affection. Symonds now knew that he could find a measure of peace when the mind was smothered and he abandoned himself to sexual indulgence. If Norman left him with any lesson, it was that sex could be an escape, a surcease from thought, a renewal of life. Yet if the wolf of lust were satisfied, the imagination and its unfulfilled ideal persisted.

CHAPTER VII

The Ambitious Years

I

WITH the *raison d'être* removed from his life, Symonds's feverish fund of energy seemed to collapse, and over the winter he was in bed with a constant series of colds and chest complaints. In the early spring of 1870 he listlessly prepared to make his annual pilgrimage to Switzerland in the elusive quest for health. Even the Alps at their loveliest failed to shake his indifference. Where only a year before he had been able to climb hills without difficulty, now even a short walk caused an acute pain in his side. 'J'ai perdu ma force et ma vie', he complained to Dakyns.[1]

Catherine passed her time as usual in sketching while Symonds turned wearily to Dante, having committed himself to giving a course of lectures on the poet to a group of Bristol women. Before they reached Switzerland, on the road between Paris and Basle, he read the *Purgatorio*, which intensified his depression. 'I think', he wrote Dakyns, 'that the effort to sympathise with a religion and a morality so sternly fixed & definite is very depressing. It brings into so strong a relief my own hopeless & abysmal state of scepticism. . . .'[2] He read on through the *Divine Comedy*, the *Vita Nuova*, and the *Canzoniere*, and with that tenacious persistence which characterized his entire life he wrote out the first draft of the lectures in a little tavern at Heilingenblut.

At Munich they received word that Dr Symonds was seriously ill. Immediately they abandoned the plans for the rest of their holiday and set out for England, travelling without rest until they arrived in Clifton in the middle of the night of 10 July. During the next weeks of worried vigil, their general anxiety was increased by the events taking place in Europe which had so many close associations for them. On the 15th they heard that France had declared war on Germany. Symonds's sympathies lay with neither side. 'The fact that these Germans are educated touches me but little', he remarked to Henry Sidgwick. 'Indeed the paradox of educated food for powder, as far as it goes, seems to give some outlook into a possible *reductio ad absurdum* of warfare. . . . All I hope for the moment is that the first shot at Paris will burst the swollen windbag of the French heroism and bring on the end.'[3] On 13 September, while crossing from Bristol to Bedminster, Symonds was told by the ferryman of the surrender at Sedan.

Sir William Jenner and another eminent physician, Dr Radclyffe, were called down from London to examine Dr Symonds. Gradually he emerged from his comatose state and Catherine was able to write to Mrs Clough:

We have been living for weeks with one idea in our heads night and day – and a shadow of sadness always over us. The shadow is lifted somehow now – yet we never dare to feel elated. Only the last two days he has looked really better, I mean he has come back to perfect consciousness and his own clear mind seems struggling with the great weight of bodily weakness. He cannot yet sit upright – but he takes interest in outside things, in the war, and in his own past weakness, and yesterday gave me a clear scientific explanation of the phenomenon of double consciousness. . . .[4]

Symonds found it almost unbearable to watch the once vigorous frame shrinking to a feeble shadow.

During this anxious autumn, in an effort to divert his mind, he began to think seriously of turning his Italian studies into an ambitious survey of Italian literature. He sent Henry Sidgwick the reassuring news that he had buried all his offending poetry: 'I want to be the historian of Italian Literature and so I trundled away my stumbling-blocks. What has become of them only C. and I know. *Illud cacoenthes poetandi* [the craze for writing poetry] is almost extinct in me.'[5] In January he blocked out the first chapter, which was to be 'a sweeping review' of Italian culture before Dante: 'I have rough hewn all this, made as it were an outline for future stippling and filling in. To get so much accumulated matter out of my head is both a relief and an exhaustion – analagous to parturition.'[6] Caught up in one of his active periods, he also began his lectures on Dante to one hundred and fifty lady students.

Dr Symonds's recuperation was short-lived; on 25 February 1871 the end came. On a soft spring day he was buried beside his wife in Arno's

Vale Cemetery. The following day Symonds wrote to Henry Sidgwick: 'I have not only lost a father but the best friend – in him the most spontaneous and unselfish love for me was combined with sympathy for my tastes and occupations, pride in my success if I ever had any, interest in every undertaking, jealous care of every interest. It is possible that the loss of a wife might bring more sorrow. I cannot think of any other loss which could bring so much sense of isolation, of having suddenly been deprived of what hitherto was vital.'[7]

Practical activities anaesthetized the first crippling sense of loss. The lectures had to be continued, the Italian book was waiting to be written. He had already started to edit Conington's literary remains and he now undertook the same project for his father's writings. Only a month after Dr Symonds's death he had completed the preface which he sent to Charlotte from Dawlish, with the plea not to show it to anyone, even T. H. Green, to whom she had recently become engaged.

I feel that I could not take advice as to sentences & modes of expression in this matter from any one but you. You & I seem to have a peculiar property in Him & in the memory of him, from w[h] it is no churlishness to exclude others now. Though he loved his children equally with that beautiful justice & unquestioning affection w[h] were so strong in him, yet ever since 1860 I have been his nearest friend & you of late years have been more than friend to him, & I think that no other has approached us in this closeness. I felt this as we stood together alone one day in his room by the beautiful pure tranquil form, from w[h] I was then almost grateful to God, that life had gone – seeing that with life all trouble & pain & weariness & possible disappointment had gone too. Therefore you alone shall say if you think this Preface adequate. You must remember it is written to be brief & for the eyes of 200 friends – not merely for ourselves.

Away from Clifton I feel what I have lost far more. There is no business to be done, no calculations to be made about money, houses furniture, w[h], sordid as they are, occupy & fatigue the mind & prevent it from dwelling in peace on spiritual things.

I am not sorry for him, nor sorry even for myself, that he is gone from the languors of the last 2 years. As far as the great Peace of Death goes, I wish that I had entered into that as holily as he has done & that for me too the world with its petty doings which I do so feebly & with its poor ambitions in w[h] I am so sordidly ambitious were at all in any sense so nobly over.

But I do stretch out my hands in vain after the vanished; I cannot help feeling that a great light is quenched & a great staff broken & that now I must live not only for my own life in w^h he took pleasure but for my children. So the past & the present seem dead & the future only remains: youth is gone & middle life spreads grey ahead.

And how small & dark & discomposed my own soul is, she only that knoweth her own bitterness, poor soul, can say. To Him happily I can never be a source of vexation or disappointment.[8]

Dr Symonds had given Charlotte and Green his blessing some months before his death, and a family conclave decided that there was no reason for the marriage to be postponed. Jowett had become Master of Balliol the previous year and Green, his trusted lieutenant, was assuming the subordinate management of the College. Charlotte would be in the sort of intellectual atmosphere she craved. The wedding took place in the house in Victoria Square on 1 July. 'Our wedding went off very well', Catherine wrote to Mrs Clough, '& nobody cried, though it was a very sober wedding. Charlotte's natural calmness did not forsake her. . . . I do believe this marriage is the beginning of much sober happiness – worthy of both.'[9] The small Symonds girls served as dignified bridesmaids, except that Lotta frequently pulled up her frock to contemplate a bruised knee. That evening Symonds sat down and wrote to Charlotte:

July 1, 1871
Clifton.

My dearest Charlotte,

A strange & heart-clutching blank has succeeded to our 4 days bustle. It is all very well to say I am cynical & do not feel things. We people of poetic temperament (!) have to grow a hard husk outside in order that the keen moments of feeling (like *this*) should not splutter over into the hours of ordinary life. I am glad I had two minutes in this room (my study) with Tom before he left. It will remain with me & make me a better man, being in my soul a judgement.

Everybody agreed that nothing could have been better than the whole business – bride, bridegroom, etc. – I shall think all night of the sea & hear it, & see it plunging on the cove; & I shall mingle with its sound the sheep & goat's bells we are, I hope, soon, to hear together.

God bless you, most dear soul. I wish I could say what I feel; but I cannot & all day I have over & around me the spirit of one who is alive & near us.

Your most loving
J. A. S.[10]

Shortly after the wedding Catherine and Symonds set off to join the Greens in Switzerland, and at Rigi Scheidech they found them both unwell. 'But marriage is an upsetting thing at first,' Symonds reminded Dakyns, 'it is oddly differentiated from free Eros.'[11]

II

Symonds had promised his father that he would move into Clifton Hill House. Much as he loved his old home, he had certain misgivings, as he confided to Mrs Clough: 'It is old & massive & too big for us. But I want to keep his things together, & if we live in England we might as well go on at Clifton. The chief objection is on the score of expense; for I shall not be much richer than I was, & the house requires more servants & pays high rates. . . .'[12] The day after they returned to Clifton – following a journey on which they were moved by the ruins of Paris and St Cloud ('most memorable sight, recalling Rome & Pompeii')[13] – Symonds described his reactions to the move to Charlotte: 'The feelings with w^h we are settling down here are very mixed. It is almost painful to find again, the same yet not the same, the household goods of two homes. A long time must elapse before they get properly fused into one harmonious whole. Yet the predominating sense is one of pleasure – & pride & of tenderness for the past that is still so recent – only 6 months, & yet what an abyss of change !'[14] In a later letter he warned her that she 'must be prepared for many changes in the *external* look of things. I have had to cut down the ilexes near the road. . . . However, I trust you will find the inside free from change – at least what changes we have are made in the spirit of the original & are *intended* for improvements.'[15]

The changes were more extensive than he led her to believe. The heavy, ornate furnishings had always stifled Catherine and she set about brightening its ponderous atmosphere with Morris papers and masses of vivid geraniums. Despite her dignified bearing, there was a strain of the gypsy in Catherine; one of Margaret Symonds's memories of her mother during this period was a recollection of her sitting on the terrace after dinner in a white dress with a red poinsettia stuck rakishly behind one ear.

She and Symonds became enthusiastic about star-gazing from the terrace behind the house, and when Dakyns married the widow of a Clifton College master in 1872, Symonds told him that he had reserved 'four tabernacles' where both couples could stand 'at a windy height'.[16] Symonds bought the neighbouring house and garden with a view to improving the property and Catherine had new gardens laid out and greenhouses built. In short, both of them viewed the move to Clifton Hill House as the beginning of a lifelong residence, and the fact that he was now master of his beautiful old home revitalized him from the languor which had gripped him during the previous months.

Symonds began to find great satisfaction in the children as they grew older, and he loved to see them playing about in the enchanted garden of his childhood. Before Dakyns's engagement, encouraging Dakyns to get married, Symonds told him: 'I do like having my children now. I wish you had some stability in life that might make up for your fading present and seem to extend itself towards futurity. This, I think, children give. We live in their youth anew.'[17] Janet was now five, Lotta four, and baby Margaret nearly two. Symonds never attempted to become a pater-familias such as his father had been; his children regarded him as a delightful, laughing companion who sometimes showed them picture-books or composed poems with funny illustrative drawings like Mr Lear's. Occasionally his Sixth Form boys would come and perform charades for them. He had a carpenter build them a set of fine blocks and brought them little wooden bears from Switzerland to mount on their castles. When Janet was still very small she was given a pony of her own and often accompanied her father seated on his mare Madge on rides across Durdham Downs, but Margaret was the one to be honoured with the nickname 'Madge' after this favourite horse. The girls tended to look on Catherine as the mature parent, Symonds as their friend.

As part of the domestic life into which they were settling, it seemed to Symonds fitting that he should now assume some of his father's civic responsibilities. In the next five years he became involved in a number of activities which would have been impossible for the tormented, intro-spective creature he had been only a short time before Dr Symonds's death. He continued the busy round of lecturing, extending his circuit to Exeter and Cheltenham; he was elected to fill his father's place on the Council of Clifton College and for a time took a keen interest in its proceedings;*

---

* The school crest bears the trefoil of the Symonds coat-of-arms, inserted there in gratitude for the help and encouragement given to the school in its early years by Symonds and his father.

he was appointed secretary of an Invalid Ladies' Home at Clifton; and he campaigned actively for Dr Percival's election to Rugby. However, these practical activities were gradually abandoned, mainly because of bad health; but the novelty also wore off after a time and he was soon talking of cutting committee meetings.

Clifton Hill House had always been famous for its hospitality and Symonds continued to fill it with visitors – Mrs Clough, Jowett, the Sidgwicks, Sidney Dobell, Andrew Bradley,* Oscar Browning, and many others. One of the acquaintances who developed into a close friend during these years was F. W. H. Myers. Symonds first met Myers in 1861 at Oxford when Myers had come from Cambridge to spend a weekend with Conington, and immediately took a dislike to the languid, arrogant young man. 'He is such a curious creature', he told Charlotte, 'not at all to my mind. Besides being conceited, he affects some uncomfortable qualities of mind, such as an entire indifference . . . contempt for merely intellectual pursuits. The account he gave of Cambridge horrified Conington – whist & boating between the supreme Sciences.'[18] However, when he met Myers again in London two years later, he began to revise his initial impression a little. 'He is a scapegrace', he admitted to Charlotte, 'but he will be a considerable man: & a turbulent, even a presumptuous & criminal youth may be ignored in silence when there is hope of so great a manhood.'†[19]

Symonds discovered that they shared more interests than he had realized, and it was to Myers that he owed his first introduction to Whitman. At this time Myers was a classical lecturer at Trinity College, Cambridge, but he loathed teaching and in 1872 he left to become a school inspector. In 1871 he suggested to Symonds that they collaborate on a study of the Italian Renaissance, but his interest in the idea was soon replaced by his growing obsession with spiritualism. Like Symonds's other

---

* Sidney Dobell, poet and critic (1824-74). His health was delicate and he spent a number of winters in Clifton to be near Dr Symonds. He and young Symonds took many walks together and discussed aesthetics and literature. A. C. Bradley (1851-1935), one of the great Shakespearean critics, was at the time an undergraduate at Balliol where he shared rooms with Norman Moor.

† Symonds is referring to the scandal surrounding the Camden Medal for Latin verse which Myers won in 1863. It was discovered that Myers had lifted about twenty-five of the hundred lines of his prize-winning poem from Oxford prize poems of previous years, and he had to return the medal (See G. G. Coulton, *Fourscore Years*, Cambridge University Press, 1943, pp. 106-8).

friends, he went through the usual period of scepticism, and in 1867 he wrote a long poem *St Paul,* the record of a personal quest for faith in which the poet turns to the Apostle as a man who was able to find spiritual peace in Christ. Everyone talked of *St Paul* as a great affirmation of faith and it went through one edition after another;* but Myers was still committed to his own questionings and by 1869 he had become passionately interested in the possibility of communion between the living and the dead.† On numerous visits to Clifton he lectured Symonds in his high-pitched, vibrant voice (the voice which led many of his friends to declare that he should have been a preacher) about his fervent belief in an after-life.

I have no doubt of convincing you (in due time for I do not want to hurry your convictions) [he wrote to Symonds in 1874] of the result of the phenomenon, – & I cannot help feeling as if you as well as myself were in some special manner called & Chosen to be hierophant of this no longer Eleusinian but Cosmic Mystery.

Our previous lives – different though they have been – seem to me both of them to have led up to some such destiny. In both there has been an incessant beating against the bars of humanity, dying down into the hopeless satiety & ruinous repose. And I believe that this new revelation was the only thing which could again awake either of us to our true life, could give an enduring object; & a profound & persistent joy.

I cannot help hoping, too, that you may find in those empty vistas of mysterious & unimaginable glory which are just beginning to open on us an inspiration to poetry still more impassioned & glowing than that which you have consecrated to irrecoverable emotions & phantasmal hopes.[20]

Symonds never became a member of the Society for Psychical Research which Myers and Henry Sidgwick helped to found in 1882 with the object of verifying paranormal phenomena,‡ but he often sent his dreams

---

* In a review of *St Paul,* signed J. S., which he contributed to *The Cliftonian,* V (March 1869), 139-42, Symonds says: 'We weary of its sustained grandeur' but admits that 'It is difficult to forget the poem after it has been read.'

† It was a source of great disappointment to him that he never experienced any personal contact with the dead. He later turned to what he called 'Phantasms of the Living' – that is, the appearance of persons still alive, though perhaps dying, to other people at a distance.

‡ William James described Myers's *Human Personality and its Survival of Bodily Death* (2 vols., 1903) as 'the first attempt to consider the phenomena of hallucination, hypnotism, automatism, double personality and mediumship, as connected parts of one whole subject'. When Myers died in 1901 he left a sealed package whose contents he intended to divulge from the other world. His followers claimed that he did communicate with them, speaking through the automatic writing of a medium.

to Myers to be analysed, and he always took a keen interest in its activities.

Symonds's long friendship with Edmund Gosse dates from 1875 when he was living in Clifton Hill House. Gosse had recently resigned his post as assistant librarian at the British Museum to become a translator with the Board of Trade; but, after a rigid Plymouth Brethren upbringing from which all art was excluded, he longed to devote his life to literature. Nine years younger than Symonds, he had begun to make a name for himself with a volume of poetry *With Viol and Flute* (1873) and a considerable amount of reviewing. He, too, was one of Whitman's early fervent admirers, and Symonds sensed in his writing a flavour of sympathetic rapport. Anxious to know more about him, Symonds wrote to ask him if he were the author of an article on Herrick which he had recently enjoyed in *The Cornhill*, and suggested that he come down to stay with him in Clifton. Gosse acknowledged the authorship and in turn professed his admiration for Symonds's writings. In his next letter Symonds inserted a cryptic comment: '. . . I should like to tell you that it was not only your essay on Herrick w^h made me want to know you.'[21] In his third letter, he ventured to be a little bolder. Gosse had sent him a copy of *King Erik* and Symonds now felt confident enough to assert: 'I note throughout this poem what I always feel as characteristic of your work, a strong & tender sympathy with the beauty of men as well as women.'[22] Apparently Gosse's reply gave him a certain amount of encouragement, yet he still did not dare to approach The Subject boldly. Instead he sent him one of his privately-printed pamphlets of poems on the theme of Greek love, emphasizing that the incidents depicted were based on sound historical fact. 'Of course this Greek love is different in quality', he assured Gosse, 'from what can be expected to flourish in the modern world, & to attempt to replant it would be anachronistic. Yet I do not see, having the root of Calamus within our souls, why we should not make the Hellenic passion of friendship a motive in art. I must beg you kindly to return the pamphlet. I have no intention of publishing these or the other poems on Greek life w^h I have written; & I have but a few copies of them in print.'[23]

Gosse seemed to be alarmed by what he read and, as on so many similar occasions, Symonds hastened to protest that he had never meant what he had so clearly been saying. 'I fear . . .', he stammered, 'lest I should have exposed myself to misconstruction, even in your mind by poems which have no didactically ethical intention . . . the two poems I sent, are distinctly archaeological. The [love?] w^h they attempt to set forth finds no place in modern life & has never found one. It is a special G^k compound of chivalrous enthusiasm & perverted sexual passion – the second of its two factors finding ample realization in Renaissance literature (chiefly Italian, but also see Marlowe's "Hero & Leander"), while the former & more spiritual has been absorbed by the romance ideal of love. . . . Pray forget "Eudiades" & pardon me for having sent it; & as you care for me at all, do not by all that is sacred dream that I want to preach its ethics to the present or a future generation.'[24]

Many such misunderstandings, denials, and apologies lay in wait to disturb their friendship.

III

A surge of energy seemed to be released in Symonds after the removal of the overwhelming dominance of his father. In his Memoirs he says frankly that, despite his great love for his father, he realized that he would never have been able to work spontaneously with the critical, concerned eye constantly upon him. Always aware that Dr Symonds expected nothing but the highest achievement from him, his literary output had amounted to little more than a number of over-written, self-conscious descriptive essays – 'word paintings' he later called them disparagingly. But his style began to appear less strained after his father's death, and the two memorials of his father and Conington, which he completed in 1871, were prefaced by simple, unaffected introductions. Significance, too, might be extracted from the fact that his first full-scale book was a study of a writer whom Dr Symonds abhorred – Dante.

Symonds continued to amass facts for the projected history of Italian culture but its plodding discipline exacerbated his frustrated poetic temperament. 'I am quite weary of erudition', he wailed plaintively to Dakyns, 'I hate it. I hate history & am not made for it – & yet I go on at it, because the muses are unkind. They give me nothing to sing of that the world will listen to; & when I think of singing, I remember the terrible words of Henry's letter in w^h he denounced my poems.'[25]

Freddie Myers and Mrs Clough – 'a clear-sighted man & a thick-sighted woman'[26] – also told him frankly that his poetry was not worth pursuing. Nevertheless, he informed Mrs Clough defiantly that he did not rebel because God 'has made me only a potential & not a real poet. I shall never cease writing poetry. It is the only thing I like. I hate the development of thought in prose.'[27] His voice was stifled because he could not speak openly of the only subject which deeply moved and inspired him. Throughout the entire course of his criticism, the principal standard by which he judged poetry was the *sincerity* of the poetic experience. He mistrusted Rossetti because he could not believe that his poetry was based on actual life.* In his own case, driven by compulsion, inhibited by society, he panted within the confines of an insoluble dilemma. 'I cannot write in verse to any purpose except on that old Subject', he explained to Dakyns. 'It keeps haunting me, emerging from the slimy Cocytus of Tiraboschi's facts now like a Siren now like a drowned Hylas now like an angry fiend now like a sad-depraved ghost of my own self that seems to wail – lost lost – forgone – forever spoiled!'[28] The only outlet he could find was to print privately his poems on homosexual themes and to distribute these among a few trusted friends.

If his own public Muse must remain silent, there were other poets at whose shrines he could lay his offering. Walt Whitman headed the pantheon. In October 1871 Symonds finally wrote him a fervent letter enclosing a copy of one of his own poems, 'Love and Death', which had been inspired by 'Calamus'. Whitman sent him a kind reply, describing his poem as 'of the loftiest, strongest and tenderest',[29] and encouraged him to continue the correspondence. Discussing Symonds one day, Whitman said, 'About every three months he writes me, O the most beautiful, splendid letters: I dare not show them to any one hardly, they are so like those tête-à-tête interviews with your chum, your mate, your comrade who throws off everything – and that is the kind of fellow Addington Symonds is.'[30] Whitman loved ardent disciples and he never had one more devoted than this man who reverently hung his photograph on the wall of his bedroom, whose poetry was written in conscious imitation of his, and who based his whole philosophy on what be believed to be Whitman's

---

* Symonds described Rossetti's sonnets as 'cabinet productions' because they lacked the note of genuine suffering ('Notes on Mr Rossetti's New Poems', *Macmillan's Magazine*, XLV, Feb. 1882, 325).

beliefs.* Unfortunately he could extract nothing but evasive replies for the next twenty years from Whitman as to the true meaning of 'Calamus', especially of No. 8 which appeared in the American edition of 1860-1, but was omitted from later editions.

Swinburne was another of Whitman's early disciples who finally won Symonds's admiration because of his devotion to the American poet, particularly after the eulogy at the close of his impassioned ode, 'To Walt Whitman in America' in *Songs before Sunrise* (1871). Symonds envied Charlotte her opportunity to listen to Swinburne discourse on Whitman at Oxford in December 1871: '... he admires him genuinely & probably had good things to say about him. . . .'[31] Three years earlier he had warned Henry Sidgwick of Swinburne's pernicious influence on young men; now he wrote to him that he was beginning to regard Swinburne as 'unapproachable in his sphere, the sphere of lyrical light and heat, now dignified by a great humane enthusiam'.[32] A year later he himself had the opportunity of meeting Swinburne at a dinner-party at Jowett's where they spent the whole evening talking together. 'He is more amiable than I expected,' he told Sidgwick, 'very modest, yet childishly pleased with his pet works and thoughts; very enthusiastic and not in any way *blasé*; clearly of a strong brain physically, and at any rate of a memory as yet unimpaired.'[33]

Not long after this meeting, Symonds summoned the courage to write to Swinburne, enclosing a sheaf of his poems. On 10 December 1872 he lamented to Dakyns: '*Here*, after two days, it seems like a stupid thing done – a third rate dream. He will certainly despise me for bothering him instead of being out with it all to the public.'[34] After what seemed an interminable wait – 'No letter from Swinburne – I am doing penance for my folly of writing to him'[35] – on Boxing Day, Swinburne replied in a long letter apologizing profusely for his delay and fulsome in praise of Symonds's poems:

---

* Symonds was even to cite Whitman as illustration of the modern version of Hellenism in *Studies of the Greek Poets*, an analogy which puzzled some of the critics. 'Strange as it may seem,' he declared, 'Walt Whitman is more truly Greek than any other man of modern times. Hopeful and fearless, accepting the world as he finds it, recognizing the value of each human impulse, shirking no obligation, self-regulated by a law of perfect health, he, in the midst of a chaotic age, emerges clear and distinct, at one with nature, and therefore Greek' (*Studies of the Greek Poets*, I, 1873, p. 422).

. . . I find them full of beauties & powers, & hope they may be but the first
sheaves of a harvest to be reaped & carried before long under the open sun of
publication. They have given me too much matter for admiration & sympathy to
be requited by windy compliments or congratulations on their rich fervour &
sweetness. The chief remark I have to make by way of qualification or deduction
comes after all in the main to this, that they have 'Les défauts de leurs qualités!'
& these, I think, might in great measure be strained off without too much re-
moulding of work already done. You have mastered the English *terza rima* with
a surer hand on bit & bridle than Byron, Mrs. Browning, or Morris in his first
noble poem. . . .'*

He then went on to comment on Symonds's paean of praise to Whitman:

With all my admiration for his great qualities of freedom & harmony in spirit &
speech I cannot, as perhaps you know, pretend to enter in full into the Whit-
manolatry or Whitmania which seems to beset the esoteric disciples of the first
American poet, with whom I am none the less proud to be on terms of reciprocal
regard; which deficiency of mine may possibly debar me from quite appreciating
or even perhaps fully apprehending the exact scope & gist of your eloquent hymn
of discipleship.

[The next passage is carefully crossed out in darker ink, perhaps by
someone into whose hands it fell after Symonds's death.]

. . . Of the three movements of your symphony I decidedly prefer the second to
the first & third, which seem to me now & then to run the risk of becoming (like
too much of Whitman's own work) what I should call blatant. A blare of excessive
sound in verse is as bad as a battle of colours that scream & swear on the canvas.
You may think that I am rebuking my own generally acknowledged faults, &
may be inclined to bid the physician heal himself; but if on coming out of school
I take the freedom to give any of my schoolfellows a tap of amicable admonition
in passing, I am quite ready to admit with all frankness that I may well have
deserved to be horsed in school till the birch drew blood at every cut. . . .[36]

Symonds replied ecstatically that Swinburne's letter was 'like the touch
of a magnetic hand'.[37]

Thus began a long correspondence, in which Symonds, the inveterate
hero-worshipper, was always the more faithful and enthusiastic partner.
When there were lapses, Swinburne was the one responsible. In one

* Swinburne is referring to Morris's *The Defence of Guinevere* (1858), a poem he admired
greatly.

letter, Symonds tried to test Swinburne's reactions to some proffered bait: 'I wonder whether you have made acquaintance at Henley with a family of Boyles. One of them, the eldest son at home, Cecil Boyle, is a very fine specimen of the young athletic Englishman.'[38] Symonds was puzzled as to what Swinburne's proclivities were, and Swinburne did nothing to clarify them for him. Although only three years older than Symonds, Swinburne's manner to him always remained slightly patronizing, and how sincere his private encouragement of him was is questionable because he never praised him in print.

Nevertheless, there were occasions when he had cause to be grateful to Symonds. In 1876 Swinburne presented the public with *Erechtheus*, a dramatic poem conforming closely to classical models. No one seemed to appreciate it – 'a mass of uninspired verbosity', Henry Sidgwick called it[39] – except Symonds. Before his favourable review was published, he wrote to Swinburne:

... I cannot refrain from telling you thus in private, better than I can hope to say in the public press, with what pure & soul-enlivening joy I have read your last poem. It seems to me the highest height to w^h you have climbed, & not only the loftiest, but placed in the clearest & keenest ether of impassioned thought — so that they whom you have taken thither return as with a glimpse of divine things to earth again. This intense beauty of conception in *Erechtheus* so satiates me that I have no critical faculty left to sum up the particular excellences w^h scholar & play reader & poetry lover & seeker after emphatic lines will severally & each to his abundant satisfaction find therein.[40]

'I must send a line of acknowledgment', Swinburne immediately replied, 'to say how much more pleasure such a letter as yours gives me than any number of anonymous published reviews written by men who may be utterly incompetent to judge, and without right to hold, much less to express, an opinion on the matter.'*[41]

1876 marked the zenith of a relationship in which each outvied the other in compliments. Symonds later recalled with pleasure that Swinburne wrote to congratulate him on the second volume of *Studies of the Greek*

---

* In print Symonds praised it for its 'classic qualities' and pointed out that at the same time Swinburne 'vitalized it with emotion that though more antique than modern, still compels our particular sympathy' (*The Academy*, IX, 8 Jan. 1876, 23). Swinburne told Andrew Chatto that this was his favourite review (See *The Swinburne Letters*, ed. Cecil Y. Lang, III, Yale University Press, 1960, p. 104).

Poets which he described as 'that delightful book (the epithet is *banal*, but here the most appropriate & genuine I can find)'.[42] Swinburne was more than delighted by Symonds's enthusiastic review in *The Academy* of *Joseph and his Brethren* by Charles Jeremiah Wells, with an introduction by A. C. Swinburne. 'Have you read "Joseph and his Brethren"?' Symonds asked H. F. Brown. 'If not, do so. It is a miracle of poetic beauty, a pearl fetched up from the deep seas of oblivion by that strong diver Swinburne.'[43] This poetic drama had been written in 1824 by Wells, an intimate friend of Hazlitt and Keats, but was forgotten until 1847 when Rossetti discovered it. In 1860 he introduced it to Swinburne but the latter could not find a publisher to re-issue it until 1876. After reading it, Symonds wrote Swinburne another ardent letter on 4 January, describing his rhapsodic reaction to the poem, and informing him that he would review it in *The Academy*. Swinburne waited impatiently for the review, and when almost convinced that it would never appear, told John Nichol sarcastically that Symonds had written him 'in a style of Corybantic enthusiasm',[44] – but had failed to produce the promised goods. At last, on 22 April, the long-awaited review appeared. Symonds praised *Joseph* because it had been written under the influence of the Elizabethan dramatists and called it 'a really great dramatic poem'.[45] Swinburne sent off yet another grateful letter: 'I have no room to thank you for a review which has given me more pleasure of a deep and more durable kind than any public praise I ever received before. It assured me that I had struck exactly the one central chord I most wanted to touch.'[46]

The relationship continued in this amiable artificiality until 1887, when it was dramatically terminated by an event which belongs to the history of Symonds's friendship with Walt Whitman.

IV

1872 saw the beginning of Symonds's long association with the publishers, Smith, Elder and Co., who wrote offering to publish his Dante lectures. These had already been turned down by Macmillan's and Longmans, and Symonds was overjoyed that Smith, Elder would pay for the cost of the printing. After his literary reputation had become established, he grew into a hard financial bargainer and would never have agreed to an arrangement by which he would receive no payment whatsoever, but at this point all he could think of was that he would now be a full-fledged author. His enthusiasm failed to be dampened even when Catherine asked, on hearing the news, 'Aren't there too many books on Dante?'

An Introduction to the Study of Dante launched Symonds on the first serious phase of his literary career. The critics were not very pleasant about it, and *The Athenaeum* reviewer sounded particularly disgruntled. He began by stating that the work did not deserve the title Symonds had given it. One of its gravest flaws was the fact that it had been based on lectures and 'familiar, slipshod phraseology . . . however admissible in a lecturer, is unbefitting an author who comes before the public in print'.[47] '. . . An Oxford Fellow who has studied Dante only at College', he went on, 'may perhaps be excused these little slips' – the sarcasm could not be missed, particularly as he proceeded to list a long series of errors. Symonds had foolishly declared that 'A clever journalist might make plenty of fun out of the Divine Comedy', a statement which would understandably inflame a hostile reviewer. 'One, without this talent, might, we humbly submit', he sneered, 'make plenty of fun out of *An Introduction to the Study of Dante.*'[48] After reading this review, Symonds sat down and wrote to Henry Sidgwick: 'I will by this post send you a copy of my book on Dante, . . . which I shall obtain at wondrous cheap price if the *Athenaeum* is right about my poor little volume. I have always wanted to know what were the sensations of an author who seasoned his breakfast with the perusal of a well-peppered, malignant review of his first book. I have this morning experienced the emotions peculiar to this condition – but I fear not with sufficient unself-consciousness for exactly learning what I wished to learn. I kept saying to myself: "that's a hard hit – that's spiteful – I wonder whether it is making me twitch and shrink the right way." But I expect that I had a pretty fair experience on the whole.'[49]

The critics might not have been encouraging, but his name was now before the public and he began to receive numerous requests for reviewing, particularly from *The Academy** whose estimate of *Dante* had been

---

* *The Academy* was founded in 1869 with the comprehensive aim, according to its first Editor, Dr C. E. Appleton, to 'survey the European literary and scientific movement as a whole'. 'Have you seen a new paper called *The Academy* ?' Symonds asked Sidgwick. 'It is very Simcoxian in its start: but I should think it might become a useful organ for writers if not for readers.' Symonds contributed to it reguarly from 1869 to 1891, but never received any payment for his reviews.

higher than that of the other periodicals. The most interesting review he wrote during this period was his piece on Walter Pater's *Studies in the History of the Renaissance*, which appeared in *The Academy* on 15 March 1873 and was inadvertently responsible for a subsequent association of their respective philosophies. This linking was ironical because, despite a mutual interest in the Renaissance, Symonds and Pater were never anything but waspishly antagonistic. Pater is said to have referred habitually to Symonds as 'poor Symonds'. On a visit to Oxford in May 1872, Symonds described Pater to Dakyns as looking 'well dressed & ghastly'.[50] Before the *Academy* article appeared, Symonds wrote to Dakyns: 'You shall have Pater reviewed by me when The Academy comes. There is a kind of Death clinging to the man, w[h] makes his Music (but heavens! how sweet that is!) a little faint & sickly. His view of life gives me the creeps, as old women say. I am sure it is a ghastly sham; & that live by it or no as he may do, his utterance of the theory of the world has in it a wormy-hollow-voiced seductiveness of a fiend.'*[51]

Feeling as he did, to review a book by Pater presented certain difficulties: very cunningly, he almost succeeded in evading them. At first reading, the review appears to be laudatory. Concentrating on what he calls the two traditional methods of criticism, the dogmatic and the aesthetic (that is, the classical and the impressionistic), Symonds lunges into an attack on the flaws in both. The criticism which attempts to formulate fixed standards of taste tends to rigidity; on the other hand, he continues, the aesthetic critic (for which read Pater), who is always testing his own sensations is apt to become a voluptuary, indifferent to the discrimination of the good from the worthless. Yet the latter critic is far more valuable than the traditionalist, he claims, because criticism is not a fixed science, nor are standards of beauty immutable. Here Symonds reflects his rebelliousness against authority, whether it be the Victorian father or bourgeois moral standards or the dominating role of the Church in the Middle Ages for which he was developing an obsessive dislike in

---

* He was probably offended, too, because, although Pater quoted three of the twenty-three sonnets of Michelangelo which Symonds had translated for *The Contemporary Review* in 1872, and described them as having been 'executed with great taste and skill . . .', he failed to name the translator. When Symonds published the complete collection of the sonnets in 1878, he referred his readers to Pater's 'refined study of Michel Angelo' – a not very complimentary word in Symonds's vocabulary.

the course of his study of Italian history. But while Symonds at this stage seethed with vague resentment, he had not yet formulated any convictions, either moral or critical. He could recognize that Pater's method was far more difficult – even more valuable – than that of the dogmatic critic, but it still remained 'comparatively isolated, indifferent to common tastes and sympathies, careless of maintaining at any cost a vital connection with the universal instincts of humanity. . . .'[52] Symonds recoiled from Pater's conviction that the impact of art on the cultivated individual was the only meaningful experience in life, as the creed of a withdrawn aesthete, anathema to a man who had learned on his pulses that art remained a pale reflection of the torments and joys of a real love. The review had sidestepped outright condemnation and yet he wondered nervously whether Pater would take offence. Reassurance arrived from Charlotte in Oxford. 'I am pleased to hear Pater liked my review', he wrote thankfully. 'I thought he might think it aigre-doux.'[53]

v

The early part of 1872 found Symonds in a moderately contented frame of mind since he had managed to find a number of projects to occupy his time. The most congenial of these was the task of translating twenty-three of Michelangelo's sonnets which were published in *The Contemporary Review* in September. At the same time he was lecturing on the artist to his ladies in Clifton and Cheltenham, a rather discouraging undertaking, for, as he asked Dakyns, 'How can I talk to them when they have never seen the Sistine Chapel & the tombs of the Medici?'[54] His literary career also made further headway this year. Apparently undismayed by the unenthusiastic reviews of *Dante*, Smith, Elder decided to bring out a collected edition of his essays on the Greek poets, some of which had already appeared in *The North British Review* and *The Westminster Review*, and all of which had their origin in the lectures delivered to the Sixth Form at Clifton College. Symonds was unable to see the book through the press because his new physician, Dr Beddoe, ordered him out of England again, and he entrusted the proofs to Graham Dakyns while he sailed off to Sicily and Greece. Before his departure he left instructions with Dakyns: 'I never told you what the title-page of my book should be. I think it may be as plain as possible:

158

Studies of the Greek Poets

by

John Addington Symonds

I do not want the repetition of Master of Arts, or late Fellow of Magdalen* etc. unless Smith desires it. Nor have I any motto: unless, stay, why not have

> *Im Ganzen, Guten, Schönen*
> *Resolut zu leben?*

(If this seems to you a worthy epigraph, please put it†).'[55]

The letters of the next two months are filled with enthusiastic descriptions of his travels, interspersed with copious instructions about the forthcoming book. 'It is pleasant to perceive at a glance, standing on an It[n] hill or by an It[n] port', he wrote from Genoa, '*why* one longs for such sights at home. It proves the hunger something real & justifies it in a way. But the pleasure of the present stores up the craving of the future.'[56] The tranquillity was disturbed by the irritating news that some of the proofs had been sent by mistake to Clifton Hill House. 'I gave full instructions to Spottiswoode & Co. about your address; but they are such unbusinesslike wretches (business people always are, I think) that I daresay they have not attended to them.'[57] In Sicily his interests were divided between the brigands threatening all the roads and his eagerness to hear from Dakyns how the 'bantling' was getting along. At two one morning he set out to climb to the top of Etna but was driven back by snow and freezing rain. He wandered happily among the temples at Agrigento and spent two days with Thucydides in hand at Syracuse: 'I think, when I go back to England, I ought to coach men at Oxford for Greats in the topography of Syracuse.'[58] The inns were filthy and overrun with fleas – 'I caught 7 one day in one pair of drawers' – but he was sleeping better than he could ever remember; and yet 'I long to be back at work upon the two books I have designed as my next work.' Athens surpassed all expectations: 'Athens is not only the most spirit-shaking but the most purely beautiful place that exists. Here one feels all that one divined in England of the G[k] Spirit. It is pure light, serenity, harmony, balance, definition, σωφροσύνη [moderation] – nothing too

---

* Ruskin habitually entitled his books in this form.   † He did. The lines are from Goethe.

large, too crushing, but all human & beautiful & fit for the cradle of the free Logos. It is worth while to be nibbled all over by cockroaches at night in rolling pitching G[k] steamers & to endure the appalling stench of an Athenian Inn for impressions of such sublimity as this.'[59]

Back in England at the beginning of June, he found that the 'wretched book' was still not out. 'Spottiswoode seems to have behaved as lazily & stupidly as only printers can. . . .'[60] At the beginning of July, *Studies of the Greek Poets* finally appeared. Swinburne wrote to tell him that he found it a 'delightful book – in the true sense of the word delight-full', and John Morley was so impressed that he asked him to join *The Fortnightly Review* as a regular contributor. The only slightly carping voice seems to have come from his old rival, G. A. Simcox, who wrote in *The Academy* with the authority in Greek literature on which he prided himself: 'Mr. Symonds's benevolent fervour, though it never carries him beyond the refinements of expression, tends to become a substitute for accuracy of thought.'[61]

He had achieved a small measure of fame and he basked in its tepid warmth. Miss North gave a dinner-party composed of lesser celebrities of the day including Francis Galton* and R. S. Poole, the recently-appointed keeper of the new department of coins at the British Museum. Symonds was urged to talk on the Greeks and later he admitted candidly to Dakyns that he found the attention delightful. 'There is egoism in telling you this. But you have often said it would do me good to get an audience. . . . However, I am bound to go forth tomorrow to the old self-musing self-corroding existence: I do it with repugnance & with fear.'[62]

Some weeks later, while riding at full gallop across Durdham Downs, he fell from his horse in a faint and remained insensible for over an hour. Dr Beddoe, convinced that he had been overworking, again ordered him abroad to keep him away from his books; but Symonds always managed to evade rest and he planned an ambitious itinerary to include Malta, Naples, Rome, and Cannes. He had already started work on the first volume of *Renaissance in Italy* and he resigned himself to his exile with the plan of gathering more material while on his travels. He had been

---

* In connection with his studies in heredity, Galton was highly interested in the Norths as the progeny of a distinguished line of forebears.

stung by *The Athenaeum's* jibe in its review of *Dante* that 'Touching the geography of Italy, the "late Fellow of Magdalen College", is not, it would seem, so well informed as a writer on Dante ought to be.' In preparation for this new book he was determined to saturate himself in the atmosphere of the country and to absorb its old chronicles.

Catherine had accompanied him in almost all his European trips but this time he would travel alone. 'The question whether Catherine should go or stay was by no means a simple one', he told Charlotte. 'I chose to insist on her giving herself to the children: but she was far from seeing it quite clearly. The first duty of husband & wife is to each other, especially in cases like this where the children would probably get on better alone than the husband. But at any rate we have settled it in this way, thinking more of the children than ourselves. One learns a good deal about life at times like this, which can be learned in no other way, I think.'[63]

The places he visited were described in *Sketches in Italy and Greece* which he dedicated to Catherine. The book appeared in 1874 after a troublesome search for a title. Smith, the publisher, vetoed Symonds's suggestion of *A Student's Sketchbook: Italy and Greece* and insisted on the name under which it was finally issued. In the briefest of reviews, *The Athenaeum* described the collection as 'the graceful papers of a man of much culture'.[64]

Meanwhile the book on the Italian Renaissance was almost completed. Smith paid him £125 for the first thousand copies and it was arranged that he would publish two successive volumes for which he would probably fix the same terms. He also approved Symonds's plan to condense the series into a final 'Cultur Geschichte [*sic*] of the Italians'. 'This is a lifework', Symonds commented soberly to Charlotte, 'I only pray that I may have strength to carry it out & energy to improve it in thoroughness of knowledge as I advance. The advantage of the plan, as thus conceived, is that I shall get possibly some valuable criticism on each section of the work, so as in a final history to bring riper judgment & more complete knowledge to the task than I could have done if I had simply begun at the beginning & gone on out of my own head. I feel the good of writing at Clifton and not in London. The quiet & freedom from flattering friends quite counterbalance what I must always miss there, good libraries. . . .'[65]

Each book extracted a heavy price in nervous exhaustion and demanded a complete recuperation. Once the *Renaissance* manuscript was submitted to the publisher, he set off for Rome but the inflammation of the eyes which he had suffered from a few years before recurred to spoil the journey. 'It is a real nuisance', he complained to Dakyns, 'for I cannot read or think or really look well at things. So I am forced back into the howling wilderness of my soul. Nothing is more pestilent to me than this – esp[y] in these great sinful cities of the South. Labor improbus is my only chance of mental health.'[66]

The Age of the Despots, the first volume of *Renaissance in Italy*, was his most ambitious work to date and he anxiously awaited word of its reception. 'I am doleful about its fate. It seems to me such a mass of pedantry & heaviness & commonplace.'[67] Although he claimed that he had re-written the lectures upon which the book was based, he later saw clearly that the structure and rhetorical tone reflected its origin. Its one great merit lay in his evocation of powerful, assertive figures like the Viscontis and the Borgias, men of imposing personality who fired the imagination of the inhibited Symonds. Pater was completely enraptured and reviewed it with a warmth absent from Symonds's review of *Studies in the History of the Renaissance* in 1873. 'The book . . .', he wrote in *The Academy*, 'presents a brilliant picture of its subject, of the movements of these energetic personalities, the magnificent restlessness and change-fulness of their lives, their immense cynicism. As is the writer's subject so is his style – energetic, flexible, eloquent, full of various illustrations, keeping the attention of the reader always on the alert.'[68] Pater praised Symonds for his dramatic imagination by which the objective tone completely masked the man who held the pen. His only complaint was an absence of 'reserve': too long a book, too opulent a style – the inevitable reaction of a man whose exquisite productions could be encased within a filigree jewel box. Symonds's hostility to Pater was abandoned momentarily. 'It is the first review w[h] has ever really pleased me of any of my books', he exulted. 'What I enjoy is his appreciation of my aims & sense of what I am about. Most reviews are mere blunderbusses charged with blame & praise, both worthless & alike disregarded by myself.'[69] He might have added that it was the first thoroughly complimentary review he had received.

The writing went on restlessly, furiously; and with one book going through the press, he was already hard at work on the next. In 1875 he published the second volume of *Studies of the Greek Poets*, ostensibly designed to fill the gaps in the first series but its more important purpose was that it gave him an opportunity of obliquely stating his views on moral and religious questions. In the last essay he abandoned the style of the impersonal essayist in order to answer the strictures which had been levelled against the first volume. Some of the critics had pointed out that in his enthusiasm for the Greeks, he ignored the fact that Greek civilization also contained slavery, the degradation of women, and pederasty. He admits that such abuses existed, but brushes them aside in a paragraph; he is prudent enough to make only one passing reference to the latter – 'even paiderastia had its honourable aspects'. The essay is devoted to the theme that Greek morality presented striking lessons to the nineteenth century, particularly because it was 'radically scientific', and the nineteenth-century mind, he reminded his readers, valued the scientific approach to every aspect of life. The whole argument is based more on enthusiasm than on any actual connection between the viewpoints of the two periods. The Greeks, he states, viewed man as an 'organic' (a word of which Symonds was growing very fond) part of the universe; the modern theory of evolution had substantiated this early 'intuitive' in-insight. 'It is only fitting', he claims, that a new religion, based on observable laws, not on 'theistic fancies liable to change', should arise.[70] As he approaches his main objective, he makes it clear that he is talking about morality more than about religion. Modern science, particularly the investigations of heredity,* had demonstrated that men act according to certain fixed laws. How foolish, then, to insist that men act 'unnaturally', in accordance with the dictates of a religion which emphasizes a mythical concept like free will!

The essay in effect is an apologia for homosexuality. Symonds was by now convinced that he had been born a homosexual and that nothing could divert his natural bias since he existed as an organic part of a cosmic system based on immutable laws. The public must be made to understand

---

* On 16 October 1875 he wrote Graham Dakyns from Clifton Hill House: 'Francis Galton was sleeping here Thursday. We had a most interesting conversation on the laws of heredity & the theory of population. He told me lots of things' (Dakyns Collection).

this, even by indirect means. While the book was in the process of being printed, a shocked compositor wrote him an indignant letter abusing him for his iniquity. Symonds had cherished the naïve hope that these Greek *Studies* might be used as a text-book, but a letter from one incensed schoolmaster soon disillusioned him. The critics, however, ignored its more dangerous implications. The reviewer in *The Athenaeum* spoke patronizingly of his 'pleasant and ingenious criticism' which would appeal to everyone except scholars;[71] G. A. Simcox in *The Academy* was pleased to see that he had pruned the lushness from his style, 'though', he added venomously, 'we sometimes fancy that the style has been stripped rather than chastened'.[72] For this second series Symonds received £50 – 'so you see', he told Mrs Clough, 'I am not yet the successful author !'[73]

VI

In February of 1876 he and Catherine fled south to the sun of San Remo. 'I do not really like the sort of life one leads in these places', he wrote disconsolately to Charlotte, '& then we have so many half-sad memories connected with them in past years. It is like resuming an old burden that I had hoped to have laid down for ever. . . .'[74] Work provided the usual opiate and he plunged into the second and third volumes of *Renaissance in Italy*, which were to deal with the revival of learning and the fine arts. When they returned to Clifton at the beginning of June his home appeared as delightful as ever. 'After an hour or two spent with the children in the garden here it is very odd to me how much pleasure some dozen trees, a few geranium plants, a fernery, a pond with water lilies & red fishes, & a well-known series of flower borders will afford. It is as though the mind, satiated with the great sights of nature & art, Italy & the Alps; harmonized by the beauty of unique places, Oxford, Cambridge; . . . a little jaded with London sights & sounds; returned to find its own peace in a handful of playthings.'[75]

But back in England, the inevitable physical maladies recurred, and the bitterness with which he surveyed them contained some of the resignation engendered by long familiarity. 'Ever since I returned to this accursed climate, as usual, the life has been oozing out of me, what with destructions by night & diarrhoea by day. There is something quite comical, if it were not so infernally ghastly, in the way one's clock runs down directly it gets fixed upon the shelf, & nature makes a movement toward the dismal equilibrium she loves in this confounded place. I survey the process, powerless, contemptuous, ironical. In a few weeks the struggle to arrest decay will begin & add a new interest to existence.'[76]

The publication of the second and third volumes of *Renaissance in Italy* distracted his mind from his bodily irritations to some degree. He was later to look back to *The Revival of Learning* and *The Fine Arts* as representing a marked advance over anything he had yet written; with the detachment born of time and distance, he could see that they bore a more professional stamp, an indication of greater control over his medium than he had yet demonstrated. At the time he felt the usual dissatisfaction with work whose value seemed relatively insignificant in comparison with the toil and effort it had cost him. When he had almost finished correcting the proofs of Volume II, he wrote to Miss Poynter:*

... it seems duller than ditchwater, incomplete, unsatisfactory, & superficial. I suppose this feeling is natural about all unimaginative work to the man who has done it, if he has a soul beyond dryasdust. The proofs are just now at the part I wrote last spring at San Remo; & every sentence reminds me of the place – morning hours of sunlight, & midnight hours of quiet with one candle, & a Scotchman's snores.† It is pleasant to have written a book all about Europe. Other pages carry me to the Bel Alp, & rides on mules over passes when I was writing in a little pocket book, & walks on glaciers when I made sentences in my head: & some are full of Chamonix, & some of Cremona, & some again of Gressonay & the little inn upon the Frustermung. . . .

There is nothing like writing to sustain life at a high pitch, even though, when the work is over, it should appear a failure. When I lose my faith in that, I shall have been played out, & it will be time to make my bow & exit and be gone from this tenaqueous [*sic*] masquerade.[77]

He was desperately anxious for the new volumes to get a good press. Who would be likely to praise them, who would be listened to with respect, and what organ would carry the most prestige? On 12 February 1877 he wrote to Edmund Gosse:

* A minor novelist and sister of the artist, Sir Edward Poynter, President of the Royal Academy 1894-1905.
† Principal Forbes of St Andrews.

It has just occurred to me to ask whether you had any connection with the Quarterly Review, & if not whether you would care to write for it?* This is not wholly a disinterested question. I hope this spring to bring out two volumes of my Renaissance in Italy, on the 'Revival of Learning' and the 'Fine Arts'; & I should be glad if the Quarterly would give me a review of my three volumes together, the first is called 'Age of the Despots'. Before approaching Dr. Smith, the Editor, which in this case I should do through common friends, Lord Carlingford, & Lady Waldegrave,* I should like to be able to say that So & So was willing to do the article if he would print it. Now there is no one I should like to be reviewed by better than you; & when I say this, I know you will understand that I am far from wishing to escape censure where I need it. I only mean that I have great confidence in your critical judgment combined with a pleasant sense of much intellectual sympathy. Therefore, before I took any steps in the matter, I should like to hear what your views on the subject are. I feel that I am asking something for myself; but I also think that it might not be otherwise than useful to you (if you are not already a writer for the Quarterly) to have entrance into that Review. I daresay I have written all this awkwardly; for it is literally the first time I have ever done anything of the sort about a book of mine. I have always cast my bread upon the waters: and I should do so still, were it not that a work in several volumes like my 'Renaissance in Italy' is more ponderous & wants a little pushing.[78]

Gosse had not yet written for *The Quarterly*, as Symonds was well aware, and jumped at the bait, as Symonds had hoped he might. 'I could not have thought of writing to you as I did unless I had thought it might be a mutual advantage', Symonds assured him in his next letter. 'I do not think that the review would need to cost you very much trouble – though you may of course like to make a solemn entry into those Ancient Halls of the Quarterly & to say your say on the Renaissance with effect.'[79] Gosse began to raise troublesome objections, protesting that he did not want to go to all the labour of writing a long article if he were not sure that Smith would print it. Symonds hastened to encourage him with a mixture of flattery and assurances of his own altruistic interest in the matter. 'I have such confidence in your literary powers that I feel sure you would send him what he would think it a bonne fortune to print', he

* Symonds had already contributed one unsigned review to it – an essay on Longfellow's translation of *The Divine Comedy* in April 1869. Smith had refused his essay on Beethoven in 1867.

† Carlingford, a former President of the Board of Trade under Gladstone, was married to Frances, Countess Waldegrave, hostess of a prominent Liberal salon.

J. A. Symonds, c. 1878

Norman Moor

Graham Dakyns

Walt Whitman

told him, 'therefore I hope you may think it worth the risk. . . .' He also felt it necessary to warn him of *The Quarterly*'s arch-conservative viewpoint:

. . . In writing for the Quarterly it would be well to remember that it is a conservative periodical, & not to *froisser* its tone by any extreme statement of liberal views. I leave the matter wholly in your hands, beseeching you not to think of me at all, but to consider simply whether you care to undertake so serious an essay under the circumstances; whether in fact you feel that you could gain a good literary connection by writing an able article on the Renaissance with my book for basis, which should put you upon the staff of the Quarterly. That is a solid aim to work for, if you judge the conditions sufficiently favourable.[80]

Gosse was again won over, and Symonds suggested an article of twenty or twenty-five pages. After prolonged negotiations, Dr William Smith finally rejected the article; Symonds attempted to comfort Gosse with the words, 'The more I think of it, the more I feel that Smith must have made enquiries about you & found that you are in the "opposite camp". His mistrust of your article is therefore a compliment.'[81] This was not to be Gosse's last brush with *The Quarterly*.

Symonds next approached Dr Chapman of *The Westminster Review* who agreed to take the article but refused to give Gosse any payment for it. In his long well-balanced essay, which appeared anonymously in October 1877, Gosse spoke highly of the three volumes but did not hesitate to record his uneasy reaction to the 'over-ornamental' style and the evidence of hurry which marred the work.[82]

Symonds eventually received attention from *The Quarterly* as well. In the issue of January 1878 it devoted a thirty-four-page leading article to *Renaissance in Italy* and Symonds was gratified to find that the three books were treated as a unit. The tone of the article was serious and respectful, with the exception of one significant sentence in which the anonymous reviewer says of the author: '. . . we find throughout his work a constant conflict between his moral instincts and his philosophical principles, the result of which is a double point of view that produces an impression of infirmity of judgment'.*[83]

* The article was actually written by W. J. Courthope, and the statement is particularly interesting as the opinion of one who knew Symonds well.

VII

Despite periodic bouts of despondency, Symonds's growing confidence in his literary powers was reinforced by the steadily mounting number of books he was producing and by the encouragement of his friends. In January 1876 Henry Sidgwick told him that he thought it would enhance his literary reputation if he could obtain the Professorship of Poetry at Oxford, soon to be vacated by Sir Francis Doyle.* Symonds's ambition was aroused, particularly as he saw his friends assuming positions of authority. Sidgwick had become Professor of Moral and Political Philosophy at Cambridge the year before, and there were rumours that Green was going to obtain the White Professorship of Moral Philosophy at Oxford.†

The idea of the Professorship appealed to him, and in the autumn he went up to Oxford to visit the Greens and make enquiries about his chances. 'These, I think, are tolerably good', he confided to Dakyns; 'I cannot hear of any formidable opponent. I find that some people expect the candidates to have proved their powers by the production of some poems; & thus the question is raised whether I ought to do so. Perhaps I shall.'[84] Since Symonds had moved back to Clifton, Arrowsmith of Bristol had been printing small pamphlets of his poems which he distributed privately to his friends. Most of these dealt with homosexual themes – hardly the subject-matter to endear him to the majority of those who would be casting votes for the Professor of Poetry. 'I am doubting', he wrote in October, 'whether it will not be foolish in the face of an election to publish verses. If the canvassed constituency clamour for it, I must make a little book of innocuous verses.'[85]

The plan to publish a volume of poetry never materialized, but the campaign to get himself elected began to assume the proportions of an obsession. He rushed about the country lining up supporters and dashed off innumerable letters to all the influential people he could think of. Green was his 'agent' in Oxford and to him and Charlotte, Symonds sent directives almost daily. Partisan feeling could not have run higher in a political battle. Besides Symonds, the earliest contenders were Walter

* A letter to Charlotte dated 22 November 1875 (University of Bristol) reveals that he was already considering the possibility.

† Green held the post from 1878 until his death in 1882.

Pater and F. T. Palgrave; there was speculation as to whether Arnold could be persuaded to stand again, but he declined on the grounds that Convocation would reject him for his theological views. Commenting on this decision, *The World* remarked cheekily that 'his unfortunate proclivities towards theology (!) have offended some of the Oxford Liberals – that being a point on which they are extremely sensitive. At all events, Mr. Pater and Mr. Symonds are immaculate in that respect.'[86]

Frank Palgrave attempted to give the impression that he was the official Balliol favourite. 'The combat thickens', Symonds wrote feverishly to Charlotte. '. . . it shows what game the Jew* . . . is playing. I hope the Master can be trusted; for he certainly told me that he should support neither P. nor me at first; & with H. S.† & Tom on my side, P. ought not to call himself the B. favourite. I think I have done as much by way of writing to people as I know how. But I am quite ready to do more under direction – or to desist altogether if that seems best.[87] Later that day he was so incensed by *The Guardian*'s reference to him as 'a writer for magazines' that Charlotte received another indignant letter: 'Please ask Tom if he thinks any notice ought to be taken of what must have been meant as injurious in the eyes of the Country parsons.'[88] Green organized a committee of support. 'I think myself it would be good to ask E. Myers, A. Lang, F. Alleyne, as working members', Symonds suggested. 'They represent general society, literature & law pretty well; & are men on

---

* i.e. Francis Turner Palgrave (1824-97). He had published the *Golden Treasury of Songs and Lyrics* in 1846, and at this time was assistant-secretary of the Board of Education. Symonds had met him at the celebrated evening at Woolner's in 1865 and had found him pompous and vain. Palgrave was extremely irritated when Mrs Clough and Symonds brought out an edition of Clough's poetry in 1869, far more complete than his own (1862). He gave vent to his animus in a poem called 'Pro Mortius' in *The Spectator* on 7 August 1869, the theme of which was that Clough's lesser poems should never have been published:

> In kind oblivion let them be
> Nor has the dead worse foe than he
> Who rakes these sweepings of the artist's room,
> And piles them on his tomb.

. . . he ought to be ashamed of himself', Symonds wrote to Mrs Clough. 'Considering his connection with the past edn, the taste of these verses is monstrously execrable. I have always heard that he was a mixture of insolence & obtuseness in all matters of delicate feeling; this is proof' (MS. letter, 16 August 1869, University of Bristol Collection). Palgrave did eventually become Professor of Poetry, 1885-95.

† Henry J. Smith was a distinguished mathematician.

whom I could reckon for help. But I suppose it would be desirable to get some more eminent names. I have asked Hugh Pearson if he would give his name thinking that he might carry weight with the Clergy.'[89] Symonds also suggested Lyulph Stanley, John Morley, Lewis Campbell, Dr Percival, Albert Dicey, and James Bryce.*

Symonds's confidence was extraordinary, considering that right from the beginning it was apparent that he had a strong body of opinion against him, both for his reputation as a liberal of advanced views and as a comparative upstart. One correspondent wrote to *The Oxford and Cambridge Undergraduate's Journal* to protest that Oxford 'had no need of an ornamental Professor to lecture to ladies in the summer term, and to print his remarks for the benefit of magazine readers'.[90] By the end of February he began to think it more prudent to withdraw. However, he was stunned by the discovery of just how violent the opposition against him was when he read the March issue of *The Contemporary Review,* containing an article, 'The Greek Spirit in Modern Literature', by Richard St John Tyrwhitt, the rector of St Mary Magdalen, and a neighbour of the Greens in Banbury Road. Tyrwhitt was also a water colourist of some talent who had exhibited at the Royal Academy, and was a fervent admirer of Ruskin, who had written a preface to his book, *Christian Art and Symbolism, with Hints on the Study of Landscape* in 1872. Tyrwhitt had withdrawn as a candidate for the Slade Professorship of Fine Art in 1869 in favour of Ruskin. He shared Ruskin's convictions on the necessity of a close relationship between art and morality, and when he read the final chapter in the second volume of *Studies of the Greek Poets* its implications did not escape him. His article in *The Contemporary Review* ostensibly included a discussion of Matthew Arnold's Hellenism, but Arnold was

---

* Ernest Myers, the poet and translator, was the younger brother of Frederic Myers. At this time he was secretary to the London Society for Extension of University Teaching.

Lang, poet, critic, and compiler of fairy tales, was a Fellow of Merton College.

Foster G. Alleyne was a barrister in Bristol.

Pearson was now Canon of Windsor. He had been one of Dr Vaughan's intermediaries with Dr Symonds.

John Morley (later Viscount Morley) was editor of *The Fortnightly Review,* 1867-82.

Lewis Campbell was Professor of Greek at St Andrew's, 1863-92. He and Evelyn Abbott collaborated to write Jowett's biography in 1897.

Dicey was appointed Vinerian Professor of English Law at Oxford in 1882.

Bryce was a distinguished lawyer and historian.

relegated to a couple of pages to make way for a lengthy and sustained attack on the immorality of a man who had the effrontery to present himself as a candidate for one of the most distinguished posts at Oxford. With icy venom, he damned Symonds with such praise as 'Mr Symonds's essays are written in the most brilliant style of the English Decadence; his eye for nature is good: he appears, as far as we can judge, to have read all his Greek poets with great accuracy and feeling, though the historians do not seem to be included in his speciality.'[91] Symonds prided himself on his knowledge of art, yet Tyrwhitt dismissed his views condescendingly as 'the result of vacation tours about the Mediterranean, and of the usual sorts of visits to Italian galleries'. Then he got down to the real core of his animus: Symonds was preaching an agnosticism, based on the more unsavoury aspects of Greek civilization, and was deliberately trying to undermine the fundamental teachings of the Christian Church. Self-distrust, restraint, a sense of sin, and suspicion of the temptations of this world were to be replaced by Walt Whitman's Hellenism – 'whatever on earth Mr. Symonds means by it'.[92] In short, Symonds's philosophy amounted to 'the total denial of any moral restraint on any human impulses'.

After reading the article, Symonds remarked tersely to Charlotte: 'It is a rather poor production, though meant to be nasty.'[93] However, only the previous day he had spoken more candidly about his concern in a note to Dakyns: 'There is a fierce onslaught upon me in the Cot: Review. I had not meant to read it; but Catherine would insist on poisoning the house by importing it. It is a good party move in the matter of the Professorship.'[94] Pride prevented him from expressing his true feelings to Gosse, to whom he announced only a fortnight later: 'My Professorial Candidature stands on the whole very fairly, I think.'[95] When Gosse brought up the subject of the *Contemporary Review* article, he replied with a nonchalant postscript: 'I fear I am only too callous & careless about such attacks as that of Tyrwhit [*sic*]. I hardly read it. Of course it was meant to be galling to me & damaging to my reputation. But I don't mind so long as I'm not forced to notice it in public.'[96]

He *did* mind – desperately – and within a few days of reading it, he was in bed with a heavy cold, which he believed he had caught in the draughty Royal Institution in London where he had been lecturing on

Florence and the Medicis. With streaming eyes and a blood-stained handkerchief pressed to his mouth, he lay there brooding about his miseries. Dr Beddoe, to whom he had dedicated *The Age of the Despots*, now appeared as an incompetent. Within the enveloping safety of bed, he longed for the strong protective mantle of Dr Symonds. To Tom Green he wrote: 'If my dear father has a personality conscious of the world of human thoughts & wishes, he must live now in the satisfaction of a beneficent past life – for he must be often hearing sufferers regret him as the only man they knew who had the power to help & sustain in sickness.'[97]

The first week in March, Principal Shairp of St Andrew's announced himself as a candidate. By the 15th another candidate, Symonds's friend, W. J. Courthope, came forward, and Walter Pater retired from the field to leave Symonds, as *The Oxford and Cambridge Undergraduate's Journal* announced sarcastically, 'the sole representative of what his friends delight to call "culture", his enemies "Paganism" or again "wishy-washy sentimentalism"'.[98] The constant comparisons with Pater added the final fillip to his bitterness.

In Clifton Dr Beddoe announced soberly that the condition of Symonds's left lung was too serious to be neglected. It served as a plausible excuse to escape from the damp English air and the complications of Oxford. Just before he left England, he wrote to Gosse: 'I have had a great deal to do about that tiresome Professorship which I think now Principal Shairp of St Andrews will get.'[99] He set off for Greece with Frank Tuckett, the Alpine climber, who was an acquaintance of long standing, fully realizing that the fight was lost, particularly as Arnold had thrown his formidable support behind Shairp. At Cannes Symonds urged Tuckett to go on without him: in his sombre state the dead world of Greece could offer him nothing. He travelled north to Lombardy and there he received word that Courthope had bowed out* and that Palgrave had urged his supporters to transfer their votes to Shairp. From Milan in a tight-lipped letter Symonds wrote to Charlotte:

Will you ask Tom if he has not already done so to put some notice of my withdrawal from the P. P. Candidature into the newspapers. . . .

I am sorry so much fuss has been made about me. If it had not been for L.

* Courthope was appointed to the Chair in 1895.

Campbell assuring me in Jany that Shairp had told him he had no intention of standing, I should not have given this trouble.

I believe it is really better for me in some ways not to have the Chair; though for my mental health I should have liked it. The Renaissance is an odd atmosphere to live in – & a bad milieu to live into. I seriously feel as if I were losing my sense of what is fitting & decorous in conduct & were adopting the moral indifference of these people. To all this the P. P. would have been a good corrective.[100]

On 24 May, *The Oxford and Cambridge Undergraduate's Journal* announced the election of Principal Shairp, whom it described with its usual bluntness as 'Honest, but dull.'[101]

In 1879 when Green suggested that he consider standing in the future, Symonds refused so emphatically that the subject was never raised again. The experience left him embittered, he seldom referred to it again, and no mention of it occurs in his Memoirs or in Brown's biography. He once alluded tersely to the campaign in an essay on Edward Cracroft Lefroy in *In the Key of Blue*,* but did not include the fact that he had been one of the candidates.†

VIII

In March 1872 Symonds had filled out one of those questionnaires so popular with the Victorians, and his answers, intended for no eyes but his own, were unusually candid:

Your favourite virtue	Loyalty
Your favourite qualities in a man	Strength & Tenderness
Your favourite qualities in a woman	Tenderness & strength
Your favourite occupation	Writing

* The reference does not appear in the original version of the essay in *The New Review*, March 1892. Lefroy, in an article, 'Muscular Christianity' in *The Oxford and Cambridge Undergraduate's Journal* on 21 May 1877 had attacked Pater and Symonds for their exhortation to live according to the dictates of one's own nature. 'The promptings of human nature', he fulminated, 'are not always so entirely beautiful as we could desire, and a promiscuous indulgence in them would probably produce more anarchy than culture in the world.' Symonds found it easy to forgive him when he learned after Lefroy's death that he shared his 'Arcadian' tastes. See p. 275.

† Tyrwhitt had a long memory too. In his sentimentalized Oxford novel, *Hugh Heron Ch.Ch.* (Strahan & Co. Ltd., 1880, p. 51), he compared the philosophy of the unnamed Symonds with that of the atmosphere of the Oxford of his youth: 'It was a rougher time in the undergraduate world. Vice was less recondite, and the devil was more of a roaring lion, and did not glide about with the polite hiss of modern days. There was coarse talk in certain sets, who had not yet been cultured into Hellenism, and accepted Nature for what she is; but, on the other hand, decency was considered decent and not "prurient".'

173

Your chief characteristic	Doublemindedness
Your idea of misery	Waking in the morning after some sorrow
Your favourite colour & flower	Green Brown Gentian
If not yourself, who would you be?	Nobody
Where would you like to live?	At home
Your favourite prose authors	Balzac Fielding
Your favourite poets	Dante Goethe
Your favourite painters and composers	Michael Angelo Beethoven
Your favourite heroes in real life	Pericles Spinoza
Your favourite heroines in real life	My baby
Your favourite heroes in fiction	Hamlet Oedipus
Your favourite heroines in fiction	Antigone Cordelia
Your favourite food and drink	Cream
Your favourite names	N or M
Your pet aversion	Ennui
What characters in history do you most dislike?	Caligula
What is your present state of mind?	Thinking of my own mind
For what fault have you most toleration?	Moral weakness
Your favourite motto	In mundo immundo sim mundus [In an impure world may I be pure][102]

The 'N or M' of the catechism provided him with a sombre jest for these were Norman Moor's initials as well, and the 'moral weakness' was his obsession for the boy. Although Norman had gone up to Oxford, Symonds continued to see him either on his return to Clifton at the end of term or during visits to Oxford. His letters to Dakyns reveal that he was suffering the same torments when he saw him, and torturing himself when Norman's letters seemed lacking in affection. 'I cannot *talk* kindly & nicely about him somehow', he complained; 'I always say something brutal, because I feel too much.'[103] In another letter to Dakyns, he cried, 'Would God that he really loved me. I do not think he does'.[104] On a visit to London, he took Norman to see the celebrated Miss Robinson, but the actress's charms were nothing compared to the 'aching joy of being with N'.[105]

After weeks of indecision, in the spring of 1872 he impulsively invited Norman on another continental tour of Switzerland and northern Italy. Although still ostensibly lovers, they both tacitly recognized that the tone of the relationship had changed. Moreover, the real Norman was replacing the image Symonds had tried to believe in, and the truth had a very acrid taste. The misery of disillusionment was poured out to Dakyns in a letter from Glion:

After selfishly seeking & loving N M, after bearing much pain & wasting much time for him, I find that error erat amor meus – O ye immortal gods! what glorious lightning & soul bathing thunderclaps! – He just cares for me; & what I thought would be worth much – his love – I have – such as it can be. But either he cannot or he will not so much as perceive – far less appreciate – what alone I have in me worth having. . . . Consequently with my inferior self I have to tally what is not the best in him; & I have to endure to see his strivings after better things go forth towards others. O fool that I am – for a moment to have loosed hold of the pure eternal spirit of my Love, to have left that star girt peak to batten on this moor. I therefore here in Switzerland carry about with me my pigmy Frankenstein, am shackled with my living corpse of a dead damned doleful passion. . . . The rage with w^h I have been writing this comes from the discovery that N does not grow in grace. He has lost his naïveté. The raw material, the δύναμις [potentiality], seems even less than it was – less mine to work upon at all events. The manufactured article, the ἐνέργεια [actuality], is but second-rate. But I do not blame him. I scourge my own folly.[106]

Still smarting from the disillusionment of love, on his return to Clifton he looked at his family with tender eyes. 'Catherine & the children are well', he told Mrs Clough, '& are daily more the life of my life to me, thank God. I found this out painfully & yet pleasantly while I was away from them for six weeks with Moor.'[107]

Love was dead, but tender regard remained. Crossing the Channel in June of 1877, Symonds was inspired by the memory of Norman to write 'Mari Magno', which later appeared in *Many Moods*.

> I met Love on the waters, and I said:
>   'Lord, tell thy servant if the fault be mine
>   Or his alone, that we who once were thine,
>   Now daily further from thy face are led !'
> 'I blame you both !' Love answered: 'You who read

The book of self-deception line by line,
Loving yourself, and fearing not to twine
Poisonous passion-flowers around his head:
Him too I blame because he was too weak
To shun your evil and to choose your good,
Too soft to serve you in the hour of need.
Thus then I pass the sentence which you seek:
Love's higher law you still misunderstood;
And love, for him, was but a wayside weed.'

Norman did well at Oxford, and returned to Clifton to become an extraordinarily popular classics master.* In 1878 he married,† had a family and died of influenza in 1895.

After Norman ceased to be the centre of his life, for a number of years Symonds formed no relationships of any consequence. The experience with Norman had left him pessimistic about finding lasting happiness through a passionate involvement with another man. His literary work served as a reasonably effective means of sublimation, but the old torments about his emotional problems and, to a lesser degree, his religious perplexities, continued to trouble him. 'Why did you not kill me?' he screamed as he emerged from the chloroform of a tooth extraction in 1873. 'Why would you not let me die?'[108] The emotional-sexual vacuum remained and there were times when his susceptibilities overcame his scruples. A letter to Graham Dakyns written from Falmouth in December 1872 describes a young cable-layer, one of the many passing strangers who attracted him –

about 22 . . . – light-haired, tall, with huge haunches – like a woman dressed in male clothes on the stage. His forehead was very broad & square & yet rounded at the temples; his eyes blue & deepsunk with dark brown hollows round them; his cheeks rather sunken; his mouth exceedingly red & strangely subtle in smiling, with white teeth. I would gladly have followed him invisibly for three days. . . . I was absorbed in the marvellous être of this man-woman, so strong & sweet & magnetic, so full of the charm of animals, so touched & flétri, somehow with the

* Sir Henry Newbolt in his *Clifton College Twenty-Five Years Ago* (F. E. Robinson & Co., 1904, p. 44) recalled Norman Moor as 'a teacher of the first rank and . . . the most sympathetic and lovable of men'.

† 'What do you think of Mrs. E. N. P. Moor?' Symonds asked Dakyns. 'I don't care much for her photograph' (MS. letter, 2 February 1879, Dakyns Collection).

fire of humanity. . . . I shall not see him again. Passing stranger – you know not how I love you! The most toothed hubbed memories in my mind are evanescent romances of this sort. How strange it is – how it deepens the incommunicable thought of w^h we spoke the other night, to feel the palpitation of a being like oneself so near one's own & not to be able to touch! Perhaps it is better not to touch, & try, & find no fusion. Mr. G. will go on laying down cables, & deepening the bistre circles round his eyes, & middle age will make his flanks & haunches undistinguishable. Meanwhile he is mine. . . .[109]

Reason told him that he was driven by *un amour de l'impossible*, that the ideal would always beckon beyond his grasp. Yet there were immediate gratifications which he found hard to resist. When Roden Noel ('the Centaur' Symonds described him to Dakyns) came to stay, he abandoned himself to sex as he had never done with Norman. He hired male models whom he attempted to draw in order to feast his eyes on their nude bodies. On one occasion he went into a London park with a soldier and touched him intimately – and had to pour his remorse into a long confessional poem, 'The Valley of Vain Desires'.*

When he transcribed his life-story in his Memoirs, he looked back on this period as one in which he might possibly have overcome his sexual bias if it had not been for one decisive event. This was the birth of his fourth daughter, Katharine, in November 1875. Catherine's black moods during this pregnancy were so frightening that after the birth of the child they again made a pact to sleep apart permanently – and this vow they kept for the rest of their lives. However, in blaming this decision for the course of his future activities, Symonds was indulging in a piece of self-deception which he seldom permitted himself in other aspects of his conduct. Like most men of his persuasion, throughout his life he envinced a facility to seize upon an incident of this kind, and convert it into a rationalization of his own conduct.

Symonds liked to believe that the decision was a relief to Catherine. In a sense he was probably right. He knew that she found sex distasteful

* The poem is included in *New and Old* (1880) and on p. 248 he added an explanatory note: 'This is an attempt to describe by way of allegory the attraction of vice that "fascinates and is intolerable", with its punishment of spiritual extinction or madness in this life. I have often doubted whether the nightmare horror which I tried to adumbrate, is a fit subject for poetic treatment. I content myself, however, by reflecting that the sense of the presentment of sin, when sternly realised, involves this horror, and that, as it is a frequent phase of spiritual experience, we are not bound to shrink from its most poignant presentation.'

and was only too aware that she could not excite him, but did he also realize that his initial inexperienced bungling on their honeymoon might have left her wary and inhibited? More important, could he have understood the anguish it must have caused her to have known that he turned to her only in desperation, indeed as a form of therapy, because he could not find what he really wanted? As she grew older, she became more silent and remote, the hurt found vent in frequent asperity, and her mouth became a thin, taut line. And this last child, Katharine, the fruit of a passionless act, was the one whom her mother loved best, the recipient of a deep, intense love which reflected the passion the woman wanted to give her husband. If there is poignancy in the struggle of a homosexual, there is as much tragedy for the woman who finds herself in love with a homosexual.

Symonds now felt freer to indulge his own desires. In February 1877 an old acquaintance (Roden Noel?) took him to a male brothel near the military barracks in Regent's Park. Here he met a strapping young soldier with whom he made an assignation for the following day. For the first time he had a profound sexual experience with someone of a lower social rank and this aspect of the encounter intrigued him as much as the delight of gazing on the beauty of the trooper's body. When his desires had been satisfied, they dressed and sat smoking and talking on the side of the bed. This part of the afternoon was idealized by Symonds as a revelation of the superb comradeship which might exist between men, even two men from entirely different classes of society, and yet – when he left the house, he hurried away in horror and disgust.

At the time he was delivering three lectures on 'Florence and the Medicis' at the Royal Institution. The first was given on the day he had arranged to meet the soldier. All the time he stood there addressing his cultured audience, he despised their self-righteous, middle-class faces gazing earnestly up at him, while he chafed with longing for the time to pass so that he could rush away to meet his soldier. In his biography of Symonds, Brown quotes the passage in the Memoirs describing the effete audience but omits the following section which gives the true explanation for Symonds's impatience. That Symonds was troubled by conscience is quite evident in a letter written at precisely this time to Dakyns in which he makes no reference to the affair with the trooper: 'If thou with thy dear poet's eyes of the soul thou could yet have seen the deaf & the dumb, the blind & the halt & the lame, & the wicked old cats of Countesses, listening to a worn weary headachy croupy semi-asthmatic-middle-aged imposter reading out . . . drivel about Florentine Guilds & dead & gone old Bankers of Florence. . . .' He goes on to describe a party at George Eliot's, and concludes: 'But I – I am as empty – as empty – as It is all a hollow horrid sham – a Marionette theatre – a rouge where the women are pasteboard if nothing worse – & the wise man lives alone.'[110]

These events took place during the fight for the Professorship of Poetry at Oxford. When he returned to Clifton he was stricken with the fierce attack of bronchitis which psychologically could be read as a collapse under the conviction of the guilt ascribed to him by the Rev. R. S. Tyrwhitt.

Whatever the cause, he lacked the strength or the will to make the long trip to Greece. He was not completely prostrated because he was able to spend the spring wandering about Lombardy by himself, but in Turin one night he became so feverish that he knew he must waste no time in getting home. The next morning he tottered out of bed to travel with the speed of desperation to Clifton. The day after he reached home, while riding on the downs, he had an experience even more serious than his fainting accident five years before. A blood-vessel in his lungs suddenly burst and he fell forward on his horse's neck with a violent haemorrhage.

For weeks during the summer he lay inert in bed. Catherine had to feed him as he could not even raise a spoon to his mouth. When he felt a little stronger he took up the sonnets of Michelangelo and Campanella which he had begun to work on before his collapse and resumed his leisurely translation, but most of the time he simply lay in a state of passive contented somnolence. However, he could not withdraw from the problems of his situation indefinitely. Gravely, Dr Beddoe told him why he must not spend another winter in England. It was in fact a death sentence. The doctors were literally counting the years left to him, and the ultimate truth inevitably produced bouts of melancholy, sometimes despair. The time had come when it was no longer possible to temporize with another set of unpalatable facts.

CHAPTER VIII

Davos Platz

I

THE immediate problem was where to spend the coming winter months. The Canaries and Australia were soon rejected because of the discomforts of a long sea-voyage, but the dry, hot climate of Egypt seemed to meet the principal requirements. Symonds and Catherine finally settled on taking Janet and Madge on a cruise up the Nile while Lotta and the baby were to remain at home with a nurse.*

Before they left England, Symonds made a trip to London to discover whether Sir William Jenner agreed with Dr Beddoe's diagnosis of the gravity of his case. The great physician's verdict was even more sobering than that of his own doctor. He advised him to settle all his affairs before he left England because it seemed more than likely that he would never recover from another cold. Symonds's tubercular sister, Lady Strachey, had been one of Sir William's patients for years. He told Symonds bluntly that he was in far more precarious condition than his sister had ever been. The news stunned Symonds. He had always regarded Mary Isabella as the real invalid while his own health, he believed, was simply that of a delicate man who had to take certain precautions.

Jenner also advised him to break his journey to Egypt in the high Alps. By coincidence, only a few days later, a letter arrived from the Greens who were holidaying in Switzerland, urging him to join them at Davos Platz. Symonds knew Switzerland well, but it was the first time he had heard of the town where he was destined to spend the rest of his life. At the beginning of August 1877 he set out with his family and servants, and

* The idea seems to have been suggested by Amelia Edwards's journey up the Nile in a dahabiya in 1873-4. Symonds reviewed the account of her voyage in *The Academy*, 27 Jan. 1877, 65, 66. Amelia Edwards was a remarkable woman who supported herself by her novels and journalism. She also became something of an Egyptologist. Symonds dedicated *New and Old* (1880) to her and contributed two poems to her *Poetry-Book* (1879).

although their mission had a grim enough purpose, it was given a bizarre air of festivity as they crossed to Ostend loaded down with pith helmets, books on Egyptian mummies, and a Union Jack which they intended to fly from their dahabiya.*

Janet suddenly developed measles *en route* and Catherine stopped at Basle to nurse her. Symonds made the rest of the journey alone by diligence, and on 7 August, weak and weary from the long journey, he had his first view of Davos. It was a grey cloudy day and this bleak valley, he could see immediately, would never satisfy the parched longings which had so often seized him as he tossed on a feverish bed. The bare plateau was enclosed not by the flowering mountains of Mürren and Glion but by the rocky Grisons with clusters of pine-trees clinging desperately to their sides. Stone and wooden farmhouses lay scattered across the broad expanse over which curved a river, the Landwasser, whose glassy surface was unbroken by the quivering foliage of trees; 'It is a river a man could grow to hate', Robert Louis Stevenson later wrote bitterly of it.[1] The town of Davos Platz itself was marked by a high church steeple around which huddled a group of ugly buildings, and the whole place had a dusty, dishevelled air with refuse heaps and abandoned sleighs littering the landscape. Symonds, always sensitive to his environment, was repelled, and at first glance could find nothing to recommend it.

At this time Davos was a small backwater town of about three thousand inhabitants. Situated close to the Tyrol, in the most easterly canton of Switzerland, it had no immediate attractions which might lead the adventurous tourist to seek it out, but it was full of health-giving possibilities. It received more sunshine in the winter months than most Swiss valleys, and the enveloping mountains protected it from icy north winds. Phthisis was unknown in the locality, and if a Davoser contracted it when travelling abroad he inevitably recovered quickly when he returned. When Symonds first came to Davos in 1877 its benefits were still known only to a few, but within a very short time it was to become famous as a health resort. In 1882 one thousand visitors spent the winter in Davos, by 1886 the number had risen to six thousand eight hundred and thirty, and in 1895 there were more than thirteen thousand temporary inhabitants.

* A passenger boat on the Nile.

The day after Symonds's arrival he was examined by the local physician, Dr Ruedi, who discovered that a cavity had begun to form in his left lung, an indication of advanced tuberculosis. At this stage the conventional treatment would have been a milk diet, and a régime of hot baths, douches of cold water, and strict confinement to bed in a warm room. Dr Ruedi, however, prescribed a new cure which had proved successful with many of his tubercular patients. The doctors of Davos were acquiring a name as revolutionary experimenters in the treatment of the disease: rooms were scrupulously disinfected after being vacated by a tubercular patient, and these medical pioneers were beginning to talk of lying-out balconies. Even at this early period the most important aspect of the new approach was the imbibing of mountain air.

For the first three weeks, following Dr Ruedi's instructions, Symonds sat all day on the gravel terrace in front of the Hotel Belvedere. At the end of this time his manservant took him in a little carriage up the side of a mountain and placed him in a hammock between two pine trees. From then on for many weeks he lay there from early morning until sunset, gazing peacefully at the clouds sailing above him or at the squirrels leaping from tree to tree. It was a glorious autumn and as the larches flamed against the brilliant blue sky and even the bare slopes of the mountains broke into a mosaic of tawny colour, he began to see that Davos could present another face more beautiful than he could have imagined. Most afternoons Catherine sat beside him reading aloud from Boswell while Janet and Madge played among the fallen leaves. As his strength gradually returned, he occasionally translated one of Michelangelo's sonnets or wrote one of his own. The series, 'Sonnets on the Thought of Death', which formed part of *Many Moods*, was the outcome of his long reflective hours in the hammock. Whenever he passed the spot in later years, he looked at it with reverence, aware of how imminent death had been.

When Graham Dakyns and his wife arrived to visit him in September, they found a tanned, rested Symonds: his fever had subsided, he had regained his appetite, and he told them proudly that he had been able to discard his respirator. They also heard an eloquent account of the local Valtelline wine which Dr Ruedi had prescribed as better than any tonic. His improvement was so marked that he could now accompany Dakyns

'Am Hof', Davos Platz

J. A. Symonds and Swiss peasants

Henry Sidgwick

T. H. Green

about a thousand feet uphill without pain or the fear of a haemorrhage. There was no doubt at all that Davos must be credited with the transformation and Symonds began seriously to entertain the idea of abandoning the trip to Egypt, a contingency dictated strictly by desperation. '. . . in spite of having got so much better, I dread with intolerable shrinking at times the prospect of wintering here', he wrote to Dakyns after his departure. 'I think we shall probably do so, because I feel helpless about going to Egypt. . . . Life goes on in a queer dream.'[2] Among his papers in the University of Bristol is a card on which Catherine listed his alternative reasons for staying or pushing on to Egypt, proof that neither alternative held any positive appeal.

DAVOS		EGYPT	
Pros	*Cons*	*Pros*	*Cons*
The Rest	Monotony	Sun & warmth & dryness	The journey
Safety from fevers	Fear of a bad cold	Amusement	The stay in Cairo
Presence of a doctor	The misery of cold	Jenner & Beddoe	The effect of Beauty on Man, etc.
			Fear of Fevers, War, & Famine
			Separation
			Cold Wind on Nile
	Snow blindness		Flies & insects
			Ophthalmia
Courage of Endurance		Courage of Good Spirits	
English Doctors Ignorant of Davos		German Doctors Ignorant of Egypt	

Davos won and they wrote home for furs and heavy winter clothing, a bottle of chloral syrup, meerschaum pipes, and a large tin box of Vesta matches.

II

Dr Ruedi promised him that if he stayed in Davos he would make him 'a very pretty little cure'.[3] Jenner, however, wrote disapprovingly that he ought to pause before he committed his 'vile body' to the Davos doctors. As the winter advanced, despite the fact that he knew his vitality was returning, Symonds sometimes thought ruefully of Jenner's advice. Not, of course, when the first snowfall turned the valley into an enchanted fairyland, and Symonds sent Dakyns an ecstatic description of his first sleigh ride:

. . . it has been such an ethereal unimaginable expedition – an aeon of enchant-ment condensed into one afternoon hour – that I must write to you about it. If you & Maggie are really thinking of coming, as I trust you are, it is right you should know what lovely things are in store for you. The strong level sunlight falls upon the snow; & where the light is, the snow-surface sparkles with a myriad stars, snow-flowers & crystals shaped like fern-leaf-moss. Where there is no light, the shadow is no less blue than the sky; so that the whole journey is like sailing through tracts of light-irradiate heavens & inter-stellar spaces of the clearest & most flawless ether. The movement is more gliding than any thing I can describe. The air as one drinks it, is like the air of highest glaciers. As we go, the bells keep up a drowsy tinkling at the horse's head. Then the whole landscape is trans-figured – lifted high up out of its commonplaceness. The little hills are Monte Rosas & Mont Blancs. Scale is quite annihilated; & nothing tells but form. Such sweeps of pure untroubled snow fold over fold of undulating softness! And the pines, some bowed with snow, glow golden-green & red & brown – each tiniest trace of colour telling. The chalets are more like fairy houses than ever: waist-deep in stores of winter wood: wonderful in their tints of madder & bistre: with fantastic icicles curving from the roof in towards the windows. The lake is not frozen; & its reflections are as perfect as ever. Words cannot convey the sense of immaterial, aerial, lucid beauty – the feeling of purity & aloofness from all sordid things – the magic of the light & movement. It is more musical – more like a spirit mood of Shelley's lyric singing than anything else. The only thing com-parable to it is rowing on the waters round Amalfi. And this is somehow more remote from earthiness.

How I wish you would give up pedagogy & come & live with me! It is not likely, I think, if I get at all better, that I shall ever settle again for long in England. Could we not manage a good existence somehow between Alps & England?[4]

Skating started early in December and although Symonds could not skate, he loved to walk over the frozen rink and peer down at the bottom 'marvelling at the myriad green splendours of frost'.[5] However, it was not long before he was oppressed by day after day of white monotony unrelieved by variations of colour, the sound of birds, the scent of flowers, or even the homely smell of cooking, if he attempted to stumble along the single track dug out for the horses and sledges. Clad in high gaiters, his frail body muffled in a heavy woollen shawl which he could pull off if the sun became too hot, in a broad-brimmed straw hat and blue spectacles to protect his eyes against the glare of the sun, he doggedly took his prescribed walk on the days when the road was passable; but often the temperature dropped to 10° below zero and the snow fell so heavily that he was confined to the hotel. During one of these imprisonments he wrote to Gosse: 'It is most horrible here now. We have been shut in the house four days & four nights while it snowed incessantly & now the average depth of snow is seven feet everywhere. As I was looking out the window yesterday I saw an avalanche fall at a short distance from the house which swept away a cart with three horses & two carters – buried them all. The men & two horses struggled out; but one horse was suffocated.'[6] To add to his sense of restriction, his room, where he took his meals in solitary grandeur, was directly above the music salon. With the strains of Meyerbeer tinkling out an unwelcome accompaniment to his Renaissance studies, he had doubts as to whether he had made the wise decision. 'I do now seriously believe', he told Dakyns, 'that if I could have got safely into a Dahabeeyah, it would have been much better for me. Yet if it were all to do again, I might still have elected to stay here, feeling the risk of getting into a Nile boat safely too great.'[7]

Symonds at least had his writing to occupy his time but, with the onset of winter, Catherine was deprived of the possibility of her only diversion, sketching, and in the narrow confines of the hotel there were no house-keeping tasks to occupy her. Christmas, always a happy time in Clifton Hill House, was a determinedly cheerful affair organized by the incongruous amalgam of continental invalids staying at the hotel. Symonds fled from the charades to his room where he wrote to Charlotte, 'We are a strange cranky society, keeping up a show of health & spirits so long as we go to bed at nine, walk like snails, & live soberly.'[8] Catherine desperately missed her babies at home. 'Four days & £20 would take me to Clifton or less',[9] she wailed to Charlotte. Eventually the desire to see them was more than she could bear, and on 1 March, undeterred by a violent snowstorm, she set off for home.

A bowl of early spring flowers sent from Cannes provided a sweetly piercing reminder of the beauties of the outside world. Nevertheless, often as they felt trapped in their mountain fastness, the external ties were by no means cut off. They knew that they could be back in England within three or four days. Letters and newspapers posted in England were delivered three days later; books and larger parcels took about a month. They were as troubled by the Eastern question as if they had still been living in Clifton. On 31 March Symonds wrote angrily to Dakyns:

All other thoughts are swallowed up in the telegrams of last night: Ld Derby resigned, & the order given to call out the reserves & hold transports in readiness! So it has come at last. I feel dumb & stupid before the news. What are we going to fight for? I suppose it is for India: but can Dizzy intend to resuscitate the dead if England comes safe out of the war, & repiece shattered Turkey? If we had to fight, we ought to have fought months ago. I know not whom to be most angry with: for I feel that the peculiarly unseasonable moment of attack has been due to Gladstone's hampering of the Government: & yet to fight at all in such a quarrel is mad.[10]

Management of the Sisson estate had taught him canniness about the investment of money,* and he was seriously concerned about whether he should sell his Russian bonds for which he had paid £500. 'Such a case as this', he warned Dakyns, 'makes one feel that all trust in investments ought to be of the most conventionally solid sort. . . .'[11] Even the sale of *Renaissance in Italy* was affected by the Eastern crisis, according to word he received from his publisher. But there were indications that he had not been forgotten in England: he was elected to the Council of the recently established University of Bristol; he was offered the Barlow Chair of Dante Literature in the University of London; and requests for reviewing continued to arrive from the literary periodicals.

The writing went on, and Symonds later attributed his recovery in large measure to the fact that he did not allow himself to atrophy in enforced idleness. He turned again to the study of the Renaissance, not

* Most of his money was invested in railways, the largest share in Canadian railways.

with the febrile restlessness of former years, but with a sense of renewed energy. The long-suffering Dakyns was bombarded with innumerable requests for books. 'You see I am going to try to fly as well as I can with clipped wings, or to try to get into my fourth volume with only a portion of my necessary books.'[12] He had committed himself to writing a short life of Shelley for the 'English Men of Letters' series published by Macmillan's, and to Dakyns he also sent off requests to comb his shelves in Clifton Hill House for everything he could find about the poet. He asked Gosse to look up information on rime royal and Antinous, the beautiful male favourite of the Emperor Hadrian, of whom he had been planning to write a study. 'It seems rather cool to use friends as living dictionaries of the most encyclopedic information', he apologized. 'But what is a poor wretch incarcerated in this frost-prison for five months to do when some problem he cannot solve passes across his brain?'[13] His subscription to the London Library had lapsed and he badly needed its copy of Painter's *Palace of Pleasure*.* 'Could I bribe a friend, I wonder, to take it out & send it to me here! I think that is what I must do.'[14] When he wanted something desperately enough, he revealed a vein of stubbornness as he coaxed, wheedled, and cajoled. In one letter to Gosse he dropped a hint that he would dearly love to see some photographs of Thornycroft's 'Mower'. Within a month he had received a 'precious roll'.[15]

While engrossed in preparing 'an exhaustive monograph' on Antinous, he wrote to R. S. Poole at the British Museum to ask if he possessed any medals of Antinous. His answer — that 'it was very courageous to ask even artistic questions about him' — infuriated Symonds. 'If he tells truth', he raged to Gosse, 'the Br. Mus. is more of a "one horse affair" than I guessed. If he conceals the truth, what is one to think of the scientific spirit in the breasts of English officials?'[16] Would Gosse be good enough to get to the bottom of the matter? To Dakyns he expressed himself even more freely about Poole's 'impudence': 'I can't tell you what a fury I was in when I got this slap in the face. The reply I sent him made him sing a different song; for he has since written to explain apologize &

---

* 'On the Relation of Painter's "Palace of Pleasure" to the English Romantic Drama' was read before the Elizabethan Society at Toynbee Hall on 1 April 1891, and reprinted in *The Fortnightly Review*, L (Aug. 1891), 235-43.

qualify. Meanwhile I have sent his answer afloat in London through Lang & Gosse, neither of whom will spare him.'[17] The incident made him all the more determined to publish a poem he had written on Antinous 'in spite of Mr. and Mrs. Grundy'.[18] 'Whether the English will stand a poem on Antinous,' he told Gosse, 'I shall probably soon discover; as I am going to publish an Euripidean sort of affair (not dramatic but narrative)* about his death I am sure I can't conceive *why* they should object.'[19] However, he felt nervous enough about their reaction to tone down 'The Lotos Garland of Antinous' which appeared in *Many Moods* in comparison with the original version which had been printed privately.†

Early in 1878 Smith, Elder published *The Sonnets of Michael Angelo Buonarroti and Tommaso Campanella*. Symonds's translation of Michelangelo's sonnets was the first complete edition to appear in English and his achievement was acknowledged with respect by the critics. In the Introduction, Symonds noted wistfully that 'nearly all Michelangelo's sonnets express personal feelings'. For years he had been longing to print the work which lay closest to his own heart, but he knew the British public would never accept his poems unless the sexes were changed and his real feelings disguised. As early as 1874 he had been negotiating with Smith, Elder to publish a volume of his poetry, but had dropped the idea when Myers warned him that it might affect the reception of *Renaissance in Italy*. Now distance from England lent him new courage.

Late in December 1877 he discussed the problem with Frances Poynter: 'I have made a volume of original poems, & this I shall soon proceed to print. The selection cost me some trouble. I think I have fairly kept out of sight all the poems which might be objected to on the score either of immorality or painfulness. I wish I felt more normally about these matters myself. It is a great plague to me that I don't & it has cost me a great "deperdition de force intellectuelle".'[20]

In June 1878 *Many Moods* (dedicated to Roden Noel) finally appeared. The reviewers all had the same reaction: Symonds might be developing into an excellent critic and a fine translator, but he was no poet. *The*

---

* Gosse had been thinking of writing a play about Antinous.

† He also wrote an essay on Antinous included in *Sketches and Studies in Italy* (1879) which he regarded 'with a parental fondness' (MS. letter to Graham Dakyns, Geneva, 2 February 1879, Dakyns Collection).

Athenaeum wondered how so perceptive a critic could ever have allowed himself to publish lines like these:

> Summer haze
> Sun-smitten were the clustering curls around
> His marble forehead; the pearly rays
> Of moonbeams are too pale for the profound
> Slumber of snow that soothed his ivory breast.[21]

Symonds was badly shaken by the critical reaction which almost convinced him that he should abandon poetry altogether. 'If I live, I may still do something with prose – for thought and feeling deepen through suffering & the hand does not lose its cunning – obedient to the still aspiring brain',[22] he told Gosse, and begged him to give him an honest opinion of his poetry. When ever-loyal Dakyns wrote to assure him of his faith in his poetic powers, Symonds replied: 'The Reviews say I am a charming writer & all that sort of thing but not a poet, in spite of my profound knowledge of style, my art, my erudition, my expenditure of labour, etc etc. Bosh! I daresay, indeed, I believe, they are right about my lacking what they call "inspiration" & not being a poet. But it amuses me to be found a *lampy* versifier. However, I need not waste ink on such topics. Thank *you* for what you say about "many moods".'[23]

With the coming of spring all the invalids were advised to leave Davos. The sun became unbearably hot, the roads were transformed into swirling rivers by the melting snow, and it was the one time of year when it seemed easy to catch respiratory infections. Symonds escaped south to Milan and Venice, but Italy sucked all the vitality out of him, a common enough occurrence among tubercular patients who had grown accustomed to the dry cold of the higher regions. Always sensitive to changes of weather, Symonds shivered in the tepid atmosphere; after warm rooms insulated by double windows, he found Venetian palazzi stagnant and chilly, and the air outside uncomfortably sultry. 'I enjoyed Venice', he admitted ruefully to Dakyns, 'but it was killing me. The strength of Davos ran out of me like water & I felt my lung a great deal. . . . The last six weeks are thus a dismal wilderness of half achievements, exhaustions, fears, & desolate comparisons between the present & the past. . . .'[24] Moreover, exposure to Italian art had its usual 'tremulous' effect on him;

after the stark surroundings of Davos, his aesthetic sensibilities were agitated disturbingly by the lush opulence of Venice.

When he returned to Davos the book on Shelley was taken up in a desultory way. Expressions such as 'I protrude my belly over Shelley & don't get on much',[25] occur in his letters during this period, and the manuscript was frequently pushed impatiently into a drawer. By July he managed to finish the first draft but was dissatisfied with the result – 'a most imperfect sketch of a life that more than any other required delicatest handling. The man Shelley grows ever more inscrutable the more I look at him.'[26]

In many respects Symonds rebelled against the standards of his day, but his preoccupation with the man behind a work of art stamps him as a typical Victorian critic. Since the poetic voice was regarded as the most profound utterance of man, it was necessary to reassure oneself about the man who ventured to assume the role of *vates*. Matthew Arnold found it difficult to believe that Shelley could produce anything noble from a background to which his reaction was, 'What a set! What a world!'[27]

To an even more pronounced degree than most of his fellow-critics, Symonds identified a work with its creator. 'I must have Keats's "Love Letters" out', he wrote Gosse, 'though I confess there is something in the personality of Keats, some sort of semi-physical aroma wafted from it, which I cannot endure; and I fear these letters will be very redolent of this. What a curious thing is that undefinable flavour of personality – suggestion of physical quality, odour of the man in his unconscious and spontaneous self-determination, which attracts or repels so powerfully, and is the very root of love or dislike.'[28] Knowing how intimately his own poetry expressed his most intense experiences, it never occurred to Symonds that there might be other values as important as an accurate recording of life; he fervently believed that his own poetry suffered if it were not scrupulous *mimesis*. Shelley's life would provide the key to his poetry and Symonds's critical task, as he saw it, was to show the close connection between the two. This attitude explains his deep perplexity over 'Calamus': how could Whitman possibly be talking about anything other than his own experience? Symonds's failure to understand Shelley reflects his own lack of creative imagination and consequent distrust of it in others; it was inevitable that he would be discouraged when the elusive poet evaded him.

His study of Shelley is a straightforward, inadequate account of the poet's life, lacking even the value of fresh biographical discoveries. Symonds's sympathies are obviously with Shelley and although he admits that Harriet seems to have had a legitimate grievance, he refuses to condemn Shelley, in the expectation that some fresh evidence may yet come to light. None of the poetry is analysed in depth. 'Alastor' – with whom he had often identified himself as a young man – is signalled out for its autobiographical interest; 'Epipsychidion' is dismissed because Symonds believed that Shelley utilized his passion for Amelia to state a favourite doctrine rather than as the expression of profound feeling. 'Brilliant as the poem is', he states, 'we cannot read it with unwavering belief either in the author's sincerity at the time he wrote it, or in the permanence of the emotion it describes. The exordium has a fatal note of rhetorical exaggeration, not because the kind of passion is impossible but because Shelley does not convince us that in this instance he had really been its subject.'[29] He dissolves into ecstasies over the 'Life of Life' lyric in *Prometheus Unbound*, but his analysis amounts to an exclamation that such beauties are beyond the scope of criticism.

He received £100 for the book – 'wh was nice,'[30] he told Charlotte gratefully – and at least one reader congratulated him on his accomplishment: Leslie Stephen wrote to tell him that 'you have made me admire Shelley as a man more than I did before'.[31] This reaction could be placed against *The Spectator*'s usual lack of enthusiasm for his work, and he described the tone of their review as 'that inconceivable . . . priggishness of wh it has remained for the Spectator to give a revelation to this last aeon of civilized humanity'.*[32]

III

There was no choice about spending the winter of 1878-9 in Davos. Much as she disliked the place, Catherine could not deny that it seemed to revitalize her delicate husband. His nervous irritability, high temperature, and fast pulse, all the symptoms of progressive tuberculosis, were

---

* *The Spectator*, in a very severe review, referred cuttingly to 'the vague religiosity of his dogmatic agnosticism' ('Mr. Symonds's *Life of Shelley*', *The Spectator*, 9 Nov. 1878, 1402).

undoubtedly modified. Symonds himself was beginning to regard Davos as a possible permanent home. They could get back to England occasionally, he reasoned; friends like Henry Sidgwick had already visited him; and he was earnestly attempting to persuade Graham Dakyns, who still chafed against his life as a schoolmaster, to join him. 'Do not forget that you could live en famille here in such luxury as Davos can afford for £600 a year', he exhorted him; '& a year of it . . . would be no bad slice of life between one nightmare & another.'[33]

As the months passed, the vague notion of making Davos into a permanent home grew into a certainty. The various problems connected with such a decision could no longer be evaded. The children, of course, remained the greatest difficulty: '. . . what are we to do with the children?' Symonds asked his sister in perplexity. 'They cannot go on like this indefinitely. It is a prospect altogether from which I shrink.'[34] Catherine had brought Lotta and Katharine back with her and began to make enquiries about putting the older girls into a school in Geneva. If they were to live in Davos, it was impractical for the family to be confined to a hotel, despite all Catherine's efforts to make their rooms into a home. And if they bought or built a house, what should they do with Clifton Hill House?

Catherine was a seasoned and adaptable traveller but her heart sank at the prospect of being isolated for the rest of her life in a bleak valley whose less obvious attractions she never learned to appreciate. The problems of housekeeping were enough to daunt the most intrepid of women: servants were difficult to find and most of them preferred to work in the hotels; the shops were inadequate, and the necessities needed for an English establishment would have to be sent from England, and imports were expensive because of high Customs levies. Moreover, Catherine had become happily accustomed to the routine of Clifton Hill House and she missed her Bristol friends and, above all, her beloved garden. When Symonds had proposed to her, and asked her if she would mind spending the rest of her life in one place, little did she know that she would be confined to Davos.

The adjustment presented Symonds with problems as well. He would be completely cut off from a literary atmosphere with its exchange of ideas indispensable for a writer. Moreover, he realized that if he continued to write scholarly books such as *Renaissance in Italy*, the difficulties were insurmountable. Davos contained only two inadequate circulating libraries, and even if he had the books from his library in Clifton sent out to him, there would inevitably be many gaps; and there would be a bothersome delay while he waited for orders to be filled by booksellers in London. If he wrote, it would have to be in the role of popularizer. The Rector of Lincoln, the formidable scholar Mark Pattison, whom Symonds always disliked, finding him at work in his room in the Hotel Buol in 1878, asked him superciliously: 'Of course, you cannot be thinking of writing a book here?' aware that this was precisely what he was doing; to which Symonds replied with some heat: 'Certainly I am – since I write for my distraction and pastime, I intend to make the best of my resources, and I hold that a great deal of nonsense is talked about the scholar's vocation: men who might have written excellent books are sterilized by starting with fastidious conceits'[35] – but perhaps in words a little less self-consciously literary!

There were other difficulties. His health was well cared for by Dr Ruedi, but some medical problems were beyond the powers of little Davos. Symonds's teeth had been causing him trouble for the past few years and by 1879 seven had to be extracted. Dr Ruedi had no faith in the local practitioners, and no dentist in any of the big centres would make the arduous journey to Davos. In desperation and pain, in the middle of winter Symonds had to travel down to Zurich where the dentist with the best reputation did a botched job; from there he stumbled on to Geneva and thence to Berne and Florence to plead with one man after another to undertake the operation before he ended up in Vevey. The inevitable consequences followed, as he wrote from Geneva to Dakyns:

The change from the pure keen air to this damp smoke-envenomed fog, from the clear sunlight to the sickly struggling beams that lose themselves among aimless wandering drifts of cloud, from the dry warm rooms to the clammy cold & draughts of this detested inn, is all a bitter pill to swallow: bad enough, if there were not that background of pain or peril too. I fear my illness has made me very timid. I think far more than I used to do, and than probably is right, about risks. But no one can have climbed so far up the hill of difficulty without being disheartened when he sees a new danger to vitality before him....[36]

Discomfort and fatigue made him all the more acutely aware of the miseries of his life and those to which he was submitting his little family.

He saw himself as 'an aged, middle aged lion, with broken teeth & aching jaws, unfed, roaring to the deserts & uncomforted. . . . Have you re-flected', he pondered bitterly, 'what it is to be a XIX Century Nomad — no Turanian with his milch-mares & his family in wicker cars upon life-giving steppes — but a broken Aryan, the effete product of an agricultural race, condemned by circumstances to wander, — without lungs, without teeth, without nerves, without sentiments — weighed down with super-incumbent filth of old habits — lugging his family about by diligence & rail in quest of nutritious localities, weighed with baggage, over-wrought with sordid cares? Even such am I. . . .'[37]

Nor was he more sensitive to the charms of Davos than Catherine; his growing affection for the place stemmed from his realization that only here could he grasp a few more years of life. After returning from Lausanne late that summer, he wrote ruefully to Miss Poynter: 'Davos looks small. There is no denying it. It looks & is tame — Its best friends must allow that. I had a sort of horrid serrement de coeur on returning to it.'[38] He, too, was homesick, especially when a letter from Gosse brought a whiff of English summer with it. 'I know how ill I should be there,' he sighed, 'but yet how delightful it all is; no poetry is sweeter than an English summer smothered deep in flowers & hay & heavy lime-laden air.'[39]

Nevertheless, Davos had to be lived in and, once they had made the decision to sink in their roots by building a house, the final break with England could be achieved only by closing down Clifton Hill House for-ever. Catherine, bowing to fate, faced the practical steps with stoic determination. In the summer of 1880, they returned to England to dispose of their old home, from which the ties with the past were to be sundered irretrievably. Clifton Hill House had to be sold or let, and they must destroy all the innumerable vestiges of a family that had transformed an empty shell into a home; but meanwhile they encamped in the house whose contents were rapidly being dismantled. Each morning a little ritual was performed when Catherine, Symonds, and their four little daughters met after breakfast in the study where the girls would arrange themselves excitedly in a circle on the floor. Then their father would drag out boxes and drawers overflowing with letters and old diaries which he emptied into an enormous pile, and they would gleefully set about tearing them to pieces. In typical Victorian fashion every scrap of paper had been carefully filed away through the years, only to end in a great bonfire in the garden. Among Symonds's own papers which were destroyed were almost all the letters he had ever received from his friends, in addition to a juvenile novel, 'oceans of verses, autobiographical nonsense, criticisms, notes for Lectures, Preparations for the *Renaissance*. You cannot conceive the quantity I have scribbled in my life', he assured Charlotte.[40] Not only did his own papers go up in smoke, but all those diaries and notebooks kept faithfully by his forebears as far back as the seventeenth century. 'Psychologically, it interested me', he later told Sidgwick, 'to note the change of tone in the letters of successive generations. Beginning with the ardent faith of the Puritan impulse; passing into earnest but formalized Methodism in the next two generations; feeling the breath of the French Revolution and physical science in my grandfather, but remaining within the limits of strict Puritan orthodoxy; in my father's correspondence with Sterling and F. Newman and F. Maurice and Jowett, taking a robust theistic complexion; and in mine with you and H. G. D. expanding finally into a free and gaseous atmosphere. The spiritual problem was the main matter of all these letters. But how that spiritual problem altered with each generation! And what – I said to myself – will be its form in *this*, the rising generation! . . .

'I feel rather like a criminal to have burned the tares and the wheat together of this harvest.'[41]

Catherine had little sympathy for these mementoes of the past, especially the sombre busts of bygone ancestors which had graced various niches of Clifton Hill House. These were loaded into wheelbarrows and carted out to a trench in the garden and when the earth had been shovelled over them, Catherine, in a wild burst of frenzy, danced over their graves. But the symbolic implications were felt very keenly by Symonds and after his home had been sold, he told Charlotte: '. . . when I left our house at Clifton I felt sure that I must sever myself from material associations with past things or be clogged or weakened for the future'.[42] England was now 'a land of passage & brief sojourning'.[43]

IV

When he returned to Davos he analysed his feelings for Sidgwick's benefit. 'My house was my home since I was ten years old, and I have sold everything that it contained. For a long time I felt very sore – like a soldier crab without his shell, molluscous properties being detected in me which my adventitious habitat had previously concealed. . . . But I feel that a new chapter is opened in life. It makes me younger, and at the same time less enthusiastic – Bohemian, cynical, and capable of boredom – all in one. I fancy I shall not care for any home again; and yet I am sure I don't want to return to the old one. Under these conditions, if I lost my interest in writing, I daresay I should go mad.'[44]

Back in Davos he was immediately plunged into the plans for his new home, but the innumerable details connected with its construction, such as quarrels with the local authorities over the sanitary arrangements, caused months of tiresome exasperation. He had eventually settled upon a site in a large meadow called Am Hof and the foundation was dug early in June 1881. During the following months he eagerly watched the house rising from the ground; fortunately it was a dry summer so that the high-pitched zinc roof could be put in place by August. To celebrate the great event, Symonds invited all the workmen to a festive dinner. The actual move took place on 25 September and the Union Jack, which they originally intended to fly from the dahabiya, was hoisted to one of the lightning rods.

The first few years in Am Hof were a particularly difficult period for all of them, but most of all for Catherine. While the house was being built, she threw herself into the plans, but once installed, routine domestic monotony deadened her spirits. She grew moody and restless and her sharp wit often turned to sarcasm. Symonds discussed her temperament very frankly with Charlotte. 'She has a nature which turns easily to discontent & irritability when she is at rest. And she has no power of communicating any movement to herself. Therefore, wherever she is, I fear she will be moody when the excitement of novelty has passed. It is really very trying for both of us that she has nothing in common with me. All I do in literature, & this takes up a good third of my time, and is almost always in my thoughts, is quite unknown to her. She does not touch it in any way.'[45] Symonds grew seriously worried about her and even confided in Jowett that he wondered whether she ought to return to England without him. Jowett, embarrassed and concerned, tried to pour oil on the troubled waters.

About your family troubles [he forced himself to write] I hardly like to speak. It grieves me that the persons who are among my dearest & kindest friends & who are loyal & affectionate to one another should not be able in time of trouble & sorrow altogether to understand one another. I am certain that there is nothing about which your wife cares more than about your health & happiness, and that there is no sacrifice which she would not gladly make for it. It would be a fatal mistake for her to come to live in England: neither of you would know any happiness afterwards. So it seems to me who love you both. She appears to have a sad impression of Davos which it is difficult for her to resist. But do not suggest that she should leave it, for it must be painful to her. She will find interests in reading & drawing & in the education of the girls. I have a great respect for her & the more so because she never spoke of her troubles to me.

These family difficulties are not matters for blame. We require to help one another as well as we can. We must not let sorrows & illnesses get upon the brain. We must get above bodily weakness if we can & at times can only lie still & trust in God....[46]

This time Jowett's comforting words had little effect. The household situation continued tense and when, after Green's sudden death in 1882, Charlotte suggested that she should come out to Davos to live with them, Symonds discouraged her:

Catherine is gloomy & depressed. I am irritable from ill health & constant aspiration. . . . You would find here no stagnant calm, neither the surf & surge of life in its intensity of suffering & action.

I have ever doubted whether our home, with its dramatic vitality, isolated, uncircumscribed by rules & precedents, would not be more painful than restful to you.[47]

It was no piece of theatricality when he proclaimed to Dakyns that life was 'a grim hard Aristophanic piece of business'.[48] In 1883 his sister Maribella succumbed to an early consumptive death, a loss which left Symonds shaken. His own poor health continued to be a burden and he felt so close to utter despair that he asked Henry Sidgwick whether he would be justified in taking his own life. Sidgwick, with that measured consideration by which he approached the problems posed in his *Methods of Ethics*, while not condemning suicide in principle, advised him against it because 'I cannot doubt that any three years you may be able to add to your life by wise management will be years of thoroughly effective human existence, – even if your power of literary work should become less vigorous & sustained.'[49]

Gradually the situation improved to some degree and in the autumn of 1882 Symonds could write to Robert Louis Stevenson and his wife, who had been in Davos the previous year: 'Things work well with me, the Lord be praised! I am not up to a high mark in health. But I have a jolly house, & a huge cellar, & a French chef, & bright delightful children; & my wife is tolerably satisfied. She, indeed, pour soul, is happier now than she ever would confess beforehand, when this building of a house worked in our bowels, that the case could be.'[50] Catherine managed in time to reconcile herself to Davos although she never ceased to complain about the ugliness of the valley, and she formed a fixed idea that its climate had undermined the girls' health. She seemed almost happy when her large frame was bent over the astounding variety of plants which she managed to grow in her small garden, a haven protected from the Föhn by stone walls and pleasantly irrigated by a little stream. But there were many emotional stresses between them from which Symonds managed to escape periodically to Italy.

The girls were removed from school in Geneva after only a single year, and were afterwards instructed by a series of governesses and, sporadically, by Symonds himself. Much of their time was spent outdoors riding or skating or tobaggoning (Katharine later became a pioneer woman skier). Symonds enjoyed having them with him. 'They are a light to me', he declared lovingly. 'Janet is like a young palm, & the baby has an aureole of tawny hair around her beautiful white forehead. They are all good – the deep-feeling taciturn Lotta & the brave & emotional Madge. . . .'[51] A fair draughtsman, he sometimes gave them drawing lessons in which he set them to copy Blake's *Job*; he also taught them some Greek and Italian and for a time paced about his study lecturing to them on Italian history. On their visits to Venice he spent his mornings conscientiously taking them to churches and art galleries where he would patiently and minutely describe the details of the paintings. It was an erratic, unconventional education, but few girls could boast such a wide knowledge of art. Above all, they benefited from their father's wide-ranging talk. Even when they were small girls he addressed them as equals, particularly Madge who looked like Catherine with her dark Dantesque colouring, but was a temperamental extension of Symonds's vibrant, nervous personality.

Another serious crisis struck them in 1884. Symonds's faith in the recuperative powers of Davos was undermined when Janet began to show alarming signs of lung disease. In an attempt to arrest its ravages, they rushed her off to San Remo and no sooner had they arrived than Madge was stricken with typhoid. With the decisiveness always elicited in him by an emergency, Symonds immediately rented Edward Lear's large unfurnished house, Villa Emily, bought furniture, and hired servants. In this converted hospital, sitting by turns at each of the girls' bedsides, he translated most of the Goliardic verses which were to make up *Wine, Women, and Song*. They returned to Am Hof as to a snug harbour after a storm.

Am Hof never took the place of Clifton Hill House but there was much to recommend it. A house with a character very much its own, it was designed as a rambling Swiss chalet with certain concessions to English tastes. Its stone exterior, punctuated with carved wooden balconies, looked like that of any prosperous farmer in the district; inside, the ceilings were covered with intricate Swiss carvings but the walls were papered in Morris. The rooms were dry and warm, each heated by a small stove which burned pine and beech logs. Turkish rugs and Murano glass provided a piquant contrast to the simple wooden furniture made by local carpenters, a curious reflection of the opposing facets in Symonds's own nature.

Symonds's inner sanctum, consisting of two bedrooms and a study, was panelled in the local cembra wood and he had carefully selected each plank so that the knotholes would form a fine pattern. In the inner room, known as the 'Carpenter's Shop', where he did his writing, he had a pretty little green porcelain stove, book-cases, and a large deal table on which he fussed over his much-loved stationery – note-paper, pens of various sizes, and paper clips. An intensely orderly man, Symonds soon had his large correspondence filed neatly away, his manuscripts stacked in various shelves, the small appurtenances – his pipes, his brass bowls, his Japanese match-boxes, and cascades of multi-coloured Venetian beads – arranged around him. Highly interested in photography, he had collected many photographs of his friends and these now found a permanent home on the walls and shelves of the pleasantly cluttered room.

The drawers of his bedroom were filled with masses of handkerchiefs, ties, and scarves, and his cupboards held his large wardrobe. Clothes were his only extravagance; he would change his attire two or three times a day, yet he slept between coarse linen sheets in a creaky old peasant bed. In his bedroom he also kept an old medicine chest. Whenever one of the children scratched a knee she ran to her father, who applied one of his many lotions or ointments with all the solicitude of Dr Symonds himself.

The routine into which life settled soon after they moved into Am Hof continued until Symonds's death twelve years later. He breakfasted alone, after which he wrote all morning. Catherine read to him for two hours every afternoon in her precise voice, after which he went for a walk with the girls and one of the Venetian water-dogs to which the family were very attached. If he were deeply engrossed in the preparation of a book, the evening would be spent in writing or research; as the proofs came in the activity in the 'Carpenter's Shop' assumed frenetic momentum. The usual orderliness was disturbed by a rapidly climbing mountain of paper which Symonds referred to as his 'precipice', and he used an extraordinary procedure to cope with the chaos. When it reached such dizzy heights that it finally toppled over into a wild cascade, he was forced to get down on his hands and knees to gather up the scattered bits of paper and file them away in their allotted places.

On the whole, his life was almost austere in its simplicity. He ate abstemiously; he loved good wine but was quite content with the local Valtelline,[52] and even more fond of the valley cream. Often generous to others, he considered £3 an excessive amount to spend on a rare book for himself. Management of the Sisson estate had instilled in him a profound respect for money, and he took a shrewd interest in all his investments. Some of his small economies seem absurd; large sums were lent or given outright to handsome young men, but he told Mrs Janet Ross that he could not afford to give her a copy of his *Life of Michelangelo* – even though she had read through the proofs for him.

The orderly pattern of his existence was frequently broken by visits from English friends. These visitors – and one seemed to be followed by another – stayed in a pretty little room papered in Morris and hung with Catherine's watercolours. The visitors were free to spend as much time as they liked by themselves and they must have enjoyed their holiday, otherwise men like Henry Sidgwick and Graham Dakyns would not have made the long trip from England so often. Symonds described one of their dinner-parties to Madge with only partial irony: 'As always in this house, the guests enjoyed themselves exceedingly. I think this is due to our fair cookery, excellent wine, & refined Bohemianism – a home & ways of its own, with a remarkable woman at its head, & a very clever man for companion. . . .'[53]

Jowett would arrive periodically with a very small suitcase containing his large books and a miniature swallow-tailed coat which he wore on Sundays to the local church, where he would fall asleep in the front pew, tiny whistling snores issuing from the pink, cherubic face. He was very fond of the Symonds girls, particularly of his godchild Lotta. With the same gravity with which he discussed the minutiae of the translation of Greek phrases with their father, he told them solemnly that no man should spend more than £30 a year on his wardrobe. On one occasion, as he was revising his proofs of Plato, he suddenly called from the next room where Symonds was working on Cellini, 'Ah, Mr Symonds! You and I are a pair of harmless drudges, are we not?'

The devotion of Symonds's old Sixth Former, Horatio Brown, was so great that when he and his mother moved to Venice, many said it was to be near Symonds. Brown never failed to visit him in Davos at least once a year, and Symonds returned his visits frequently. Brown's unqualified adulation of Symonds did much to compensate for the distance that now separated him from Dakyns. Indeed, by 1882 Symonds had appointed Brown his literary executor although in 1866, at the height of his friendship with Dakyns, he had asked Dakyns if he would assume the responsibility. Intensely serious, slightly pompous as he grew older, Brown fussed over Symonds, flattered him, and genuinely loved him. There was more than a hint of Boswell in the stolid little Scot, who took himself very seriously indeed but whose self-satisfaction was relieved by a colourful streak of Bohemianism.

In addition to its many visitors, the monotony of Davos was also frequently interrupted by what the Symonds family called 'Little Changes'. On these excursions, Symonds with one or two of the girls, would make short journeys of exploration over various Alpine passes and spend the night at humble little inns. Then each spring there was a general exodus to Venice, and in the late summer or autumn another long journey to Italy or England. Although Symonds enjoyed the heady beauty of Venice or the round of social activities in England, he was always thankful to return to Davos. Occasionally he would sound a theatrical note such as his lament to Swinburne that 'I lead a difficult life, condemned by slow disease . . . to exile in a monotonous valley of the Alps, where I freeze, where the pulses of enjoyment & energy fail, where there is but little companionship, where books are scarce & have to be dragged over passes nearly the whole year deep in snow.'[54] A far more characteristic mood was expressed to Janet Ross by a weary traveller in a letter written on a return from Italy in 1891: 'And finally, as so often happens, out of the unutterable fog and filth of Lombardy, the drenched squalor of the Gothard, the repellent dullness of lower Switzerland, we emerged before sunset into the aerial splendour of our snowy mountains, with their pure clear air and graceful summits cleaving upward to the stars. It is like getting back into an enchanted crystal palace after the humdrum of a mediocre world.

'The luxury too of finding a house with perfectly dry air in it and an equal temperature. Many as are the drawbacks of spending one's life at Davos, it has aesthetically and sensually the greatest pleasures which an epicure can hope for.'[55]

v

Apart from a warm house in a dry climate, in Davos he found a sense of freedom and relaxation from the disapproving eyes of Mrs Grundy who was never absent from the English scene. It did not take him long to realize that the Graubünden peasants were closer to Walt Whitman's ideal democracy than any people he had ever met before. They were a proud people whose traditions extended far back into the past, yet Symonds was impressed by the fact that they seemed completely free from class-distinctions. Close family feeling existed among the members of this patriarchal society, the different members of which might be lawyers, carters, teachers, or guides, and yet each man's work was treated with equal respect. At haymaking the magistrate would roll up his sleeves and wield a pitch-fork with the rest of his neighbours. The valley was essentially a farming community, but there was no tenantry and each farmer possessed his own 'alp'. There were no excesses of wealth or poverty, and servants and masters shared the same simple meal of bread, cheese, and dried meat.

Symonds was immediately attracted to the sturdy muscular men with their flowing beards, and proud manly bearing. Inevitably he soon fell in love with one of them. Christian Buol was a magnificent-looking youth of nineteen, the youngest of a large family who, in any other society, would be regarded as aristocrats, but in Davos he worked as sledge-driver with the same matter-of-factness that Symonds admired in his other compatriots. Christian reminded him of a noble young Greek charioteer as he stood erect in his sledge, driving his four horses at a brisk trot. Symonds's first overture was to approach him as he stood smoking at the door of a cow-shed, and to offer him a meerschaum pipe as a New Year's gift. During the first months of 1878 the intimacy grew rapidly, the pattern reminiscent of the early stages of his relationship with Norman. He invited Christian to dine in his rooms in the Hotel Belvedere; in turn Symonds was invited to join Christian's birthday celebration. As he looked around the simply-furnished room, with the candlelight flickering on the cembra panelling, it seemed to him that he was witnessing a scene out of one of Walt Whitman's poems.

It came to his ears that Christian's brother, Caspar, was in grave financial difficulties and was threatened with the loss of his hotel. Symonds jumped at the opportunity of indirectly helping Christian by offering to lend Caspar the £1,000 he had originally planned to spend on the abandoned dahabiya. He told Catherine what he intended to do, and was deeply touched when she agreed to the plan, even though she was fully aware of his infatuation for Christian. In the following years he helped the Buols in many ways. He later lent them a further £2,000 which they scrupulously repaid little by little, so that a considerable part of the loan was paid off before Symonds's death. He also moved his family to the Hotel Buol, and through his influence it became the centre of the English colony at Davos. Further indirect help resulted from an enthusiastic article, 'Davos in Winter', which he sent to *The Fortnightly Review* in May 1878, and which was responsible, he believed, for encouraging large numbers of English people to visit Davos.

In his Memoirs Symonds makes a great point of emphasizing his generosity to the Buols as an example of the sort of altruism that could spring from a passion which most people would connect only with lust and degradation; yet he immediately goes on to state that his financial gifts served as a means of cementing his friendship with Christian. Self-deception, as he often declared, is the besetting sin of mankind. Nevertheless, he was convinced that this was the healthiest physical relationship he had ever formed with a man. There was none of the tortured analysis with which he had probed Norman's every gesture, and it was impossible to associate vice and squalid passion with a simple, guileless creature like Christian. When he took him to Italy with him that first spring, the young man had never before travelled beyond his own canton, and Symonds experienced the same sort of fatherly pleasure in his enthusiastic reaction to all he saw as he had from Norman's first visit to London. 'He is quite a comrade', he wrote to Dakyns, '& is besides what a thorough gentleman rightly understood means. Je l'aime de tout mon coeur. It is a splendid sight to see him asleep with the folded arms & the vast chest of a young Hercules, innocent of clothing. A better way of satisfying the plastic sense than many others.'[56] Christian returned Symonds's feeling for him with a simple, warm affection and even when he told him that he wished to get married, the feeling between them remained unaltered. When domesticity and duties on the farm prevented him from accompanying Symonds on further Italian journeys, he was replaced on several occasions by his young cousin. Thus it was that *Italian Byways* was dedicated to the two Christians.

Through Christian Buol Symonds soon came to know most of his Davos neighbours, and the local carters, postmen, and farmers were encouraged to visit him for a smoke and a chat. He longed to be accepted as one of them. It seems extraordinary that this over-cultivated man was able to make friends so easily with these simple people, yet the fact remains that he genuinely enjoyed their company and they responded to his warm laugh and intense interest in them. They invited him to join their clubs, he rolled up his sleeves and helped with the haymaking, and he was eager to give them advice or financial help when they sought it. H. F. Brown recalled one bacchanalian scene in which Symonds and his Davos friends, each perched tipsily on a hogshead, roared out a bawdy song in unison.

Symonds tightened his connection with his new home by gradually buying up a number of farms in the area. His only real brush with his adopted villagers occurred over a matter of drains. Perhaps as a result of his medical background, Symonds was obsessed with hygiene and highly disturbed by the drainage conditions in Davos, particularly after he had decided to settle there permanently. In order to convince the stubborn townsmen, he wrote letters about the problem to a number of European newspapers, including *The Pall Mall Gazette* in October 1882.* Many of the Davosers were so incensed by this action that a number of them stopped speaking to him. However, in time tempers simmered down and Symonds got his drains.

He liked to think he was performing a worthwhile service for Davos. He loved tobogganing and when the idea occurred to him that Davos might become the centre of an international toboggan race, he enthusiastically set about organizing the first one which was held in 1883 and aroused enormous interest. As President of the Tobogganing Committee for a number of years, he acted as pacifier to its often turbulent scenes, a role which eventually so strained his patience that he resigned in 1889, but the same year he also gave a substantial sum to the building of a large gymnasium. Various 'literary' societies sprang up and Symonds was much sought after as a lecturer: for a time he held forth on the Elizabethan dramatists to a fascinated audience in the dining-room of the Hotel Angleterre. Although not orthodox in his beliefs, he contributed much time and money to the little church which arose to serve the growing English colony. With the coming of the railway in 1890, and the interest that developed in ski-ing through the late eighties, Davos was rapidly being transformed from the dull little backwater on which he had first set eyes.

Symonds came to believe that only in Switzerland could he achieve the 'self-effectuation' he had always craved. As a true son of Walt Whitman, he was ardently convinced that the most genuine, spontaneous people were simple, unlettered folk. Only too aware that he was 'nothing if not cultivated', [57] he winced when a reviewer once accused him of carrying culture around Europe like a pedlar's pack, for culture never ceased to have inhibiting connotations for him. In a late essay, 'Culture:

---

* The £2 he received for it struck him as ironical, considering the furore it had raised.

its Meaning and Uses', he describes true culture as the development by the individual of all his potentialities, no matter how humble in their own sphere; he viewed false culture as the priggish condescension of a man like Matthew Arnold or the esoteric aestheticism of Pater. Symonds fervently believed that the Kingdom of God could be attained more easily by those rough tillers of the soil who had not been exposed to evenings of poetry-readings. His attitude to these people was a Rousseauesque idealization of the noble savage who appeared to be in touch with the natural springs of affection. While his sincerity was unquestionable, he also tended to cultivate and sentimentalize his unsophisticated neighbours in his attempt to make them match his ideal. Constantly talking about how much he 'learned' from them and how much more valuable their company was than that of literary men, he was never very explicit what these lessons were beyond the fact that, unhampered by bourgeois restrictions, they were far more tolerant towards sexual deviation. When Charles Kains-Jackson remarked that he could not see the beauty of the Swiss, Symonds replied by quoting the belief of a friend that 'You do not feel the beauty of a nation till you have slept with one of them.'[58]

Symonds often complained of his isolation from the English literary scene, but he more often declared that he would exchange a literary coterie any day for the genuine simplicity of a Christian Buol.

I tell you, after very long experience [began one of his typical exhortations to Madge], that what is called conversing with people of distinction has very little pleasure or profit in it – unless it be carried on in that perfectly intimate way which you have been so amply initiated into in your home. . . .

The sort of conversation I had at Florence with various literary men, and more or less literary ladies and pretty countesses and ugly Scotch dowagers, is of absolutely no use to any human soul except in the way of superficial pastime. You only touch the epidermis of these people, and the *obiter dicta* of somebodies are as unsatisfying to the spirit as the remarks of nobodies. Indeed, the table-talk of nobodies, if they are peasants and artisans, seems to me really more succulent than that of somebodies – unless you are living with the people of importance in close intimacy and sustained sympathy.[59]

VI

In 1891 Margaret Symonds wrote a delightful parody of life at Am Hof which she called *A Visit to Castle Slapping*. Intended only for the eyes of her family, it is the account of the visit of a proper young English gentleman to this Bohemian home and his bewildered reaction to their downright, eccentric ways. In the following passage, he has just been introduced to 'Mr S':

'Humm-Haw', yawned Mr. S. It struck me that he was intolerably bored.

The door stood open behind me, and the men who had carried up my luggage, now came tramping down stairs. Mr. S espied them; and immediately his face, his whole figure, were transfigured and full of joy. 'Jacob, Jacob', he cried, springing to the encounter of my heavy-faced driver – 'Why do you never come to see me? Ah, what a pleasure to look at you! You must stay. You must have a glass of wine. Come in. Come in', and he seized the stolid young fellow by the arm.

'No,' answered the driver slowly, 'I'll have to be seeing to my horses.' He was not exactly embarrassed, and as for looking in any way out of place, he seemed a part of the room, standing there in his coarse home-spun coat, his rude gaiters covered with melting snow.

'Ah me, ah me,' sighed his eager host. 'Well then, Jacob, you must go, I suppose. But come, come very soon to me again.'

'I'll maybe come in this evening', said the youth, in a sort of condescending manner, and then he slouched off, and we heard him drive his horses down the hill.

Mr. S stood meditating in the middle of his study. 'What a man,' he mused, 'what a thorax! A model for Michelangiolo [sic]. But poor Michelangiolo! he couldn't draw anything half so beautiful', he added sadly, 'Art's a delusion', and tragically humming some immortal lines, he lighted a bedroom candle and preceded me upstairs. And thus I entered Castle Slapping.

CHAPTER IX

The Literary Life

I

On 4 November 1880 another literary invalid arrived in Davos in a state of collapse. Robert Louis Stevenson, accompanied by Fanny, his American bride of six months, and his stepson, Lloyd Osbourne, had come to Davos in the hope of arresting his acute chronic catarrh. Although he had not yet been diagnosed as a tubercular case, at the age of thirty his extreme weakness and other allied symptoms were far more serious than Symonds's had been ten years before when he was the same age.

Symonds had heard of Stevenson only in the most casual way as a promising young writer – he was even uncertain how to spell his name – but in his isolated mountain eyrie he was anxious to meet anyone from the world of letters. Stevenson came with a letter of introduction from Edmund Gosse, but in his eagerness Symonds made the first gesture by walking over to the Hotel Belvedere to meet him the day after he arrived. They immediately seized on one another as kindred spirits. On 17 November Symonds wrote to Horatio Brown: 'There is a very interesting man come – Louis Stevenson – a friend of Lang and Leslie Stephen – really clever, and curious in matters of style. I find him a great acquisition.'[1] To Sidney Colvin, Mrs Stevenson wrote: 'We find many pleasant people here, and Louis and Mr. Symonds are, so to speak, Siamese twins.'[2] And Stevenson himself described his reaction to his new friend: 'I like Symonds very well, though he is much, I think, of an invalid in mind and character. But his mind is interesting, with many beautiful corners and his consumptive smile very beautiful to see. We have had some good talks; one went over Zola, Balzac, Flaubert, Whitman, Christ, Handel, Milton, Sir Thomas Browne: do you see the liaison?'[3]

Stevenson spent two winters in Davos and the only thing he seemed to like about it, other than the tobogganing, was Symonds's companion-ship. Dr Ruedi told him that he was suffering from chronic pneumonia, but the cold winter air did not have its usual miraculous effect on him. Most of the time he was bored and restless, and when Colvin*visited him in January he found him extremely depressed. Stevenson complained that his 'old gypsy nature' felt trapped – 'like a violin hung up I begin to lose what music there was in me'.[4] He lacked the energy for a long book and, on Symonds's suggestion, filled his time with a little reviewing.[5] Some of his work, however, had definite connections with his convalescence at Davos. His first collection of essays, *Virginibus Puerisque*, came out early in 1881 shortly after he arrived. He had already worked out the plot and written part of an adventure story which he related to Lloyd that first winter in Davos, and on the many occasions when Symonds found them stretched out on the floor, poring over the map that illustrated the tale, he had no idea it would become famous throughout the world as *Treasure Island*.

At first Symonds was excited by the hope that he had discovered another fellow-disciple of Walt Whitman. A few years earlier, Stevenson was one of the many young men stirred by the American poet, but his initial enthusiasm had been tempered by critical maturity. Two years before Symonds met him, he had written an essay on Whitman, but the first draft sounded so adulatory that he tore it up in disgust. By the time he completed the final version,[6] he found that he had modified his attitude considerably. He told Symonds of this experience and Symonds, dis-pleased by such backsliding, later described the essay as 'frigidly appreci-ative'.[7]

Symonds and Stevenson liked each other as men, but they never admired each other's work. Symonds had to admit that *Virginibus Puerisque* was brilliant writing, although he dismissed it as a little too 'flashy' for his taste.[8] Both were intense creatures, eager to seize all that life offered, yet there was a wide difference in their talents. Symonds's laborious scholarship, on which he stolidly built up his edifice of facts, could not have been more divergent from Stevenson's quicksilver creativity. In his attitude to the younger man there was also something of the condescension he himself had received from Swinburne as a relative

* Colvin was Slade professor of Fine Art at Cambridge, 1873-85.

newcomer in the world of letters, one whose presence would be tolerated providing he kept his place. Stevenson had read the classics only through the Bohn translations, and Symonds's writing struck him as stuffily donnish. The perceptive Scot captured Symonds's reserve towards him in this description: 'His various and exotic knowledge, complete although unready sympathies, and fine, full discriminative flow of language, fit him out to be the best of talkers; so perhaps he is with some, not *quite* with me – *proxime accesit*, I should say.'[9] For his part, Symonds could not fail to be attracted by the slight boyish figure who combined a touch of the Bohemian in his black shirts and high boots, with a hint of the radiant-eyed Shelley. Yet, was Stevenson quite a gentleman?[10] It was all very well to be a child of nature, a Davoser peasant, even Walt Whitman in America, so long as one remained in one's native primitive habitat. Nor did Symonds admire Stevenson's intellectual capacities. 'I have apprehensions about his power of intellectual last', he confided to Brown. 'The more I see of him, the less I find of solid intellectual stuff. He wants years of study in tough subjects. After all, a university education has some merits. One feels the want of it in men like him.'*[11] Was Symonds a little disgruntled because his disciple, H. F. Brown, had struck up a close friendship with Stevenson? He reacted with similar petulance on one occasion when he heard that Brown was going on a trip with Roden Noel.

When Stevenson embarrassed him by asking him to write a testimonial for him in support of his highly unlikely candidature for the Chair of Constitutional Law at Edinburgh, Symonds dwelt on the fact that he had many attractive qualities but skilfully made it clear that they were not those required by a professor of law. 'Though he has early made a mark in English literature by compositions which do not touch the province of a Chair of History and Constitutional Law', he concluded, 'this success, to those who know him, is no proof of his incapacity to deal with severer intellectual subjects. At the same time, this success is a guarantee that he would treat grave studies with the fine touch and attractiveness which belong to a master of expression.'[12]

Stevenson once described his friendship with Symonds as 'an adventure

---

* In actual fact Stevenson had been called to the Bar in Edinburgh, after having taken the engineering course at the University as well.

in thornwood'[13] – in other words, a very prickly business. The suppressed tension of their relationship was sharpened by Stevenson's outspoken criticisms of Symonds's poetry. Here was no devoted, unquestioning Dakyns, but one who 'hardly disguises his opinion that I cannot write poetry at all, and am a duffer at prose. But having said this, he has no interest in the affair. Whether or not I have what is worth saying to say in verse, is utterly beyond his scope – not the scope of his intellect, but his being. In other and simpler words, he does not know one red cent of me – as he would say – and hardly anybody does.'[14] Symonds was smarting from his second unsuccessful poetic venture, *New and Old*, and during that first winter of anxiety and indecision in Davos, his nerves were often at the breaking-point. However, determined to publish a further volume of verse, he sent over some poems with a request for Stevenson's opinion. Although no poetry could be more personal than his, it was quite extraordinary how eagerly Symonds submitted it to the scrutiny of other eyes. Much to his surprise, this time both Stevenson and his wife reacted enthusiastically to those poems dealing with philosophical themes. Symonds had already considered *Vagabunduli Libellus* as a good title for a volume of verse; now R. L. S., with his flair for inventing titles, suggested the substitution of *Animi Figura*. Symonds happily agreed, despite a slightly uneasy suspicion that Stevenson wished to bag the earlier title for himself.

The Stevensons returned to Scotland for the summer of 1881 but were back in Davos by October. This time they moved into a small house known as the 'Chalet am Stein', on the slopes immediately above the Hotel Buol. Now the relationship between the two men underwent a fresh development, for during this second winter they were less reserved towards each other. 'He is very nice', Symonds reported to Brown in November. 'I get to like him more. Perhaps I am less masterful than last year.'[15] Many of Stevenson's letters during this period contain comments on Symonds such as, 'He is a far better and more interesting thing than any of his books.'[16] Symonds spent many evenings in good talk at Chalet am Stein, but while he was enchanted by Mrs Stevenson's vivacity, his methodical nature had to brace itself to overlook her untidy housekeeping. Both Stevensons, moreover, began to appreciate the fundamental soundness of Symonds. 'Symonds grows much on me', Stevenson admitted to Gosse; 'in many ways, what you would least expect, a very sound man, and very wise in a wise way. It is curious how Fanny and I always turn to him for advice: we have learned that his advice is good.'[17]

During this second winter Mrs Stevenson's health also became cause for anxiety. Davos obviously did not agree with her either, and she began to gain an alarming amount of weight, a condition Dr Ruedi diagnosed vaguely as a disease of the stomach. By now Stevenson had regained sufficient strength – between bouts of weakness – to begin writing seriously again. In April he could tell his mother that he had written forty thousand words, including a volume of poetry, *Underwoods*, which he dedicated to Dr Ruedi, the remainder of *Treasure Island*, and *The Silverado Squatters*. 'I begin to hope', he declared, 'I may if not outlive this wolverine upon my shoulders, at least carry him bravely like Symonds and Alexander Pope.'[18] At the end of April, Stevenson, Fanny, and Lloyd left abruptly for France. It was a considerable break to leave the by now very congenial company of Symonds, but his hatred of Davos had reached such a pitch that even Symonds's vivid eloquence provided insufficient compensation.

In the next ten years Symonds and Stevenson were to meet only once again – in 1887 in Bournemouth, where Symonds was grieved to see that Stevenson had 'gone downhill terribly'.[19] During these ten years they maintained an intermittent correspondence and occasionally sent each other copies of their most recent work. In August 1882 an essay by Stevenson, 'Talk and Talkers', appeared in *The Cornhill*. 'Get it, read it, & see if you can guess a person I had in my eye', Stevenson wrote back to the Macmorlands, a Scottish pastor and his wife who had long lived at Davos. The cryptic reference was to Opalstein, and Opalstein with 'his troubled and poetic talk' could not be taken for anyone other than Symonds. In his essay Stevenson wrote of him: 'He is not truly reconciled either with life or with himself; this instant war in his members sometimes divides the man's attention. He does not always, perhaps not often, frankly surrender himself in conversation. He brings into the talk other thoughts than those which he expresses; you are conscious that he keeps an eye on something else, that he does not shake off the world, nor quite forget himself.'[20] Courthope had also referred to his 'double point of view' in the review of *Renaissance in Italy* and Symonds himself had noted 'double-mindedness' as his worst fault.

Symonds had no difficulty in recognizing himself and he did not conceal his annoyance at this frank portrait drawn after one of their nights of animated talk. He sent an annotated copy of the article back to Stevenson, and in the accompanying letter, he remarked: 'So far as I perceive, with far blunter artistic sensibilities, with perhaps wider though diviner intuitions into the possibilities of talk, I should say that you have discoursed upon the Species as though it were the Genus.' Then followed a trenchant piece of advice cast in pompously patronizing terms which revealed all too clearly the differences between the men:

In your Individuality, combined with your rare power of condensation by the might of style, you hold a potent fructifying instrument. It is of course double-edged, cutting some folk to the quick with its truth, others on the surface with its limitations.

The great quality of this fact in you is that it comes fresh from self & from personal experience. Its defect is that it has not absorbed into itself a hundred things w^h have occurred to other men of other selves & other experiences. I give this as a hint for growth, for the next Manner. Possibly wiser? ⎫ * reading;
                                                                        deeper ⎭
possibly more omnivorous sympathies; might make the brilliance of the art still more imposing.[21]

Perhaps his pique over Opalstein contributed to the violence of his reaction to *Dr Jekyll and Mr Hyde* when it appeared in 1886. 'I doubt whether anyone has a right', he admonished Stevenson, 'so to scrutinise the abysmal depths of personality. . . . At least I think he ought to bring more of distinct belief in the resources of human nature, more faith, more sympathy with our frailty, into the matter than you have done.' It was a harsh judgment, spoken with the voice of a man who believed he could chide from the heights of ten years' additional experience, but his natural warmth overcame him, and he added: '. . . I seem to have lost you so utterly that I can afford to fling truth of the crudest in your face. And yet I love you & think of you daily.'[22] Stevenson replied mildly enough: 'Jekyll is a dreadful thing, I own; but the only thing I feel dreadful about is that damned old business of the war in the members. This time it came out; and I hope it will stay in, in future.'[23]

---

* The word 'deeper' was added later.

213

Despite the undeniable tensions of their relationship, there remained an underlying depth of feeling between these two invalids which never diminished. Knowing Stevenson's love of Villon, Symonds dedicated his collection of Goliardic verse, *Wine, Women, and Song*, to him in 1884. On 11 November 1888 Stevenson sent Symonds from Tahiti a proposed dedication for a travel book which was never published. In the soft summer night R. L. S. had a vivid image of Symonds so many thousands of miles away:

The glittering frosty solitudes in which your days are cast arose before me: I seemed to see you walking there in the late night, under the pine-trees and the stars; and I received the image with something like remorse. . . . It was you, dear Symonds, who should have gone upon that voyage and written that account. With your rich stores of knowledge, you could have remarked and understood a thousand things of interest that escaped my ignorance; and the brilliant colours of your style would have carried into a thousand sickrooms the sea air and the strong sun of the tropic islands. But it was otherwise decreed. But suffer me at least to connect you, if only in name and only in the fondness of imagination, with the voyage of the 'Silver Ship'.[24]

Shortly before Symonds's death, he was seized with a longing to write to Stevenson.

My dear old friend [he wrote], After all these years, since that last sight of you in Bournemouth, I come to write to you. How strangely different our destinies have been! Here I am in the same straight valley, with the old escapements to Italy and England, with the regular round of work – I forget how many books I have written since we conversed; and I do not want to record their titles. You have been thrown into such very different scenes – and a sort of injustice has been done to our friendship, by the wistfulness I have for all that South-Sea life. Not that I am unhappy. I have found a great deal of happiness by living with the people here, though it is chequered with disappointments and pains.

I sometimes think I may still set sail, an old Ulysses, for those islands of magic charm. But I am past the age of doing more than dream of them.[25]

What impulse prevented Symonds from posting one of the best letters he ever wrote – a letter with ironic echoes of Stevenson's own writing – one can only speculate.

When he heard of Symonds's death in 1893, Stevenson wrote to Gosse:

Catherine Symonds

J. A. Symonds, 1886

'And now the strange, poignant, pathetic, brilliant creature is gone into the night, and the voice is silent that uttered so much excellent discourse. . . . I should be half tempted to write an *In Memoriam*, but I am submerged with other work. Are you going to do it?'[26]

Stevenson himself was to die only a year later.

II

The beginning of 1879, the first full year in Davos, was a time for totting up accounts. Symonds could see quite clearly that the door was being shut decisively on a stage in his life, one that he could now view as a period of initiation. Whenever a question of success was involved, his thoughts always turned to his father.

I often think [he confided to Charlotte], remembering my father's love of literature & respect for men of letters, how pleased he would have been if he could have lived to share what has been pleasant in this development. I do not mean that I have done more than I ought reasonably to have done or have succeeded better than was to have been expected from the moderate use of moderate faculties. But when he died, I had, so to speak, done nothing; & the sort of thing he liked has come to me in plenty since – so that if my health does not revive & I am to have no further career, I may still think (& he would have thought) that *pro virile parte*, with the strengths & parts allotted to me, I have lived. . . .[27]

The achievement amounted to this: a growing reputation as a prolific writer of essays and articles, written in the style of a cultivated traveller; a recognition by the critics of his ability to reanimate the past; a qualified admiration for his persevering scholarship; and a tolerance of his self-conscious poetry. By 1879 he was being regarded as a writer of some substance; he might not have grasped fame, but the achievement was not inconsiderable when he reflected that it had been the result of less than ten years' labour.

Above all, he wanted to publish another volume of poetry. This time he was anxious that it should be a real love child, uncensored and unchanged, expressing his actual feelings and experiences. But how much would the British public stand? His pessimism was reflected in a sad comment to Dakyns on some of Horatio Brown's poetry for which he had asked Symonds's opinion: 'I am sorry that he has chosen to tread the wearifully barren & solitary & heart-saddening path of paiderastic poetry.'*28

As for himself, in addition to *Many Moods* which he presented to the public in 1878, he printed privately five copies of a slim collection of poems, entitled *Rhaetica*, which he longed to flaunt courageously, but the danger seemed too great. Wavering indecisively about what he should do, he sent copies to various friends,† asking for advice and suggestions about which poems they thought it would be possible to publish without repercussions. Henry Sidgwick's reaction might have been expected. When Symonds arrived in Geneva in June 1879 in his search for a dentist, he found 'an awful letter' awaiting him. 'The gist is that I am on the brink of a precipice [he paraphrased it for Dakyns], on the verge of losing my reputation & bringing disgrace on Henry & you & all who call me friend. Rhaetica, if smelt out by a critic, would precipitate me altogether. I think I ought to ask you, under the conditions, to destroy the peccant pamphlet, together perhaps with all my confounded verses in print or out of it. I am sure they are not as well worth keeping as they seem to be perilous, & to you they must only now be very ancient bores – pathetic perhaps & a little humorous, if we think about them in the past. ... I think this is due to Henry, who is really in a state.'29 This was the last time he ever showed any of his poetry to Sidgwick. It was only too clear that he would never be the sympathetic reader Symonds craved, and he did not even send him a copy of *Vagabunduli Libellus* after its publication.

A feeling of defeat and general discouragement followed Sidgwick's harsh bluntness: 'I am used up with work & feel as though the English language had no words left – which simply means I suppose that I have written myself dry.'30 However, this period of despair was relatively shortlived, and when Norman visited him during the Christmas holidays he found him excited about a new volume of poetry which he had been busy compiling during the autumn. He entrusted the manuscript to Norman to take back to Dakyns in Clifton with the request 'to cut out offending members' and send it on to Smith, Elder. Symonds, in the meantime, warned 'the Elder' of 'the imminent παρουσία [presence,

* The only volume of verse Brown ever published was *Drift* (1900), in which there are veiled homosexual allusions.

† The friends seem to have been Brown, Dakyns, Henry Sidgwick, and either Herbert Warren or Arthur Sidgwick.

coming] of poems with or sans testicular appurtenances'.[31] Symonds seems to have had extraordinary faith in Dakyns's judgment because he willingly agreed to all his suggested omissions, even those with a 'cunning falsification of the sexes'.[32] Curiously enough, Dakyns did not blue-pencil 'The Valley of Vain Desires', the expression of Symonds's remorse after the incident in the park with the soldier. The volume appeared in 1880 under the title, *New and Old*, which received little more attention from the critics than *Many Moods* two years before.

Symonds's poetry was beginning to appear in various anthologies.* He viewed his contributions to these volumes as indications of his failure as a poet. 'Poetry, I perceive from my one experience', he sighed to Dakyns, 'must work through subterranean channels. The best chance for a not Olympian singer is to creep through selections into literature.'[33]

The compulsion to write poetry could not be stifled for long, and more poems were dashed off with his usual fluency. In September 1881 he informed Dakyns that he had completed about one hundred and twenty-five sonnets during the summer, 'ranging over a wide surface of emotion & reflection with some merely picturesque episodes. . . . I find the Sonnet form convenient for saying a good many things w^h have accumulated in my mind.'[34] By April 1882 he had written nearly a hundred more, but intended to condense these to about half the total number under Stevenson's suggested title, *Animi Figura*. 'The key to the whole I may not publish', he told Dakyns sadly.[35] These poems were written during the period of deep depression after he had moved into Am Hof. Catherine hated Davos, Janet was beginning to show signs of lung disease, his own desires were still finding no permanent outlet. 'These are just a rind of a fruit so sour & bitter that I think there can be no cure but a pistol or a poison for my cancer', reads one of the most despairing of his letters.[36]

In 1884 he brought out a volume of medieval Goliardic songs never before translated into English,† *Wine, Women, and Song*, and a book of

---

* e.g. *A Poetry-Book* by Amelia B. Edwards (Longmans, Green & Co., 1879); *The Garland of Rachel* (Oxford: H. Daniel, 1881); and *Sonnets by Living Writers* (George Bell and Sons, 1881).

† As early as 2 February 1879 he wrote to Dakyns about his discovery of these drinking songs of wandering students of the twelfth and thirteenth centuries. 'Latin in these satires, drinking songs, & love lyrics takes a wonderful new form akin to that of the great Hymns of the Church: but with strange rhythms & Monumental turns to phrase that give a high notion of the creative force of those nameless singers' (Dakyns Collection).

217

his own verse, *Vagabunduli Libellus*, of all his published poetry the most intimate expression of his feelings. To Charlotte, he explained why *Vagabunduli Libellus* meant so much to him:

I believe there are in this book the truest truths that I can utter, up to the present phase of my enlightenment. . . . I believe the whole series entitled 'Stella Maris' is the most thoroughly moralized of the book. The Sonnets written up here 'Among the Mountains' have the most of my actual self in them – & the last section, about Doubt & Dread & Death, has the most acutely poignant. But in 'Stella Maris' I have tried to sound the perplexities of a nature in w^h passion & duty conflict & neutralize each other – with a result w^h is but too common, & w^h is not worse than human life exhibits in its medley. Some things in the exposition may strike you (&, I expect the public) as too bold or too spasmodic. It is very difficult to get just graduations of light & shadow in Sonnets, w^h are records of intense moments. . . .[37]

To Dakyns he was even franker:

. . . one section is a very realistic delineation of an improper love liaison. I wanted to supplement & explain *Animi Figura* – to *motiviren* the soul's self-condemnation by showing how the soul had sinned in intemperate passion. For this I constructed a certain doubtful episode with a Venetian Stella. There is some good poetry in the forty or odd sonnets on this topic. But I do not feel sure that the motive is not ridiculous – a Much Ado about Nothing affair. And I have nobody to consult. Also the style is oddly mixed, in obedience to changing moods. In fact I have raised more in the episode than I know how to reckon with. And now I am, as the Venetians say, 'in secco', high & dry, with nothing obvious to do, in want of work.[38]

He took infinite care about the design of the book – a black binding with the Symonds coat of arms (a gold shield enclosing three black trefoils)* – in one corner. He went to even greater pains to make the poems acceptable to the public. For example, in a poem such as 'I had two loves', the line 'or she whose mouth mixed passion like a cup' was changed from the masculine of the original in *Rhaetica* (from which many of the poems had been borrowed). In the Preface he declared that he was trying to portray a man in whom, after he has been overmastered by passion, 'his

---

* Lest Whitman recoil from the 'feudalism' of the coat of arms, he explained to him that he regarded the shield as a symbol of 'The Whole, the Good, the Beautiful', Goethe's phrase which had always appealed to him.

acquired habits of self-analysis necessitate doubt and conflict at the very moment of fruition, and how he becomes aware of a discord not only between his own tone of feeling and that of the woman who attracted him, but also between the emotion she inspired and his inalienable ideal of love'. Miss Poynter told him frankly that no one would be deceived by the fact that he professed to be depicting a fictional character. She was also distressed that he had seen fit to speak with so little reticence. Symonds began to have qualms himself. 'I have doubted myself upon the propriety of speaking out so fully without speaking out more', he replied. 'I rather feel that from the literary point of view, I fell between two stools.'[39]

The chilling blast from the critics was strong enough to blow out any flame of inspiration. They condemned *Wine, Women, and Song* for its not-quite-nice title and *The Westminster Review* did not mince words about its estimate of *Vagabunduli Libellus*: '. . . the subject is an unwholesome one, and the motive strikes us as inadequate. . . . We cannot commend work of this kind, however cunning the hand of the artificer might be . . . we repeat what we have urged before, that there are moods and phases of passion which do not lie within the domain of art.'[40] It might have been better if Henry Sidgwick had glanced over 'Stella Maris', thoughtfully stroking his long silky beard, a concerned frown creasing his brow, turning from time to time with a note of weariness in the soft, high-pitched voice to say, 'That won't do, Johnnie, that won't do at all.'

Symonds never published another volume of poetry. In part he blamed the public; more fitfully, himself. He was clear-sighted enough to realize that while he might be a competent craftsman, he lacked the fire of real genius, and in a moment of insight he once compared himself to a second-rate poet like Southey. On the other hand, the public never saw the real Symonds who had to present his wares in various conventional disguises. What they received was a poor, truncated version of the original *cri de coeur*. Some of the copies of the privately-printed *Rhaetica* survived the edict for their destruction, and on re-reading them after Symonds's death Brown told Gosse: 'I feel, as you do, the tragedy of these poems, not of course in the poems themselves, but as expressions of Johnnie's inner life. I hardly think on reading them again that there is much good poetry in them; & yet they are consistently the most individual, genuine, characteristic work that Johnnie ever did.'[41] In the poetic medium alone could he find a measure of cathartic relief. There was also a certain esoteric satisfaction in evolving an elaborate system of hieroglyphic symbols such as 'Chimaera', 'the valley of vain desire', and 'Maya', the significance of which only the initiated would understand. Whether or not the reader knew the real meaning of these poems depicting the friendship of comrades, he could not fail to grasp their pervasive theme: an anguished longing for an ideal love, the despair intensified by the realization that it would never find fulfilment. The language tended to be pompous, the tone humourless, but the emotion was knuckle-bare.

III

Symonds's letters during the early years at Davos are filled with complaints about the boredom of literature – and yet it was literature which maintained the vital link with his former life in England: the arrival of friends with the latest literary gossip, Henry Sidgwick's monthly newsletter, periodicals pouring into the house, manuscripts sent off to publishers, the returning of proofs to be corrected. In 1886 he had his most productive year to date: the proofs of the two final volumes of *Renaissance in Italy* were corrected; an article on Tasso was submitted to the *Encyclopaedia Britannica*;* two biographies – *Sir Philip Sidney* and *Ben Johnson* – were completed; he edited and contributed introductions to selections from Sir Thomas Browne and Ben Jonson; and translated the autobiography of Benvenuto Cellini. For all these efforts he received the princely sum of £400 – the largest amount he had ever earned in a year. But the reviews made him reflect on whether he should 'lay down my pen for ever. Over & over again I take it up again for $\dot{\alpha}\nu\alpha\gamma\omega\gamma\dot{\eta}'s$ [lifting up of the soul] sake.'[42]

In prose he was assuming the confidence of an experienced craftsman. His pen seemed dipped in fluency, and while he lacked the patience of Pater to linger meticulously over a phrase until he had polished it to gem-like perfection, Symonds was highly conscious of style. Perhaps he

* He had already written a long article on Italian history for the *Encyclopaedia Britannica* in 1880 and one on Machiavelli in 1882.

disliked Pater's style because it had so many affinities with his own, but Pater was able to achieve a uniquely distinctive effect that always eluded Symonds. Paradoxically, although his writing was often attacked as ornate, he admired the clear, direct crispness of Sainte-Beuve or Renan. When Graham Dakyns was puzzled by the critics' denigration of the style of his *Xenophon* as allusive, Symonds had some interesting words of advice for him:

I think in style there are two things to do: either to aim at lucidity of say Renan or Macaulay; or to develop idiosyncrasy to the very utmost with Carlyle. I have no hesitation in preferring the former aim as the really nobler if attained, & the more modest if failed in. But it requires a good deal of enunciation. One has to give up making certain points; & after much self-denial & labour, to bear the reproach of having been fluent or commonplace or even perhaps rhetorical. The latter aim is a kill or cure affair – to be succeeded in by a kind of coup d'état if lucky, or (if less favoured by fortune, then) by persistent beating of your own drums backed with very considerable force. Carlyle & Browning banged themselves into reputation. But these two men are both very great – & yet neither is likely to be an English classic. Carlyle's chance is gone already. Browning's is going. . . .

What I should recommend, for the excursus-writer, is an aiming at the standard of Ste Beuve or Renan. You will know well that both of these great authors are at all hazards clear, direct, luminous, sacrificing prophecy & passion & humour & poetry & all to that one object of saving the reader trouble & impressing him with the agreeable sense of his own capacity.[43]

But he did not follow his own advice sufficiently to satisfy Jowett, who, using Catherine as an intermediary, sent him some avuncular suggestions for pruning his style. 'Give my love to Johnny', he said. 'Notwithstanding ill health he has really made something of a literary life & attained for his age very great distinction. If he could only acquire the habit of rewriting & gaining in concentration without losing in simplicity he would greatly improve in writing. But nothing perfect is ever done 'currente calamo' though his gifts in that way are extraordinary. So you see I lecture him through you according to my judgement, as I might have done 18 or 20 years ago.'[44]

Symonds's relations with publishers and editors were usually amicable, although he could explode with wrath if he discovered sloppy misprints. When the brash new editor of *The Fortnightly Review*, Frank Harris, sent him frantic requests by telegram for an article, 'A Page of My Life', and then ignored his corrections on the proofs, so that it was printed riddled with errors, Symonds sent off a furious protest to Harris as well as an open complaint to *The Pall Mall Gazette* about his 'villainously ill-edited essay'.[45] The irrepressible Harris replied blandly that he had been unwell when the magazine went to press, and his substitute had not been familiar with 'the peculiarities of Mr Symonds's handwriting' – an explanation too far-fetched for the Editor of *The Pall Mall Gazette*, who added a note that 'the only peculiarity we have ever noticed about Mr Symonds's handwriting is that it is peculiarly clear and scholarly'.[46] Nevertheless, *The Pall Mall Gazette* chose 'A Page of My Life' as the most interesting article in the best magazine of the month, an accolade that mollified Symonds to some extent.

Symonds was always extremely generous in giving time, help, or advice to other writers. Horatio Brown continued to regard him as the teacher he had admired in the Sixth Form and submitted every poem and essay he wrote for Symonds's scrutiny and judgment. Symonds had little confidence in Brown's abilities – ('What I doubt is, whether Brown has the quality of success')[47] – but he knew that he longed to be a writer and he used his influence to get various articles placed for him. With the beautiful young poet-novelist, Agnes Mary Robinson, whom he met through Frances Poynter in 1880, he maintained an extensive correspondence, analysing her various works in detail. He was so enthusiastic about her poems of peasant life, *The New Arcadia* (1884), that he suggested paying her the supreme compliment of sending a copy to Walt Whitman. When it was badly reviewed in *The Spectator*, he immediately sent off a word of comfort: 'I think you are suffering from what success at the beginning always brings – a certain cruel & spiteful reaction – which is also not unjustified. I have gone through this – perhaps am in it, owing to my inability to soar above into undisputed regions where the critics do not bark or bite.

'And I know, regarding myself, that there is a certain equity in their instructive & often rather malevolent attempt to poise the balance.' Then he added, 'How I should like you to go & live somewhere away from clever women & clever men for some long while.'[48]

When she asked him if he would review a book of poetry by 'Vernon

Lee's'* stepbrother Eugene Lee-Hamilton and arrange to have it published in *The Academy*, he replied sanctimoniously: 'I so abhor the undignified modern system of arranging beforehand for the reviews of books, that I will have nothing to do with it, & always refuse requests of this sort from my friends wʰ are pretty frequently made me.'†[49] Had he forgotten his own unsuccessful attempt to place Gosse's review of *Renaissance in Italy* in *The Quarterly Review*? In this case, too, he eventually acquiesced to Miss Robinson's request to review Lee-Hamilton's *Apollo and Marsyas*, but made it quite clear that he did it only for her sake. 'I have ascribed to it more than I believe its ultimate value really is', he admitted reluctantly.[50]

Although there is no mention of her in his Memoirs, Symonds appears to have been more than slightly enamoured of the tremulously feminine Miss Robinson who was sixteen years his junior. When he did not hear from her for some time after their first meeting, he wrote plaintively to Miss Poynter that seeing him must have broken 'the spell of romance'.[51] There is a particularly tender note in all his many letters to her in which he repeatedly implores her to visit him in Davos or Venice. When Gosse chaffed him about rumours he had heard of the many letters passing between them, Symonds replied sheepishly that the reports had been exaggerated.

Symonds also carried on a lengthy correspondence with Miss Robinson's constant companion, the aggressively masculine 'Vernon Lee'. Symonds's dislike of 'Vernon Lee' was so intense that he appears to have written to her only to get news of Mary. 'She is a charming friend in every possible way', Symonds remarked fervently to 'Vernon Lee' of her friend; 'a more beautiful & gentle spirit I have never met with. And to get this in combination with her intelligence.'[52] Symonds hated to see the domineering influence 'Vernon Lee' had over Mary Robinson and it is obvious whom he had in mind when he warned Mary to get away from 'clever women'.‡

'Vernon Lee' had lived in Italy for years and Symonds could not help

---

* Pseudonym of Violet Paget (1856-1935).

† But he often arranged meetings with editors for his friends. His nephew, St Loe Strachey, and Arthur Symons, both wanted to review for *The Academy* and Symonds gave them letters of introduction to J. S. Cotton, the Editor.

‡ Havelock Ellis later suggested to Symonds that the pair might serve as a possible case-history for the section on Lesbianism in *Sexual Inversion*.

admiring the remarkable books on Italian aesthetics* which she produced while still so young a woman, but her sense of her own importance drove him to complain waspishly to Miss Robinson that her friend 'becomes more insufferable in her ignorant conceit every day'.[53] To 'Vernon Lee' herself he spoke with unusual bluntness. 'I feel', he lectured her, 'that you imagine yourself to be so clever that everything you think is either right or else valuable. . . . I cannot help thinking you would be really greater & more effective, if you were (to use a vulgar phrase) less cocksure about a heap of things.'[54] Nor did the extravagant praise she paid to *Shakspere's Predecessors* in her *Academy* review compensate for the fact that she dedicated *Euphorion* to Walter Pater. 'Vernon Lee' continued to be so certain about her own views that, although she continued to live in Italy during the 1914-18 War, she made no attempt to conceal the fact that her sympathies lay with the Turks and the Germans.

Nevertheless, if Symonds disliked another writer's work – even that of 'Vernon Lee' or Walter Pater – he made a great effort to understand and appreciate it. When Pater's *Marius the Epicurean* was published in 1885, he wrote to Miss Robinson:

Mr. Pater's Marius will of course be read by me – I hope in a gondola. My brain is so badly made that I cannot easily bear the sustained emotions of refinement in his style. To that exquisite instrument of expression, I daresay that I shall do justice in the langour & the largeness of the lagoons – better than I can in this larger air of mountains, where everything is jagged & up & down & horribly *natural*.

I cannot sympathize with Pater's theory of life; as this book seems to give it elaborate utterance, I do not want to study it in discordant circumstances:— for I want at least to respect it.†[55]

Symonds took particular pains to come to grips with work to which he could not respond if the author happened to be a friend of his. Gosse's poetry was one such instance. 'There is something in your style which I have not yet assimilated', he admitted candidly, ' – a something which I can best at present describe negatively as a defect of fluidity & morbidezza. It is something which I daresay my prolonged study of not the best

* *Studies of the Eighteenth Century in Italy* (1880); *Belcaro* (1882); *Euphorion* (1884).

† To Henry Sidgwick he spoke more frankly: '"Marius" I have not read. I suppose I must. But I shrink from approaching Pater's style, which has a peculiarly disagreeable effect upon my nerves – like the presence of a civet cat' (Brown, p. 401).

Italian poets has accustomed me to, & which my own instincts of composition incline me to aim at weakly. It is something which also bars my thorough sympathy with a great deal of Rossetti's work.'[56]

It was a brave man who dared to criticize the touchy Gosse. Always ready to take offence against any implied denigration, Gosse would rush to his study to pour out vituperation on his attacker in letters, many of which his wife managed to circumvent. Symonds was the bewildered recipient of one of these in 1879. In an article, 'Matthew Arnold's Selections from Wordsworth', in the November issue of *The Fortnightly Review*, Symonds had spoken condescendingly of 'the carved cherry-stones' of some poets, and Gosse, for some inexplicable reason, assumed that he had been referring to his, Gosse's, poetry. Symonds tried to treat the matter jokingly, but even Gosse could not doubt the sincerity of his concluding remarks: 'I would have most gladly cancelled any sentence that should have seemed to say a word against you. Please forgive me for what was so utterly un-meant – for what was so absolutely penned without the memory of your existence . . . do not let me lose a friend. . . .'[57]

Further trouble arose in 1884 over the 'English Worthies' series edited by Andrew Lang. Gosse raised a wail of protest when he heard a rumour that Symonds was to contribute monographs on both Sir Philip Sidney and Ben Jonson. The bemused Lang had obviously forgotten what he had promised to whom. Gosse was told that Symonds had indicated 'with furious fervour'[58] that he wanted Jonson, but Lang could not remember having promised Sidney to him as well. Attempting to appease both men, he also told Symonds that Gosse was furious because he 'coveted' Ben Jonson. Symonds then tried to calm Gosse with the information that it was for Morley's 'Men of Letters' series he had promised to write a biography of Sidney, but he would not be 'so churlish or so foolish as to want to have both Jonson & Sidney!'*[59] He could not refrain from

* Had Gosse forgotten that he knew as early as 1882 that Symonds was contemplating a work on Sidney? At that time he wrote to Stevenson: 'Please give my kindest regards to Symonds. Do not let him hasten over his Philip Sidney. The subject wants digestion. I know why he chose him for a hero, but they would send me to the Tower if I wrote the reason in a letter. O naughty world ' (E. E. Charteris, *The Life and Letters of Sir Edmund Gosse*, William Heinemann Ltd., 1931, pp. 150, 151.) Gosse is probably referring to the speculation about the relationship between Sidney and Hubert Languet. Moreover, Gosse also sent him information about the location of a Sidney MS. and said, 'I look forward to a charming book from you on Sidney' (MS. letter, 29, Delamere Terrace, 27 April 1882, University of Bristol).

inserting an acid addition: 'Sir Philip Sidney is really a better choice. But you have the opportunities in London for doing it so far better than I could, that I am sincerely glad to renounce any slight hold I may still be supposed to retain on him (as advertised to write his life in the "Men of Letters" series) in favour of your abler pen.' Somewhat shamefacedly, Gosse backed down, and Symonds ended up by writing *Sir Philip Sidney* for the English 'Men of Letters' and *Ben Jonson* for the 'English Worthies' series. When Symonds wrote to A. H. Bullen of the difficulties Gosse was raising, Bullen replied: 'For Gosse's scholarship I have no extraordinary regard, and I don't much care for his verse. He deserved to be successful, but his success is spoiling him; he lacks Austin Dobson's modesty.'[60] Writing to Gosse some months after the tempest had subsided, Symonds, in a naïvely obvious attempt at appeasement, deprecated the value of writing on a man such as Sidney: 'I found it difficult to make Sidney interesting to myself, & so I fear that I shall have failed to present him in an interesting light to the public.'[61] Yet, of all his books, none surpasses the *Sidney* for its tone of adulation.

Any differences between them were forgotten when both were flayed by that scourge of the late-Victorians, Churton Collins. The attack in both instances was based largely on shoddy scholarship, and in Symonds's case the charges were levelled against *Shakspere's Predecessors in the English Drama*.

This was a book which should never have been written – or, more precisely, it should perhaps have been written seventeen years before, in 1866, when Symonds, 'in rage, fury, love, depression, illness',[62] had shoved a manuscript on the history of the Elizabethan drama into his 'desolation box'. In 1882, when he pulled it out again, the document seemed worth resuscitating and expanding into a full-length study. His anxiety never to be left without some engrossing work made him turn to it once more, although the heat of his early passion for the Elizabethans had long since diminished. Nevertheless, he hesitated for some time, and his uncertainty is reflected in the letters which he wrote to friends, asking whether they considered such a work worth the abandonment of his Italian studies for a year. He received enthusiastic support from A. H. Bullen, son of George Bullen, the keeper of the printed books in the British Museum library. The younger Bullen had already published a number of reprints of Elizabethan literary works, and was recognized as one of the leading contemporary authorities on the literature of the sixteenth and seventeenth centuries. To Bullen, Symonds outlined his plan of tracing the development of the Elizabethan drama from its origins in the early miracles and moralities. Bullen agreed with him that scant justice had been done to this early period by Lamb or by the modern critics. 'I think it is now time for some one of authority to speak out on the other side', Bullen encouraged him.[63] During the preparation of the book they were in constant communication; Bullen supplied him with necessary information gleaned from the British Museum, and eventually checked the proofs of the book.

In the Preface Symonds stated that he had not attempted to write a scholarly book, but rather an expository study intended to stimulate general interest in this early period. In actual fact, however, he was carried away far beyond the title of his book. Symonds was characteristic of his period in his preoccupation with what Matthew Arnold called 'the science of origins', and in this volume he attempted to apply an idea which had been intriguing him since he had first read Herbert Spencer in the early 'sixties, and to which he had given tentative expression in *Studies of the Greek Poets*. This was the concept that works of art underwent the same evolutionary process of growth, maturity and decay as any other organism. In such a development Shakespeare would represent the fruition of a long series of preparatory efforts, valuable not so much in themselves as for their germinal contribution to the development of the drama. After Shakespeare an inevitable decline could be demonstrated, a period marked by imitation and artificiality because the original dramatic energy had exhausted itself.

Unfortunately, *Shakspere's Predecessors in the English Drama*, which was published in 1884, is a failure of intentions beyond the author's capacities. The evolutionary approach may have appealed to Symonds as a contemporary one in keeping with nineteenth-century currents of thought, but he obviously did not ponder all its implications. Symonds's mind was quick to respond to new ideas, but it lacked the depth to assimilate them or the constructive audacity to transform them to his own purposes. The first part of the book, in which he traces the early liturgical origins of the drama, successfully evokes the spirit of the times;

but he failed to prove his overall thesis that these early plays form the base of a pyramid with Shakespeare reigning at the apex, and that his successors utter the dying gasp of the dramatic impulse. Despite Symonds's repeated insistence on the organic development of his subject, his own book emerged as a glaring example of disorganization. He discussed at length many of Shakespeare's contemporaries, including a detailed study of Ben Jonson; an analysis of Shakespeare's genius he sedulously avoided; and for his views on the period of decadence following Shakespeare, one must hunt out various articles he wrote for the periodicals. In other words, for the scale which Symonds postulated in his approach to the drama, a single volume work is lamentably incomplete. Moreover, as Swinburne pointed out to him, the lack of an index in a book of this nature is slipshod and frustrating. Symonds himself never cared for the book, which he described as 'a dull pompous volume',[64] and he realized that instead of reworking the earlier study, he should have destroyed it and begun again, since the result was 'a piece of inartistic patchwork'.[65]

The reviewers were undeceived by Symonds's promises of an orderly scientific study. Far more serious, the critic in *The Dial* found him guilty of 'padding'. 'That this is a most serious charge', he admitted, 'to bring against one of the foremost Englishmen of letters of the day, the present writer is painfully aware; but several passages of trivial or irrelevant matter compel the conclusion that its author felt bound by some exigency to make a book of a given size, and that not possessing the requisite amount of sound material, he was driven to shifts unworthy of his reputation in order to "bombast out" his chapters, some of which read as if they had been hastily concocted for some ephemeral magazine.' The verdict: '. . . there is nothing new in the book, nothing that has not already been as well or better said, nothing that makes it indispensable or even useful to the student who has already broken ground'.[66]

Worse was yet to come. Far more damaging to Symonds's reputation was the unsigned attack by Churton Collins in *The Quarterly Review*. Collins opened his review innocently enough with the assertion that *Shakspere's Predecessors* deserved consideration because 'it promises to be the most voluminous history of our national drama which has yet been attempted'. He then proceeded to leave no doubt as to why it should be dismissed from any consideration at all. Indeed, he considered it a dangerous book: 'A bad book is its own antidote; a superlatively good book appeals to few; but a book which is not too defective to be called excellent, and not too excellent to become popular, exercises an influence on literary activity the importance of which it is scarcely possible to over-state. And of such a character is the volume before us.' Collins deplored its many inaccuracies – for example, Symonds's description of Euphues as the inventor of Euphuism – and hyberbolic generalizations such as his statement that the Elizabethan drama was draped with 'a tragic pall of deep Teutonic meditative melancholy'. Collins represented the author as a member of a new school of writers whose leader was Swinburne, and in following his example, 'they out-Ossian Ossian in the tumid extravagance of their epithets and turns'.[67] With such a critical reaction it was not surprising that Smith, Elder did not encourage Symonds to contribute a second volume.

Bullen wrote him a consolatory letter: 'The review in the Quarterly struck me as very unfair. Anybody could see that some of the writing in your book was early work. It would have been quite enough to hint at this, without dwelling so elaborately on the subject. I was amused to find the author of the Introduction to Cyril Tourneur* (for I guessed at once that the Quarterly article was by him) calling you to task for your Swinburnianisms. . . . It would take the ability of 100 Collinses to produce the finished English of the Introduction to *Wine, Women, and Song*.'[68] But a puzzle remains: when Bullen was correcting the proofs, why didn't *he* catch all the factual errors? In a letter of 12 October 1882 he spoke only of some 'trifling mistakes' in dates.[69]

Collins next opened his guns on Gosse. In *The Quarterly Review*, October 1886, he reviewed Gosse's *From Shakespeare to Pope*, and the list of inaccuracies he discovered was very serious indeed for a man who by now held the Clark Professorship of English Literature at Cambridge. Gossip had it that Collins, a Balliol man, who fancied himself as a serious scholar, was smarting with chagrin at his failure to secure the Merton Professorship of English at Oxford the previous year while Gosse, with no academic qualifications, had insinuated his way into Cambridge by showy superficial journalism which passed with the credulous as scholar-ship. Collins's attack was the first serious rebuff Gosse had suffered and he

* Collins edited a two-volume collection of Tourneur's plays in 1878.

let out the roar of a wounded lion. Letters of outrage demanding sympathetic support went off to all his friends. Andrew Lang characteristically laughed the matter off with a sophisticated quip. Symonds, on the other hand, who had already been stung by the adder, poured solicitude on his wounds:

I can hardly see how literature is to be carried forward if this tyranny of journalism continues [he lamented].

It will be necessary to keep our thoughts locked up in our hearts & studies. When I think what we earn in wages by the thankless Muse, and what we are exposed to in annoyance, time can be better employed in breaking stones than in giving the best we have of our mind and heart to an ungrateful public . . . you can see how painfully I feel, and how distressed I am not only for yourself but also for the whole commonwealth of letters. I hope and feel sure that you will be sustained by the sympathy of friends. I know that your work can endure even this fiery ordeal, and that your reputation will survive it. But it is terribly hard to bear.[70]

The Athenaeum agreed to publish a long rebuttal by Gosse in the issue of 23 October 1886. It sounded aggrievedly self-righteous, and Symonds, while still sympathetic, was now inclined to believe that Gosse's wisest course would have been to admit the justification of some of Collins's charges. To Miss Robinson he spoke candidly: 'It seems to me clear that Gosse had been spitefully & unfairly dealt with; but he made a most ridiculously feeble reply to the Quarterly. . . . Gosse is certainly an inaccurate writer.'[71] In a letter written the same day to Gosse, he modified his tone somewhat:

By this time I sincerely trust that the great Quarterly row with all its unutterable baseness of blackguardism will have subsided. I had a long letter from Arthur Sidgwick about the matter, wrote taking your side. He asks me whether I do not think it is absurd to lay so much stress on a few slips here & there, & none at all upon a man's power to stimulate the interest of his audience. He says he hears on good authority that Ch. Collins is himself a very inadequate & inaccurate Greek teacher at some Crammer's.*

* Collins taught Greek and English literature at W. P. Scoones's coaching establishment but, despite Sidgwick's innuendo, he was a literary figure of some consequence. A prolific reviewer, Collins had already published three books, and was prominently connected with the University Extension Society. He later (1904) became Professor of English Literature at Birmingham.

Robert Louis Stevenson

J. A. Symonds, 1886

I believe you might have made a far better answer to the Quarterly than you did & have stopped the matter sooner. I should have enumerated all the slips; & mistakes w^h I acknowledged very briefly in the first place; & have then proceeded to deal with the unfairness & misrepresentation & animus of the article more in detail. It is quite preposterous to suppose that a man should be impeccable in every detail.[72]

Churton Collins had not yet finished with either of them. Gosse invited trouble by an article on Sir Philip Sidney in *The Contemporary Review* of November 1886, in which he spoke enthusiastically about – ironically – Symonds's forthcoming book on Sidney; Symonds, however, was not altogether pleased with such excessive praise and told Gosse that it made him feel 'almost uncomfortable'. 'You are wrong', he continued, 'when you say that I am a sound scholar. I take indeed great trouble about any bit of work I do: & I have burrowed myself into one small section of the world's history in Italy. But otherwise, I am not & cannot here make myself a scholar in the supreme sense of that word.

'I wonder also whether I have the fire that burns in you for literature ! I love it, but I love life more.'[73]

As Symonds feared, 'that beast'[74] Churton Collins, in *The Pall Mall Gazette*, seized upon *The Contemporary* article as an example of the literary log-rolling he had been deploring – 'in matters of this kind reciprocity is everything', he sneered.[75] On 16 December Symonds wrote to Gosse: 'What has embittered Mr. Collins against me, I cannot imagine, and it is indeed too bad to insinuate that you and I have been log-rolling ! I was fearful lest he should come down upon us in this very way when I read your kind words in the Contemporary about my forthcoming "Sidney". Do you observe how a creature like Churton Collins omits in his review all real discussion of the material in books, confining himself to the one object of carping sneering and personal insult ? He must be a most unhappy man – poor little wretch !' His weary conclusion: 'Literature is becoming a most ungrateful task, and I think I shall give it up. After really trying to do my best in my vocation for fifteen years, I find myself getting more kicks than half-pence. . . .'[76]

Gosse immediately sent off a plea to him not to give up: '. . . You are getting to be looked upon as a figure whose mark is made, a leader in living literature. On all sides I see you now so spoken on [*sic*] with high respect. . . . You are one of the first six or seven personages which take rank immediately after the old Olympians like Tennyson & Ruskin. . . . There is not a single man in England, born since 1840, who holds such a place in literature as you do. . . . In ten years' time, your influence & status will be enormous. The public knows you, trusts you, reads you – they will presently begin to take you for an oracle. . . .'[77]

Collins always claimed that he drew a sharp distinction between the man and his work, and that there was no personal malevolence in his attacks. He had often been a guest in Gosse's home, but such personal factors were irrelevant when attempting to reach an objective estimate of a book he was reviewing. When he reprinted the article on *Shakspere's Predecessors* in *Essays and Studies* two years after Symonds's death, he justified its inclusion in the following words: 'Exception may perhaps be taken to the strictures of Mr Addington Symonds' book, and I should like to add that when I heard of his lamented death I determined, should the article ever be reprinted to suppress them. But on reconsideration I found I had no choice. Nothing could have justified the appearance of those strictures during Mr. Symonds' lifetime if they are not equally justified when he lives only in the power and influence of his writings . . . it was in no spirit of personal hostility that I wrote what I thought it a duty to say nearly ten years ago; and it is with the liveliest sense of the great loss which English literature has sustained by his death that I again perform what I conceive to be a duty in reprinting what I then wrote.'[78] And in 1898 he was to make an even more devastating assault on Gosse's *A Short History of English Literature.*

Both Gosse and Symonds confused criticism of a work with a personal attack on its author, as Symonds indicates in a letter to Miss Robinson written only a few months before Collins's review of *Shakspere's Predecessors*. 'I get more & more to feel', he informed her, 'that criticism should not inflict pain. Books (unless published by men of great authority, whose authority when used for evil has to be resisted) should be praised in silence, if we object to them. This it is principally which makes me now so shy about undertaking reviews. If I write, I must write them genially towards the authors.'[79] Unfortunately, through this dread of inflicting or receiving pain, Symonds hesitated to make any decisive statements, and his readers were often left uncertain as to what his views really were.

IV

Much against his will, Symonds was drawn into an even more famous literary controversy involving Whitman and Swinburne. In the course of the years, the early enthusiasm of Swinburne's impassioned 'To Walt Whitman in America'* had soured to distaste for the poet's formlessness. In his life of Swinburne, Gosse attributed Swinburne's change of attitude to 'the slow tyranny on Swinburne's judgment by the will of Watts'[80] – an incomprehensible explanation in view of the fact that as early as 1872 Swinburne had publicly drawn attention to the difference between Whitman as poet and as 'formalist';[81] and to Gosse himself he made his attitude quite clear in a letter he wrote to him in 1885 on Gosse's return from America where he visited Whitman.[82] Nevertheless, there was no previous hint of how radically Swinburne's views had altered and Whitman's supporters were stunned by the virulence with which he suddenly attacked Whitman in the pages of *The Fortnightly Review* in August 1887. In an article, entitled 'Whitmania', Swinburne assured his readers that he had 'never meant to imply what most assuredly I have never said – that I regard Mr Whitman as a poet or thinker in the proper sense. . . .'[83] As Swinburne proceeded, his tone became almost hysterical: '. . . Mr Whitman's Eve is a drunken apple-woman, indecently sprawling in the slush and garbage of her over-turned fruit-stall: but Mr Whitman's Venus is a Hottentot wench under the influences of cantharides and adulterated rum.'[84]

Caught completely off guard, Symonds simply did not know how to handle the situation. He felt called upon to defend his idol, yet he found himself trapped in a dilemma because he did not want to offend Swinburne, even though they were no longer writing to each other.† On 21 August 1887, he wrote to Whitman's friend, W. S. Kennedy: 'I sent to the Fortnightly about ten days ago a temperate rebuke to Swinburne for his ignoble attack on Whitman.'[85] 'Temperate' was an extravagant term to describe his pallid defence. In an attempt to adopt the voice of reason, he begins by agreeing with Swinburne that Whitman is not a

---

* In *Songs before Sunrise* (1871).

† The correspondence ended somewhat tensely in 1882 when Symonds wrote a moderately critical review of *Tristram of Lyonesse* (*The Academy*, XX, 5 Aug. 1882, 93, 94).

poet in the technical sense of the word. But then he seems to succumb to the enemy completely: he will not 'defend Mr Whitman's method of treating sexual matters, which is far too physiological' for his taste, he states sanctimoniously, and he weakly maintains that Whitman's Eve is the 'exact opposite of Mr Swinburne's caricature'. His apologia for Whitman is contained in the following passage:

We may not care for Whitman's gospel of the sexes. We may think, as I for one do, that it is bawled with superfluous vehemence into our ears. Yet we ought not to forget that Whitman's familiarity with the American proletariat convinced him that this message, delivered through a speaking trumpet, was needed, in order to bring men back to sound ways of thinking and feeling upon matters fundamentally important to society. Against the dram-drinker, the slave to secret vice, the victim of habitual excesses, the adulterous couple, the obscene dreamer, the nympholept of unnatural erethism, he deemed it his duty to protest. He felt that the core of material life in the great American cities ran a risk of being corrupted by such folk. Accordingly he promulgated his own conception of the primal attraction of normal womanhood for normal manhood, he glorified an idea of average and natural reciprocity between the sexes.[86]

In this hypocritical recital the only perversion he omitted was his own.

That he was ashamed of his timidity is only too apparent in the stammered circumlocutions of another letter sent to Kennedy on 17 September: 'I am afraid that his friends may have thought my rebuke to Swinburne (in the Fortnightly of this month) lukewarm. It was printed, or rather misprinted, without my being able to modify my utterance upon that proof. I meant to keep my tone very low, and to say far less than I feel; for I am sure that this is the right way to win a wide recognition of Whitman's merits. Yet when I saw my note in print, I felt very sorry that I had not been allowed the opportunity of striking out a phrase here and there. It does not represent my thought. It is almost impossible to say exactly anything about so astounding and incommensurable a thinker and writer as Whitman is. . . .'[87]

Although Whitman was disconcerted at the time – he called Symonds's defence 'such a milk and water affair'[88] – he felt no rancour for him because he realized that his hesitancy stemmed from cowardice. He knew very well why Symonds responded so ardently to his poetry. 'What Mr Symonds admires in my books is the comradeship', he told his friends the

Gilchrists; 'he says that he had often felt it, and wanted to express it, but dares not.'[89] Symonds might have been living in Switzerland but his roots were still in England, and he was fearful about antagonizing conventional opinion. Through the numerous newspapers and periodicals to which he subscribed, he was well aware of the contemporary moral atmosphere of England. After the passing of the Labouchere Amendment it was only a matter of time until the Oscar Wilde case brought the new law and the old prejudice into scandalous prominence.*

Symonds tried to make amends to Whitman by an essay, 'Democratic Art. With Special Reference to Walt Whitman', included in *Essays Speculative and Suggestive* (1890), and a monograph on Whitman, published in 1893. In the latter, he still could not bring himself to issue more than a mild rebuke to Swinburne, 'lavish of . . . hyperboles of praise and blame', and in a brief reference to Swinburne's controversial article he remarked casually, 'I forget the exact verbiage of the scurrility; and I do not impute the change of attitude implied in it, so much to Mr Swinburne's levity, as to the bewilderment created in his mind by Whitman's incongruities.'[90]

* See Chapter XI, p. 283.

CHAPTER X

Symonds's Italy

I

'I DO not know what there is here', Symonds wrote to Rutson from Sorrento in 1864, 'but I feel in Italy a continual unsatisfied desire. . . .'[1] From the time of his first visit to northern Italy with his father in 1861 until his death in Rome more than thirty years later, Italy exerted the fascination of the unreal, the exotic, and the forbidden. The letter to Rutson goes on to describe its beauty as affecting him with 'the sense of what can never be'. Italy, with its warm sunshine, its vibrant colours, and its languorous atmosphere, was a heady wine to be savoured in slow sips.

It is significant that after his periodic visits to Italy, Symonds frequently spoke of 'fleeing' or 'escaping' from its coils. He returned to the sharp clear air of Davos as though emerging from the spell of an enchanter. The real world – *his* world – was not to be found among olives and oleanders but in the grim mountain fastness, 'where the feet of the seasons pace so monotonously'.[2] Italy devoured him, body and soul. Its climate drained the strength from his frail body, its pleasures aroused his sensibilities to their highest pitch. 'Here', he wrote from Venice to Miss Robinson, 'I am simply slack & to be played upon, with great detriment to the strings of the instrument.'[3]

But he could not shake himself free from 'this dreadful Italian pathology'.[4] Within his study in Am Hof he invoked its scenes and recalled its history in countless books and articles. Even when he wrote on English subjects, Italy was not abandoned. In *Shakspere's Predecessors* he turned constantly to Italian models for comparison and contrast. At the risk of offending Shakespeare lovers, he pronounced Bandello's ending of the Romeo and Juliet story far more tragically effective than Shakespeare's. Before writing his monograph on Shelley, he revisited the

Italian scenes where the poet wrote many of his poems, in order to steep himself in their atmosphere. On one occasion when he was too ill to make his annual spring visit to Venice in 1885, he consoled himself that 'Italy lies in my memory & heart enough to be now that better thing than a heard melody – an unheard one'.[5]

His response to the beauty of the country was recorded in numerous descriptive essays, originally contributed to various periodicals, and later assembled in three collections, *Sketches in Italy and Greece* (1874), *Sketches and Studies in Italy* (1879), and *Italian Byways* (1883). Many of these had been worked up from passages in his letters or diaries, and their lack of spontaneity bears the mark of Dr Symonds who had trained him to note every detail of a scene. The peasants' cottages, the wild flowers, the changing hues of the sky, nuances of colour, variations of light, are noted with the perceptive eyes of an enthusiastic tourist with his note-book open, determined to capture any item of local colour. All too frequently the finely-stippled effect is marred by a final passage of self-conscious comment. The description of sunrise on Monte Generoso must be rounded off with the sober reflection that 'the thoughts which it suggests, the images with which it stores our mind, are not without their noblest uses. The glory of the world sinks deeper into our shallow souls than we well knew; and the spirit of its splendour is always ready to revisit us on dark and dreary days at home with an unspeakable refreshment.'[6]

Symonds always remained the perpetual tourist, and despite his intense reaction to Italy, he never felt very comfortable with Italians. He admired their beauty and their grace, he envied their relaxed gaiety, but he could never establish the rapport that he felt with his Swiss neighbours. The exceptions included a few gondoliers to whom he became deeply attached, but with them the relationship was of a nature that transcended barriers of nationality. In an essay, 'The Gondolier's Wedding', his muted pleasure in the festivities is very different from the sheer delight of the christening party he attended in Mürren many years before with Rosa. In Swiss gatherings he loved the complete absence of self-consciousness only possible in a classless community. Italy, on the other hand, was a rigidly hierarchical society and Symonds found himself constantly annoyed by the respect with which underlings treated the *Signor*. The gondoliers and

their families could never be made to understand that the English gentleman wanted them to accept him as one of themselves, and their flattery
and exaggerated politeness only irritated him. Language presented another
barrier in communication. Symonds had a wide knowledge of Italian
literature, yet he was seized with shyness when it came to speaking the
language. Although highly flattered when the Italian scholar, Ernesto
Masi, remarked that 'The Italian language has no secrets for Mr
Symonds', he was uneasily aware that he did not deserve such praise. His
nervousness probably stemmed from the fact that he had studied Italian
as an adult, whereas he had little difficulty in conversing with the Davosers
in German, a language he had learned as a boy from Sophie Girard.

If Symonds had difficulty in establishing personal relationships with
Italians, he also had little sympathy for the nationalistic aspirations of
modern Italy. As a young woman, Catherine had worn the fashionable
coloured shirts called 'garibaldis', but during the same period, despite
frequent visits to Italy, Symonds remained completely unmoved by the
enthusiasm for the emerging nation which swept up Swinburne and the
Brownings. Totally preoccupied in his own problems, he felt nothing but
exasperation for Swinburne's espousal of Italian *Unità*. 'The South hates
the North', he informed Charlotte in 1873 in one of his rare remarks on
the subject. 'The only way of uniting Italy would be to put the whole
South under martial law and at the same time to make railways and
encourage trade in every way. For the Italians are very keen in their
perception of material advantage.'

Except for Venice, the cities of Italy failed to capture him completely.
Rome was too impressive to take to one's heart. Its magnificence bewildered him. 'Rome is an awful place', he warned Miss Poynter; 'the
only way is to tackle it with nonchalance, leaving unseen at least 70% of
its θαυμάσια [wonders]. . . .'[7] He hated to see its stately beauty being
destroyed by modern encroachment. In 1891, he lamented, 'The Rome I
loved in 1863 is lost. But I cannot deplore change when change means
prosperity. Does it so here? The Ludovisi Villa has become a nest of
bourgeois habitations. . . . I see little of real wealth about. The faces of
the shops in the vast new quarters are poor, like stores set up by squatters
in some California mining stations.'[8]

However, for all his qualifications about Rome, he preferred it to

Florence. In *Renaissance in Italy* he described Florence as the cradle of Renaissance intellectual activity, and he could appreciate it intellectually; he could also love its autumn evenings lit by the warm glow of the chestnut toasters in the Piazza del Duomo; but once again there were moods in which he described it as 'a place I detest'.[9] Rome and Florence were admired, appreciated, and sometimes spurned: Venice alone engulfed him. 'I have thought of nothing but Venice, Venice, since I left', he wrote Brown after his visit in the spring of 1881. 'The name rings in my soul.'[10] It was small enough to be comprehended, the variety of its life excited him, and in its opulent art he could indulge his repressed craving for extravagance. Images of water and immersion recur frequently in his references to 'the divine city'. He spoke of recovering 'from the sea-bath of Venetian existence, into w^h I plunged. . . .'[11] 'It is difficult to get unmoored from this divine place', he sighed contentedly on one of his last visits.[12] Venice exerted a soporific effect on the Puritan strain in his nature, the element in him that distrusted imagination and luxuriance and sensuality.

Here he could drift in a gondola and immerse himself in *Marius the Epicurean* and Tennyson's 'Lucretius', works too refined for the brisk empyrean of Davos where trees and mountains and chalets were outlined with uncompromising clarity. Venice was a floating dream-city:

. . . when you are at Venice it is like being in a dream, and when you dream about Venice it is like being awake. I do not know how this should be, but Venice seems made to prove that *La vita è un sogno*. What the Venice dream is all the world knows. Motion that is almost imperceptible, colour too deep and gorgeous to strike the eye, gilding so massive and ancient as to wear a mist of amber brown upon its brightness, white cupolas that time has turned to pearls, marble that no longer looks like stone, but blocks cut from summer clouds, a smooth sea that is brighter and more infinite than the sky it reflects – these are some of the ingredients of the dream which are too familiar for description. Nothing can describe the elemental warmth of the days, the sea-kisses of the wind at evening, the atmosphere of breathless tepid moonlight in the night. Some people dislike this part of the dream. It just suits me – only I dream of myself in it dressed in almost nothing and very lazy.[13]

So he wrote to Dakyns in 1872, and this dream of Venice was reinvoked in the opening paragraphs of his chapter on Venetian painting in

The Fine Arts, the third volume of *Renaissance in Italy,* in prose which reflected the city's overripe splendour.* Not unexpectedly, his favourite painters were Titian, Veronese, and Tintoretto; and Lena Waterfield has recorded how he would sit for hours in front of Tintoretto's 'Last Communion of St Lucy'.[14]

After he settled in Switzerland Symonds soon developed the habit of moving between Davos and Italy as mood and weather dictated. The pattern was initiated the day they moved into Am Hof, when he left Catherine to cope with the disorder while he escaped south to Venice. Then, every spring, reversing the seasons, 'like a stork at the top of a steeple',[15] he descended from his eyrie, and flew south to warmth and beauty – and away from Catherine's difficult moods, because, as he told Stevenson bluntly, they found that they got along best when they were apart. For a number of years he stayed in a series of palazzi, then in 1887 Horatio Brown suggested that he take a small flat attached to the house Brown and his mother had bought at 560 Zattere. It was ideal as a *pied-à-terre* for its great advantages were sun and warmth, and Symonds suffered cruelly from damp Venetian interiors. In the spring of 1888, with Madge's help, he moved into the empty mezzanino, which they gradually filled with a colourful jumble of furniture. Here he encamped each year for a month or so, enjoying the view of the ships anchored outside his windows and the life of the people in the streets and canals behind Ca' Torresella, whose colour he evoked for Gosse in a letter of November, 1890: 'My window here, where I write, is charming: the whole via of the Zattere and the Canal of the Giudecca, in part, crowded with all kinds of craft, yellow and red sails, etc., leading on to the distant mainland and the Euganean Hills behind w^h the sun sets. I am just above a bridge (it is an entresol I live in) up & down w^h go divine beings: sailors of the marine, soldiers, blue vested & trousered fishermen, swaggering gondoliers. I can almost see their faces as they top the bridge. By rising from the chair a little – I do so at once, and get some smiles from passing strangers. . . .'[16]

Symonds was only too happy to establish some sort of semi-permanent

* In 1883 Henry James sent him his essay on Venice 'as a small acknowledgment of the pleasure his own writing about Italy has given me' (Virginia Harlow, *Thomas Sergeant Perry: A Biography,* Durham, N.C., Duke University Press, 1950, p. 313). This essay was 'From Venice to Strasburg' in *Foreign Parts* (Leipzig: Bernhard Tauchnitz, 1883).

home in Venice. Through the years he had made many friends among the international colony, from Browning to Sir Henry Layard and the Princess of Montenegro, and his life there had become 'a jumble of palaces and pothouses, princesses and countesses, gondoliers and *faccini*, hours and hours by day upon the lagoons, hours and hours by night in strange places of the most varied description'.[17] Nowhere, except in Venice, could he range through the whole social gamut with such nonchalance.

These lazy, dream-like holidays were shared with Horatio Brown who had become a regular 'Inglese Venezianato'. They drifted together through the lagoons* in Brown's colourful *sandolo*, the 'Fisole', its orange sails emblazoned with a fleur-de-lis; or, if they felt more active, they joined Brown's gondolier Antonio for a game of *tre sette* or *bocce*. At Brown's Monday receptions, which were to become famous through the years as an integral part of the Venetian social calendar, Symonds helped him to entertain large miscellaneous groups of people. Symonds was also keenly interested in Brown's researches into the Venetian state papers. After the death of Rawdon Brown† in 1883, the British Government asked the younger Brown to continue his editing of those papers connected with English history, and Symonds encouraged him to pursue the task because it provided him with a fascinating preoccupation which would arrest the listlessness into which he had been drifting. With Symonds giving him aid and stimulation, Brown eventually produced *Venetian Studies* (1887), *The Venetian Printing Press* (1891), and *Venice, an Historical Sketch* (1893).

Although fourteen years separated Symonds and Brown, their interests and temperaments fused agreeably: both were lovers of fine wine and handsome young men. Sitting together one May afternoon in 1881 in the garden of an *osteria*, Brown pointed out a striking young gondolier, the servant of General de Horsey. Symonds was immediately entranced by an electric quality that seemed to run through the young man. For the next few days he was haunted by the memory of a hoarse voice, a mass of dark hair, and dazzling teeth under a short blonde moustache. In his waking

---

* These scenes are described by Brown in *Life on the Lagoons* (1884).

† Rawdon Lubbock Brown (1803-83), no connection of the younger Brown, did extensive research into the Venetian archives and aroused interest in the news-letters which the Venetian ambassadors in London had sent to the republic during the sixteenth and seventeenth centuries.

dreams he imagined himself as a different being, even a woman who was loved by the vibrant gondolier.

A few nights later, in a state of trembling agitation, he stood waiting in front of the Church of the Gesuati, while the young man strode nonchalantly towards him. Symonds had no difficulty in persuading him to go back to his room in the Casa Alberti where he was then staying. Here he questioned him about his life and learned that his name was Angelo Fusato, he was twenty-four years old, and had just completed three years' service in the Genio. Angelo assumed that Symonds was just another English gentleman of perverted tastes which he was willing to satisfy for a stipulated number of *lire*. The indignity of the situation appalled Symonds and he could not bring himself to touch him. In a turmoil of emotion, the next day he left abruptly for Monte Generoso. Here he wrote the series of sonnets called 'The Sea Calls', expressing his longing to return to Venice, poems which were later included in *Vagabunduli Libellus*; and most of the sonnets in the series 'Stella Maris' in the same volume were also inspired by Angelo.* In *Animi Figura*, 'L'Amour de l'Impossible' should be followed by 'Self-Condemnation', 'O, si!' and 'Amends' as the record of his moral struggle during their early intimacy.

By September he realized that 'Sonnet writing will not suffice for the human soul',[18] and he returned to Venice, determined to establish some sort of permanent relationship with Angelo. This time he took rooms in the Casa Barbier where the gondolier began to visit him at night. Symonds was completely infatuated and showered Angelo with presents and money, but the reckless way the young man squandered it made Symonds understand why his friends called him *il matto* (the madcap). However, he seemed to have formed a serious attachment for a girl who had borne him two sons and he would have married her, he claimed, if he had enough money. For two months Symonds tried desperately to convince Angelo that his interest in him extended beyond a passing amour. To his great joy he finally persuaded him to leave General de Horsey's

---

* To Miss Robinson's objections that no one would believe the statement in his Preface that he was describing imaginary experiences, he replied: 'As for people not believing my preface it will be very nasty of them if they don't. Stella never existed, except in my brain, & I never passed through any such experience with any woman – "nor" (to reverse Hamlet) "man neither"' (MS. letter, Davos Platz, 14 November 1884, University of Bristol).

service and become his own gondolier at a fixed wage so that he would now be able to marry his mistress.

Symonds's pleasure at the course events were taking is reflected in a letter to Dakyns written on his return from Venice in November: '. . . the six weeks or so w^h have elapsed since I scrawled a hasty note to you on the eve of my departure for Venice have been so full not of literature but of vehement life: — so full that that problem of what to work at, has not only retired but seems insignificant. . . . I have gained a complete blurr [*sic*] of all merely literary preoccupations, & the entrance into a new stage of living.'[19] Gradually Angelo responded to Symonds's fervent sincerity, and in time the relationship almost developed into his ideal of 'comradeship'.

Despite his numerous visits to Venice, by 1892 Symonds estimated that he had lived in the mezzanino only eight months out of five years. He wondered whether he should continue to pay out the rent of £36 a year to Brown, but he could not bring himself to part with it. Angelo and his wife acted as caretakers in his absence and Maria served as housekeeper during his visits. It was pleasant to be rowed about by Angelo, and where else but in Venice would he allow himself the indulgence of flaunting his coat of arms as he did on his gondola? Occasionally Angelo visited him in Davos and they took many trips together. Angelo grew to trust him so completely that he concealed nothing from him and he continued to serve him until Symonds's death in 1893. Sometimes he gave vent to outbursts of Italian passion but his disposition was, on the whole, sunny and kindly, and in his company Symonds could relax without the constant strain of being amusing or profound as he had to be with his more cultivated friends.

It was neither the periodic relaxation which his driving temperament craved, nor the aesthetic satisfactions denied to him in Davos, that made it difficult to part with his life in Venice. Here his sexual longings found partial fulfilment, and many cryptic references in his letters reveal that the price was high, for his experiences extended far beyond Angelo: eventually he had to limp back to Davos, exhausted, trembling, vaguely dissatisfied. Sometimes, after a particularly turbulent experience, he looked forward to returning to Davos. 'There is no wine, no work, & too much etc. here', he once wrote to Dakyns from Venice.[20] When, in 1891,

Brown urged him to come to Venice, he replied with a flash of bitter clarity, 'The problem of life and self is not . . . to be solved by change of place.'[21]

II

While Symonds's relationship with contemporary Italy was ambivalent, hectic, and disturbing, his interest in its history provided its most enduring fascination for him. To understand the background of this preoccupation, it is necessary to go back to the youthful inception of his *Renaissance in Italy*, and follow through the years of his maturity the writing, publication, and reception of his *magnum opus*.

It was E. M. W. Tillyard's belief that 'if one could have questioned a typical Victorian of the later nineteenth century on the Renaissance, the result would have been somewhat as follows. The Renaissance was a manifestation of new life, an outburst of virtuous floridity after the cramping restraints and withering asceticisms of the Middle Ages. In the Victorian's mind the movement would be connected generally and principally with Italy and would carry with it specific, if little formulated, associations with Florence and Amalfi, carnivals, poisonings, orange trees and red wines, the Brownings, honeymoons on Lake Como, and churches full of highly-coloured paintings.'[22] Such a conception of the Renaissance was derived in no small part from Symonds's seven-volume *Renaissance in Italy*, the first full-scale study of the period in English – and, in W. K. Ferguson's view, it can still be described as 'the only history of Renaissance civilization by a single author that can be compared to Burckhardt's'.[23] Yet the legacy of the romanticized Italy it evoked has survived the sober historical reputation and it is significant that Edmund Wilson, in his description of the 'mock-Elizabethan' home of 'The Princess with the Golden Hair', notes that Symonds's *Life of Michelangelo* and his history of the Renaissance have a place on its shelves, adding that proper *recherché* touch.[24]

When Symonds first began to think seriously of undertaking a major work on the Renaissance, Jowett told him: 'No Englishman probably has ever been so well qualified to undertake it by previous study as yourself.'[25] The child in Clifton Hill House had become familiar with engravings of many of the *cinquecento* masters, and his father later took him on the

Grand Tour, in which he had conscientiously made notes of all the note-worthy historical and artistic monuments. As a young man he was nourished on the plethora of nineteenth-century literature about the exotic figures of the Renaissance. He pored over Shelley's *Cenci*, George Eliot's *Romola*, and Browning's Renaissance portraits, all of which provided an exciting escape for a restless young Victorian suffering from the *maladie du siècle*. In preparation for the Chancellor's Prize Essay in 1863 he read Michelet's *Histoire de France* and Sismondi's *History of the Italian Republic*; between 1863 and 1871 his knowledge was deepened by Roscoe's biographies of the Medici, Grimm's life of Michelangelo, and Villari's *Savonarola*.

Originally his attention had been drawn to the Italian Renaissance through the Elizabethan drama. As he enlarged his reading of these early plays, he was repeatedly led back to their Italian sources, and the exuberance which infused both Elizabethan and Italian Renaissance literature thrilled him with the sense of discovery experienced by Keats on first opening Chapman's Homer; yet an even more significant enthusiasm than the Elizabethans heightened his interest in the Renaissance. No one embraced the nineteenth-century cult of Hellenism more ardently than Symonds. The Hellenic ideal, which satisfied all his longings, seemed impossible of fulfilment in his own day – 'The Greek voice rings in accord with few souls now', he lamented to Dakyns.[26] None the less, it had been revived in the Renaissance and he found a close connection between the discovery of the classics and the discovery by man of himself and his world. The Renaissance interested him inasmuch as it seemed to have assimilated the spirit of the Greeks, although he realized that its turbulence fell far short of their repose, and he experienced frequent bouts of emotional hostility when he traced the process by which the Church regained control over men's minds. After he had completed the final volume of *Renaissance in Italy*, he remarked wearily to Miss Robinson, 'It was very different when one used to write about Greeks! They gave everything. One had only to express in inadequate words one's sense of the blessing.'[27]

Despite his wide reading, the Chancellor's Essay Prize, and his Bristol lectures on various aspects of the Renaissance, it required considerable temerity for a young man in his early thirties to undertake an ambitious survey which eventually comprehended almost every aspect of the Renaissance. The task was made more formidable by knowing that he would address a wide audience who had acquired a taste for history, and that his work would inevitably be compared with models like Buckle, Grote, and Michelet. The determination with which he began to draw up a plan for the work in 1871 was closely connected with his father's death. When the first shock had passed, he began to feel liberated from a loving but oppressive restriction, and it was more than coincidental that he concentrated on a period characterized by freedom and defiance. And, paradoxically, to his own sense of freedom was coupled a resolve to honour his father's memory, to prove to the father's ghost that the son's feeble body could accomplish impressive feats of which Dr Symonds had never really believed him capable. Although the original project was far more modest than the seven-volume study eventually presented to the public, from the outset Symonds viewed it as a work of immense importance which he approached in a spirit of sober dedication.

Symonds has sometimes been accused of basing *Renaissance in Italy* on secondary literary sources, and it can be argued that it is patently the work not of a professional historian but of a man of letters who viewed history with the same personal bias he brought to an evaluation of literature. The seven volumes reflect the prejudices, passions, and problems of a complex temperament. Symonds's wistful absorption in strong personalities vitalizes the ruthless egoists of *The Age of the Despots*, and even their vices intrigued him as manifestations of the courage to flout conventional morality.[28] His intense interest in the human drama and the aesthetic aspects of the period tended to make him overestimate these so much that he almost totally ignored the great social and economic changes taking place at the time; nor, for all his professed interest in science, did he give more than a passing nod to contemporary developments. Even in the realm of art his inadequacies were apparent, for while his highly developed visual sense was utilized effectively as he placed his reader squarely before Ghiberti's bronze doors of the Baptistry in Florence, or if he could exploit his predilection for an artist like Michelangelo, his limitations in taste (which distressed Bernard Berenson) were revealed by the short shrift he gave to Leonardo. His preoccupation with detail, his inability to select, his anxiety to include everything he could glean about the period, were responsible for a wealth of incidental anecdote, repetition, and sometimes tedious prolixity.

His method was to block out the main sections of each volume and then to overlay them with a mass of ornamental detail, an approach in which he had great confidence as he explains in a letter to Charlotte in 1871: 'What you notice', he says, 'as having struck you is exactly what I want people to notice – I mean my attempt to give a clear view of the Renaissance as a whole, & to build my view up by accumulated details.'[29] His own over-luxuriant prose and fondness for exaggeration often destroyed the objective lucidity which he attempted to impose on his style, an imperfection described by Disraeli in a letter to Lady Bradford: 'I have now read 2/3rd of the Renaissance volume with unflagging interest', he wrote in 1875; '. . . the writer is a complete scholar, and has a grasp of his subject wh., from the rich variety of its elements, can never be one of simplicity, and yet wh., from his complete hold, he keeps perspicuous.

'As he warms with his theme, he even evinces some spark of that divine gift of imagination, in wh. he appeared to me at first deficient. . . .

'What he fails in is style; not that he lacks vigor but taste. He writes like a newspaper man, "our own correspondent", but wants the stillness and refinement and delicacy and music, wh. did not fall to the lot of the active journalist.'[30]

In addition to the personal bias Symonds brought to the subject, *Renaissance in Italy* also reflects a number of late nineteenth-century attitudes. In his acceptance of a sharply-defined period to which he applies the term 'Renaissance', Symonds was accepting the changing contemporary view of the period. In the first part of the century the idea of the Renaissance as an epoch separable from the Middle Ages had not yet emerged. When Macaulay wrote on Machiavelli in 1827 he emphasized many of the characteristics which were to become standard Renaissance associations within a few decades – the new learning, the stimulus of science; while in his description of Machiavelli he summarized the dramatic contrasts which contributed to the exaggerated image of Renaissance man – 'a phantom as monstrous as the portress of hell in Milton, half divinity, half snake, majestic and beautiful above, grovelling and poisonous below'.[31] Nevertheless, Macaulay still referred to the period as 'these Middle Ages'. As the century advanced, through the dominant influence of Comte and Hegel (both were read avidly if not always sympathetically by Symonds), of Taine's racial traits theory (which creeps into *Renaissance in Italy*), and with the demonstration of a process of development by the biological scientists (an idea excitedly embraced by Symonds), historical periods began to be marked off in distinct eras, each with its own peculiar characteristics. Almost invariably, for all who wrote of it – with the single great exception of Ruskin – the Renaissance emerged as one of the great peaks in civilization.

Symonds frequently denied setting up rigid demarcation dates to mark the confines of the period; as early as 1863, while preparing his essay for the Chancellor's Prize, he wrote to Rutson: 'I toil daily at the Renaissance period, but I have not yet come to understand what it is. Each day carries me a step back, and I put the time of reawakening earlier by a century. And each day convinces me that the true period of enlightenment is not yet come, so that the dim past is connected with a Future as yet uncomprehended. In fact there is no such thing as the Renaissance. There is a certain sure growth and development of human nature, there are special laws which regulate the decay and regeneration of Art, there is a sudden madness of reverence for Antiquity, but there is nothing like a clear definite all including movement.'[32] In the Preface to *Wine, Women, and Song*, and in *Renaissance in Italy* to a lesser degree, Symonds echoed Pater's belief expressed in *Studies in the History of the Renaissance* that the origins of the Renaissance could be traced back into the Middle Ages. Yet the fact remains that the Middle Ages were always depicted by him as the Dark Ages: the Church was repressive, the Crusades were hopelessly futile gestures, free enquiry was stifled, man was enslaved by obscurantism. Moreover, as he became increasingly obsessed with his subject, he began to enclose the Renaissance within the hundred years between 1450 and 1550, an era whose characteristics stood out in dramatic contrast to those of the period preceding it.

Symonds had few Roman Catholic friends* and, like most Victorians, he regarded the Church as a strange, slightly sinister institution, an image aggravated by the promulgation of the doctrine of Papal Infallibility in 1871. In his case, this attitude was reinforced by his recoil from the pomp

---

* An exception was the critic and poet, Aubrey de Vere, who was a frequent visitor to Clifton Hill House.

of the services he witnessed in Italian churches. In the final volumes of *Renaissance in Italy* Symonds left no doubt that he attributed the quenching of the enlightenment to the Counter-Reformation, yet he did not altogether disown the view expressed in his early letter to Rutson that the Renaissance was a term which could be applied generally to the progress of mankind; if the advance had suffered a temporary setback it was being liberated again by the discoveries of science.

Renaissance in Italy is a testament to Symonds's faith in science. He formed part of the second wave of reaction to the implications of *The Origin of Species*: evolution was beginning to serve as an affirmation not a gloomy denial of man's potentialities for progress. While he often echoed the nineteenth-century lament that '*Je suis venu trop tard dans un monde trop vieux*', and while he was bewildered by an environment in which traditional stability had been shattered by scientific revelations and men were left to formulate their own faiths, nevertheless, particularly as he grew older, he tended to view the scepticism engendered by science as characteristic of the free, far-ranging mind. One of the longest sections in the entire series was devoted to Bruno, who embodied qualities Symonds admired most – idealism, venturesome thought, and the courage to defy conventions – qualities which he also associated with his modern hero Whitman.

Symonds's devotion to science, first stimulated in him by his father and later deepened by his reading of Comte, Darwin, and Spencer, was so enthusiastic that he attempted to apply the theory of development to the entire culture of the Renaissance, just as he did on a more limited scale to the material of *Shakspere's Predecessors*, written between the appearance of the third and fourth volumes of *Renaissance in Italy*. Such an approach provided him with a convenient means of placing either works of literature, men, or events at various stages of evolution. History became the 'biography of man'. There was something slightly naïve in his eager unreflective espousal of the theory of evolution as offering the explanation for all human phenomena, in which various periods were compared to the youth, maturity, and old age of an individual; and, inevitably, he was led to contradiction, in some cases distortion, of history in his anxiety to accommodate fact to theory. Lacking any real understanding of science, he felt justified in extracting from it those elements which appealed to him. Frequently he claimed that if one viewed life as a predetermined cycle of growth, maturity, and decay, in which the advance of man could be observed in a series of spiral movements, one could only regard the men and works belonging to periods of decline as inevitable consequences of forces beyond their control. Yet, deterministic as this belief tended to be, Symonds shared his generation's faith in progress, attempting to reconcile the two apparently contradictory concepts by a curious leger-demain. The Middle Ages and the Counter-Reformation were inter-preted as temporary halts in the forward march; these interruptions could be explained in modern terms as the periodic conflict between the forces of progress and retrogression, rather than between good and evil as an earlier generation might have explained them. Such Olympian detach-ment enabled him to state at one point that 'unchecked, it is probable that the Renaissance would have swept away much that was valuable and deserved to be permanent'.[33] But in a private letter he expressed his real views: 'I have just finished the last two volumes of my Renaissance in Italy. They are on the Catholic Reaction & the Spanish Hegemony. It is a dismal subject – the tragedy of a nation, the disappointment of a great European hope. I am very glad to have finished it.'[34] The abeyance of tolerance is evident, too, in these final volumes, where he related the history of the Counter-Reformation, particularly in his indignant account of the Spanish Inquisition, even though he had to admit that it did not belong to the story of the Italian Renaissance.

Renaissance in Italy was never conceived as an organic whole, but evolved rather from a series of piecemeal compromises. In 1875 when Symonds finished *The Age of the Despots*, he planned to complete two further volumes, *Italy and the Counter-Reformation* and *Italy in the Middle Ages* which would be rounded off with a final volume, a condensation of the entire series 'into one Cultur Geschichte [*sic*] of the Italians'.[35] However, for a variety of reasons, the original project was radically altered. *Italy in the Middle Ages* – what such a volume would have been is difficult to imagine! – was entirely abandoned. One of the compensa-tions of moving to Europe, he soon realized, was that even if he did not have libraries immediately available, he had access to original sources in Italy, and could expand his original design. The two volumes which were intended to supplement the first volume grew into four – *The Revival of*

Learning, The Fine Arts, and the two volumes of *Italian Literature* – a surprising omission from the first scheme, considering Symonds's interest in the arts. Finally, *Italy and the Counter-Reformation* was transformed into the two parts of volumes VI and VII of *The Catholic Reaction.* In 1880 Symonds told Charlotte that works of this sort 'never seem complete'.[36]

Despite the sweeping scope of the entire series, Symonds's involvement in the Renaissance was dissipated by the fact that for a number of years he contemplated writing a monumental history of Italy, of which the Renaissance would form only one part. In September 1881 he first mentioned the plan to Graham Dakyns. When he broached the idea to Jowett, the latter enthusiastically suggested that he might collaborate with Horatio Brown, a proposal Symonds did not take long to reject. By the time he reached the final volumes of *Renaissance in Italy* he had lost interest in the more ambitious scheme; the preparation of the first draft of *The Catholic Reaction* had deteriorated into dogged persistence, and by November 1885 he confessed to Stevenson that he did not feel strong enough to pursue his research further. Inevitably, the cohesiveness of *Renaissance in Italy* suffered from these constant interruptions and adaptations.

The changes can be attributed in some measure to the impact of Burckhardt on Symonds. There has been a considerable amount of speculation as to what extent Symonds was influenced by the Swiss historian,[37] but there seems no reason to doubt Symonds's own testimony. In the Preface to *The Age of the Despots* in 1875, he stated that Burckhardt's *Die Kultur der Renaissance in Italien* had come to his notice when he had almost completed his first volume.* 'It would be difficult indeed', he goes on to say, 'for me to exaggerate the profit I have derived from the comparison of my opinions with those of a writer so thorough in learning and so delicate in his perceptions as Jacob Burckhardt.'[38] In *The Revival of Learning* he again acknowledged his debt to Burckhardt, but at the same time stressed that 'I have made it my invariable practice . . . to found my own opinions on the study of original sources.'[39] No one can fail to notice that Symonds's sprawling work lacks the tight coherence of Burckhardt's single volume, and it seems probable that Symonds expanded

---

* Originally published in German in 1860; an English translation by Middlemore appeared in 1878.

his work to such an immense length in order to avoid comparison with Burckhardt. Sheer bulk did not necessarily encompass comprehensiveness, for, while both historians followed Michelet's definition of the period as the discovery of the world and of man, Symonds gave far greater prominence to the impressive personalities, the literature, and the revival of learning than did Burckhardt, whose *Kulturgeschichte* was intended to evoke the general spirit of the age by exposing in turn each facet of its culture.

There were other influences which determined the final shape of *Renaissance in Italy*. Symonds must have thought constantly of Pater's collected *Studies in the History of the Renaissance* which he reviewed before he had finished his own first volume; Pater's book might not have appeared to him as an object for emulation, but at least it was a challenge to be surpassed. *His* work on the Renaissance would be far more scholarly, far more substantial than the delicacies concocted by the Brasenose dilettante. Paradoxically, hostile as Symonds felt towards Pater and his epicureanism, he shared Pater's ardent response to the Hellenism of the Renaissance, but his own delight gradually sobered into disillusion with a brief enlightenment quenched abortively by the massive hand of obscurantism.

Another figure whom Symonds could not have failed to take into consideration in the preparation of *Renaissance in Italy* was that of the great Italian literary critic, Francesco De Sanctis, whose *Storia della Letteratura Italiana* had appeared in 1870-1.* Strangely enough, De Sanctis's name never appears in the two volumes on Italian literature (1881), yet the approach of both writers to the literature of the period is too close to be merely coincidental. Both conceived the development of Italian literature from the Middle Ages through the Renaissance to modern times in Hegelian terms as a triad represented respectively by Dante, Ariosto, and Alfieri, although De Sanctis, instead of accepting the death of art in modern culture, saw it rescued from extinction by the persistence of *form*. Implicit in both writers is the didactic assumption that literature expresses the moral fibre of a nation, and occasional passages in Symonds echo De Sanctis's exhortations to his compatriots to stir themselves to new life. Both regarded the Renaissance from an

* I am indebted to Iain Fletcher for drawing my attention to this.

uncompromisingly Protestant viewpoint, except that Symonds's Protestantism was all too clearly allied to scepticism.

The years of close research, the elaborate organization of a chaotic mass of material, and countless hours devoted to describing, explaining, enlarging, qualifying, and revising, had convinced Symonds that his *magnum opus* could be nothing less than an impressive contribution to historical knowledge* – 'the subject is not uninteresting or unimportant', he told the ever-admiring Charlotte, '& for myself, I think I may say without conceit that to treat it from so many points of view as I have done, indicates a somewhat unusual complex of intelligence & information'.[40] Not without reason, he felt bitter because neither the pecuniary emoluments nor the critical recognition were commensurate with the labour it had cost him. His depression following the muted praise of the first volume dogged him throughout the work. 'Nobody knows or cares about Italy', he complained to Miss Robinson in 1881, '& what they say about my "eloquence" is stereotyped. Creighton who does know, took occasion to write a dull slighting notice in the Academy, touching my book with dry fingertips.† This sort of lack of comradeship in literature grieves me a little. But what does it all signify? I have got my heart set on other work, & I cannot expect the English public (to use the old proverb) to drink out of my pond, even if I bring it up to their very noses.'[41]

Symonds's definition of the Renaissance as 'the resurgence of personality in the realm of thought', has been criticized as a romantic simplification, the view of a man who was determined to find in the period elements lacking in his own century, and eager to emulate the audacity of its vital figures. In other words, his interpretation of history

---

* J. H. Shorthouse, the author of *John Inglesant*, records that Symonds, as the Italian authority he saw himself, '*with the irritating stupidity of great men*', thought little of Shorthouse's impressionistic account of the 'Palace of Umbria' (*Life and Letters of J. H. Shorthouse*, I, Macmillan and Co., 1905, p. 274).

† Mandell Creighton, the historian and subsequently bishop of Peterborough and later London, was at the time working on the first two volumes of his own *History of the Papacy* which were published in 1882. Despite Symonds's disappointment, Creighton praised *Italian Literature*: 'It is full of just criticism, and is free from exaggerated admiration' (*The Academy*, XX, 13 Aug. 1881, 112). Symonds's all too frequent inconsistency is demonstrated by the fact that he wrote both to Creighton and to the Editor of *The Academy* to say how much he liked the review. As for Creighton's work, Symonds found it 'a really great book' (Brown, p. 429).

was shaped by his own desires and frustrations. Moreover, the seven volumes are too detailed, their impact weakened by too many diffused interests. This lack of integration reflects Symonds's central weakness as a writer, as a scholar, and as an historian. He found it difficult to involve himself so completely in a subject that he could not be deflected by other temporary attractions. 'I have got my heart set on other work. . .' And in turn the other work would be abandoned for a fresh enthusiasm. *Renaissance in Italy* was written to impress with its bulk, to make a name for himself with the importance of its theme; the prodigious labour it necessitated served as an opiate for his own problems, while the passages of romance and colour offered the vicarious satisfactions of a less inhibited age. But it was not a labour of love, and as he was finishing its final pages, he sighed, 'It is odd to be always filling note books and writing chapters upon things w^h do not very greatly signify to any human soul.'[42]

III

The completion of *Renaissance in Italy* did not mean the end of his Italian studies. In the spring of 1886 A. H. Bullen wrote him that J. C. Nimmo, the publisher of handsome library editions, had arranged to publish a fine edition of Benvenuto Cellini's autobiography but had found that the man commissioned to do the translation was lamentably incompetent, and had asked Bullen to enquire of Symonds whether he would be willing to take over the job. Nimmo offered him an honorarium of £100 and specified that the translation must be finished by the end of August, when he proposed to print five hundred copies. Symonds was not averse to the scheme because the personality of Cellini fascinated him, but Nimmo's terms were completely unacceptable. Through Bullen's intervention the fee was eventually raised to two hundred guineas and Bullen also tried to extract from Nimmo a promise to print a thousand copies.

Symonds plunged into the work enthusiastically. Memoirs exerted a particular fascination for him as the most genuine revelation of a man, of far more interest than the work of the artist. The restless, passionate Cellini, the complete Renaissance man, who developed and expressed all his capacities, stirred Symonds's imagination so greatly that during the months he worked on the translation he achieved an almost total identification with his subject, 'bones, marrow, flesh, and superficies'.[43] The curious point is that Cellini's life was the complete antithesis of Symonds's frustrated existence. 'His autobiography is the record of action and passion', Symonds wrote in the Introduction. 'Suffering, enjoying, enduring, working with restless activity, hating, hovering from place to place as impulse moves him, the man presents himself dramatically by his deeds and spoken words, never by his ponderings and meditative broodings.'[44]

As Nimmo had advised him not to produce too literal a translation, he set out to achieve the effect of Cellini's unself-conscious, animated talk without changing the original content. Despite the looseness of the translation, he went to enormous pains to discover the exact meaning of certain words current in Cellini's time. For many years Symonds had admired Goethe's translation, but he was very critical of Thomas Roscoe's expurgated version in which entire episodes of Cellini's uninhibited life were misrepresented. Just as he had urged Mrs Clough many years before not to exclude any of Clough's poems from the 1869 edition, so now he reiterated his conviction that, 'if a book is worth translating, it ought to be set forth in full'.[45] This enabled him to take a sly poke at Victorian hypocrisy: 'I hold him for a most veracious man', he said of Cellini. 'His veracity was not of the sort which is at present current. It had no hypocrisy or simulation in it.'[46] Catherine showed unusual interest in the book and wrote out large portions of it to Symonds's dictation. Once he had begun, he rushed the book through to completion and laid his pen down just before midnight on 10 November, his twenty-second wedding anniversary.

To Symonds's disappointment, Nimmo brought out only the five hundred copies he had originally stipulated, with an additional two hundred and fifty copies for America, in an ornate two-volume edition with etchings by F. Languillermie. Symonds, when sending a complimentary copy to Sir Henry Layard, apologized for these etchings as being 'middle class below contempt'.[47] Nevertheless, *Cellini* proved an immense success and was sold out in record time, to be followed in 1888 and 1889 by a second and third edition.

Nimmo was so delighted that he suggested that Symonds now undertake a translation of the memoirs of an eighteenth-century nobleman,

Count Carlo Gozzi. The picturesque aspects of Venetian decadence intrigued Symonds, and here again he had the opportunity of penetrating to the very soul of a man. However, Gozzi failed to absorb him as Cellini had done. 'Gozzi will not do', he told Brown. 'And yet I do not see my way of getting out of Gozzi . . . his Memoirs are hardly worth translating, and their interest depends upon such trivialities. . . .'[48]

Other difficulties arose. The National Vigilance Association were sniffing after publishers who printed what they considered improper translations. In 1888, through their instrumentality, Henry Vizetelly was charged for publishing an obscene libel in Zola's *The Soil (La Terre)*, fined £100, and placed on a year's probation. The following year he was again charged at the Old Bailey after he had defiantly reissued Zola's works in a slightly expurgated form. This time he went to prison for three months and his health broke down under the strain. Alarmed by these pressures, Nimmo suggested that Symonds agree to a privately printed edition of the Gozzi memoirs.* Symonds indignantly refused because such an arrangement would mean that the whole responsibility would be thrown on his own shoulders. The problem was eventually resolved by the suppression – despite all Symonds's previous indignant statements on censorship – of the love stories which might cause offence, while the Preface was written primarily to reassure that section of the public for whom he felt most contempt. He emphasized that Gozzi's candour was 'the candour of a cleanly heart',[49] yet he abjectly confessed that he believed it necessary to remove 'those passages and phrases which might have caused offence to some of my readers'. But then, Gozzi did not mean very much to him.

The translation occupied a year of his time. 'Having begun it, I stuck to it out of pure cussedness',[50] he admitted to Dakyns when he finally finished the book in March 1889. The only importance even Symonds could find in it was the fact that no one in England, with the exception of 'Vernon Lee', had previously known anything about Gozzi. But he had to agree with Brown that the book was boring – 'Think how bored I must have been, boiling him down and trimming him up !' he exclaimed.[51]

In November 1890 Nimmo wrote to offer him the unexpectedly large

---

* *Giovanni Boccaccio*, a short monograph written for Nimmo in 1887, was held up by the publisher until 1895 for the same reasons.

sum of five hundred guineas for a life of Michelangelo. Despite his own comfortable private income, Symonds was always acutely concerned about the money he received for his work. He constantly expressed contempt for bourgeois values, yet at times he seemed to estimate success in terms of cash received. However, his preoccupation with literary earnings was by no means entirely self-centred because he was genuinely disturbed about the financial plight of English writers, a subject on which he frequently held forth eloquently. Five hundred guineas, especially from the hard-bargaining Nimmo, was a windfall of the first order, and the possibility of writing a life of Michelangelo presented an exciting challenge. Nevertheless, even in Davos he was beginning to complain of constant tiredness. The thought of the immense labour necessary for a monumental work (for such it would have to be) oppressed him. 'I want to sleep more than to think', he sighed wearily.[52]

He could not resist work for long. By March 1891 he was working nine hours a day on the biography and had written the first chapter. During the next year Michelangelo became so compulsively engrossing that Symonds seemed possessed by the spirit of the man. He read and re-read every study of the artist he could lay his hands on; he bombarded Michelangelo scholars with queries by post; he travelled the length and breadth of Italy tracking down everything related to the artist. Am Hof overflowed with photographs of Michelangelo's works,* but because he failed to have them mounted, most of them lay 'curled up like so many hundreds of Aaron's rods turned into serpents on my tables & my floor'.[53]

The initial problem was to make a new Life 'fresh'. Although he felt optimistic that he could 'clarify the whole liquid of his biography',[54] he was unable to present a new interpretation unless he could obtain permission, hitherto denied to scholars, to examine the archives in the Casa Buonarroti in Florence. Through the influence of his friend, Mrs Janet Ross, the Italian Government finally granted him permission to work in the Archives for two months, and October 1891 found him reading his way through six large folios of unedited letters. A German scholar, Professor K. Frey, who was also working on Michelangelo's papers, caused certain difficulties. 'He hates me', Symonds complained

* Sidney Colvin, who was now keeper of the prints and drawings in the British Museum, arranged to have most of the museum's collection of Michelangelo's drawings photographed for him. Edward Poynter was responsible for the final selection of the illustrations for the book.

to Brown, 'and tries to keep all the MSS. to himself. It is really very annoying. We have to use the same index to the Codices, which causes a perpetual rub.'[55] Still, this minor irritation was overlooked in his exciting discovery that certain of Michelangelo's letters had been suppressed and distorted by previous biographers.

When he had extracted the vital information, he went off to Rome to refresh his memory with Michelangelo's principal works. He was convinced that Michelangelo, as an architect, was 'incredibly unequal, a veritable amateur in this branch, as he always said he was',[56] an opinion he transmitted in more modified form to the biography. To Herbert Horne, the architect and editor of *The Century Guild Hobby-Horse*, he admitted that of all the arts, architecture was the one for which he had the least sympathetic understanding; as for Michelangelo's efforts, 'I am fairly puzzled & at sea. So much of his work in this way seems mere decorative quibbling; & yet the total effect is so pictorially impressive. It seems so wrong in its principles & still so genial in its results.'[57]

Symonds's temperamental difficulty in appreciating anything with which he could not fully sympathize led him to regret the emphasis on the other-world in the frescoes of the Sistine Chapel. With his Greek sensitivity to the beauty of the male body, it was the sculpture that particularly appealed to him. When he revisited the statue of David at the Accademia in Florence, he was struck as he had never been before by its exquisite beauty. 'Among other things', he told Gosse, 'penem juvenis et testiculos mirabili arte ad verum effigium modelli sui singulariter conformati perfecit sculptor.'*[58] When he came to write of David in the biography, he remarked that the statue was unique among Michelangelo's figures as it 'strongly recalls the model',[59] whereas so much of the artist's later work was characterized by a generalized 'monotonous impressiveness'. He pointed out that David's torso was not in scale with his enormous hands and feet, and that he 'wants at least two years to become a fully developed man'.[60] His description of David as 'a colossal hobbledehoy' irritated Herbert Horne, and in an otherwise favourable review of the book in *The Fortnightly Review* he singled out the phrase as an indication of Symonds's lack of any real knowledge of the arts. What Symonds was

* This is jargonized Latin: 'The sculptor, with wonderful skill, made the youth's penis and testicles in the true likeness of his extraordinarily shaped model.'

looking for, as he did in all art, was human passion or the physical presence of a real man behind the work. Architecture could not reveal this and so it had little interest for him.

Between June and September, while he grew visibly more haggard and thin, he continued to write as though possessed, with the briefest of intervals spared for food and rest. 'The pace is killing', he admitted ruefully to Gosse. 'And I can hardly say *why* I have steamed along so. Nor do I know in the least what the literary result is; for I have read over nothing, being able to carry every detail of the work done in my head, so as to avoid involuntary repetitions and omissions without turning backward.'[61] Madge eased the strain to some extent by copying out the quotations. Occasional escape was found in 'crude life', in drinking and sleeping with young Swiss ('There is my life expressed. Ardent literature and moving fact: each reacting on the other, & driving the soul of the man to what God only knows his destiny will be...').[62] The immediate drive behind his frenetic industry was his compulsion to learn definitely whether Michelangelo was a homosexual or not. 'With the man's spirit I am intoxicated', he confessed to Gosse in another letter. 'I have wrestled with his "psyche" so that I seem absorbed in him. But I cannot say that this close study makes me sympathetic to his artistic ideal.'[*63] He added, 'if he had any sexual energy at all (which is doubtful) he was a U.'[†] What Symonds suspected from the suppressed letters, and from such works as David and the red chalk drawing of the archers at Windsor Castle, was that Michelangelo had homosexual leanings which he sublimated in his generalized studies of the human form. In a discussion of the sculpture, he stressed the crudity of his treatment of the female body: 'The woman is, for him, an allegory, something he has not approached and handled.'[‡64]

---

* As Symonds explained to Charles Kains-Jackson, the book would not 'expound the Principles of Renaissance Art so much as explain the psychology of a very peculiar artist-nature. Out of fifteen chapters only three are devoted to distinct criticism of art: one dealing with MAB's ideal of form & successive manners; another with his architecture; the third with his poetry & its underlying emotions' (letter dated Davos Platz, 4 March 1892, Weeks Collection).

† He is referring to the term 'Urning' devised by Carl Heinrich Ulrichs to denote a homosexual. See Chapter XI.

‡ Symonds had been fascinated by the Italian psychiatrist and criminologist, Cesare Lombroso's *L'uomo di Genio*, which was published in 1888. He could not accept Lombroso's close connection between genius and insanity, nor could he agree that Michelangelo's complete indifference to women was an anomaly.

In Chapter XII, 'Michelangelo as Poet and Man of Feeling', – the chapter which he found the most difficult in the whole book to write – he had to discuss his findings in the Buonarroti Archives and to analyse the nature of Michelangelo's sexuality. Some biographers and historians had made much of the artist's friendship with Vittoria Colonna. Symonds discovered that Michelangelo's nephew had perpetrated a 'pious fraud' by falsely stating that certain ardent letters from Michelangelo were written to a woman whom he revered as a close friend but for whom he had no sexual feeling. The letters were in fact, Symonds found, addressed to a young Roman nobleman. 'There is something inexpressibly pathetic', he wrote to Dakyns after his visit to the Archives, 'in turning over the passionate letters & verses, indited by aged genius & youthful beauty, after the lapse of four centuries and a half. . . .'[65] With the discovery of the previous suppressions, he realized, as he told Gosse, that 'My book will, to some extent, be revolutionary. But I am afraid of the task before me: truth-telling, without seeming to dot i's wilfully. I need not say that I have discovered no scandal about MA.'[66]

Truth had to be told, especially when Symonds knew his discoveries to be the result of serendipity rather than deliberate search for scandal, but the truth was too blunt for most of his readers and had to be approached circumspectly. The chapter emerged as a skilful blend of tact, candour, and propagandizing. When he came to discuss Michelangelo's relation-ships with Vittoria Colonna and the young Roman, Tommaso Cavalieri, he stressed that the suppression and distortion of facts had been a betrayal of truth; to explain away 'the obvious meaning' of the letters and sonnets was to injure all the human beings concerned. He then went on to demonstrate that Michelangelo's poems are pervaded by the doctrines of the Phaedrus and the Symposium – a connection which had first whetted Symonds's interest in them many years before – and he pointed out their many references to Uranian and Pandemic, celestial and vulgar Eros: 'The tap-root of feeling is Greek.'[67] Michelangelo is described as 'one of those exceptional, but not uncommon men, who are born with sensibilities abnormally deflected from the ordinary channel'.[68] But Michelangelo's emotion, he assured his readers, remained 'ideal, imaginative, chaste: such, in fact, as the philosophers in the best age conceived and formulated'.[69] With his readers' fears allayed, two pages further on he slipped in one significant sentence about men of Michelangelo's temperament: 'In Hellas they found a social environment favourable to their free development and action, but in Renaissance Italy the case was different.'[70]

In his review of the book on its publication in 1893, Herbert Horne drew attention to the fact that Symonds had been confronted with the problem facing a critic who was forced to analyse the letters of Languet to Sir Philip Sidney or to discuss the relationship of Shakespeare to 'Mr W. H.'* Symonds's interpretation, he concluded, was completely successful because it was not 'a series of pleasing speculations, but a delicate chain of arguments, based upon authoritative documents'.[71]

In Venice, Symonds, as we have seen, had his only profound experience of Italy. His visual sense was satisfied by its art and its natural beauty, but he remained always the perceptive, appreciative, detached tourist. He journeyed to Italy with his mind stored with literary associations, and he looked for a past that he was destined never to find.

He could reinvoke it through historical research but even here he experienced disappointment. The explanation for Symonds's reluctance to commit himself completely to the Renaissance is clear. It was a period of release, of renewed energy, of individuals comparatively free to achieve self-development — but not as free as the Greeks had been. What had been sanctioned in Greek society was castigated and suppressed by the Church. Had Michelangelo lived in Athens, his letters would not have contained that note of wistful yearning.

* In his study of Sir Philip Sidney, Symonds does not drop the slightest hint that there might have been something slightly irregular in the relationship between Sidney and Languet. The ambiguity of Shakespeare's friendship with Mr W. H. intrigued him for years, and he exchanged letters with Wilde on the subject.

CHAPTER XI

The Problem

'THE PROBLEM' – homosexuality – was the overwhelming obsession of Symonds's life. His inclinations affected his friendships, his sympathies coloured his tastes, and all his writing – biography, criticism, poetry, or history – was influenced by this central fact about the man. The satisfactions which he was able to extract from his situation gave his life its most significant meaning, but more frequently its frustrations made his existence a torment.

To attempt to probe into the psychological depths of his neurosis would be beyond the scope of this book. Symonds himself believed that his condition was congenital; modern psychiatrists in the wake of Freud attribute inversion to some early conditioning, usually a fixation on a female (in most cases, of course, the child's mother). According to Symonds he had only the faintest memory of his mother, who died when he was four. This obliteration in itself does not rule out the possibility of her death having left the child with an irreparable sense of loss, for 'childhood amnesia' is a very common condition among children who want to blot out some painful memory. Unfortunately, there is no evidence beyond hypothesis to reconstruct his life before the age of four, but his mother must have been his greatest source of love, especially as he was the only one of her sons to survive. Even as an invalid, she would want to have her children around her bed and her room would have been the centre of the household.

Symonds did retain a very clear recollection of the incident in the carriage with his mother when the horses bolted. The experience was so traumatic that it is understandable that his memory of her appearance should have been inseparably associated with it – the white frightened face, extremely pretty and feminine, framed by a mass of golden curls under a pink bonnet.

Madge, Katharine and Lotta Symonds, 1893

Janet Symonds

Agnes Mary Robinson

Benjamin Jowett

Havelock Ellis, 1891

Edmund Gosse

Miss Sykes, a forceful aggressive woman, never took the place of his mother. The lovable Sophie Girard might have done so if he had had more opportunity of being with her. The first woman for whom he formed any strong emotional attachment was his sister Charlotte, and there undoubtedly existed between them an unusually intense relationship bordering on the romantic. As a young woman, Charlotte was also extremely close to her father, a complex situation in which Symonds closed the tight triumvirate, unconscious of the subtle overtones of an intimacy upon which his emotions fed ravenously. When he first began to be aware of women, it is significant that he attached himself to older married women – Jenny Lind and Mrs Butler – from whom there would be no danger of any romantic demands. The girl whom he eventually chose for a wife was an austere, dark, big-boned creature, utterly unlike his mother. This difference, and the fact that she did not attract him physically, may have made her easier for him to pursue, since pursuit would involve no betrayal of his mother. Repeatedly he described Catherine as his 'friend', and it is not surprising that neither man nor wife found satisfaction in the physical aspects of their marriage. But there were two women to whom he was strongly drawn aesthetically and physically – Rosa Engel and Agnes Mary Robinson. Both were enchantingly pretty, ultra-feminine blondes with the same type of beauty as his mother, especially Miss Robinson with her absurd little parasol and enormous hats trimmed with cabbage roses. Attractive as he found Rosa, the thought of marrying her never crossed his mind, and he was already married when he met Miss Robinson. The implications to be drawn from his reactions to these various women are highly interesting, and all the threads of the network seem to lead back to the frail figure of his mother.

Then there was the formidable figure of Dr Symonds, dominating the first thirty years of his life. Competent, self-assured, in vigorous health, his father seemed everything the sickly little boy could never be. In all seriousness, in middle life, Symonds still described his father as representing the apex of the Symonds line, and himself as a symbol of its inevitable decline. He always tended to associate himself with his mother's side of the family who were delicate and prone to nervous disorders. As he grew older, another role was superimposed upon the ideal conception of his father – that of the moral censor. His father spoke for society at large when he disapproved of his son's aesthetic ideals, and impressed him with the gravity of his antisocial behaviour. It was only after his father's death that Symonds began to twist his way out of the tight coils of conventional pressures which had been choking him for over half his life. It is probably significant that in his subsequent relations with young men, he treated them with a distinctly fatherly attitude.

At a very early age Symonds began to manifest homosexual tendencies. While it is true, as Freud pointed out, that the sexual drive is initially undifferentiated, it does not follow that those who persist in a preference for their own sex therefore prove the existence of an inborn bias, as Symonds claimed. In his Memoirs and letters to Havelock Ellis, he laid triumphant stress on the fact that while he and his young male cousins shared early homosexual experimentation, the interests of the latter were later diverted to women. What Symonds failed to realize was that his own bias might have been formed irrevocably by some trauma predating these early intimacies.

Until his middle thirties, Symonds's overt sexual impulses were romanticized in poetic daydreams, and any physical contact was confined to the gentlest of caresses. The abrasive conflict between moral dicta and compelling need rubbed like a canker at the core of the man, and his repressions and longings inevitably found an outlet in symbolic form within his dreams. The residue of troubled dreams haunted him for days afterwards. In one, which had a particularly oppressive effect, he dreamt that he was the owner of a magnificent estate through which he wandered happily, examining every part of it with proud possessiveness, though now and then his pleasure was assailed by a vague, disquieting sense of unease. Then his eldest daughter, Janet, rode up to him on her pony – just as she had often done in the days when they lived in Clifton – accompanied by a robust young groom. He looked up into the lad's eyes, and suddenly recognized the 'devil's brand', the evil that disturbed his tranquillity – 'the misery that levels and makes prisoners of all men who are marked by it'.[1]

Through his interest in the Society for Psychical Research, Symonds began to record many of his dreams and sent some of the more unusual ones to F. W. H. Myers. Others he noted down in his journal and attempted to interpret their content; although, in a pre-Freudian era, the

existence of substitute symbols and displacements escaped him. Yet
frequently he was struck by the disparity between apparently trivial
content and the disturbed reaction of the dreamer. Some dreams he
actually published, naïvely unaware of the implications which would
immediately strike later readers, sophisticated in the lore of Freudian
analysis. To a long poem, 'Midnight at Baiae', published in *The Artist* of
March 1893* he appended a note that the poem had actually been dreamt
by him. The atmosphere is reminiscent of an Edgar Allen Poe fantasy as
he slips stealthily, compelled by irresistible control, through a dark palace
whose eeriness is heightened by the barking of watch-dogs in the distance.
His footfalls are muffled by warm silky furs. Eventually he enters a high
narrow room whose walls are lined with phallic horns holding amber oil
and creamed essence. On a couch lies a beautiful young man who, on
closer examination, is found to be dead, his throat slashed and his body
bruised and battered by the onslaughts of a vicious passion. The whole
dream is charged with a Huysmans' fascination in exotic evil.

Desolate terrain is the most common landscape of his dreams. High
rocky mountains fall into sharp declivities, plains open into chasms and
flaming lakes. Often the dreams are softened by the piercing sweetness of
Willie Dyer's first kiss, or by the vision of a handsome youth who
stretches out longing arms to him. But all too frequently the inhabitants
of his dream-world are sinister, menacing figures. The following dream is
particularly indicative of his deepest fears, his most repressed desires, and
the rationalizations by which he managed to suppress the id even in this
somnambulant state.†

It seemed [he recalled] that a friend had come to me, and told me that, in
the town where we then were, there was a Wax work show. It was worth a
visit, he heard, and one only paid 4 francs for entrance. But the worst folk in
the place frequented it; and the men who gained by it, were *Chanteurs* who
made a sinister profit by the passions they aroused in its frequenters. I said that
it was surely our business, as students of humanity, to go there, and that as concerned the *Chantage*, I guessed we could hold our own. When we got inside, I

---

* It is difficult to attribute a date with any certainty to these dreams. A form of this poem
originally appeared in the privately printed *Lyra Viginti Chordatum*, probably published in the
early seventies.

† It is also an extraordinarily sophisticated version of his early childhood reverie. See above
p. 20.

soon lost sight of my friend, and was mixed up with a set of men, and all men, who interested me by their manifold types of crime and lust and hereditary vice.

The objects, cunningly presented to us in waxwork, were all of them exquisite and far-fetched *Simulacra* of obscenities. And the showmen, like devils, pressed them upon our attention, seeming to divine each casual spectator's hidden proclivities, and threatening us in coarse terms when we refused to order copies at considerable sums of money. To have shown our faces there, they said, was enough to ruin our reputations, and we might just as well square them by taking home with us a memento we could put up in our houses and serve like domestic deities of pleasure.[2]

After Symonds moved to Europe and began to abandon himself freely to his impulses, he enjoyed many forms of sexual activity with a wide variety of men. In his Memoirs, and in his anonymous case-history slipped unobtrusively into *Sexual Inversion*, he made a special point of stressing the fact that his health improved appreciably after his long-repressed desires were gratified. There is probably some truth in this belief to which he clung so tenaciously. On the other hand, the greater truth seems to have been that the dry clear air of Davos benefited him more than anything else; when he visited England or Venice, where he also had many sexual experiences, his health declined again.

Symonds's attitude to homosexuality* was riddled with contradictions and rationalizations. He was attracted to handsome, athletic young men of the lower classes, a preference he justified with the explanation that he sought 'some uncontaminated child of Nature'.[3] Symonds did not share Arnold's view of the brutalized working classes. Invariably influenced by his own inclinations, he regarded their greater tolerance to sexual deviation as an emancipated contrast to the inhibited, hypocritical bourgeoisie – *ergo*, the working classes were honest in their dealings, spontaneous in their reactions, capable of genuine emotion. He did not approve of the attitude prevalent among many of his own generation and class that the working classes provided fair game for sexual exploitation; unlike Wilde and Lord Ronald Gower, the sculptor who served as the original of Lord Henry in *The Picture of Dorian Gray*, Symonds did not seem to find any perverse pleasure in 'slumming',† but he found it

---

* A term he almost never used. He preferred 'unisexual love' or 'Comradeship' or various generic terms derived from Ulrichs' coinage, 'Urning'.

† But see dream on p. 265.

possible to rationalize a situation in which his partner was totally free
from a sense of guilt or one which would not be complicated by the
problems of social intercourse among equals. On the other hand, he could
not divest himself entirely of his own middle-class background and its
inherent suspicion of sex. Sexual intimacies must always be romanticized
or idealized into 'comradeship' or 'adhesiveness', and he was shocked to
the core by the defiantly unsentimental approach of Roden Noel and
Lord Ronald Gower.

Symonds also laid a great deal of emphasis on the fact that there were
two kinds of inversion. Here again he reflected a basic Victorian distrust
of sex in his distinction between casual carnality and the purer, more
idealized comradeship of the Greeks with its manly, athletic overtones.
Of Lord Ronald and another friend with similar inclinations, he wrote
disapprovingly: 'They saturate one's spirit in U . . . threm* [*sic*] of the
rankest most diabolical kind.'[4] When an admirer, Oscar Wilde, sent him
a copy of *Lippincott's Magazine* (July 1890) containing 'The Picture of
Dorian Gray', he was distressed by 'the morbid and perfumed manner of
treating such psychological subjects',[5] which, he feared, would only
confirm the worst suspicions of the uninformed. His own wish, he
claimed, was to establish a permanent relationship not unlike a marriage,
and this he certainly attempted to do with Christian Buol and Angelo
Fusato. On the other hand, he was often seized with a desire for a passing
stranger. In the period between 1878 and 1890 he made advances to
scores of men, yet the anomaly between principle and action never seemed
to disturb him unduly. The complexities of Symonds's motivations were
so intricately enmeshed that it is almost impossible to disentangle factual
truth from poetic truth.

There was a further contradiction embodied in his admiration for
Greek literature. On that memorable night when he was eighteen and
had sat up until dawn in the house in Regent's Park reading the *Phaedrus*
and the *Symposium*, the true nature of his emotions seemed to be revealed
to him and given a poetic, idealistic sanction. The Greek conception of
love between men remained the greatest influence of his entire life, yet in
middle age he began to condemn the teaching of Greek in schools. In
January 1891 on the appointment of Glazebrook as Headmaster at

* See p. 280.

Clifton, Symonds expressed strong views about the future of Greek: 'I hope they are going to give up the study of Greek', he told Dakyns. 'They teach it so infernally that it had better be done away. And the Greek voice rings in accord with few souls now.

'Will the Greek classics survive in translations? I doubt. That, as you know, is Jowett's hope. But they do not form a Bible – have no relation to religion and the bourgeoisie, & finally unless "Set to the tune of Amanda" are indecorous.'[6] Less than a fortnight later, in reply to Dakyns's protests, he had changed his mind, and declared, 'I am of opinion that all engaged upon the work of translation from the Greek are doing good service to culture.'[7] But when Jowett was translating the *Symposium* in 1888, Symonds warned him of the dangers of exposing impressionable young men to its doctrines, and the ingenuous old man shook his head in bewilderment, maintaining that Plato was using only a figure of speech.* The following year he thwarted a plan of Jowett's to write an essay on the subject. 'He is so thoroughly off the spot that no good could come of it', he wrote with relief to Dakyns. 'He says, par exemple, that παιδεροτία [pederasty] in the Phaedrus, the Symposium, the Charmides, the Lysis, is "a matter of metaphor". What he means I cannot imagine. But an excursus written to demonstrate this point of view could not fail, I think, to be infelicitous, & might lead to scoffing criticism upon his sophistic habit of mind. The fact is that he feels a little uneasy about the propriety of diffusing this literature in English, & wants to persuade himself that there can be no harm in it to the imagination of youth. We went through the whole Symposium last summer word by word; & I must say I thought it very funny to be lending my assistance to a man of his opinion in the effort to catch the subtlest nuances of that "anachronistic" dialogue.'[8]

In actual fact, Symonds was quite unconcerned about the effect of Greek literature on young men. Almost mischievously he was trying to draw Jowett's attention to the anomaly of a situation in which Plato was held up as the greatest of the classics. Teachers tried to pretend that his very clear message could be interpreted only as a series of metaphors; whereas, he tried to tell Jowett, if Plato were read correctly, he would be

---

* Symonds also wrote to Oscar Browning urging him to point out to the public the dangers of Greek literature (H. E. Wortham, *Oscar Browning*, Constable & Co. Ltd., 1927, p. 261).

found to advocate something from which the Victorians would recoil in horror.

Symonds had alluded to this same aspect of British hypocrisy three years before when he sent a public letter to *The Academy*, protesting against the horrified outcry that had arisen over the publication of Sir Richard Burton's *Arabian Nights Entertainment*. 'In the lack of lucidity, which is supposed to distinguish English folk', he declared bluntly, 'our middle class *censores morum* strain at the great gnat of a privately circulated translation of an Arabic classic, while they daily swallow the camel of higher education based upon minute study of Greek and Latin literature. When English versions of Theocritus and Ovid, of Plato's *Phaedrus* and the *Ecclesiasusae*, now within the reach of every schoolboy, have been suppressed, then and not till then can a "plain and literal" rendering of the *Arabian Nights* be denied with any colour of consistency to adult readers.'*[9]

The fact that Symonds was undisturbed by the possible 'corruption' of the young is borne out by his deep-rooted conviction that homosexuality was congenital. Of Schrenk-Notzing's theory of suggestion, he wrote to Havelock Ellis: 'The weakness of Suggestion as a principle seems to me to be this. All boys are exposed to pretty much the same sort of sexual suggestions & associations in early life, & all of them are certainly very soon familiar with the male organ in other individuals. The fact that the majority are uninfluenced by these suggestions, while the minority feel the stirrings of sexual instinct under the impact seems to prove that in the sace [*sic*] of the latter, there is an inborn bias toward homosexuality.'[10] One might ask why, feeling as he did, he should (as late as 1889) have expressed horror at the pernicious influence of Dr Vaughan over the boys in his charge at Harrow?† Time and again he reiterated that he himself was obeying the inexorable law of his own nature, yet he frequently tripped over contradictions in his arguments. At one point in his Memoirs he suggests that his drives might have been normalized as a

---

* A. H. Bullen was shocked by Symonds's defence and wrote to tell him that, in his opinion, 'those notes of Burton are often intolerable. The Marquis de Sade would have shaken his head over some things. Of late the demand for bawdy books has become startlingly large. If the study of "Anthropology" goes on at this rate heaven only knows what we shall reach in the next generation' (MS. letter, dated Residence, British Museum, 12 Oct. 1885, University of Bristol).

† When he was collecting his case-histories for *Sexual Inversion* he told Ellis that schoolboy vices seemed to play an insignificant part in the formation of sexual patterns.

young man if his father had encouraged him to frequent brothels: then immediately he realizes that he could not have followed this course because of his fear of venereal disease; and later he speculates as to whether he might have had a normal marriage if his wife had not found sex so distasteful. Symonds was so tormented and bewildered by the unpalatable truths which he was forced to face about himself, that he desperately flung about among various explanations in his anxiety to achieve some sort of *modus vivendi*.

As a young man in England, he was extremely careful to conceal his proclivities from all but his closest friends. After he moved to Switzerland he became much bolder about his liaisons, and by the time he died a large group of people were aware that he was a homosexual, although the information was generally divulged by a lifted eyebrow or a cryptic hint. On 26 March 1884 Henry James recorded in his notebook:

Edmund Gosse mentioned to me the other day a fact which struck me as a possible *donnée*. He was speaking of J. A. S., the writer (from whom, in Paris, the other day I got a letter), of his extreme and somewhat hysterical aestheticism, etc: the sad condition of his life, exiled to Davos by the state of his lungs, the illness of his daughter, etc. Then he said that, to crown his unhappiness, poor S's wife was in no sort of sympathy with what he wrote; disapproving of its tone, thinking his books immoral, pagan, hyper-aesthetic, etc. 'I have never read any of John's works. I think them most *undesirable*!' It seemed to me *qu'il y avait là un drame – un drame intime*; the opposition between the narrow, cold, Calvinistic wife, a rigid moralist; and the husband, impregnated – even to morbidness – with the spirit of Italy, the love of beauty, of art, the aesthetic view of life, and aggravated, made extravagant and perverse, by the sense of his wife's disapproval.[11]

The result of the *donnée* was 'The Author of Beltraffio' which appeared in the *English Illustrated Magazine* in June and July 1884. On 9 June James sent a note to Gosse by hand: 'Perhaps I *have* divined the innermost cause of J. A. S.'s discomfort – but I don't think I seize on p. 57 exactly the allusion you refer to. I am therefore devoured with curiosity as to this further revelation. Even a post-card (in covert words) would relieve the suspense of the perhaps-already-too-indiscreet-H. J.' And at the bottom of the note he ordered his messenger, '*Wait answer.*'*[12]

* James must be referring to the MS., because the story in the *English Illustrated Magazine* begins on p. 563. The protagonist of James's story is a novelist, Mark Ambient, who bears

The information did not need to be conveyed so secretly because, as he grew older, Symonds became almost reckless in his proclamation of the fact. When he visited England in the summer of 1892 he was accompanied by Angelo, and his friends were informed that it would be impossible for him to stay with them unless they could find accommodation for Angelo as well. However, only two years before, he had chosen his words carefully when he wrote to Mrs Janet Ross asking her if he might bring Angelo with him on a visit to Poggio Gherardo: 'He is an old peasant, has been with me for ten years, & is a very good fellow. Just now I am really dependent on him while travelling.'[13] Mrs Ross's reaction, when confronted by a dazzlingly handsome 'old peasant' of thirty-three, is not recorded!

In a moving letter to his beloved Madge, written during the last summer of his life, he attempted to explain to her his conception of love.

When I was your age [he confided], & for a long time after, I contented myself . . . with seeing & admiring people, entering by imagination into sympathy with their lives. I now want to love them also. I do not much believe in knowing anybody, even oneself. But I am sure one can love immensely. And I love beauty with a passion that burns the more I grow old. I love beauty above virtue, & think that nowhere is beauty more eminent than in young men. This love is what people call aesthetic with me. It has to do with my perceptions through the senses, & does not affect my regard for duty, principle, right conduct. I know well enough that there are more important things in the Universe than beauty. But there is nothing I was born to love more.

With my soul & heart I love you more than the world. With my aesthetic perceptions I love physical perfection. . . .[14]

From the time he first started to write, he was bitter because he could not speak freely of the over-riding motive-force of his life. Nevertheless, he displayed a good deal of courage in speaking out as frankly as he did. The final chapter on Greek love in *Studies of the Greek Poets*, he was convinced, lost him the Chair of Poetry at Oxford in 1877. Despite this

many unmistakable resemblances to Symonds, both in appearance and in aesthetic tastes. His wife also accords closely with the report James heard of Catherine, and she too declares, 'I consider his writings most objectionable.' But the central theme of the story, the struggle for the child, is entirely James's creation. I have been unable to ascertain definitely the allusion to which Gosse refers. Perhaps it is this sentence: 'I saw that in his books he had only said half of his thought . . . [he] had an extreme dread of scandal.'

setback, he felt compelled to continue to praise the beauty of what Edward Carpenter called 'homogenic love', and to educate the public towards greater understanding and sympathy for a practice most Victorians regarded as an abomination. Yet, if he spoke without evasion, he realized that his audience would necessarily have to be small. In 1873, while absorbed in the first series of his Greek studies, he wrote a long essay, 'A Problem in Greek Ethics', in which the fervour was balanced by an impressive knowledge of Greek history and customs; but he did not dare to publish this in pamphlet form until 1883 when only ten copies were printed for private circulation. To all the friends who received a copy went the warning – 'please be discreet about it'. In a mood of discouragement, he wrote to Gosse on 28 February 1890:

When I last wrote my soul was troubled and perplexed not so much with any sorrows of my own – for I can truly say with S. Augustine and yourself 'Jam tempore lenitum est vulnus meum' [my wound has now been soothed by time] – but I had been musing on the insolubility of the whole problem and the terrible amount of pain and misunderstanding in the world of men around us – due more to wondering whether nothing can be done to put things straighter and saner. You will not doubt, I am sure, that what you call 'the central Gospel' of that essay on the Greeks, has been the light and leading of my life. But I had to arrive at this through so much confusion of mind and such a long struggle between varied forms of inclinations and abstentions that a large portion of my nervous force and mental activity was engaged in the contention during the years when I most needed them for tranquil study and patient labour at art. It was also the main reason for the break-down of my health.

It seems to me not only sad and tragic, but preposterous and ludicrous that this waste should have to be incurred by one man after another when the right ethic of the subject lies in a nutshell.

'To refine and cultivate': yes, that is the point. To see the making of Chivalry where the vulgar only perceive vice. To recognize the physiological and psychological differences in individuals, wʰ render this process of elevation necessary, & the process of extirpation impossible, that is the duty wʰ Society neglects.[15]

He would have felt more confident about making a frontal attack if he had been successful in lining up enthusiastic supporters. The greatest disillusionment of all was the apostasy of Walt Whitman. Ever since Symonds first wrote to him in 1871, enclosing a poem inspired by 'Calamus', he continued to drop hints as to how much he longed to know its real meaning. The meaning was clear enough to him, but he wanted Whitman to spell it out explicitly and uncompromisingly. Whitman answered his letters courteously; sent him photographs; but for twenty years he turned a deaf ear to his pleas. After receiving from Whitman a complete edition of the poems – albeit with the omission of 'Long I thought that knowledge alone would suffice me', which had been left out of all editions after 1860 – Symonds was emboldened to put the question once more. On 3 August 1890, he wrote more urgently than he had ever done before, asking specifically if 'adhesiveness' included sexual relations between men; he justified the persistence of his demands with the explanation that he could not write the study of the poet which he had long been contemplating unless Whitman's intention was absolutely clear to him. The letter is a very ingenious piece of subtilizing – and Whitman would have been a fool to have fallen into the trap so skilfully – and so obviously – laid for him. Symonds in effect challenged him to state his position because he, Symonds, and Whitman's other disciples, often found themselves defending him against the charge that his doctrines led to degradation – even though they weren't quite sure what his doctrines were! Ingenuously Symonds went on to say that he agreed with Whitman's detractors that, since some men *did* have a bias towards their own sex, 'Calamus' might encourage them in sexual intimacies; yet, for his part, he could see nothing anti-social in such behaviour. Did Whitman leave the physical nature of a relationship to the individual conscience? There follows a passionate exclamation that he is sure Whitman would speak candidly to him if they met in the flesh! Then, in a final careless aside, as if to reassure Whitman, he concludes with the casual remark that he is really not interested in the subject at all, but enquires only because it is a necessary part of Whitman's philosophy which he hopes to disseminate to the world.

Whitman had had enough. The anger fairly burns from his scalding reply of 19 August; yet he was concerned enough about the interpretation Symonds might make of his words, to work them out carefully in a pencilled draft before the final answer went off. He first admits to having six illegitimate children (scattered far and wide !), the implication apparently being that he was a perfectly normal man. Then the voice roars out in righteous indignation: 'About the questions on "Calamus", etc., they quite daze me. *Leaves of Grass* is only to be rightly construed by and within its own atmosphere and essential character – all its pages and pieces so strictly coming under. That the Calamus part has ever allowed the possibility of such construction as mentioned is terrible. I am fain to hope that the pages themselves are not to be even mentioned for such gratuitous and quite at the time undreamed and unwished possibility of morbid inferences – which are disavowed by me and seem damnable.'[16] After twenty years Symonds finally had his answer.

His reaction was bitter disappointment,* but he rallied himself to reply with dignity, although the hurt and bitterness broke through into his letter. He tells Whitman that he is most grateful for the clear exposition of his views – and adds that they were exactly what he had expected. Did he really believe Whitman would be undeceived by this volte-face? He is still enough on his guard to adopt the tone of the detached observer who cannot fail to see the obvious implications of intense male friendship, yet his stance is that of one who is not personally involved in the question. Bluntly he reminds Whitman that the language of 'Calamus' is closer to the enthusiasm with which the Greeks described comradeship than anything else in modern literature; hints that Whitman's horror is unscientific in the light of modern knowledge about the constitution of certain individuals; and apologizes for annoying him with distasteful but necessary questions.

It was the end of a long idyll. His 'Master' had not only failed him lamentably but, unkindest cut of all, had turned viciously upon him. Nevertheless, the affection and admiration which had lit his life for over twenty years could not be eradicated completely; besides, he had committed himself to writing the long-projected study once Whitman had given him an explicit answer. He dashed it off in twelve days, partly because he wanted to discharge his duty swiftly, partly because the sentiments flowed so readily from his heart. The book is a statement of Symonds's interpretation of Whitman's philosophy, and, while he acknowledges the position declared by Whitman in his letter, again and again he insinuates that Whitman meant more by 'Calamus' than he

---

* 'I am extremely glad to have this statement,' he told Ernest Rhys, 'though I confess to being surprised at the vehemence of the language' (Ernest Rhys, *Letters from Limbo*, J. M. Dent & Sons Ltd., 1936. p. 43).

knew.* No longer will he commit himself entirely to Whitman: 'I sincerely regard him, and have long regarded him, as a man born to remind the world of many important and neglected truths, to flash the light of authentic inspiration upon many dark and puzzling questions, and to do so with the force of admirable courage, flawless candour. But the ways he chose for pushing his gospel and advertising his philosophy, put a severe strain on patience.'[17] The ardent protestations of an impetuous young man were now muted into the slightly cynical irony of middle age.

Whitman, it will be remembered, once told his friends the Gilchrists that Symonds could not bring himself to speak openly of comradeship, the theme which he admired so much in Whitman's poetry. Symonds cannot be blamed for his timidity when account is taken of the legal penalties and social pressures of the time. Referring to the difficulty of speaking out frankly, Symonds once remarked: 'I have to think of the world's verdict – since I have given pledges to future in the shape of my four growing girls.'[18] As a consequence, while he felt impelled to speak, he had always to use an oblique approach in which ingenuousness and craft were cunningly allied. An example of this *pis-aller* is an essay, 'The Dantesque and Platonic Ideals of Love', which he submitted to *The Contemporary Review* in 1890, waiting with bated breath to learn whether the Editor would realize that it was in effect a paean to the glories of homosexuality. Another essay, 'Edward Cracroft Lefroy', which appeared in *The New Review* of March 1892, praised an obscure poet whose verses celebrating the beauty of young men seemed to him saturated with the 'aura', a suspicion confirmed after Lefroy's literary executor allowed Symonds to read his letters.

Symonds felt a sense of personal triumph when he found a painting, a poem, or a novel which seemed to glow with masculine love. He wrote excitedly to friends about a painting of Hack Tuke's which was bathed

---

* Some of Whitman's admirers responded to Symonds's persistence with indignation. In the Preface to *Reminiscences of Walt Whitman* (Alexander Gardner, 1896, p. vii) W. S. Kennedy wrote: 'Mr Symonds was singularly unfortunate in his published utterances on the man he loved most passionately of any on earth. We here in America were astounded that it seemed to him necessary in his work on Walt Whitman to relieve the Calamus poems of the vilest of all possible interpretations. It was a sad revelation to us of the state of European morals, that even the ethical perfume of these noblest utterances on friendship could not save them from such a fate. But Symonds had the best of motives.'

in the 'aura'. 'What a number of Urnings are being portrayed in novels now !' he exclaimed to Gosse. '*Un Raté, Monsieur Vénus,* this *Footsteps of Fate* – I stumble on them casually & find the same note.'[19] With friends of similar inclinations he exchanged bundles of photographs of young male nudes (Gosse was driven to steal glances at a photograph Symonds had sent him, all through Browning's funeral service in Westminster Abbey). 'The male body', Symonds declared in *A Problem in Greek Ethics,* 'exhibits a higher organisation of the human form than the female.' In an unpublished undated essay, 'Notes on the Relation of Art and Morality', far more candid than the one dealing with the same subject in *Essays Speculative and Suggestive,* he describes sex as the root of the aesthetic sense; sex, he claims, is responsible for blinding most men to real beauty: '. . . men regard the female form as more essentially beautiful than the male. The contrary to this belief can be abundantly demonstrated. The male form is infinitely richer in a variety of lovely qualities, and is incomparably nobler in its capacities of energetic action.'[20] What Symonds wanted, above all, was a frank recognition of male beauty, a rending of the veil in which Victorian prudery enveloped nudity. He reacted enthusiastically to an account of a circus Madge had attended in England:

When I read your letter about Barnum, how I did envy you! The acrobats, the charioteers, the lightly clad girls & well-set-up tall men, in Nero! I should like to give Toby a guinea for saying after it was over, that he wanted to be naked. That was a fine word. It expresses much w^h goes to the very root of our passions. We desire the savage, *l'homme primitif,* as Loti says, when we are deeply stirred.

This is not the gospel of Wordsworth or Mat Arnold; but perhaps of Whitman, certainly of me.[21]

If the contemporary public was too obscurantist to accept his message, there remained the possibility that a future generation might be more enlightened. With this hope for posterity, in 1889 he began to set down his Memoirs, an idea which had long been germinating in his mind. The autobiographies of Cellini and Gozzi had intrigued him as revelations of men, the essential nature of whom could not be captured so successfully in any other form of literature; as early as 1863, while wrestling with the truth of his own emotions, he wrote to Rutson: '. . . I have often thought that, if I lived to do nothing else, I should write Confessions which would be better for the world to read than Rousseau's & not less interesting. I sometimes think that I am being trained for this.'[22] Nearly thirty years later, in March 1889, he now wrote to Dakyns:

My occupation with Cellini & Gozzi has infected me with their Lues Autobiographica; & I have begun scribbling my own reminiscences. This is a foolish thing to do, because I do not think they will ever be fit to publish. I have nothing to relate except the evolution of a character somewhat strangely constituted in its moral & aesthetic qualities. The study of this evolution, written with the candour & the precision I feel capable of using, would I am sure be interesting to psychologists & not without its utility. There does not exist anything like it in print; & I am certain that 999 men out of 1000 do not believe in the existence of a personality like mine. Still it would be hardly fair to my posterity if I were to yield up my vile soul to the psychopathical investigators.

I do not know therefore what will come of this undertaking. Very likely, I shall lay it aside, though the fragment is already considerable in bulk & curious in matter – & I feel it a pity, after acquiring the art of the autobiographer through translation of two master-pieces, not to employ my skill upon such a rich mine of psychological curiosities as I am conscious of possessing.

This may appear rather conceited. But it is not so. I speak as an artist, who sees 'a subject' of which he is confident. *Infin de' corti* I believe I shall go forward, & leave my executors to deal with what will assuredly be the most considerable product of my pen.

You see I have 'never spoken out'.* And it is a great temptation to speak out, when I have been living for two whole years in lonely intimacy with men who spoke out so magnificently as Cellini & Gozzi did.[23]

Symonds became so engrossed in his recollections of *temps perdus* that all other work was relegated to the background for a period of about eighteen months although the Memoirs were not actually completed until 1893. 'A thing of this sort', he told a friend, 'ought to be a master's final piece of work.'[24] Word got abroad of what he was about, and in a report of his work in *The Pall Mall Gazette* in 1890, the writer speculated archly on what naughty anecdotes might be divulged about the semi-Bohemian life of Oxford in the sixties.

Symonds might have smiled grimly at the possibility of being interested

---

* This phrase was a familiar one to the Victorians in connection with Arnold's description of Gray – '*He never spoke out*' (*Essays in Criticism*, Second Series, Macmillan & Co., 1888, p. 81).

in such trivia. When he learned that the writer was Ernest Rhys,* he wrote him a troubled letter: 'I only wish . . . that you had not mentioned an autobiography of mine w^h is something very different from what you described. But that is not your fault – mine rather, who ought not to have mentioned to anyone that I was engaged on what will probably be consigned to the fire.'[25] When Ernest Rhys wrote to apologize, Symonds replied:

With regard to my autobiography, please do not think that I resent what you said in the PMG, or that this would make me suppress the work. I meant only to remark that now – when the thing is almost done – I do not see how it could be published.

What I did demur to was the description of the autobiography. If you had read it, you would have seen that it is a close psychological study, & that there is very little anecdotal matter or gossip about people in it. I do not like to acquire the reputation of preserving for publication things about 'the people I have met'. On the other hand I feel that the intelligent & careful study of any person's development, psychical history written from inside with sincerity, is what he may legitimately give to the world if he likes, & what is a valuable contribution to our documents of human experience.[26]

What he was concerned with was an *apologia pro vita sua*, an explanation, a description, a justification for the tormented struggle which had torn at him through the whole of his unfulfilled existence. The writing became a cathartic experience, and when he recalled some of the more poignant moments with Willie Dyer or Norman Moor, he was so overcome with emotion that he had to lay down his pen. The autobiography is not a record of the external events of his life but an account of the emotional forces which shaped the man who was now nearly fifty. With the exception of a fairly lengthy account of Jowett's impact on him, the years at Oxford are passed over in a few paragraphs; social contacts are scarcely mentioned; there is no reference to Gosse or Stevenson or Swinburne; no account of his children. In a curious anticipation of later psychoanalytic emphasis, Symonds laboured to reinvoke memories of childhood, and inserted clinical descriptions of his early sexual patterns. 'According to my conception of such a work', he told Brown, 'the years

* Ernest Rhys (1858-1946) had begun his literary career in London in 1886. He was editor of the Camelot Classics (1886-91) and of the Everyman's Library (1906-46).

Angelo

J. A. Symonds in Venice   Horatio Brown

Horatio Brown's house on the Zattere, Venice

of growth are the most important, and need the most elaborate analysis. . . .
It is a fascinating canvas, this of *Lebensschilderung*, for a man who has been
hitherto so reticent in writing, and who is so naturally egotistical and
personal as I am.'[27] The autobiography emerges essentially as the history
of Symonds's sexual life; it is not the lusty boasting of a Frank Harris but
the anguished record of a man whose energy had been drained by the
struggle to reconcile his instincts with the mores of society. As such, it is a
profoundly moving document, and he earnestly hoped that its future
publication might serve to create greater understanding for others like
himself. It was not by his wish, but through Horatio Brown's decision,
that it has been locked away all these years.

One of the great miseries he endured throughout his life was the conviction that he was a pariah, a creature unlike other men. This is the
significance of the phrase '*L'amour de l'impossible*', which threads his
writings like an anguished refrain. However, in the course of writing his
Memoirs, his attention was drawn to various studies of homosexuality
which opened his eyes to its wide, if little acknowledged, incidence among
all classes in every society. One of these was Sir Richard Burton's terminal
essay to the *Arabian Nights*, in which Burton put forth the ingenious
but hopelessly ill-informed theory that homosexuality was prevalent in
certain societies influenced by a combination of particular geographic and
climatic conditions. A far more impressively factual book was *Psychopathia
Sexualis*, published in 1889, in which Dr R. von Krafft-Ebing, a professor of psychiatry in Vienna, assembled two hundred histories of inverts.
Krafft-Ebing advanced the theory that homosexuals could be divided into
two groups – congenital inverts, and those who have developed the
characteristics of the former through undetermined influences. Another
important tome, Dr Albert Moll's *Die Contrare Sexualempfindung* (1891),
discussed the hereditary and environmental factors contributing to
homosexuality. German physicians were leading the pioneer investigations
into the field, and Symonds also became acquainted with the work of
Westphal, Caspar Liman, and Schrenk-Notzing. However, it was not
the writing of a doctor, but of a former Hanoverian legal official, which
left the greatest impression on him. During the sixties, Carl Heinrich
Ulrichs, under the pseudonym of 'Numa Numantius' had issued a series
of pamphlets intended to alter the stringent laws against homosexuality in

Germany. From Plato's Uranos of the *Symposium*, he coined the word 'Urning' to denote a homosexual, while a heterosexual lover he described by the term 'Dioning'. Uranismus, he claimed, was a congenital abnormality in which a female soul had become encased in a male body; such a mystical conception Symonds could not accept, but Ulrichs's terminology, with its poetic associations, delighted him. In latter years Ulrichs had abandoned his propagandizing, and in 1887 had settled in L'Aquila in southern Italy where he published a Latin periodical.

These scientific studies which objectively tried to explain and understand a phenomenon that had hitherto aroused general horror, inspired Symonds with the idea of publishing a semi-scientific study of his own, a modern counterpart of *A Problem in Greek Ethics*, to be called *A Problem in Modern Ethics*. In the early stages of preparation Henry Sidgwick came out to Davos to stay with him and when they discussed the project, Sidgwick's viewpoint was obviously as divergent as ever from Symonds's. 'Good Lord !' Symonds exclaimed to Dakyns, 'in what different orbits human souls can move. He talks of sex, out of legal codes, & blue books. I talk of it from human documents, myself, the people I have known, the adulterers & prostitutes of both sexes I have dealt with over bottles of wine & confidence.

'Nothing comes of discussions between a born doctrinaire & a born Bohemian. . . .

'Shall we ever be able to see human nature from a really central point of view ! I doubt this now. Though we redouble our spectacles, put scores of our neighbours' glasses on our own, in order to obtain the typical impression, shall we reach the central standpoint ?'[28]

One man with whom he did achieve complete sympathy was Edmund Gosse. Symonds's resolute determination to continue his investigations elicited Gosse's admiration and moved him – after fifteen long years of friendship – to admit at last the truth of Symonds's suspicions. 'I know of all you speak of', Gosse wrote, '– the solitude, the rebellion, the despair. Yet I have been happy, too; I hope you also have been happy, – that all with you has not been disappointment & the revulsion of hope? Either way, I entirely & deeply sympathise with you. Years ago I wanted to write to you about all this, and withdrew through cowardice. I have had a very fortunate life, but there has been this obstinate twist in it ! I have reached a quieter time – some beginnings of that Sophoclean period when the wild beast dies. He is not dead, but tamer; I understand him & the trick of his claws.'[29]

On 6 December Symonds wrote to Madge, then staying in England, that the book (too important, he believed, to be described as an essay) was finished. 'If I were to publish it now, it would create a great sensation. Society would ring with it. But the time is not ripe for the launching of "A Problem in Modern Ethics" on the world. The MS. lies on my table for retouches; & then will go to slumber in a box of precious writings, my best work, my least presentable, until its day of Doom.'[30] Early in 1891 fifty copies were printed privately. A booklet of one hundred and four pages, the style 'acid and severe',[31] its contents included an historical survey of homosexuality, various modern theories of the causes of the phenomenon, and a concluding section dealing with suggested amendments in legislation. Symonds's object was to stimulate discussion, and the various recipients were asked to return their copies with comments noted in the wide margin. 'I am eager about the subject for its social & juristic aspects', Symonds told Dakyns. 'You know how vitally it has in the past interested me as a man, & how I am therefore in duty bound to work for an elucidation of the legal problem.'[32]

Sir Richard Burton was sent a copy because, though 'not exactly sympathetic he is a perfect mine of curious knowledge about human nature'.[33] All during 1891 Symonds and Ulrichs were in daily correspondence, although Ulrichs failed to give Symonds the help he had expected. 'He does not seem to care for Urnings any more. How odd!' Ulrichs wrote to ask him if he would translate Tennyson's 'Crossing the Bar', whose Latin version by Montagu Butler, now Master of Trinity, he had read. Symonds was struck by the ironical aspects of the request: 'Is it not for me & Ulrichs, me only interested in him because he championed the slave-cause of the Urnings, & him mainly interested in me because I can expound Tennyson's odd English – is it not funny I say, for us to be brought together upon this extraordinarily trivial trifle – the Master of Trinity's Latin translation of the Poet Laureate's "Vale" to the public – when our original *rapport* was in the *hearts* & *viscera* & potent *needs* of thousands of our fellow-creatures.

'So goes the world. And – well I will not say what I was going to say:

only I fear that a free legal course with social sympathy attending, will not be given to my brethren – the Urnings.'[34] However, when he travelled down to L'Aquila to visit Ulrichs in October he found the 'beautiful & dignified old man',[35] who was living in great poverty, far more willing to talk about The Problem face to face.

The booklet moved from hand to hand, and aroused furtive, excited interest. After reading *A Problem*, Henry James described it as 'infinitely remarkable'. Then he went on to tell Gosse:

It's on the whole, I think, your place to plant the standard of duty, but he does it with extraordinary gallantry. If he has, or gathers, a band of the emulous, we may look for some capital sport. But I don't wonder that some of his friends and relations are haunted with a vague malaise. I think one ought to wish him more *humour*, it is really *the* saving salt. But the great reformers never have it – & he is the Gladstone of the affair.[36]

The letters from homosexuals recording their histories, almost all of them lives of conflict and furtiveness, came flooding in to Am Hof. One after another echoed Gosse's statement that 'the position of a young person so tormented is really that of a man buried alive & conscious, but deprived of speech. He is doomed by his own timidity and ignorance to a repression which amounts to death. . . . This corpse, however, is obliged to bustle around and make an appearance every time the feast of life is spread.'[37] Symonds was saddened by this testament of human misery but he had moments of exultation when he envisaged a new hope for these inverts, a time when their love would not be treated as something shameful, but rather as a civilizing and ennobling element in society, such as courtly love had contributed in the Middle Ages, or, more powerfully still, the Platonic concept of love in Ancient Greece. 'This sort of thing, at my time of life,' Dakyns was told, 'is much more amusing – than re-cooking the jaded cabbage of a Florentine sculptor.'[38]

The changing of the law in connection with homosexuals had been of intense concern to him ever since the passing of the Criminal Law Amendment Act in 1885. This law was the outcome of investigations by the reforming editor of *The Pall Mall Gazette*, W. T. Stead, into the current traffic in adolescent girls. In order to reveal to the public how easy it was to procure one of these girls, Stead himself obtained one, but neglected to get permission from her father as well as her mother, and, by an ironical twist of fate, was imprisoned for three months for abduction. But his zeal bore fruit in the passing of the law raising the age of consent from twelve to sixteen. However, with the memory of the Cleveland Street Scandal* and its revelations of male prostitution still lurid in the memories of the shocked, an extra clause, known as the Labouchere Amendment, was slipped in, by which indecencies between males, even if practised in private, were made a criminal offence punishable with two years of hard labour.

Symonds had no sympathy for Stead, who had been one of Vizetelly's persecutors, and felt positive hostility for the cause he championed. He believed that *The Pall Mall Gazette* was thoroughly hypocritical in its claim to be exposing vice which amounted only to a cheap yellow journalistic trick. His old friend, Mrs Butler, was one of Stead's closest allies and even appeared in court on his behalf, conduct which infuriated her once-adoring Symonds. '. . . I regard his present sentence as too easy', he raged to Gosse, '& . . . I should like to see his instigatrix Mrs J. E. Butler in prison too. A bourgeois Anglo-Saxon pack of Jesuits! Violating law: doing evil that good may come! Without even the solemnity, inscrutability, & perfect art of the real Jesuits!'[39] Gosse replied wittily: 'The friends of social purity will be glad to learn that Mr Stead is to be appointed the first Josephine Professor of Comparative Prostitution.'[40]

Symonds was roused to passionate indignation by these do-gooders because their meddling had been responsible for the Labouchere Amendment which he described to Charles Kains-Jackson as 'a disgrace to legislation by its vagueness of diction & the obvious incitement to false accusation'.[41] The Labouchere Amendment stood out conspicuously as one of the most stringent laws for a sexual offence in Europe. In 1889 an act was passed in Italy abolishing punishment for sexual relations between men as long as they were not accompanied by violence, infringement of the rights of minors, or outrages to public decency. In Symonds's belief this law had been brought about by the efforts of the distinguished psychiatrist, Cesare Lombroso, to create an informed public opinion. In France the Code Napoléon protected minors, but no legal measures were

* An article in the *North London Press* exposed the fact that a house at 19 Cleveland Street, off Tottenham Court Road, was being frequented by aristocrats for homosexual purposes. Although the Editor could produce evidence to support his charges, he was sentenced to a year's imprisonment for slander.

taken against adult homosexuals, although strong social feeling was organized against them. In Germany and Austria the laws were still severe, but the practice was widespread and regarded far more tolerantly than in most countries.

Symonds wanted to see the English law changed '*without discussion*'; he was convinced that 'the majority of unprejudiced people would accept the change with perfect equanimity'[42] but they dreaded the scandal of a public discussion. *A Problem in Modern Ethics* elicited such an interested response that Symonds was encouraged to pursue his quiet efforts for social reform. 'I am quite surprised', he told Dakyns, 'to see how frankly ardently & sympathetically a large number of highly respectable persons feel toward a subject which in society they would only mention as unmentionable.

'The result of this correspondence is that I sorely need to revise, enlarge, & make a new edition of my essay; & I am almost minded to print it as a *published* vol: together with my other essay on Greek Morals & some supplementary papers.'[43] He planned to assemble his case-histories as Krafft-Ebing had done, but he was fully aware that the conclusions a literary man might draw from them would not carry the same weight as those of an established medical man. In 1890 an exciting possibility occurred to him after reading a book called *The New Spirit*, by a handsome young doctor-cum-writer, Havelock Ellis. Ellis had first come to Symonds's attention in 1885* when he received a copy of *Time* with an article, 'The Present Position of English Criticism', written by Ellis. In later years, Ellis believed that he had 'over-estimated'[44] Symonds, but in 1885, after reading *Renaissance in Italy*, he regarded him as the doyen of English critics, the one with 'the most marked catholicity' in contrast to a critic like Pater who has 'the advantage or disadvantage of a definite method'.[45] However, the essay was not simply an unqualified display of hero-worship, and Symonds appreciated the objectivity with which Ellis analysed his writing. Ellis pointed out Symonds's tendency to over-indulge in analogies drawn from all the arts, and he concluded with the statement: 'It is doubtful whether Mr Symonds possesses the dangerous gift of a keen intuition.' 'What you say about myself gratifies me', Symonds wrote in reply.

* Ellis had also been closely acquainted with Symonds's old friend, Roden Noel.

It is the first word spoken clearly, which shows that anybody has taken my drift in criticism, and understood what I had been always aiming at. You could hardly have stated my intention better, or have more kindly pointed out the impedimenta in the way of manner or descriptive tendency which I long used to carry about me. . . . What you say about my not possessing the 'gift of a keen intuition' is quite true. Perhaps I owe to this défaut the qualité of seeking to set at all events, I will not say succeed in setting the things I have to deal with in relations to the whole.

That has been my steady purpose, and all my life through I have resolutely pared away my own personal proclivities when I had to formulate or pass a judgment — indulging them, as you rightly observe, quite enough in places where I thought I might describe.[46]

A year later Ellis asked him to contribute an introduction to Marlowe for the Mermaid series of Elizabethan dramatists which he was editing for Vizetelly.* When Ellis printed for the first time in the appendix the complete charges of blasphemy and immorality brought against Marlowe by an informer before his death, Symonds added his protests to Swinburne's shocked disapproval of any distortion of the ideal image of Marlowe, whose importance they had both championed.† In the edition which appeared in 1887, Vizetelly mutilated the complete text.

In 1890, Ellis, then less than thirty, challengingly echoed Huxley's credo in *The New Spirit*,‡ a copy of which he sent to Symonds: 'To promote the increase of natural knowledge and to forward the application of scientific methods of investigation to all the problems of life to the best of my ability, in the conviction, which has grown with my growth and strengthened my strength, that there is no alleviation for the sufferings of mankind except veracity of thought and of action, and the resolute facing of the world as it is, when the garment of make-believe, by which pious hands have hidden its uglier features, is stripped off.'[47] Ellis proceeded to

* When A. H. Bullen heard of the arrangement, he wrote indignantly to warn Symonds of what an unscrupulous character Vizetelly was. His main complaint seems to have been that Vizetelly was underpricing Nimmo's series on the Elizabethan dramatists which Bullen was editing (MS. letter, dated West Hampstead, 31 May 1886, University of Bristol).

† In *Sexual Inversion* Ellis stated quite categorically his conviction that Marlowe was a homosexual, a suggestion Symonds had put forth obliquely in *Shakespere's Predecessors*, with his emphasis on Marlowe's *'l'amour de l'impossible'*.

‡ Symonds was so impressed with the title that he used it for an article on the Renaissance in *The Fortnightly Review*, LIII (March 1893, 427-44). He wrote to Ellis apologizing for his plagiarism.

praise writers such as Tolstoy and Whitman who described life as it really was rather than as the sham people expected them to make of it. Symonds was highly excited by Ellis's candour, but the critics flew in for an attack, the virulence of which far surpassed any of the gentlemanly sarcasms Symonds had received through the years. The chapter on Walt Whitman was the target for their fiercest abuse. Whitman had been depicted by Ellis as almost the re-incarnation of Christ, and they were incensed by his claim that for the first time since the beginning of Christianity, a man had appeared who embodied the instincts of a complete man.

Nothing could have delighted Symonds more, and he told Ellis that he recognized 'a deep critical sympathy between us'. When Ellis, replying to the inevitable questions, stated his belief that Whitman did not exclude sexual intimacy from male friendships, Symonds was completely convinced that he had found his man.* Nevertheless, their subsequent collaboration was by no means the brain-child of Symonds alone, even though in both *Sexual Inversion* and *My Life*, Ellis creates the impression that all the overtures came from Symonds. In July 1891 Symonds received the following communication from Ellis: 'I was interested to hear from my friend, Dr Tuke,† and others that you are thoroughly working out this question of Greek love in modern life from the moral side. Whenever you are in London I hope I may have an opportunity of talking over this question with you. I am not sure that I should altogether agree with you, but the question is one that constantly forces itself on one's attention.'[48] Symonds in his reply emphasized his belief that the main problem connected with inversion was repressive legislation which could not be changed so long as public opinion was guided by the outdated theories of obscurantist medical men. The whole subject, he continued, 'ought to be scientifically, historically, impartially investigated, instead of being left to Labby's‡ inexpansible legislation'. Finally, he

---

* His faith was reinforced by Ellis's objective study of *The Criminal* (1890), contributed to the Contemporary Science Series, which Ellis was editing.

† Dr Hack Tuke, father of the artist Symonds admired, had been a friend of Dr Symonds. At this time he was editor of the *Journal of Mental Science*. Symonds had tried to talk to him about homosexuality when he was writing *A Problem in Modern Ethics* but was very disappointed by his indifference. As an older man, he was not illiberal for his day and age, but he disapproved of a detailed approach to sex.

‡ i.e. Labouchere.

stressed that it was absolutely necessary for Ellis and himself to reach a clear understanding about principles and sympathies, although he felt sure that they would not 'disagree at bottom about the ethical views'.[49]

Was Ellis suffering from an old man's lapse of memory, or was he anxious to dissociate himself from the notoriety that had persisted in clinging to *Sexual Inversion*, when he stated in his autobiography that he had hesitated for over a year before committing himself to the collaboration? The evidence presented very clearly in the letters exchanged between Symonds and Ellis indicates that in June of 1892 Symonds wrote to Arthur Symons (with whom he had been corresponding for some time), and who was sharing rooms at the time with Ellis, asking him to sound out Ellis on the possibility of their collaborating on a joint study of homosexuality. Symons brought the subject up at a music hall one night, and the following day Ellis wrote Symonds that he himself had been planning to present a paper to the forthcoming Congress of Criminal Anthropology but, as for a full-scale book, 'the difficulties are certainly serious'.[50] At this point, Symonds, as if to spur Ellis on, divulged that he would probably publish a book under his own name if Ellis were reluctant to commit himself to the venture. 'Then', he added in a postscript, 'you can criticize & exploit me.'[51] (In *My Life*, Ellis emphasized that Symonds was determined to go ahead, if need be, on his own, an exaggeration of Symonds's statement.) Symonds's most persuasive argument was that 'it is a field in which pioneers may not only do excellent service to humanity, but also win the laurels of investigators & truth-seekers'.[52]

If Ellis continued to have grave doubts about the venture, he did not divulge them to Symonds, because the collaboration seems to have been definitely settled in the next letters exchanged between them. Ellis had recently been married, and in a postscript Symonds added a word of congratulation: 'I hope it may prove as true a source of happiness as mine upon the whole has been to me.'[53]

Symonds had hoped that the work might form part of the Contemporary Science Series which Ellis was editing, but Ellis quickly discouraged this idea: 'Several of the volumes approach various forbidden topics as nearly as it is desirable, and I am inclined to agree with the publisher that there is too much at stake to involve the Series in any risky pioneering experiment.'[54] Symonds then suggested that they try to get some medical organization to sponsor it, but here again Ellis believed that such an imprint would narrow the circulation of the book and that they would do better to approach some reputable general publisher like Macmillan's or Smith, Elder. It was an ironical discussion in view of subsequent events.

However, there were problems of more immediate concern which had to be ironed out. Both men had read most of the same sources and had come to many of the same conclusions; both were determined to break through the old shibboleths connected with inversion such as the widespread belief that the brain degenerates as a result of 'unnatural' pleasures; finally, both were vitally concerned that the law should be changed. Yet there were important differences of temperament and approach: in the correspondence Ellis displays the cool lucidity of the scientist in contrast to the emotionalism of Symonds who, although widely read in the literature on the subject, always tended to give greater consideration to the evidence which reinforced his own views. On many occasions Ellis warned him that their case could be presented more effectively by avoiding discussion of the question's social bearings. Ellis always feared that Symonds would be carried away by a wave of emotion – 'It seems to me . . . that we should adopt a rather austere style in this book avoiding so far as possible a literary or artistic attitude towards the question – appealing to the reason rather than to the emotions. (For this reason some passages in your modern *Problem*, ought, I think,' he added tactfully, 'to be omitted.')[55]

The most fundamental question on which they had to reach agreement was their respective views on the origin of homosexuality. As the entire collaboration had to be conducted by post, they have left a fascinating series of letters in which they argued the merits and defects of the various theories of hereditary and environmental factors. Symonds was obviously worried by the fact that Ellis seemed to approach the subject with too open a mind. As a homosexual himself, Symonds indignantly rejected the 'morbidity' hypothesis advanced by Lombroso and various other psychiatrists of the day, and tried desperately to convince Ellis of the compulsive drives of the invert. He was willing to accept Ellis's statement of the intention of their investigations as being primarily a study of a psychological anomaly, but, while he would admit neurosis as a frequent accompaniment of inversion, he made it very clear that he would never accept it as a cause. With that calculation amounting almost to craft which he could assume if something meant enough to him, Symonds then blandly suggested the difficulty that might arise in an historical analysis through the impossibility of concealing 'the fact that sexual anomaly (as in Greece) is often a matter of preference rather than of fixed physiological or morbid diathesis. This may render the argument *ad legislatores* complicated.'[56]

Ellis reassured him by a judicious combination of tact and common sense. 'Collaboration is difficult,' he replied placidly, 'as a whole not worth the trouble of attempting, but in this case the advantages to be gained seem quite enough to make it worth while to smooth out the difficulties.'[57] He flattered Symonds by saying that his point of view was probably in advance of modern scientific opinion: 'But I do not wish to put myself in opposition to the medical psychologists, the people who have most carefully studied the question; to do so in any case would be bad policy: I simply wish to carry their investigations a step further.'[58] Symonds had no choice but to agree: 'I think that we may now consider that all important disagreement on the fundamental points is at an end,' he wrote on 29 September 1892.[59]

Once this basic question of causes was settled, the organization of the book had to be decided. Ellis sketched out a plan by which he proposed to write the introduction, and handle the clinical aspects of inversion, while Symonds would deal with the historical background and perhaps write the conclusion. In his autobiography, Ellis states that Symonds reluctantly agreed to the plan, although he objected that Ellis had chosen all the best chapters for himself. There is not the slightest evidence for this charge in Symonds's letters. The plan struck him as admirable and he even insisted that Ellis place his name first on the title-page – a suggestion which Ellis was not unwilling to accept, 'as that happens to be the alphabetical order'.[60]

In dealing with the historical aspects of inversion, Symonds emphasized that it was essential that the Greek situation should receive the greatest attention, and wanted to incorporate *A Problem in Greek Ethics* into the text. Here Symonds revealed his bias towards propaganda: the inclusion of the pamphlet would not only enable him to display homosexuality in its most attractive light but also show it to be a perfectly normal phenomenon, because, as he pointed out to Ellis, the significant point about the Greeks was their attraction to both sexes: they married and went on taking boys. He was extremely worried about how he could treat the transition to modern times as the situation began to grow far more complicated. Since homosexuality was frowned on by cultures after the Greeks, it was impossible to know how widespread the practice had been in private, and consequently, hundreds of years of history had to be passed over in a sweeping superficial survey. His investigations into Michelangelo's diathesis, where he had the advantage of copious documents to study, had warned him how much more difficult it would be to speak authoritatively on cases like Marlowe, Shakespeare, James I, and Frederick the Great. In great alarm, Ellis wrote back warning him against mentioning Shakespeare – 'not only does it seem difficult to throw light on the matter but one would arouse the fury of devout Shakespeareans. . . .'[61] Marlowe's case he was willing to consider, and it did eventually appear in *Sexual Inversion*, as we have seen.

Although Symonds's part in the collaboration was largely confined to the historical aspects, he was also responsible for contributing a large number of the case-histories. He gathered these by means of a questionnaire which he drew up based on his study of Krafft-Ebing's and Ulrichs's methods, a form of approach Ellis approved. In his prefatory remarks in *Sexual Inversion*, Ellis rather minimizes Symonds's share, and while it may be true that after Symonds's death Ellis decided to reject many of the case-histories submitted and to augment them with his own, nevertheless, on 3 January 1893 he confessed to Symonds, in connection with the casehistories, 'It seems to me that my contribution of fresh material to the book will be a very humble one compared to yours.'[62] However, since Symonds seemed completely indifferent to the question of Lesbianism – another indication of his lack of objectivity – Ellis had to conduct this investigation entirely on his own.

Ellis and Symonds planned to meet when Symonds visited England in the summer of 1892. By then the collaboration had been agreed upon; some of the difficulties had been ironed out but many remained. One might assume that Symonds would be desperately anxious to meet Ellis, but in his busy round of social engagements he did not seem able to wedge him in between 'the dukes and the hair-dressers', and on 21 September he wrote to Ellis from that edifice of respectability, the Athenaeum (to which he had been elected in 1882), that he had decided to quit England abruptly the following day. 'I have been here nine weeks rushing all over the country, & am afraid of having some break-down in health if I continue this sort of life.'[63]

During the following winter many letters were exchanged, and in February Symonds suggested that they discontinue the use of 'Mr' in addressing each other. At this point Symonds seemed to be the one most concerned about completing their project, while Ellis was unable to devote as much time to it as to his own *Man and Woman*. In April, when the organization of the material was still far from complete, Ellis received word that Symonds had died suddenly in Rome. Later, when claiming that he was never fully won over to the idea of the collaboration, Ellis confessed that he experienced a sense of relief that the partnership had fallen through. He believed that the dissimilarity of style might create an uneven effect; and, even more important, the fact that one of the compilers was widely known as a homosexual, might make the work suspect as a case of special pleading. Nevertheless, he decided against abandoning the project, and obtained permission from Brown, Symonds's literary executor, to use some of Symonds's material.

It soon became evident that Ellis was going to have difficulty in finding an English publisher. As a result, the study first appeared in Germany in 1896, translated by a friend of Ellis's, Dr Hans Kurella, under the title *Das Kontrare Geschlechtsgefuhl*, and was soon acclaimed in German scientific circles as a pioneering work, just as Ellis and Symonds had hoped. In England, however, the trial of Oscar Wilde had taken place between the time of Symonds's death and the appearance of the German edition; Brown, Henry Sidgwick, and the Symonds family became alarmed at the prospect of the scandal an English edition might cause. When *Sexual Inversion* was finally published in 1897, by Wilson and Macmillan, Brown attempted to buy up the entire edition, but a number of copies slipped through the net.

Some of the material in the German edition had been deleted; a good deal had been added; and the whole, according to Ellis, carefully revised. *A Problem in Greek Ethics*, which Ellis stated frankly as of not much scientific value, was printed in full. Portions of *A Problem in Modern Ethics* were distributed throughout the book, usually in footnotes, whose origin in each case was acknowledged. A few fragments of letters from Symonds to Ellis were quoted. Ellis claimed that about half the case-histories had been collected by Symonds, the others by himself. He did not differentiate in this case, he explained, because each had used almost precisely the same type of questionnaire.

Ellis deliberately left the reader with the impression that Symonds's contribution was of little consequence. He allowed Symonds to speak in the section on Greek Ethics as one versed in classical literature; his case-histories had been admitted because he pursued a method similar to Ellis's. But the sections analysing contemporary theories of inversion, those suggesting changes both in the public's attitude and in the law, belong entirely to Ellis. There is no praise of Symonds, no platitudes gratefully acknowledging his contribution; Ellis emphasizes that the project was originally suggested by Symonds and that he had only reluctantly been drawn into it. Ellis was willing to relinquish the responsibility of the volume to Symonds, but he also made it clear that the credit for anything valuable it contained belonged entirely to him. In the second edition published later that year, Symonds's name was omitted completely and he was referred to cryptically as 'Z' or 'one of my correspondents'. Symonds's essay on Ulrichs (by 'Z') remained, but Symonds's material in the foot-notes was absorbed into the text, and *A Problem in Greek Ethics* was not to be found. Otherwise, the content remained the same.

The subsequent history of *Sexual Inversion* belongs more to Ellis's story than to Symonds's. In 1898 a copy was found among the stock of a bookseller, George Bedborough, who was being arrested on a charge of suspected anarchy. The publisher received a stern warning, and as a result of the publicity, *Sexual Inversion* was regarded as an obscene publication by the majority of the public, a prejudice which has clung to it until this day in uninformed quarters. None the less, this first volume in the series *Studies in the Psychology of Sex*, which Ellis subsequently completed, does remain a pioneer work in the investigation of homosexuality. Ellis and Symonds challenged the prevalent Victorian attitude that inverts* were

---

* Ellis preferred the word 'invert' or even 'homogenic' to 'homosexual' which he considered a barbarously hybrid word.

either criminals or madmen, by a presentation of an impressive list of case-histories collected from men, many of them pillars of society.* Homosexuality, instead of appearing as the acquired vice it was generally supposed to be, was described as a 'constitutional abnormality' in which the 'sexual instinct turned by inborn constitutional abnormality towards persons of the same sex'.[64] Ellis was unwilling altogether to dismiss the possibility of early acquired patterns, and his hypothesis anticipates Freud's description of infantile fixation in which relationships, normal enough in childhood, become abnormal if persisted in through adulthood. 'We must regard the inversion of later life,' he said, 'if it persists, as largely due to arrested development.'[65] The modernity of Ellis's view was remarkable for his understanding that latent sexual ambivalence exists in everyone. Freud, however, totally rejected Symonds's belief that homosexuals constituted 'a third sex'. Whereas Ellis had wavered when Symonds turned the full force of his passionate arguments on him, Freud was to declare decisively:

The claim made by homosexuals or inverts, that they constitute a select class of mankind, falls at once to the ground when we discover that every single neurotic evidence of homosexual tendencies is forthcoming and that a large proportion of the symptoms are expressions of this latent inversion. Those who openly call themselves homosexuals are merely those in whom the inversion is conscious and manifest; their number is negligible compared with those in whom it is latent.[66]

The question of origins aside, there remained the problem of the homosexual in society. Both Ellis and Symonds deserve credit for the courage to say publicly that the homosexual should be left free to live his own life, unhampered by fear of legal or social persecution. He could achieve self-development, in their view, only if he were not forced to become a 'mere feeble simulacrum of a normal man'. As for the Labouchere Amendment, its attitude towards what constitutes 'indecency' was anachronistic. Indecency, Ellis claimed, lay in the eyes of the beholder: an indecency was committed only if those participating regarded the act

---

* Even among medical men feeling was so strong that in 1904 a doctor in the *Maryland Medical Journal* could indignantly reject the possibility that Symonds might have been an invert. 'I am aware', Dr George Gould wrote, 'of the scurrilous clubman's nonsense as to the reason for his leaving Oxford; no word of correction is needed' ('The Life Tragedy of John Addington Symonds,' *MMJ*, Aug. 1904, 282). He also atttibuted Symonds's tuberculosis to eye strain!

as indecent, or if it were considered such by an onlooker. Countless lives could be rescued from misery only by a simple change in the law – that of erasing the words 'in private'. The remarkable similarity of the views expressed in *Sexual Inversion* to the Wolfenden Report of 1957 is self-evident – but *Sexual Inversion* was published only two years after Oscar Wilde's trial.

CHAPTER XII

The Last Years

SYMONDS's last years alternated between bouts of excessive anxiety to grasp as much life as he could, and periods of prostration in which he sank back exhausted from the effort. Warm human relationships were cultivated with his usual obsessive intensity. To his friends the gay, outgoing side of his nature was far more in evidence than the introspective brooding of former years. In May 1891 he wrote to Dakyns: 'I suppose no human being really *changes*. But I am now 50, & am as unlike what I was at 30 as it is possible for two men to be.'[1] He knew that there was nothing more he could do to enhance his literary reputation and the game seemed scarcely worth the candle. Constantly he reiterated his belief that art was a trivial substitute for real life, whereas his efforts towards sexual reform were an attempt to leave something of solid worth behind him. A premonition of death clung to him and he was desperate to cram in as much as he could while there was yet time.

The death of his eldest daughter Janet in 1887 sharpened his awareness of mortality more than any other event. Years before, Janet had been the beautiful child who enchanted Edward Lear into writing nonsense rhymes for her amusement. Sitting sturdily on her pony with her golden curls blowing behind her, she had joined her father for rides across Durd-ham Downs and her quick responsive mind delighted him when he gave her Greek lessons in his study after breakfast. Symonds encouraged her love of music with the gift of a piano of her own. When she was fourteen she began to exhibit unmistakable signs of tuberculosis, and had been rushed off to San Remo in an effort to arrest its ravages. For the first few years the disease did not seem to progress rapidly, yet she was never again able to be very active, and while she lay quietly for days at a time on a sofa, Symonds grew closer to the restless, energetic Madge who became his companion on many of his numerous journeys.

By the beginning of 1887 they knew that Janet's condition was hope-less. During that spring Symonds had been unable to shake off a persistent cold, and early in April Dr Ruedi advised him to get away from Davos, reassuring him that Janet would hold out until the middle of May. Shortly after he reached Ragatz a telegram arrived from Dr Ruedi with the news that Janet was growing very weak but in no immediate danger, and that there was no necessity for him to return. Nevertheless, he found that he could not rest with anxiety fretting at him, and he returned to Am Hof on 6 April in time to spend an evening of quiet talk with her. Later, her death seemed all the more poignant when he recalled how her face lit up with pleasure on his arrival and how she was able to talk with renewed energy about the possibility of moving to a lower level where she would be able to breathe more easily. The end came very quietly that night.

No death, not even his father's, touched Symonds so profoundly. Janet had lived in Am Hof more closely than any of the others, and the whole house seemed crying out for her as he wandered sadly from room to room, touching her belongings with gentle fingers.

I did not know [he wrote to Madge and Lotta who were visiting in England] how much I loved her, & I am always regretting that I did not do more for her while there was yet time. I know she felt for me a deep & peculiar affection; & I might have given up some of my eternal scribbling which engrossed me always & made me irritable & nervous, in order to read to her or to talk about things she liked. Instead too of sitting with the door ajar in my room smoking & thinking, 'how nicely Janet is playing', I might have pleased her by going in & listening. . . . And also I think it would have been kind if I had more often alluded to her symptoms of illness. She liked talking about such things. But I deliberately avoided doing so, for I judged her life would retain more of naturalness if its painful elements were not constantly touched upon.

Being our first-born, we did not understand how to treat her health; & our experience has been of advantage to you & little K. And now that she is the first to die, she will I hope make me less neglectful of small matters if any of you come to suffer in like ways.

Your mother embroidered a golden daffodil upon a little satin cushion for her head in the coffin; & I made her add beneath it these Greek words οὐκ ἔθανες πρῶτε. These are the beginning of a beautiful Greek epitaph: 'Thou are not dead my Protë.' Prote means 'the first'. She looked wonderful in her coffin – like a bride – only as Greeks would say 'the bride of death', or better as the early Christians would say 'the spouse of Christ'.

I find myself always saying to myself 'Ah, I will tell Janet that!' & then catching myself up with 'I can't'. I used to refer many things to her & told her a great deal about my work.[2]

Symonds was touched by the large number of Davosers who turned out for the funeral, and as they threw spring flowers into the grave he remembered Webster's dirge:

> All the flowers of the spring
> Meet to perfume our burying;
> For these have but their growing prime,
> And man doth flourish but a time.

In the following months thoughts of God and immortality concerned him as they had not done since the agnostic speculations of his early manhood. The conception of God as a living presence had been occupying his thoughts before Janet's death, and now such religious questions assumed more urgent significance. In answer to Madge's probing queries, he wrote:

You ask me what I think about those whom we loved in life being present with us after death. In a spiritual sense I feel Janet nearer to me now than when she lived. I do not mean that she comes & speaks to me, or that I imagine her soul is in the air unseen. But her thought, her ideal self, what she truly was for me, seems to be more inside my own spirit now than when she was there – an objective human being with her own personality in contrast to mine. This Christ promised to his disciples; & this explains how the memory of Christ developed into a religion.

I believe it to be my own duty not to be anxious about the question of survival after death. I feel that we are unable to know. And the purest religion seems to me to consist in leaving this absolutely to God. But there is no reason in the world why one should not exercise both faith & hope upon this topic. The immortality of the soul, even after the Christian Revelation, is a matter of faith not sight.

. . . I am sure He makes allowances for us, w[h] we have no right to make for ourselves. I am sure that in some way sin & pain & disease & unrest are educational; & that a liberated soul, like hers, if it is still aware of them, cannot be distressed by them because it knows what they are intended for. . . .[3]

The religious scepticism of his earlier life was being resolved into a vague pantheistic faith in which he conceived God as an immanent presence in nature. It was a personal credo which had borrowed elements from Walt Whitman and modern science to emerge as something with the grandiloquent title of 'Cosmic Enthusiasm'. Symonds was obviously moved when he spoke of the peace such acceptance of the universal order had brought him but, highly subjective as he always tended to be, his religion amounted in effect to a rationale of the place every atom had in the total scheme of things – even homosexuals such as himself. When he had embraced this comprehensive view, when he had accepted the fact that he was as much a part of the cosmic order as any other man, then he could exclaim, with a phrase he had picked up from Robert Louis Stevenson, that nothing was 'worth a red cent except the possession of a quiet conscience & submissive will'.[4]

He grew very gentle, and his periods of nervous irritability were less frequent. He needed all the patience he could muster to handle Catherine's deep glooms which were becoming more pronounced with advancing age. She spent solitary hours working in her garden which obsessed her to the exclusion of all other interests. 'Your mother has been exceedingly difficult to live with', Symonds confided wearily to Madge, '& her behaviour to me is something extraordinary: such an odd mixture of dead indifference with peevish disapproval. She has hardly spoken about anything except flowers. I always liked flowers, but it annoys me to see them placed far above all human interests. I am glad your mother has the resource, but it seems to me monomania, & I really think it deadens her sympathies toward people.'[5]

The womenfolk generally were cause for distress. 'There are 11 females in the house,' he moaned to Charlotte in 1885, '& I the one man, living a bachelor life among them all. It is rather more of the so-called fair sex than I like. . . .'[6] It was a household of strong personalities and fierce tensions. The girls, in their comparatively isolated life, played hard and fought stormily. Small talk wasn't tolerated and they either sat in sullen silence at the table or discussed a topic with complete and savage thoroughness. The bewildered 'Mr Moor' endured this fiery ordeal in *A Visit to Castle Slapping*:

In Castle Slapping conversation never flags. There is a continual and colossal warfare of words, waged between two members at least of that intensely interesting family, in which the other members join at intervals and keep their own smouldering fires ablaze by bellows which may blow more gently but none the less surely. Every one is hauled over the coals of these two fires, man, woman, and beast – the most trivial gnat bite, the ghastliest suicide, are all worthy of the dissecting knife of J. A. S., his wife and progeny. . . . I had a sense of being in a beleaguered City. The cannon-balls rushed around my unprotected limbs as they would in a nightmare. . . .

Despite his theatrical groans, Symonds was deeply attached to his daughters and his long letters to them are unusually loving. In 1887 he and Catherine felt that the time had come for Margaret and Lotta to return to England, and his tender concern followed them in letter after letter:

Tell me, both or either of you, if you want anything to make the life you are now living more agreeable.

Enjoy yourselves both, & learn; that is my wish. There is an immense amount for both of you to learn where you now are, which you could not learn at Davos. I believe you will learn most by enjoying simply & healthily.[7]

He was proud of the fact that he had brought them up according to his own emancipated principles, and he felt a victory had been achieved when Madge wrote from England that she found most of the families she was visiting stuffy in comparison with her own.

I am glad [he replied] that you have discovered that your family is liberal in soul beyond most people. I think that we are. Your Mother & I form a rare combination. There is nothing middle class or *bourgeois* here. Many & many a time have you heard me prate about the gospel of the spirit. Not words, serious facts, are there. A large part of human life, the largest part, is involved in not being bourgeois. I do not know whether one gets felicity thereby. I rather think that doubtful. But I am sure the spirit lives – suffering perhaps, enjoying greatly, sinning deeply, risking the passage from this world into another in a state of nudity & keen vitality. When we find God, if we ever do find Him face to face, it will be well for us, I fancy, to have been as true, as naked, as incisive, as active, as vital, as devoid of prejudices & conventions, as we can be. Only, we must bear in mind that we shall face God, & be held responsible for our deeds & feelings & desires. In some way or other, here in this life, or elsewhere in the everlasting life, God will ask about the soul committed to us – the spark of his divine existence, which we help to constitute. And that conviction abides with me ever, controlling me.[8]

His emphasis on the life of the spirit did not mean that he intended them to abandon the conventional amenities of social intercourse – instructions were sent out from the house so far from England about visiting cards, how much to tip servants ('15s. spent at the house you stay at is enough')[9] and, above all, the duty they had to make themselves agreeable to their hosts. Even that Victorian institution, the house-party, could produce something of genuine value. Symonds recalled that, when he was a boy a Marchioness had once said to him: 'Dear boy, take care never to over-stay a three days' visit.' 'I made a mental memorandum', he told his daughters, 'to avoid people with whom such precepts passed as oracles. Life, I thought, was not worth living on that scale of philosophy.

'With time, I found out that the three days' visit has its uses & its charms, & also that the people brought together in this social scheme can often diverge into beautiful relationships.'[10]

In 1889 Madge returned to England for a more lengthy visit to stay with the Leslie Stephens and study art. 'You need not my telling you', her father wrote her, 'with what anxiety & sympathy we watch all these first steps of yours in a life away from us: –

'I began to live this life of a personality making itself in the world – at 13, when I went to Harrow. And I know all the stages of it.

'It is my firm belief that parents can help their children best – & older people, the younger whom they love – by providing them with wholesome surroundings, chosen at first & mainly for their social advantages.'[11] This time Madge was completely captivated by England, and wrote long letters home in which, with the thoughtless exaggeration of the young, she found Davos inferior at every point to England. Symonds was deeply hurt. All his old anxieties about exiling his family to a confined life, in which their potentialities for self-development were restricted, reasserted themselves. After an afternoon of sleighing, he sat down and reminded her of the beauties *he* found in Davos:

As I drove down, it snowed softly incessantly & was very cold. There is a chastity, the chastity of a wild animal or of a strong shy young man in all this winter world which has not ceased to take my fancy. If we find no excitement, we have no noise, no dirt, no darkness caused by human habits.

I wish it were possible to combine what is good in this life with what is good in England. For myself, I will never voluntarily go to live in London. I should not live. I might not die. It would be death-in-life, against which, if I were strong enough to react at all, I should react by outbursts of excitement dangerous to my health. But I have always thought that your mother & you girls might do something to make an English home for yourselves. I do not see why your young life should be condemned to the limitations which suit my old life, & out of which I draw some satisfaction. . . .[12]

But there were other moods of increasing frequency in which there seemed little reason to go on living. 'Perhaps I have reached the point at which it would be better to quit the scene or be removed from it – if only one could "fade upon the midnight without pain".'[13] Madge, with that warm impetuosity so like her father's, reassured him of her love and he, in turn, admitted that, without her, 'I am a man who has lost a finger.'[14] There was, as he described it, a 'very subtle & vibrant' bond between them – the same love of beauty, the same restless craving for experience, the same ardent responsiveness. Madge had ambitions to write; Symonds bent solicitously over her initial efforts, advising her to prune 'self-important bustle'[15] from her style. To give her a taste of authorship, he collaborated with her in a collection of essays, *Our Life in the Swiss Highlands*,* which was published in 1892. He beamed with fatherly pride when she produced *Days Spent on a Doge's Farm* all by herself, but was concerned by a familiar note which he thought he recognized. 'What, by the way,' he asked her, '*is* the undercurrent of melancholy in your work? Neuropathy?'[16]

Two years before he died, Symonds confessed to Madge that 'I have often felt that what in me gave pleasure to friends & strangers, was not in its right place in my family.'[17] For such a 'Flying Dutchman of the Spirit',[18] family life had inevitable limitations, and his craving for emotional response was insatiable. The net of friendship was thrown so wide that it embraced an astounding variety of men and women, and the letters that flowed in and out of Am Hof make the literary output all the more remarkable. He had let distance diminish the friendship with Graham Dakyns and he now attempted to cement the former bond between them; even his old friend Gustavus Bosanquet, a country parson

---

* His first idea for the title was *Our Life in the High Alps*. 'I wish you would invent a good one,' he begged Mrs Ross, 'I have no talent for this' (MS. letter, dated Davos Platz, 10 December 1891, University of Bristol).

for many years, was startled when he suddenly began to receive letters from Davos. A new intimacy with Rutson, free from the torments and recriminations of the past, was re-established. 'We make a beginning – a title-page – a sketch,' he wrote to Gosse after a long intimate talk at the Savile Club in 1889; 'and then we find that the threshold has hardly been crossed, the real serious good work of life and friendship scarcely touched upon.'[19]

But one of his closest relationships had changed irreparably. Charlotte was no longer the adoring support she had once been to him. After Green's death Symonds was distressed by the state of deep melancholy into which she allowed herself to sink for a time. 'I was conscious of being really brutal to you; and this made me unhappy',[20] he apologized after one of her visits, yet he could not restrain his anger when she found morbid consolation in the brevity of life. 'I have not a very defined religion, but that attitude of mind strikes me as distinctly irreligious', he lectured her. 'Suppose you were to die & find yourself out there alone, with what is called eternity before you; where would you be then if your life on earth had not provided you with courage & unselfish sympathies, but had taught you only to expect the end – the end *then* of something wh ex hypothesis could never end.'[21] Eventually, on his advice, she roused herself to take a nursing course and cared for Jowett through one of his last illnesses. Miss Sykes had come to spend her last days with her and it was a difficult period of adjustment for both women. Symonds's very loving concern for their welfare is illustrated in his advice to 'Auntie': 'You must take great care of your diet, & learn even now at the eleventh hour, to masticate your food well so as to get the maximum of nutrition. Mr Gladstone says that he chews each piece of meat 36 times before he consigns it to his stomach. And see what he is! Able to break up the Liberal Party & shake the very pillars of the English Empire !'[22] With Charlotte, as with all to whom he was deeply attached, he continued to worry about her problems as intensely as if they were his own, but marriage had broken the immediacy of their relationship, and the place she once occupied was now filled with other close friendships.

Some of Symonds's homosexual friends could not bear the company of women, but he immensely enjoyed being with them, particularly if the women were intellectually inclined, and, more important still, if they had strongly marked, masculine personalities. With the exception of the very lovely Agnes Mary Robinson, femine, clinging women did not appeal to him; he preferred the more boisterous tomboys like Margot Tennant, the daughter of Sir Charles Tennant. In her *Autobiography* she relates the amusing circumstances of their first meeting in 1885 when she was only twenty-one. She had come to Davos to nurse one of her six sisters, Pauline Gordon Duff, and when she presented herself at Am Hof a servant showed her into a room where she was left alone for what seemed an eternity. Eventually slippered feet shuffled behind a screen and a low voice asked, 'Has she gone?' 'No, I am afraid she is still here', Margot replied pertly. At this point Symonds presented himself with a charming smile, and the ebullient Margot immediately began to charm him with her uninhibited *joie de vivre*, just as she was to enchant her future husband, Herbert Asquith, and so many other distinguished men. Every night, after putting her sister to bed, she made her way to Am Hof, where she and Symonds would sit until the early hours reading aloud from Plato, Voltaire, Browning and, of course, Whitman. Symonds agreed with Jowett that Margot was 'the best educated ill-educated woman I have ever met'. Margot's two passions were fox-hunting and good talk, and she described Symonds as a superb conversationalist. Neither Stevenson nor anyone else, she contended, 'could ever really give the fancy, the epigram, the swiftness and earnestness with which he not only expressed himself but engaged you in conversation. This and his affection combined to make him an enchanting companion.'[23]

Symonds was fascinated and a little envious of her aggressive good health – as he had been of his father's and of Whitman's – and he advised her to grab life by the forelock: 'Live well. Live happy. Do not forget me. I like to think of you in plenitude of life and activity. I should not be sorry for you if you broke your neck in the hunting field. But, like the Master,* I want you to make sure of the young, powerful life you have – before the inevitable, dolorous, long, dark night draws nigh.'[24] When he was reading the journal of Marie Bashkirtseff, he was struck by Margot's resemblance to the Russian painter: 'No two leaves on one linden are really the same. But you and she, detached from the forest of life, seem to me like leaves plucked from the same sort of tree.'[25] In 1890 he

* i.e. Jowett.

dedicated *Essays Speculative and Suggestive* to 'Miss Margot Tennant, in Memory of Long Dark Winter Nights at Davos, made Luminous by Witty Conversation'. Symonds grew absolutely devoted to this vibrant young woman; and to her brother-in-law, Gordon Duff, he wrote: 'She makes people to be in love with her. But she is able to make them go further, to love her.'[26]

Another woman of immense character to whom Symonds was greatly attached was Mrs Janet Ross, the daughter of Sir Alexander Duff-Gordon, and wife of Henry Ross, who had assisted Sir Henry Layard with the excavation of Nineveh. From the Poggio Gherardo outside Florence, she ruled the English colony with all the autocratic confidence of a *grande dame*. Symonds had met her at a house-party at Aldermaston many years before. Mrs Ross had been asked to entertain the guests after dinner with a recital of Tuscan folk songs, into which she flung herself with passionate gusto, only to be confronted by a ring of phlegmatic English faces. Suddenly from behind her, she heard the sound of applause and a friendly voice shouting, 'Bene, brava.' It was the beginning of a warm friendship, and Mrs Ross once felt moved to express her admiration for Symonds in the following poem:

> Faithful and truthful, generous, modest, kind,
> Many the virtues which in thee I find,
> So wise art thou that flattery is vain
> To fill with vanity thy steady brain.
> Made to discern the charms of men,
> And calmly trace their real meaning, when
> They would dissemble. Large and just thy view
> Of all humanity, and clear and true
> Thy judgment, which nor fear nor favour rules,
> But justice metes to sages and to fools.

'Symonds's brilliant conversation and great charm of manner', she wrote after his death, 'are impossible to describe; his talk was like fireworks, swift and dazzling, and he had a wonderful gift of sympathy – even with the fads and foibles of others. No struggling young writer ever appealed to him in vain, both his brains and his purse were at his service.'[27], Symonds was even willing to go to 'detestable' Florence to see her – 'She is a very old friend,' he told Gosse; 'and though most people do not like her, I do. A thorough *bon camarade*.'²⁸ Mrs Ross's influence was responsible for opening the Buonarroti Archives to him and when she read the proofs of *Michelangelo*, he listened carefully to her advice. At Poggio Gherardo she fussed over 'My Historian', as she called him, and he teasingly nicknamed her 'la tiranna' when she sent him off to bed early. 'For this poor wanderer on the world', he wrote her after a visit in 1891, 'your room in the evenings, with you & Mr Ross, both so tolerant of nonsense, & so delicately kind to weakness, will retain an abiding and uneffaceable impression of genial and active life.'²⁹

As Mrs Ross says, Symonds retained a lively interest in young writers and literary experimentation right up until his death. A new magazine like *The Century Guild Hobby Horse* appealed to him because its editor, Herbert Horne, and its contributors were young, fresh, and vigorous. As he grew older he contributed more and more to the new magazines like Alfred Douglas's *Spirit Lamp*, *The New Review*, and *The Artist*. His own collection of essays, *In the Key of Blue*, issued in February 1893, was a book which Holbrook Jackson described as 'so typical in some ways of the Nineties that it might well have been written by one of the younger generation'.*³⁰ He shared Gosse's interest in the importance of English translations of continental writers; his friends were constantly advised to read Tolstoy, Dostoievsky, Loti, Bourget. French literature began to intrigue him, and he was particularly delighted when his *Dante* was translated into French in 1891.

He was also interested in the young English writers who were emerging at the end of the century. He wrote to Hardy to tell him how much he enjoyed *The Return of the Native* and in reply Hardy praised him for 'silently doing your good & enduring work in the romantic place in which you live. . . . I have spread out the map of Switzerland, the better to realize where you are, & it lies before me while I write.' 'Years before we met', he went on to say, 'I used to read your essays (as correctives to those of M. Arnold, which are in need of the counterpoise that some of yours afford).' He also had some interesting remarks to make about

---

* A few copies of the first printing of the book appeared in violent 'Ricketts' Blue (quickly replaced by a cream cover, but the earlier copies are now regarded as collectors' items). *The Artist* found the effect 'not quite fortunate' – 'A Blare of gold on his cover may suit a charlatan of genius like Oscar Wilde,' it declared, 'it is hardly suitable for a follower of the Greek Sophrosyne like Mr Symonds.'

the sombre view of life pervading his novels which had offended the critics:

The tragical conditions of life imperfectly denoted in The Return of the Native & some other notices of mine I am less & less able to keep out of my work. I often begin a story with the intention of making it brighter & gayer than usual: but the question of conscience soon comes in; & it does not seem right, even in novels, to wilfully belie one's own views. All comedy is tragedy, if you only look deep enough into it. A question which used to trouble me was whether we ought to write sad stories, considering how much sadness there is in the world already. But of late I have come to the conclusion that the first step towards cure of, or even relief from, any disease being to understand it, the study of tragedy in fiction may possibly here & there be the means of showing how to escape the worst forms of it, at least, in real life. . . . I, too, am in a sense exiled. I was obliged to leave town after a severe illness some years ago – & the spot on which I live here is very lonely. However I think that, though one does get a little rusty by living in remote places, one gains, on the other hand, freedom from the temporary currents of opinion by which townspeople are caught up & distracted out of their true course.[31]

Symonds was enchanted with *Soldiers Three* and wrote to tell Kipling so.

On my word [Kipling exclaimed], I cannot see how to thank you for all the generous praises you have seen fit to bestow on an unknown manufacturer of books – a savage from among savages. In regard to my three friends whatever merit lies in my work comes from the fact that I loved em – very much, I take it, as you loved a man called Benvenuto Cellini and in your translation showed that love – so that he became alive and swaggered and brawled and beat his way across the pages. . . . At present the tide goes with me and I hope to bring the three men to the notice of the Englishman. But there is no light in this place, and the people are savages living in black houses and ignorant of everything beyond the Channel. I'll send you samples of stuff that I do, that you may warn me when I slide from decent work. Seven years of the grind of journalism lays a man open to the scamping and taking of his duty. Some day if God pleases we shall meet. Meanwhile if there is anything in my power that I can do for you in England from the purchase of cigars to the capture of dogs (forgive me if I do not know your tastes and judge all from my own weaknesses) you may command me and throughout believe in

Yours sincerely
RUDYARD K[32]

However, by the following November Symonds was beginning to be disillusioned in Kipling, as he indicated in a letter to Gosse:

I was always afraid that Kipling would go up like a rocket to come down like a stick. If you remember, I talked enthusiastically last autumn about him, before he was widely known. But this was wholly on the strength of 'Soldiers Three' and 'Studies in Black and White'. As he multiplied, it seemed to me that what one felt to be the weak side of his work became more apparent, while the stuff dwindled for want of aliment.

He is so young that he may yet find the *via artis*, which is very different from the *via vitae* strongly felt and lively seized.

Probably his milieu is not a metropolis. . . . I fear he is determined to force himself up; and no talent can do this with impunity. . . . Distinction he lacks.[33]

When it came right down to it, the novel, as a form of communication, seemed to him hopelessly inadequate. 'But how stupid all these efforts are to say the big things of our lives "by indirections". It is only the coarse rank cheek-by-jowl comradeship which pays for our immortal soul's destiny – one way or the other.

'I feel that Loti, the novelist, or that an essayist evades the main point of the situation. What that main point is, the ultimate issues of life-contacts, remains insoluble of expression, the burning-point for our vitality & future.'[34]

What Symonds was looking for was 'raw native humanity' in literature, characters who were spontaneous men of action, uninhibited either by conventional standards of behaviour or by introspection, the sort of men upon whom Symonds had been modelling himself for years. 'Symonds has got into our crowd in spite of his culture', Whitman told his friend Horace Traubel: 'I tell you we don't give away places in our crowd easy – a man has to sweat to get it.'[35] And Symonds had sweated – to stifle his Amiel-like broodings, and to live a vigorous life among simple, uncomplicated working men. He idealized democracy as a semi-Paradise in which simple, generous men would mingle in a state of fraternal equality. Like Morris, Symonds believed in a sort of mythical 'people' whose turn it now was to express themselves in art. 'The People', he exulted, 'lives and acts and feels. It is possible that the new apotheosis, if one there is to be, may rise from the proletariate [*sic*], as Christianity, as Buddhism, as the Mosaic Theocracy before it.'[36]

With these standards, it is understandable that he would be irritated by Henry James's delicate, tortuous probing of the psychological depths of the cultivated leisured classes. That he did not think very highly of James is indicated in a letter to Margot Tennant in which he raves about the journal of Marie Bashkirtseff which he had just been reading: 'The episode of Pachay, short as that is, is masterly – above the reach of Balzac; how far above the laborious beetle-flight of Henry James! Above even George Meredith. It is what James would give his right hand to do.'[37] Symonds gave expression to his faith in a new type of literature in a long lyrical essay, 'Democratic Art', included in *Essays Speculative and Suggestive* (1890), in which culture was dismissed as 'good enough in its way; but it is not what forms a manly personality, a sound and simple faith'.[38] Modern artists needed to assimilate the spirit of 'primeval forests', to be braced by principles of brotherhood, equality, individuality, freedom, comradeship.

Symonds always claimed that fame was an empty bauble and yet when some of its glitter fell his way he was quick to report it to his friends with childlike pleasure. He frequently expressed contempt for the standards of the middle classes, but when he heard of his election to the Athenaeum in 1882 the honour delighted him as a sign that his literary achievement was finally being recognized. The same year he was flattered when *Harper's Magazine* asked him to go to India to write a series of descriptive travel essays, with the added inducements of an artist to illustrate them and a proposal that he set his own fee. On a more exalted level, he was chosen by Oxford in 1888 as one of its three delegates to the eleventh centenary celebrations of the University of Bologna.

Then there was the pleasure of mingling with the famous on equal terms. In Venice he discussed the problems of writing with Browning. In 1865 he had sat in the background at Woolner's while his father talked of the Eyre case and Greek prosody with Gladstone and Tennyson; but by 1887, at a lavish dinner-party at Sir Charles Tennant's, he was seated next to Gladstone to provide the old man with a stimulating conversationalist. In 1891 he visited Tennyson at Aldworth, and the Laureate displayed a gratifying knowledge of *Renaissance in Italy*. Dr Symonds could not have asked for more.

Despite his protestations that he was through with literature, the beckoning lure of one last 'big' book continued to tempt him. Early in

1889 he disclosed to Dakyns his plans for a book embodying many ideas which had been discussed in sessions around the stove in his study with Dakyns and Arthur Sidgwick, who by now had left Rugby and was a Fellow of Corpus Christi College, Oxford, during visits to Davos. 'It will be a collection of Essays on all sorts of things. . . . Do you think "Suggestive Essays" would be a good title, & not too ambitious, for such a publication? This expresses my intention, which is to stimulate thought & to arouse speculation rather than to treat the subjects I handle *ex cathedra* or in an exhaustive way.

'My chief difficulty about the book is that the essays have been written at different times & in very different moods. Myself has changed rapidly, &, of late, immensely, since I began to think of the collection. . . . I wish I could talk with some competent friend. At times I feel inclined to chuck the whole scheme up, & to keep silence from these words for ever.' The letter ended on an even more sombre note: 'I am more & more doubtful about my own capacity to say anything which could be of the least use to anybody.' Then, in a sentence which had obviously been added later, he scrawled: 'I think I have been nearly mad, & am not sane now.'[39] Dakyns encouraged him not to abandon the work, but it meant so little to him that he did hardly more than assemble a number of essays which had already been published in various periodicals. Abstract thinking had never been his forte; and the transition to the mental discipline required for a statement of aesthetic principles after the concrete detail of the biography of Gozzi left him depressed with a sense of inadequacy to deal with unfamiliar philosophic problems.

No book ever received a worse press than *Essays Speculative and Suggestive*. 'Mr Symonds on Things in General', *The Pall Mall Gazette* headed its review, a cutting allusion to the breadth of subject-matter covered in a vague, repetitive fashion. Its failure can be judged only by turning to the four essays, 'Notes on Style'. Unlike many of the other essays in the collection, none of these had been published before; Symonds probably felt that he had to state his views on style in a book purporting to deal largely with aesthetic subjects. Pater's famous essay on style which had appeared in *Appreciations** in 1889, shortly before he

* 'I tried Pater's *Appreciations* today, and found myself wandering about among the "precious" sentences as though I had lost myself in a sugar-cane plantation' (letter to Brown, 20 June 1889, Brown, *Biography*, p. 451).

tackled the subject himself, was obviously in the forefront of his mind as he composed his own series of undistinguished comments. He takes issue with Pater where no issues exist; he deals with most of the same points, but how trite, how commonplace, how ponderous is anything he has to say in comparison with Pater's glittering finesse! The truth of the matter was that he could not work up the slightest interest in Pater's pre-occupation with art aspiring to the condition of music or the fusion of form and content. It all seemed so utterly trivial.

He believed he had nothing anyone wanted to hear; the self-deprecation of a letter to Margot Tennant is almost embarrassing:

What the critics say is that I have uttered truisms in the baldest, least attractive diction.

Here I find myself to be judged, and not unjustly. In the pursuit of truth, I said what I had to say bluntly – and it seems I had nothing but commonplaces to give forth. In the search for sincerity of style, I reduced every proposition to its barest form of language. And that abnegation of rhetoric has revealed the nudity of my commonplaces. . . .

So, when I finally withdraw from further appeals to the public, as I mean to do, I cannot pose as a Prospero who breaks his staff. I am only a somewhat sturdy varlet in the sphere of art, who has sought to wear the robe of the magician – and being now disrobed, takes his place quietly where God appointed him, and means to hold his tongue in future. . . .[40]

On the eve of his departure for a visit to England in 1892, he wrote to Madge:

What vexes me is the thought that not only am I growing old, but that I have some unconquerable malady to face – death in fact is near. My soul keeps whispering this to my spiritual ear.

And before I go hence & see the lovely earth no longer I want to do so much still. I want to write my History of Graubünden, to publish my work on Sexual Aberrations, & to get my Autobiography finished.

I do not think I should have written so candidly to you as I have done under this cover, were I not starting soon for a journey to England with this Fear upon me. I regard you, & always have regarded you more as a comrade than a daughter. And I say now to you, as we shall not meet before you leave Italy, what I say to no one else.

Think well of me, when all is over. I have been a very unhappy man, as you will find out if you read the history of my life. But I have tried to be a brave one, & to work.[41]

He had no appetite, perpetual diarrhoea made life wretched, and he tossed restlessly on his old peasant bed night after night. A photograph taken of him during this period reveals feverish, anxious eyes, underlined by deep grooves; the haggard face is too young for the experience that has been etched upon it. Madge was greatly distressed by its expression of utter misery; it was too nakedly unguarded without even a beard to soften the truth. 'I am sorry', he apologized to her, 'I depressed & saddened you so much, & that you hate my photograph. It is easy enough, if I choose, to let my mangy grizzled beard grow again. Only I think I am better without it. What you do not like is the look of spiritual fatigue, of being haunted eternally, w[h] my face in a photogaph carries. I cannot help that. I was born with a temperament w[h] has given me immense worry & distress all through my life. It is, luckily, mixed up with great capacity for enjoyment & being happy.

'I do not feel easy about my health. But no doctors can help much. Who can minister to a mind diseased? Neither divine nor physician. And the mind corrodes its organ the nervous system, with me. Of rest there is no possible question left.'[42]

As death seemed to draw closer, so the longing intensified to embrace as much life as he could before the shadows obliterated everything. During the last two years of his life he grew very intimate with Lord Ronald Gower, of whose abandoned sensuality he had never quite approved. But now, with so little time remaining, Gower's lack of restraint appealed to the desperation in him. 'With me life becomes ever more intense', he wrote to Dakyns, 'as my real strength wanes, & my days decrease. It seems to me sometimes awful: the pace at which I live in feeling – inversely to the pace at which my self is ebbing to annihilation. . . . I never seem to have lived until quite lately; & just when the times are out of joint for self-externalizing life, I seem drawn into it.

'It is true I go on writing books, & even poems. But literature has long since lost for me reality of interest.

'One reads certainly. Copious reading fills the vacuum which remains when feeling & sensation are abeyant.'[43]

He was asked to deliver a lecture on the Renaissance in Oxford at the end of July 1892, and he became unusually excited about the prospect of a visit to England on which Angelo would accompany him. The time in England passed in a whirlwind of activity and varied experience. In London, where he stayed with T. H. Warren, one of his Sixth Formers who was now President of Magdalen College, Oxford, he rushed around to art galleries and publishers and old friends. He saw his new collection of essays, *In the Key of Blue*, through the press. He arranged to spend the Sisson bequest on good works. He took Angelo to the theatre several times, and found the same pleasure in his naïve response as he had so many years before with Norman. After he delivered his lecture at Oxford (said to have been attended by over a thousand) he and Lord Ronald Gower travelled to Stratford to look at Gower's new statue of Shakespeare, then on to Yorkshire to stay with Gower's relative, Lord Carlisle, at Castle Howard. There Symonds was intrigued by the gaunt old man shuffling about the cavernous rooms and corridors, whose darkness was lit only by the flickering light of candles. A day or so later they set out again, this time to find a complete contrast in 'The Glen', Inverleithen, the home of Margot Tennant's parents – 'a house too flowing with wine beer food & flunkeys'.[44] Here he saw a side of Margot not generally revealed to the world. 'I like Margot in her home', Symonds told Madge. 'She is the life of it. The girl at heart is deeply religious & conservative in her feeling about life. She has a very singular naïveté & innocence underlying her fast ways.

'She over-lives life, & is very pale, & much thinner.

'Politics & correspondence with people in the swim of the great world are still her main interest. I don't think, however, that she enlarges her circle very much. The clique is not a wide one but it touches society at several points. I see that Margot suffers, as most people do, from want of fixed work.'[45]

In all, he stayed in nineteen private houses and seven hotels during these six weeks in England, and just as he sensed the danger signs of imminent collapse he abruptly cut short all his plans, including, as we have seen, the meeting with Havelock Ellis, and headed back for Am Hof.

His interminable restlessness made Davos intolerable and the early autumn found him in Venice, where he resumed his complex double life; but its pace, combined with ambitious new literary plans, was too much for him. His spirit demanded excitement, but the rebellious body craved rest. 'I get so dreadfully tired sometimes,' he complained in his last letter to Gosse in January 1893, 'and yet I cannot stop. The little threads that entangle are so shy and subtle. Days and weeks go by in a dream of fusses w^h mean nothing. And when the moment of rest comes, the tired brain writes a sonnet or a study of "Venetian Melancholy".

'. . . The real thing is that I was not made to live in the Category of Time.'[46]

The following month Brown received a disturbing communication from him: 'Last Sunday night, I was lying awake, thinking of death, desiring death; when, lost in this sombre mood, to me the bedroom was at a moment filled with music – the "Lontan lontano", from Boito's "Mefistofele", together with its harp accompaniment.

'"Lontan lontano" has not left yet my auditory sense – stays behind all other sensations – seems to indicate a vague and infinite, yet very near. . . .'[47] This sober mood was reinforced by a letter from Charlotte telling him that Jowett lay gravely ill.

Symonds had been invited to deliver a lecture in Florence on 15 April; but realizing that he could not stand the strain of addressing a large group of people, he asked Mrs Ross to arrange for someone else to read it for him. As though endowed with some curious intuition of just how much strength remained to him, he was determined to conserve his small resources to enjoy these last weeks. At the beginning of April he set off with his much-loved Madge on what in effect amounted to a pilgrimage of fulfilment. Intending to move through southern Italy as whim dictated, he was frantic to absorb every nuance of pleasure he could extract from the experience, and never before had any of his innumerable journeys comprehended such a variety of activity.

He had always said that the best way to appreciate a city was by night, and through the dark streets of Bari, Taranto, and Naples he wandered with that rapt, eager expression he assumed when his senses were acutely aroused. The early spring flowers brought him the same intense delight he had experienced on the visit to Italy with Cecil Bosanquet in 1863, and each day he would pick a tall spike of asphodel to carry about with him on his walks. They stayed with Sir James Lacaita* at Leucaspide where one night Symonds joined in the pizzica dancing but was mortified to find how stiff his joints were. 'How I envied the scullion-boy's beautiful toes!' he confessed ruefully to Mrs Ross. His delight in the absurd asserted itself after a visit to the temples of Paestum when, in the railway-carriage, he could hardly restrain his laughter when he realized that the German tourist sitting opposite him had secreted a fragment of the Temple of Neptune in an old plaid shawl. At Naples he took Madge on a perilous sailing expedition in which they were almost wrecked on the rocks. They even attempted to climb Vesuvius, although here his enthusiasm outran his resources and he had to stop before they reached the top.

Back in Rome he hurried Madge round to his favourite places, all the time talking volubly, animatedly, feverishly. It was as though he had to make one last attempt to encompass all the glory of that bewilderingly beautiful city, and to help her to see it with his eyes. He had a slight cold, but the only shadow to cross their days was an intermittent anxiety about Catherine, who lay ill in Venice with gastric fever.

No words could surpass Margaret Symonds's moving account of the last days of her father's life, which Brown appended to his biography of Symonds. She has described how he took her especially to see one of his favourite sketches, Dürer's 'Rabbit'; how she held his coat while he stretched dangerously over a ledge to gather some mignonette; how he stopped the carriage one morning above the city in order to point out not the buildings but the Campagna, the hills, the quality of the air, those things that struck him as the essential beauties of Rome; and how he lingered thoughtfully over the inscription on a cardinal's tomb, 'Labor et gloria vita fuit, mors requies'.

There was an epidemic of influenza in Rome and on Sunday night, the 16th, he complained of a sore throat. The following day it was worse, and Madge called in a friend of her father's, Dr Axel Munthe,† who told

---

* Sir James Lacaita (1813-95) was an Italian scholar and politician whose interests were divided between Italy and England. He was knighted for his services as secretary to Gladstone's mission to the Ionian Islands in 1858. At one time he had been an unsuccessful candidate for Librarian of the London Library. During the past fifteen years he had wintered at Leucaspide where he had large land-holdings.

† Axel Munthe (1857-1949), was the Swedish physician and author of *The Story of San Michele*. In 1893 he was practising medicine in Rome.

her to poultice his throat, but reassured her that there was no cause for alarm. Symonds was desperately tired, but from his bed he continued to talk volubly; at night he choked and panted in the clammy Roman air, even though they were staying in a large room on the fifth floor of the Hotel d'Italia where they had hoped they might find a fresh breeze. The next morning – Tuesday – it was immediately apparent that he had become much weaker and his mind seemed to be wandering slightly. The uproar in the street outside was deafening: the King and Queen of Italy were celebrating their silver wedding anniversary and crowds were pouring into the city for the festivities. Up to this point Madge and Angelo had been nursing Symonds by themselves, but he began to sink so rapidly that the distraught Madge, in a futile act of despair, called in an English Catholic sister. During the day Symonds once roused himself to ask for some paper to write a note to Catherine. He found it difficult to hold his head up and could only scrawl the last lines, but he carefully folded the paper and with a final gesture of his customary neatness, drew his three trefoils as a seal for the envelope.

He did not suffer. He never complained of the heat or the noise but thanked his attendants gently for whatever they did for him. He muttered incessantly to himself. 'He seemed to be wandering back through the *thoughts*, not the experience of his old life', Margaret later recalled. 'His body was exhausted, but his mind, though detached from the present surroundings, was strangely strong. Though delirious with fever, he maintained that extraordinary command over his brain, which only years of protracted suffering can procure.'[48] He had only one request – late in the day he asked her to hand him his mother's small book of spiritual texts which he had carried with him on all his travels.

By Wednesday there was no possible doubt that he was dying. Dr Munthe brought another doctor to examine him, and they told Madge that his condition was hopeless since both lungs and the heart were being paralysed by pneumonia. Symonds had become pitifully weak, and although he never stopped talking earnestly to himself, it was impossible now to catch his words. By noon the talking ceased, he sank into a deep sleep, and his breathing became painfully laboured. During this last hour of his life he seemed happy; the lines on the face smoothed out and the head struck Margaret as strangely transformed into that of a young boy.

She cradled him in her arms as he slept, and, as he lay with his head on her shoulder, in the heat of a cloudless Roman day, the breathing stopped.

A short time later, a Swiss porter from the Graubünden mountains timidly entered the room with a large bouquet of lilac. The enormous fellow, obviously deeply moved, reverently laid the bouquet beside his dead friend. It seemed appropriate that this should be the first remembrance Symonds received and it was followed by masses of flowers from his many friends in Rome.

That afternoon Madge travelled through the hot, noisy congestion of the city to the tranquillity of the Protestant Cemetery, then at its loveliest with the graves covered with spring flowers. Lines from 'Adonais' had been flowing through her mind and she chose a spot close to Shelley's grave. That night, as Symonds lay still and untroubled, Rome thundered with fireworks and rejoicing.

The funeral was delayed until Saturday in order to give Catherine and Charlotte time to reach Rome. All those who gathered round his grave spoke to each other of the beauty of the vernal setting where they left their friend, whose spirit remained so young. 'How it would have thrilled him!' T. E. Brown exclaimed, when Dakyns told him that Symonds lay not far from Shelley...[49] Jowett, who was to die only a few months later, wrote the epitaph that appeared on his grave:

INFRA JACET

JOHANNES ADDINGTON SYMONDS

VIR LUMINIBUS INGENII MULTIS

ET INDUSTRIA SINGULARI,

CUJUS ANIMUS

INFIRMO LICET IN CORPORE

LITERARUM ET HISTORIAE STUDIO ARDEBAT

BRISTOLII NATUS V. OCT. MDCCCXL.

REQUIEVIT IN CHRISTO XIX AP. MDCCCXCIII

AVE CARISSIME

NEMO TE MAGIS IN CORDE AMICOS FOVEBAT

NEC IN SIMPLICES ET INDOCTOS BENEVOLENTIOR ERAT.

And below these words they added Symonds's translation of Cleanthes's hymn:

Lead thou me, God, Law, Reason, Motion, Life,
All names for Thee alike are vain and hollow:
Lead me, for I will follow without strife,
Or if I strive, still must I blindly follow!

A few days later Catherine wrote to Dakyns: 'More & more I feel what a fitting end it was to his life that he should die just so, & *there*, in Rome – & be buried there under the cypresses. Only I wish I might have been there. He was overworked so terribly in the last months at Davos, how could he help breaking down? He seemed to have collected all the work of all his friends besides his own – & to be doing it all at once himself – And he was so dreadfully tired & yet would *never rest.*'[50]

CHAPTER XIII

Aftermath

W H E N Catherine arrived in Rome, Madge handed her the note which
Symonds had written so painfully a few hours before his death.

My dearest Catherine [she read], there is something I ought to tell you, and
being ill at Rome I take this occasion. If I do not see you again in this life you
remember that I made H. F. Brown depositary of my printed books. I wish
that legacy to cover all M.S. Diaries Letters & others matter found in my books
cupboard, with the exception of business papers. I do this because I have written
things you would not like to read, but which I have always felt justified and
useful for society. Brown will consult & publish nothing without your consent.

Ever yours

J. A. SYMONDS

Rome. April 19. 1893.

You are ill at Venice & I have fallen here. No time for more.[1]

To this he added a pencilled scrawl; 'I want to write all I have to say.
The doctor particularly wants to see it,' and, in the margin, 'Show this at
once to him.' There were also a few Italian words trailing off into
illegibility. Apparently he had made an overwhelming effort to summon
up enough strength to write this vital message, its strange formality a
reflection of the urgency which possessed him; and then, exhausted from
this last struggle, he surrendered completely.

A few months later, Catherine copied out the note for Dakyns, with
the comment: 'These were his last words in pencil – hardly legible – wh.
they gave me when I reached Rome that morning. You see how the great
question was supreme in his mind to the very last. Are we right in being
cowardly & suppressing it? I am glad to have Henry's wisdom for *final*
reference. I trust Horatio fully & want to help, not hinder him as you
know. I think if I write a very short preface embodying part of this

318

letter, it will make his position clear to the outside world (not his friends, I mean) but the critics & relations.'[2]

During the following year the perplexing problem of the autobiography remained more troublesome than the disposal of Am Hof and the plans for a permanent return to England. Catherine, Brown, and Sidgwick agreed that the Memoirs were impossible to publish in their full 'fond outpourings', as Henry James described them. Symonds's daughters had regarded his attachments for young men with affectionate amusement, but the full implications of these relationships had been sedulously concealed from them, and it seemed perilous suddenly to overturn the carefully constructed house of cards. On the other hand, people's suspicions might be aroused if the autobiography were not published, particularly when it was widely known that Symonds had regarded it as his most important work.

An arrangement was finally worked out that Brown would write a 'biography' in which passages from the autobiography would be linked by comment from Brown and by sections of letters written by Symonds and some of his friends. Graham Dakyns, who might have been offended because the literary executorship had been handed over to Brown in 1882 without, apparently, Symonds even consulting him, freely lent almost six hundred of Symonds's letters which he still possessed. Brown had nearly two thousand of his own through which he had to sift, discarding all those that might be too candid. Cautious Henry Sidgwick exercised a firm censor's eye over the whole project. It seemed that anyone who had any connection at all with Symonds had objections to raise, most of them of course concerned with the importance of suppressing the inversion. 'I suspect,' Brown said of one of these, Symonds's nephew, St Loe Strachey,* who was just starting out on his journalistic career, 'that St Loe regrets the waste of reputation, consideration, etc more than anything else in connection with Johnnie's Urningtherism.'[3]

'It is immensely difficult', Brown complained to Dakyns, 'to hit the just line which will not express more than the family & Sidgwick think advisable & will yet leave a not altogether unveracious "counterfeit presentment" of Johnnie.'[4] In the Preface, Brown skilfully skirted the

---

* In 1896 Strachey became editor of *The Cornhill* and from 1898 to 1925 was editor and owner of *The Spectator*.

reasons for not publishing the full autobiography and simply claimed that
he had been influenced by 'ordinary and obvious reasons which render
the immediate publication of autobiographies undesirable'. Then he
hurried on to assert that a biography would be far more valuable than an
autobiography because, as Symonds himself pointed out, 'autobiographies
written with a purpose . . . are likely to want atmosphere. A man, when
he sits down to give an account of his own life, from the point of view of
art or of a particular action, is apt to make it appear as though he were
nothing but an artist, nothing but a lover, or that the action he seeks to
explain were the principal event in his existence. The report has to be
supplemented in order that a true portrait may be painted.'[5] Therefore,
claimed Brown, the inclusion of letters and diaries could give a far more
comprehensive picture of a man than the distorted lens of the ego itself.
His argument failed to be convincing because the framework chosen by
Brown was in effect a highly selective autobiography, and Symonds's voice
was still almost the only one to be heard, usually in a tone of anguish
that highlighted one aspect of his life. Moreover, Brown failed to note
that a biography which falsifies a man, changes events, and omits important
facts, is less than truth. The conspiracy of silence was largely successful
and when Gosse, who had read the Memoirs, reviewed the biography for
the St James's Gazette 1895, he mentioned casually that the autobiography was 'too bulky for publication'.[6]

So many friendships had to be omitted, so many activities had to be
suppressed, so many motives had to be accounted for in innocuous terms.
In some cases, the attempt at concealment was absurd: Mrs Josephine
Butler, for instance, was referred to as 'Mrs B.' When Gosse expostulated
with Brown for not including the Opalstein description by Robert Louis
Stevenson, Brown justified its omission with the explanation that
Symonds had been offended by it. Norman Moor* and his wife were still
alive and no reference could be made to his friendship with Symonds.
Angelo might be accounted for as the traditional loyal servant. Rutson
could not be mentioned except in the most casual way. A veil of silence
had to be drawn over the traumatic events at Harrow; it was impossible
not to give some brief explanation for Symonds's withdrawal from
Magdalen, and as Shorting had retired into oblivion, he could be referred

* Norman died in 1895, the year the biography was published.

to cryptically as a false friend who had betrayed him. Consideration had to be given to the feelings of Catherine, who was not to die until 1913, so the truth about their courtship and marriage must be glossed over. Walt Whitman could be described as a powerful philosophic influence but the question posed by 'Calamus' was far too delicate to be raised. Naturally. *A Problem in Greek Ethics*, *A Problem in Modern Ethics* and Havelock Ellis were best forgotten.

What was left? Well, one could always turn to religion. All the tormented young Robert Elsmeres of the period were being perplexed by doubt and harassed by scepticism, so why not Symonds as well? 'Those marvellous out-pourings' (Henry James again) could be interpreted as the anguished gropings of a deeply religious man. In the Preface, Brown wrote: 'The central, the architechtonic, quality of his nature was religious. By religious, I mean that his major occupation, his dominating pursuit, was the interrogation of the Universe, the search for God.' Brown amassed and juxtaposed Symonds's comments on religion in such overwhelming magnitude that the general conception of Symonds has been that of L. E. Elliott-Binns who has said of him and Henry Sidgwick that 'vaguely aware of a supersensual reality which they could neither find nor forget, they became waifs in an alien world, or, to adopt a more modern figure, dispossessed and stateless persons'.[7] Those sections in which Symonds could not have spelled out the situation more clearly Brown omitted out of consideration for Mrs Symonds and under pressure from Henry Sidgwick. While it is true that Symonds's life was engaged in 'an earnest search for truth in painful God-forgotten wildernesses', his 'dominating pursuit' was not a quest for God but for a *modus vivendi*, an apologetic which would satisfy both his Nonconformist conscience and the mores of society and at the same time reconcile these with his own overpowering instincts.

After reading Brown's biography, Henry James told Gosse: 'I have been reading with the liveliest – an almost painful – interest the 2 volumes on the extraordinary Symonds. They gave me an extraordinary impression of his "gifts" – yet I don't know what keeps them from being tragic.'[8] It was probably the false impression of a self-consciously tragic stance, the wallowing in self-pity without any specific cause for grief, that prevented James from responding with complete sympathy. Those who had known Symonds well were not so easily satisfied with the Amiel-like figure constantly beating his chest troubled by some vague spiritual malaise. 'I confess that I had not known Symonds', the puzzled T. E. Brown wrote Horatio Brown after reading the biography. 'That is, I had not known what an important part in his life was borne by the sceptical agony, or, rather agonizing. Are you quite sure that, through some co-affinity of temperament or experience, you have not exaggerated this? I mean relatively. . . . I fancy I can recollect a different Symonds, full of enthusiasm for favourite authors, outspoken, critical, of course, but brimming with love for those he preferred. What has become of this rapture? I think it was the normal mood, & the other the abnormal.'9

His daughters, who had also known a gay, delightful human being, were disappointed that this side of his nature was not revealed in the official biography. In 1899 Margaret wrote from Clifton to Dakyns: 'His spirit seems to haunt Clifton – the sadder or more sentimental . . . side of him is here. There was another side – strong, healthy, joyful even which only the Graubünden, its men & mountains & home life called forth.'10 In order to give a more complete portrait of her father she wrote her recollections, *Out of the Past* (1925), and Katharine was moved to contribute her own in *Hearts and Pomegranates* (1940).

In the letter in which a perplexed T. E. Brown asked what had become of the Symonds he had known, he went on to berate Brown, Dakyns, and Sidgwick for encouraging Symonds in his role of the anguished poet *manqué*. 'Pardon me when I blame you', he stated bluntly, 'for not in every way discouraging those flashes and ebulitions of a despair which, in him, had no ground in the actual. You ought to have ducked & dived beneath these outbursts, not sympathised with them, not admired them. Was there not something of an *abonder dans son sens* in your intercourse with him, & all your encounters with what I must not hesitate to call the evil spirit in him. I know the difficulty. The astounding dialectic vigour of Symonds overpowered you. The method – his madness was magnificent. You could not stand up to it. Sidgwick might have had a chance; but no one else. Who would bell the cat?'

Undoubtedly there is a good deal of truth in Brown's description of the hypnotic power Symonds seemed to exert over his friends. In his close relationships, Symonds was obsessive, absorbing, insistent. He made tremendous claims on his friends' sympathy and they could not resist his demands to condole with his frustrations. On the other hand, they seemed equally ready to accept the swift reversal of mood to the engaging gaiety of the *bon viveur*. To be a friend of Symonds's became an engulfing experience in which one ranged through the entire spectrum of emotion. Perhaps part of the explanation for his hold over his friends lay in their realization that he was willing to give as much as he received – and they had to be willing to receive it. No man ever embraced the Hellenic spirit of comradeship more passionately.

At his death, Henry Sidgwick wrote to Gosse: 'He gave the world all he could: but how much more he gave his friends cannot be told.'[11] Henry James was intrigued by the legend of the vibrant firefly, and after Symonds's death wrote to Gosse:

I am very glad of the emotion that led you to write me immediately after the sudden – the so brutal & tragic extinction, as it comes to one, of poor forevermore silent J. A. S. I had never even (clearly) seen him – but somehow I too can't help feeling the pang – & with a personal emotion. It always seemed as if I *might* know him & of few men whom I didn't know has the image so much come home to me. Poor much-living much-doing passionately out-giving man! Various things, however, seem to me to have been made – to have contributed to make – his death – in the conditions – fortunate and noble. The super-abundant achieved work – I mean, the achieved maturity – with age & possibly aberration (repetition & feverish over-production) what was mainly still to come; and now, *instead*, the full-life stopped and rounded, as it were, by a kind of heroic maximum – and under the adored Roman sky. I hope he will be buried there – in the angle of the wondrous wall where the Englishmen lie – & not in his terrible Davos. He must have been very interesting – & you must read me some of his letters. We shall talk of him. . . .

Do let me know of any circumstance about Symonds – or about his death that may be interesting.[12]

The people of Davos among whom Symonds had lived for sixteen years presented Catherine with a memorial scroll whose stiff formal language did not conceal the very real regret they felt at the loss of their friend and benefactor. But the obituary writers were presented with a problem more difficult than simple grief when it came to evaluating his ambiguous literary career. In a private letter Gosse might write to

Stevenson: 'Symonds was a very dear and charming creature, a loyal friend, courageous in the face of piteous troubles from within and without, by the very nature of his isolation singularly free from prejudice – I think of him with genuine affection and most real regret.'[13] Yet, in the unsigned obituary he wrote for *The Saturday Review*, he described him as 'one who aimed at the highest things and came a little short'.[14] One of the few unqualified eulogistic notices came from Lord Alfred Douglas. 'The world', he sighed, 'has lost [in] him a sweet poet, and a biographer, translator, and essayist, as learned, as graceful, and as brilliant as any that it has ever known.'[15] *The Artist* published an unusually frank memorial poem, of which one stanza read :

> O loyal-hearted, O comrade dear,
> What words shall serve for our grief or ruth,
> Soul found flawless from fleck or fear,
> Lover of Art and Nature and Youth.
> You that have lifted the world's heart higher,
> Drawing the hearts of us nigher and nigher,
> 'Let men be lovers,' your voice rang clear,
> 'Let men be lovers, and Truth be Truth.'[16]

Those who were not his friends or sympathetic to his views were not so charitable. One of the harshest judgments was voiced by Oswald Crawford who did not soften his blunt opinion even for an obituary notice: 'Mr John Addington Symonds will not go down to posterity as a great writer of English, though it has been the fashion of late to praise his style. A little of it goes a long way for in truth the readers who can stand more than half-a-page at a time of intentional word-painting are not very numerous.'[17]

And Swinburne, who had once flattered him in the most unctuous terms, only a year after his death, in his recollections of Jowett, wrote of 'such renascent blossoms of the Italian renascence as the Platonic amorist of blue-breeched gondoliers who is now in Aretino's bosom. The cult of the calamus, as expounded by Mr Addington Symonds to his fellow-calamites, would have found no acceptance or tolerance with the translator of Plato.'[18]

Today Symonds's writings can be analysed as the expression of the unreconciled elements of his nature. Sensuous and artistic, he loved the colour and texture of words, but he lacked the restraint of the true artist in handling his medium. When he attempted to discipline the exuberance of his style, the result was all too often the flat banality of declarative statement. In his poetry, where he felt less compulsion to confine the torrent, the uninhibited indulgence in emotional hyperbole can embarrass the reader with its exhibitionist display. As for the wide range of subject-matter, while it indicated a fine breadth of interest, it also reflects his inability to probe very deeply, except perhaps in some features of the Renaissance.

Symonds approached every aspect of life, be it art or human relationships, with the same intense fervour. Ideas were seldom analysed for their logical content, but tested against the degree of his emotional response. '. . . a man of a thousand moods,' said T. E. Brown, 'a Proteus always, a Philoctetes occasionally'; the swift reversal of mood from Teutonic gloom to the high spirits of a larking schoolboy were clearly the characteristics of an unbalanced temperament, but his neurosis was a complex amalgam of various important influences, each of which might have unsettled the most stable of men.

One significant aspect of the man which cannot be overlooked is that he was the victim of tuberculosis. His disease as such was first diagnosed at twenty-five; sporadic attacks of blood-spitting preceded a severe haemorrhage when he was thirty-seven; at forty-two the 'mischief' in his right lung was also detected; and at fifty-two he died of a paralysis of the lungs following a severe attack of influenza. His whole life was a battle with wretched health: heavy colds, bronchitis, severe headaches, inflamed eyes, insomnia, troubled dreams, fever, rheumatism – it is a dreary chronicle of enforced idleness and lassitude. In the intervals of temporary relief he hurled himself into work or strenuous exercise, frantic to cram in as much activity as he could before the inevitable consequences of his over-indulgence overwhelmed him.

As though such a handicap were not strain enough, he had to reconcile his homosexuality with the rigours of Victorian morality. Even in his own day and age, he might have found himself in certain stations in life where the pressures to conform were not so exigent, but from the time he was a small child it had been impressed upon him that it was his duty to be a credit to a noble father who held a respected position in society.

Driven by the compelling sexual demands of his nature, he was as much torn by the dictates of conscience and the moral attitudes of his class. Most of the world saw only the harassed features of the mask assumed by a marginal man, tragically aware of his alienation from society at large.

A third pressure aggravated the dilemma of his situation. This was the necessity to 'prove' himself. It is a commonplace that anything less than success was deemed a failure by the Victorians, and in Symonds's case his early indoctrination by his father and by Jowett confirmed in him an irretrievable determination to grab fame by the forelock. With the torment of bad health and moral problems undermining every project he undertook, his perseverance emerges as rare courage, even more remarkable when he clearly understood that he was equipped only with a keen intelligence and moderate talents. Dogged industry, in the face of all odds, was an attempt to counterbalance the lack of genius.

Little wonder, then, that Symonds has left an impression of narcissism as he grappled with the intricacies of his problems. On the other hand, neither his personality nor his failure can be judged apart from the context of his own times. He died just before the turn of the century and he was touched by many of the currents that had swept men into a flood of perplexity, doubt, and at times, despair. His far-ranging mind would have been more at home in the critical climate of the Renaissance in which spiritual disintegration was checked by an underpinning of faith. His true milieu would have been a Periclean Athens where his passion for sensuous expansion could have developed more freely; but, granted that there were environments more attuned to his capacities, it would be an inadequate description of the man to portray him as entirely out of step with his century. He was excited by its scientific discoveries, he shared its interest in historical research, and his Hellenism was an intense form of an enthusiasm far wider than his own. His comprehensive attitude, his eagerness to sally through the arch of experience, stamp him as a far more typical nineteenth-century figure than a narrow aesthete like Pater.

Symonds's writings have not deserved the obscurity to which they have been relegated. His *Renaissance in Italy* might find a far wider audience than the scholars who still regard it as one of the most important contributions to the period made by any Englishman. His literary criticism, derivative and confused though it often is, reflects many of the conflicting standards of his time. His poetry, despite its artificiality of diction, betrays a note of genuine feeling.

Taut, guarded, perennially anxious, Symonds remains something of an enigma. He never succeeded in fusing the contradictory facets of his complex personality. A romantic, he longed always for the impossible. A realist, he knew only too well that the sensuous beauty of a world symbolized by the passing gondolier would forever elude him.

NOTES AND SOURCES

PROLOGUE *pp.* 1-4

1 MS. letter to Margaret Symonds, Venice, 4 November 1892 (University of Bristol).
2 'Venetian Melancholy', *The Fortnightly Review, LIII* (Feb. 1893), 260.
3 MS. letter, *op. cit.*
4 *Ibid.*

CHAPTER I — CLIFTON *pp.* 5-21

1 Thomas Carlyle, *The Life of Sterling* (Chapman & Hall, 1851), p. 239.
2 Horatio F. Brown, *John Addington Symonds, A Biography* (Smith, Elder & Co., Second Edition, 1903), p. 14.
3 D. Hack Tuke, *Prichard and Symonds in Especial Relation to Mental Science* (J. & A. Churchill, 1891), p. 34.
4 MS. letter, Davos Platz, 20 December 1888 (University of Bristol).
5 MS. letter (University of Bristol).
6 Brown, *op. cit.*, p. 6.
7 MS. letter, Bavluo, 25 May 1866 (Dakyns Collection).
8 Brown, *op. cit.*, p. 4.
9 *Ibid.*, p. 12.
10 *Ibid.*, p. 31.
11 *Ibid.*, p. 27.
12 *Ibid.*, p. 6.
13 *Ibid.*, p. 39.
14 *Ibid.*
15 MS. letter, Davos Platz, 20 April 1887 (University of Bristol).
16 Brown, *op. cit.*, p. 10.

CHAPTER II — HARROW *pp.* 22-41

1 Horatio F. Brown, *John Addington Symonds, A Biography* (Smith, Elder & Co., Second Edition, 1903), p. 47.
2 Anthony Trollope, *An Autobiography*, 1 (W. Blackwood & Sons, 1883), pp. 5, 6.
3 MS. letter to Charlotte (University of Bristol).

4 MS. letter to Charlotte, 6 June 1857 (University of Bristol).

5 Brown, *op. cit.*, p. 58.

6 MS. letter, 15 June 1857 (University of Bristol).

7 MS. letter to Charlotte (University of Bristol).

8 MS. letter (University of Bristol).

9 MS. letter (University of Bristol).

10 MS. letter (University of Bristol).

11 *The Times*, 29 April 1854, p. 10.

12 Percy Thornton, *Harrow School and its Surroundings* (W. H. Allen & Co., 1885), p. 448.

13 MS. letter to Charlotte (University of Bristol).

14 MS. letter to Charlotte (University of Bristol).

15 MS. letter to Charlotte, 2 November 1856 (University of Bristol).

16 MS. letter, 15 June 1857 (University of Bristol).

17 Augustus Hare, *The Story of My Life*, I (George Allen, 1896), p. 242.

18 *Harrow School*, ed. E. W. Houson and G. F. Warner (Edward Arnold, 1898), p. 198.

19 Margaret Symonds (Mrs W. W. Vaughan) *Out of the Past* (John Murray, 1925), p. 40.

20 *Ibid.*, p. 42.

21 Brown, *op. cit.*, pp. 53, 54.

22 MS. letter, 8 March 1857 (University of Bristol).

23 Arthur P. Stanley, *The Life and Correspondence of Thomas Arnold* (B. Fellowes, Sixth Edition, 1846), p. 423.

24 *Harrow School*, *op. cit.*, p. 113. Percy Thornton in *Harrow School and its Surroundings* (W. H. Allen & Co., 1885), p. 294, asserts: 'The years 1844-59 will be remembered on the whole for a steady progress (which even out-stripped the national advance) in the standard of morals, learning, and discipline, while, with the single exception of the Platt-Stewart case, public controversy was unheard in connection with Harrow.'

25 F. D. How, *Six Great Schoolmasters* (Methuen & Co., 1904), p. 138.

26 MS. letter to Charlotte, 22 February 1857 (University of Bristol).

27 Edward Graham, *The Harrow Life of Henry Montagu Butler, D.D.* (Longmans, Green & Co., 1920), p. 29.

28 MS. letter to Charlotte, 17 May 1857 (University of Bristol).

29 J. G. Cotton Minchin, *Old Harrow Days* (Methuen & Co., 1898), p. 100.

30 *Harrow School*, *op. cit.*, p. 110.

31 MS. letter to Charlotte, 24 June 1858 (University of Bristol).

32 Graham, *op. cit.*, p. 119.

33 Charles John Vaughan, *Memorials of Harrow Sundays* (Macmillan & Co., 1859), pp. 490, 491.

34 Thornton, *op. cit.*, p. 299.

35 Graham, *op. cit.*, p. 129.

36 In an unwittingly ironical passage in *Our Public Schools* (Swan Sonnenschein & Co., 1901), p. 148, J. G. Cotton Minchin remarks: 'Charles John Vaughan must have been born under a happy star. Everything to which he put his hand prospered. As Head Master, Rector, Master of the Temple, Dean, he was equally successful. His success we might not wonder at. . . . The secret of his influence lay in his rare gift of self-renunciation. It is a great stake to play, but the man who plays it wins the game. Every suffrage is secured by him who is indifferent to the prizes which others seek. . . .

'It is . . . a fact, little known, that the Bishopric of Rochester was offered to Dr Vaughan and accepted by him, but a few days after his acceptance of the mitre he wrote to Lord Palmerston asking to be excused, if the matter had not gone too far.'

37 MS. letter, September 1859 (University of Bristol).

38 MS. letter (Dakyns Collection).

39 Graham, *op. cit.*, p. 130.

40 One Who Has Kept a Diary, *Collections and Recollections* (Smith, Elder & Co., 1898), p. 221.

41 L. A. Tollemache, *Old and Odd Memories* (Edward Arnold, 1908), p. 119.

42 *Harrow School, op. cit.*, p. 109.

43 Vaughan, *op. cit.*, p. 203.

CHAPTER III — OXFORD *pp.* 42-68

1 MS. letter, Harrow, 1858 (University of Bristol).

2 MS. letter to Charlotte, Balliol, 1858 (University of Bristol).

3 MS. letter to Charlotte, Balliol, May 1859 (University of Bristol).

4 Horatio F. Brown, *John Addington Symonds, A Biography* (Smith, Elder & Co., Second Edition, 1903), p. 69.

5 MS. letter to Charlotte, Balliol, 19 February 1861 (University of Bristol).

6 MS. letter to Charlotte, Balliol, November 1859 (University of Bristol).

7 MS. letter to Charlotte, Balliol, 11 March 1860 (University of Bristol).

8 MS. letter to Charlotte, Balliol, May 1859 (University of Bristol).

9 MS. letter to Charlotte, May 1859 (University of Bristol).

10 *Ibid.*

11 *Ibid.*

12 *Memorials of Albert Venn Dicey*, ed. R. S. Rait (Macmillan & Co., 1925), p. 39.

13 Brown, *op. cit.*, p. 79.

14 MS. letter to Charlotte, Balliol, April 1859 (University of Bristol).

15 Brown, *op. cit.*, p. 84.

16 MS. letter to 'Auntie', Balliol, 7 February 1861 (University of Bristol).

17 MS. letter to Charlotte, Balliol, June 1859 (University of Bristol).

18 Brown, *op. cit.*, pp. 130, 131.

19 MS. letter to Charlotte, Balliol, November 1859 (University of Bristol).

20 Brown, *op. cit.*, p. 132.

21 'Jowett's Life', Introduction to *The Interpretation of Scripture* (George Routledge & Sons, Ltd., 1906), p. ix.

22 Goldwin Smith, *Reminiscences* (New York: Macmillan Co., 1910), p. 83.

23 *The Poems and Prose Remains of Arthur Hugh Clough*, 1 (Macmillan & Co., 1869), p. 174.

24 MS. letter, Balliol (University of Bristol).

25 Brown, *op. cit.*, p. 73.

26 *Ibid.*, p. 78.

27 *Ibid.*, p. 84.

28 *Ibid.*, p. 87.

29 *The Quarterly Review*, 109 (Jan. 1861), 274.

30 Brown, *op. cit.*, p. 87.

31 MS. letter to Charlotte, Oxford, 16 February 1861 (University of Bristol).

32 Brown, *op. cit.*, p. 311.

33 MS. letter to A. O. Rutson, Sutton Court, 13 March 1864 (University of Bristol).

34 MS. letter to Charlotte, 21 November 1861 (University of Bristol).

35 MS. letter, Chur, 19 November 1882 (University of Bristol).

36 Geoffrey Faber, *Jowett, A Portrait with Background* (Faber & Faber, 1957), pp. 302 ff.

37 MS. letter to Charlotte, Balliol, 4 March 1861 (University of Bristol).

38 Brown, *op. cit.*, p. 99.

39 MS. letter to Charlotte, Balliol, October 1859 (University of Bristol).

40 MS. letter to Charlotte, Balliol, 25 November 1861 (University of Bristol).

41 MS. letter to Charlotte, Balliol, 6 June 1861 (University of Bristol).

42 MS. letter to Charlotte, Balliol, 25 November 1861 (University of Bristol).

43 Brown, *op. cit.*, p. 78.

44 MS. letter to A. O. Rutson, 1863 (University of Bristol).

45 Brown, *op. cit.*, p. 134.

46 MS. letter, Clifton, 2 October 1863 (University of Bristol).

47 Brown, *op. cit.*, pp. 108, 109.

48 MS. letter to Charlotte, Oxford, 1 December 1861 (University of Bristol).

49 MS. letter (University of Bristol).

50 MS. letter, Oxford, 12 March 1862 (University of Bristol).

51 Brown, *op. cit.*, p. 149.

52 MS. letter, Oxford, 20 October 1862 (University of Bristol).

53 MS. letter, Magdalen, 2 November 1862 (University of Bristol).

54 MS. letter to Charlotte, 25 October 1862 (University of Bristol).

55 *Ibid.*

56 Brown, *op. cit.*, p. 151.

57 MS. letter, Magdalen, 5 November 1862 (University of Bristol).

58 MS. letter to Charlotte, Magdalen, 30 January 1863 (University of Bristol).

59 *Ibid.*

60 MS. letter to Charlotte, Balliol, 13 May 1861 (University of Bristol).

61 MS. letter to Charlotte, Magdalen, 21 February 1863 (University of Bristol).

62 Brown, *op. cit.*, p. 154.

63 *Ibid.*

64 *Ibid.*, p. 155.

CHAPTER IV – THE YOUNG BACHELOR *pp.* 69-93

1 MS. letter, Clifton, 26 December 1865 (Dakyns Collection).

2 Horatio F. Brown, *John Addington Symonds, A Biography* (Smith, Elder & Co., Second Edition, 1903),p. 77.

3 MS. letter, London, 8 April 1864 (University of Bristol).

4 MS. letter, Oxford, May 1859 (University of Bristol).

5 MS. letter, Oxford, 5 October 1862 (University of Bristol).

6 MS. letter, Magdalen, 29 May 1863 (University of Bristol).

7 Brown, *op. cit.*, p. 158.

8 MS. letter to Charlotte, Seelisburg, 7 July 1863 (University of Bristol).

9 Brown, *op. cit.*, p. 160.

10 *Ibid.*, p. 162.

11 *Ibid.*, p. 161.

12 MS. letter to 'Auntie', Mürren, 18 August 1863 (University of Bristol).

13 Margaret Symonds (Mrs W. W. Vaughan), *Out of the Past* (John Murray, 1925), p. 50.

14 MS. letter to Charlotte, Dresden, 12 September 1863 (University of Bristol).

15 MS. letter (Dakyns Collection).

16 Brown, *op. cit.*, p. 167.

17 MS. letter, 26 January 1864 (Dakyns Collection.)

18 Brown, *op. cit.*, p. 167.

19 MS. letter, Florence, 9 December 1863 (Dakyns Collection).

20 Brown, *op. cit.*, p. 172.

21 MS. letter, Oxford, 31 January 1861 (University of Bristol).

22 MS. letter to Charlotte, London, 8 April 1864 (University of Bristol).

23 MS. letter, 19 May 1864 (Dakyns Collection).

24 MS. letter, 23 March 1864 (Dakyns Collection).

25 MS. letter, 1863 (University of Bristol).

26 Vaughan, *op. cit.*, pp. 55, 56.

27 MS. letter, London, 3 May 1864 (Dakyns Collection).

28 MS. letter, 23 May 1864 (University of Bristol).

29 Vaughan, *op. cit.*, p. 56.

30 Marion Holmes, *Josephine Butler* (Women's Freedom League, 1913), pp. 6, 7.

31 Brown, *op. cit.*, p. 124.

32 MS. letter, Earley Court, 17 April 1864 (Dakyns Collection).

33 *The Cornhill Magazine*, XIV (Sept. 1866), 304.

34 MS. letter, 1 April 1964 (Dakyns Collection).

35 MS. letter, 19 June 1864 (Dakyns Collection).

36 MS. letter, 19 May 1864 (Dakyns Collection).

37 MS. letter, Earley Court, 17 April 1864 (Dakyns Collection).

38 MS. letter, 1863 (University of Bristol).

39 MS. letter, London, 15 July 1864 (Dakyns Collection).

40 MS. letter, London, 19 July 1864 (Dakyns Collection).

41 MS. letter, 23 July 1864 (Dakyns Collection).

42 MS. letter, 24 July 1864 (Dakyns Collection).

43 MS. letter, Buxton, 25 July 1864 (Dakyns Collection).

44 MS. letter, Earley Court, 2 July 1864 (University of Bristol).

45 MS. letter, Buxton, 27 July 1864 (Dakyns Collection).

46 MS. letter to Charlotte, Clifton, 30 July 1864 (University of Bristol).

47 MS. letter, Pontresina, 10 August 1864 (University of Bristol).

48 MS. letter to Dakyns, Pontresina, 14 August 1864 (Dakyns Collection).

49 MS. letter to Charlotte, Pontresina, 14 August 1864 (University of Bristol).

50 MS. letter, Pontresina, 14 August, 1864 (University of Bristol).

51 MS. letter (Dakyns Collection).

52 MS. letter, Cadenabbia, 12 September 1864 (Dakyns Collection).
53 MS. letter, Venice, 6 September 1864 (University of Bristol).
54 MS. letter, Union Club, 25 October 1864 (University of Bristol).
55 MS. letter, 11 October 1864 (Dakyns Collection).

CHAPTER V — THE RESTLESS YEARS *pp.* 94-127

1 Horatio F. Brown, *John Addington Symonds, A Biography* (Smith, Elder & Co., Second Edition, 1903), p. 116.
2 MS. letter, 11 November 1864 (University of Bristol).
3 MS. letter, Bonchurch, 19 November 1864 (Dakyns Collection).
4 MS. letter, Freshwater, 24 November 1864 (University of Bristol).
5 MS. letter, Freshwater, 23 November 1864 (Dakyns Collection).
6 MS. letter, 14 January 1865 (University of Bristol).
7 MS. letter, 30 January 1865 (University of Bristol).
8 MS. letter, Temple, 23 March 1865 (Dakyns Collection).
9 MS. letter, 7 February 1865 (Dakyns Collection).
10 Brown, *op. cit.*, pp. 185, 186.
11 *Ibid.*, p. 191.
12 *Ibid.*, p. 193.
13 *Ibid.*, p. 195.
14 MS. letter, Hastings, Easter Eve, 1865 (University of Bristol).
15 MS. letter, London, 30 January 1865 (University of Bristol).
16 'Orvieto', *The Cornhill Magazine*, xi (Feb. 1865), 157.
17 MS. letter, Malvern, 17 April 1862 (University of Bristol).
18 MS. letter, Sutton Court, 20 August 1865 (Dakyns Collection).
19 MS. letter, 47 Norfolk Square, 21 June 1865 (Dakyns Collection).
20 MS. letter, Temple, 7 November 1865 (Dakyns Collection).
21 I am indebted to Dr Laurence Evans of Northwestern University for the attribution of this article.
22 'Alfred de Musset', *The North British Review*, xlix (Dec. 1868), 300.
23 MS. letter to Dakyns, 47 Norfolk Square, 19 May 1867 (Dakyns Collection).
24 MS. letter, London, 5 October 1965 (University of Bristol).
25 MS. letter, Oxford, 14 February 1862 (University of Bristol).
26 MS. letter to A. O. Rutson, Clifton, 21 January 1863 (University of Bristol).
27 'The Prophet of Culture', *Macmillan's Magazine*, xvi (Aug. 1867), 271-80.
28 MS. letter to Dakyns, 22 August 1868 (Dakyns Collection).

29 MS. letter to Dakyns, San Remo, 7 April 1866 (Dakyns Collection).

30 MS. letter, 19 August 1866 (Dakyns Collection).

31 MS. letter, London, June 1864 (Dakyns Collection).

32 MS., undated (University of Bristol).

33 MS., undated (University of Bristol).

34 Sigmund Freud, *Introductory Lectures on Psycho-Analysis* (George Allen & Unwin Ltd., 1949), p. 259.

35 MS. letter, 31 May 1865 (University of Bristol).

36 MS. letter, 47 Norfolk Square, 1 July 1865 (University of Bristol).

37 'The Love of the Alps', *The Cornhill Magazine*, xvi (July 1867), 27.

38 MS. letter, 47 Norfolk Square, 16 November 1866 (Dakyns Collection).

39 MS. letter, Union Club, 22 October 1866 (Dakyns Collection).

40 MS. letter, 47 Norfolk Square, 12 October 1865 (Dakyns Collection).

41 MS. letter, 18 January 1866 (Dakyns Collection).

42 MS. letter, 20 January 1866 (Dakyns Collection).

43 MS. letter (Dakyns Collection).

44 MS. letter, 47 Norfolk Square, 27 October 1865 (Dakyns Collection).

45 MS. letter, Temple, 7 November 1865 (Dakyns Collection).

46 MS. letter, 23 November 1865 (Dakyns Collection).

47 MS. letter, Union Club, 30 November 1865 (Dakyns Collection).

48 MS. letter, Clifton, 26 December 1865 (Dakyns Collection).

49 MS. letter, 47 Norfolk Square, 30 January 1866 (Dakyns Collection).

50 MS. letter, 47 Norfolk Square, 22 February 1866 (Dakyns Collection).

51 MS. letter, Sutton Court, 20 August 1865 (Dakyns Collection).

52 Brown, *op. cit.*, p. 212.

53 MS. letter, Mentone, 29 March 1866 (Dakyns Collection).

54 *Ibid.*

55 MS. letter, San Remo, 7 April 1866 (Dakyns Collection).

56 Brown, *op. cit.*, p. xiv.

57 MS. letter to Dakyns, San Remo, 7 April 1866 (Dakyns Collection).

58 Brown, *op. cit.*, p. 139.

59 MS. letter, Milan, 16 May 1866 (Dakyns Collection).

60 MS. letter, Bavluo, 25 May 1866 (Dakyns Collection).

61 MS. letter, Macugnagna, 8 June 1866 (Dakyns Collection).

62 *Ibid.*

63 MS. letter, Clifton, 22 August 1866 (Dakyns Collection).

64 MS. letter, Union Club, 2 November 1866 (Dakyns Collection).

65 MS. letter, 47 Norfolk Square, 16 November 1866 (Dakyns Collection).

66 MS. letter, London, 20 November 1866 (Dakyns Collection).

67 MS. letter, 26 November 1866 (Dakyns Collection).

68 MS. letter, Clifton, 22 August 1866 (Daykns Collection).

69 *Ibid.*

70 MS. letter, 8 June 1866 (Dakyns Collection).

71 MS. letter, 26 November 1866 (Dakyns Collection).

72 MS. letter, 1 December 1866 (Dakyns Collection).

73 *Ibid.*

74 MS. letter, Christmas Eve 1866 (Dakyns Collection).

75 MS. letter, Hastings, 8 February 1867 (University of Bristol).

76 MS. letter, Clifton, 4 January 1867 (Dakyns Collection).

77 MS. letter, Clifton, 20 January 1867 (Dakyns Collection).

78 MS. letter, Hastings, 29 January 1867 (Dakyns Collection).

79 MS. letter, 1 December 1866 (Dakyns Collection).

80 MS. letter to Charlotte, 47 Norfolk Square, 24 June 1867 (University of Bristol).

81 MS. letter, Hastings, 2 February 1867 (Dakyns Collection).

82 MS. letter, Clifton, 22 August 1868 (Dakyns Collection).

83 MS. letter, Clifton, 8 April 1967 (Dakyns Collection).

84 Horace Traubel, *With Walt Whitman in Camden* (New York: D. Appleton & Co., 1908), p. 72.

85 MS. letter, 47 Norfolk Square, 15 April 1867 (Dakyns Collection).

86 MS. letter, 26 November 1866 (Dakyns Collection).

87 MS. letter, 19 August 1866 (Dakyns Collection).

88 'Mr Swinburne's Poetry', *The Westminster Review*, N.S., XXXI (April 1867), 461.

89 *Ibid.*, 470.

90 MS. letter, Cannes, 9 November 1867 (University of Bristol).

91 MS. letter to Charlotte, 47 Norfolk Square, 19 July 1867 (University of Bristol).

92 MS. letter, Hastings, 6 March 1867 (Dakyns Collection).

93 MS. letter, Cannes, 4 January 1868 (Dakyns Collection).

94 Brown, *op. cit.*, p. 247.

95 *Later Letters of Edward Lear*, ed. Lady Strachey (T. Fisher Unwin, 1911), p. 92.

96 MS. letter, 47 Norfolk Square, 16 September 1868 (Dakyns Collection).

97 MS. letter, London, 3 April 1864 (Dakyns Collection).

98 MS. letter to A. O. Rutson, Clifton, Easter Sunday 1864 (University of Bristol).

99 MS. letter to Lady W. Parrish, Monaco, 3 April 1868 (College of St Mark and St John).

100 *Later Letters of Edward Lear, op. cit.*, p. 152.

101 MS. letter to Dakyns, 47 Norfolk Square, 16 September 1868 (Dakyns Collection).

102 MS. letter, Hastings, 20 October 1868 (Dakyns Collection).

CHAPTER VI — THE TURNING-POINT *pp.* 128-40

1 MS. letter, Sutton Court, 10 February 1869 (Dakyns Collection).

2 MS. letter, Sutton Court, 14 February 1869 (Dakyns Collection).

3 MS., undated (Dakyns Collection).

4 MS., undated (Dakyns Collection).

5 MS. letter, 7 Victoria Square, 13 January 1869 (Dakyns Collection).

6 Horatio F. Brown, *John Addington Symonds, A Biography* (Smith Elder & Co., Second Edition, 1903), p. 132.

7 MS. letter, Malvern, 7 August 1862 (University of Bristol).

8 'Clough's Life and Poems', *The Cornhill Magazine*, XIV (Oct. 1866), 412.

9 *Ibid.*, 416.

10 MS. letter, 47 Norfolk Square, 15 October 1866 (University of Bristol).

11 MS. letter, Hastings, 27 December 1866 (University of Bristol).

12 MS. letter, 47 Norfolk Square, 21 July 1867 (University of Bristol).

13 According to Katharine Chorley, Clough would not allow his wife to read 'Dipsychus' during his lifetime (*Arthur Hugh Clough, the Uncommitted Mind*, Oxford University Press, 1962, p. 260).

14 'Arthur Hugh Clough', *The Fortnightly Review*, XXIV (Dec. 1868), 591.

15 *Letters and Papers of John Addington Symonds*, ed. Horatio F. Brown (John Murray, 1923), p. 30.

16 MS. letter, Hastings, 26 September 1868 (Dakyns Collection).

17 Margaret Symonds (Mrs W. W. Vaughan), *Out of the Past* (John Murray, 1925), p. 120.

18 MS. letter, Hastings, 10 November 1868 (Dakyns Collection). In another letter Symonds told Dakyns that he had helped Mrs Clough to write the memoir, a fact not recorded by Mrs Clough in the Preface: 'The editor desires gratefully', she says, 'to acknowledge the valuable assistance which she has received in making these selections and in arranging these volumes from Mr John Addington Symonds, to whose taste and judgment any measure of success that may have been achieved is chiefly due.' There seems to be little doubt that he did assist her in the memoir as well, judging from a remark he later made to her in 1871 while he was editing his father's literary

remains. 'You will not have a good opportunity of picking holes in me', he exclaimed, 'when I come to write a little memoir all by myself!' (MS. letter, 9 July 1871, University of Bristol).

19 MS. letter (Dakyns Collection).
20 MS. letter, 22 March 1869 (Dakyns Collection).
21 MS. letter, Hastings, 15 April 1869 (Dakyns Collection).
22 MS. letter, Sutton Court, 1 May 1869 (Dakyns Collection).
23 *Ibid.*
24 *Ibid.*
25 MS. letter to Dakyns, Sutton Court, 10 March 1869 (Dakyns Collection).
26 MS. letter (Dakyns Collection).
27 MS. letter, 3 Victoria Street, 30 May 1869 (Dakyns Collection).
28 MS. letter, 18 July 1869 (Dakyns Collection).
29 MS. letter, Maderaner Thal, 16 August 1869 (Dakyns Collection).
30 MS. letter to Charlotte, Hastings, 4 November 1864 (University of Bristol).
31 MS. letter to Dakyns, Hastings, 30 October 1869 (Dakyns Collection).
32 MS. letter, October (?) 1869 (University of Bristol).
33 MS. letter, 2 October 1869 (Dakyns Collection).

CHAPTER VII – THE AMBITIOUS YEARS *pp.* 141-79

1 MS. letter, Monte Generoso, 5 June 1870 (Dakyns Collection).
2 *Ibid.*
3 *Letters and Papers of John Addington Symonds*, ed. Horatio F. Brown (John Murray, 1923), pp. 42, 43.
4 Margaret Symonds (Mrs W. W. Vaughan), *Out of the Past* (John Murray, 1925), p. 154.
5 Brown, *Letters, op. cit.*, p. 43.
6 *Ibid.*
7 *Ibid.*
8 MS. letter, Dawlish, 26 March 1871 (University of Bristol).
9 MS. letter, 7 Victoria Square, 4 July 1871 (University of Bristol).
10 MS. letter (University of Bristol).
11 MS. letter, Rigi Scheidech, 20 July 1871 (Dakyns Collection).
12 MS. letter, Dawlish, 27 March 1871 (University of Bristol).
13 MS. letter to Charlotte, Clifton, 5 September 1871 (University of Bristol).
14 *Ibid.*
15 MS. letter, 5 December 1871 (University of Bristol).

16 MS. letter, Clifton Hill House, 16 April 1872 (Dakyns Collection).
17 MS. letter, Clifton Hill House, 22 April 1871 (Dakyns Collection).
18 MS. letter, Oxford, 10 June 1861 (University of Bristol).
19 MS. letter, London, 20 April 1863 (University of Bristol).
20 MS. letter, Education Department, Whitehall, 5 December 1874 (University of Bristol).
21 MS. letter, Clifton Hill House, 11 August 1875 (The Brotherton Collection).
22 MS. letter, Clifton Hill House, 14 January 1876 (The Brotherton Collection).
23 MS. letter, Clifton Hill House, 16 January 1876 (The Brotherton Collection).
24 MS. letter, Clifton Hill House, 20 January 1876 (The Brotherton Collection).
25 MS. letter, Spring 1872 (Dakyns Collection).
26 MS. letter, December 1871 (Dakyns Collection).
27 MS. letter, 12 December 1872 (University of Bristol).
28 MS. letter, Spring 1872 (Dakyns Collection).
29 Brown, *Letters, op. cit.*, p. 48.
30 *In Re Walt Whitman* (Philadelphia: David McKay, 1893), p. 302.
31 MS. letter, 5 December 1871 (University of Bristol).
32 Brown, *Letters, op. cit.*, p. 47.
33 *Ibid.*, p. 51.
34 MS. letter (Dakyns Collection).
35 MS. letter, December 1872 (Dakyns Collection).
36 MS. letter, Holmwood, 26 December 1871 (obviously misdated by Swinburne) (University of Bristol).
37 MS. letter, Clifton Hill House, 27 December 1872 (Boston Public Library).
38 MS. letter, Clifton Hill House, 20 January 1873 (Boston Public Library).
39 A. & E. M. Sidgwick, *Henry Sidgwick, A Memoir* (Macmillan and Co., 1906), p. 293.
40 MS. letter, Clifton Hill House, 30 December 1875 (Boston Public Library).
41 MS. letter, Holmwood, 2 January 1876 (University of Bristol).
42 *Ibid.*
43 Brown, *Letters, op. cit.*, p. 77.
44 *The Swinburne Letters*, III, ed. Cecil Y. Lang (Yale University Press, 1960), 175.
45 '*Erechteus: a Tragedy.* By A. C. Swinburne', *The Academy*, IX (8 Jan. 1876), 23.
46 MS. letter, Holmwood, 1876 (University of Bristol).

47 *The Athenaeum* (30 Nov. 1872), 694.

48 *Ibid.*, 695.

49 Brown, *Letters, op. cit.*, 52.

50 MS. letter, Oxford, Spring (?) 1872 (Dakyns Collection).

51 MS. letter, 20 February 1873 (Dakyns Collection).

52 '*Studies in the History of the Renaissance*, by Walter Pater', *The Academy*, IV (15 March 1873), 103.

53 MS. letter, Clifton Hill House, 24 March 1873 (University of Bristol).

54 MS. letter, Clifton Hill House, 22 April 1872 (Dakyns Collection).

55 MS. letter, 3 Victoria Street, 27 March 1873 (Dakyns Collection).

56 MS. letter, Genoa, 31 March 1873 (Dakyns Collection).

57 MS. letter, Palermo, 9 April 1873 (Dakyns Collection).

58 MS. letter, Leonforte, 30 April 1873 (Dakyns Collection).

59 MS. letter, Corfu, 12 May 1873 (Dakyns Collection).

60 MS. letter, Oxford, 2 June 1873 (Dakyns Collection).

61 '*Studies of the Greek Poets by J. A. Symonds*', *The Academy*, IV (15 July 1873), 262.

62 MS. letter, Union Club, 27 October 1873. (Dakyns Collection).

63 MS. letter, Clifton Hill House, 22 October, 1873 (University of Bristol).

64 *The Athenaeum* (18 April 1873), 523.

65 MS. letter, 3 Victoria Square, 26 January 1875 (University of Bristol).

66 MS. letter, Rome, 6 May 1875 (Dakyns Collection).

67 *Ibid.*

68 '*Renaissance in Italy; the Age of the Despots*', *The Academy*, VIII (24 July 1875), 105.

69 MS. letter to Charlotte, Clifton Hill House, 30 July 1875 (University of Bristol).

70 *Studies of the Greek Poets* (Smith, Elder and Co., 1876), p. 386.

71 *The Athenaeum* (24 June 1876), 858.

72 '*Studies of the Greek Poets*. Second Series', *The Academy*, X (8 July 1876), 25.

73 MS. letter, Clifton Hill House, 22 January 1876 (University of Bristol).

74 MS. letter, San Remo, 25 February 1876 (University of Bristol).

75 MS. letter to Mrs Clough, Clifton Hill House, 4 June 1876 (University of Bristol).

76 MS. letter to Dakyns, Clifton Hill House, 17 September 1876 (Dakyns Collection).

77 MS. letter, 3 Victoria Street, 17 December 1876 (University of Bristol).

78 MS. letter, 3 Victoria Street, 12 February 1877 (The Brotherton Collection).

79 MS. letter, 3 Victoria Street, 13 February 1877 (The Brotherton Collection).

80 MS. letter, Clifton Hill House, 20 February 1877 (The Brotherton Collection).

81 MS. letter, Clifton Hill House, 9 July 1877 (The Brotherton Collection).

82 'Renaissance in Italy', *The Westminster Review*, LII (1 Oct. 1877), 351-74. I am indebted to Dr Paul F. Mattheisen of Harpur College for the attribution of this article.

83 'Renaissance in Italy', *The Quarterly Review*, 145 (Jan. 1878), 3. I am indebted to Professor Walter Houghton of Wellesley College for the attribution of this article.

84 MS. letter, 18 October 1876 (Dakyns Collection).

85 MS. letter, Union Club, 29 October 1876 (Dakyns Collection).

86 *The World* (31 Jan. 1871), p. 11.

87 MS. letter, Clifton Hill House, 2 February 1877 (University of Bristol).

88 MS. letter, Clifton Hill House, 2 February 1877 (University of Bristol). *The Guardian* described him as 'well known to magazine readers as a writer on literary subjects' (21 Feb. 1877, p. 262).

89 MS. letter, 3 Victoria Street, 16 February 1877 (University of Bristol).

90 *The Oxford and Cambridge Undergraduate's Journal* (8 March 1877), 291.

91 'The Greek Spirit in Modern Literature', *The Contemporary Review*, XXIX (March 1877), 556.

92 *Ibid.*, 559.

93 MS. letter, Clifton Hill House, 7 March 1877 (University of Bristol).

94 MS. letter, Clifton Hill House, 6 March 1877 (Dakyns Collection).

95 MS. letter, Clifton Hill House, 14 March 1877 (The Brotherton Collection).

96 MS. letter, Clifton Hill House, 15 March 1877 (The Brotherton Collection).

97 MS. letter, Clifton Hill House, 30 March 1877 (University of Bristol).

98 *The Oxford and Cambridge Undergraduate's Journal* (19 April 1877), 325.

99 MS. letter, 5 April 1877 (The Brotherton Collection).

100 MS. letter, Milan, 25 May 1877 (University of Bristol).

101 *The Oxford and Cambridge Undergraduate's Journal* (24 May 1877), 425.

102 University of Bristol Collection.

103 MS. letter, Clifton Hill House, 16 December 1871 (Dakyns Collection).

104 MS. letter, Union Club, 13 March 1872 (Dakyns Collection).

105 MS. letter, Union Club, 11 January 1872 (Dakyns Collection).

106 MS. letter, 3 August 1872 (Dakyns Collection).

107 MS. letter, Clifton Hill House, 13 September 1872 (University of Bristol).

108 MS. letter to Mrs Clough, 40 Wilton Crescent, 18 February 1873 (University of Bristol).

109 MS. letter, Falmouth, 10 December 1872 (Dakyns Collection).

110 MS. letter, 11 February 1877 (Dakyns Collection).

CHAPTER VIII – DAVOS PLATZ *pp.* 180-207

1 *Essays of Travel* (Chatto & Windus, 1905), p. 214.

2 MS. letter, Davos Platz, 2 October 1877 (Dakyns Collection).

3 MS. letter from Catherine Symonds to Mr and Mrs Dakyns, Davos Platz, 11 September 1877 (Dakyns Collection).

4 MS. letter, Davos Platz, 27 November 1877 (Dakyns Collection).

5 MS. letter, Davos Platz, 12 December 1877 (Dakyns Collection).

6 MS. letter, 19 January 1878 (The Brotherton Collection).

7 MS. letter, Davos Platz, 27 November 1877 (Dakyns Collection).

8 MS. letter, 23 December 1877 (University of Bristol).

9 MS. letter, Davos Platz, 24 February 1878 (University of Bristol). The first class fare from London to Davos in 1878 was estimated at £9–£10 (*Davos Platz* by One Who Knows it Well, Edward Stanford, 1878, p. 222).

10 MS. letter (Dakyns Collection).

11 MS. letter, Menaggio, 15 April 1878 (Dakyns Collection).

12 MS. letter, Davos Platz, 20 March 1878 (Dakyns Collection).

13 MS. letter, Davos Platz, 19 January 1878 (The Brotherton Collection).

14 MS. letter, Davos Platz, 20 July 1878 (The Brotherton Collection).

15 MS. letter, Davos Platz, 23 October 1884 (The Brotherton Collection).

16 MS. letter, Davos Platz, 8 March 1878 (The Brotherton Collection).

17 MS. letter, Davos Platz, 20 March 1878 (Dakyns Collection).

18 MS. letter, Davos Platz, 8 March 1878 (The Brotherton Collection).

19 MS. letter, Davos Platz, 1 February 1878 (The Brotherton Collection).

20 MS. letter, Davos Platz, 23 December 1877 (University of Bristol).

21 *The Athenaeum* (29 June 1878), 820.

22 MS. letter, Davos Platz, 9 June 1878 (The Brotherton Collection).

23 MS. letter, Davos Platz, 21 June 1878 (Dakyns Collection).

24 MS. letter, Mendrisco, 24 May 1878 (Dakyns Collection).

25 MS. letter, Davos Platz, 9 July 1878 (Dakyns Collection).

26 MS. letter, Davos Platz, 9 July 1878 (Dakyns Collection).

27 *Essays in Criticism*, Second Series (Macmillan & Co., 1888), p. 237.

28 Horatio F. Brown, *John Addington Symonds, A Biography* (Smith, Elder and Co., Second Edition, 1903), p. 141.

29 *Shelley* (Macmillan & Co., 1878), p. 141.

30 MS. letter, Davos Platz, 7 January 1879 (University of Bristol).

31 F. W. Maitland, *The Life and Letters of Leslie Stephen* (Duckworth & Co., 1906), p. 331.

32 MS. letter to Dakyns, Davos Platz, 21 November 1878 (Dakyns Collection).

33 MS. letter, Davos Platz, 17 July 1878 (Dakyns Collection).

34 MS. letter, Davos Platz, 7 January 1879 (University of Bristol).

35 Brown, *op. cit.*, p. 349.

36 MS. letter, Geneva, 2 February 1879 (Dakyns Collection).

37 MS. letter, Argentière, 4 July 1879 (Dakyns Collection).

38 MS. letter, Davos Platz, 9 August 1879 (University of Bristol).

39 MS. letter, Davos Platz, 20 July 1878 (The Brotherton Collection).

40 Margaret Symonds (Mrs W. W. Vaughan), *Out of the Past* (John Murray, 1925), p. 185.

41 *Letters and Papers of John Addington Symonds*, ed. Horatio F. Brown (John Murray, 1923), p. 105.

42 Vaughan, *op. cit.*, p. 188.

43 MS. letter to Dakyns, Athenaeum Club, 8 June 1880 (Dakyns Collection).

44 Brown, *op. cit.*, p. 357.

45 MS. letter, Davos Platz, 9 December 1881 (University of Bristol).

46 MS. letter, Chur, 19 November 1882 (University of Bristol).

47 MS. letter, Davos Platz, 31 December 1882 (University of Bristol).

48 MS. letter, Davos Platz, 23 March 1883 (Dakyns Collection).

49 MS. letter, Cambridge, 13 August 1883 (University of Bristol).

50 MS. letter, Davos Platz, 5 November 1882 (British Museum).

51 MS. letter, Davos Platz, 4 July 1879 (Dakyns Collection).

52 See 'Bacchus in Graubünden', *The Cornhill Magazine*, XLVII (Jan. 1883), 50-61.

53 MS. letter, Davos Platz, 1892 (University of Bristol).

54 MS. letter, Davos Platz, 6 August 1882 (Boston Public Library).

55 Janet Ross, *The Fourth Generation* (Constable & Co., 1912), p. 311.

56 MS. letter, Menaggio, 15 April 1878 (Dakyns Collection).

57 Brown, *op. cit.*, p. 305.

58 Typescript copy of a letter, Venice, 24 April 1892 (Weeks Collection).

59 Vaughan, *op. cit.*, p. 210.

CHAPTER IX — THE LITERARY LIFE *pp.* 208-35

1 *Letters and Papers of John Addington Symonds*, ed. Horatio F. Brown (John Murray, 1923), p. 111.

2 E. V. Lucas, *The Colvins and their Friends* (Methuen & Co., 1928), p. 150.

3 W. G. Lockett, *Robert Louis Stevenson at Davos* (Hurst & Blackett Ltd., 1934), p. 190.

4 *The Letters of Robert Louis Stevenson*, i, ed. Sidney Colvin (Methuen & Co., 1899), p. 187.

5 He wrote four articles on the Alps which appeared in *The Pall Mall Gazette* in February and March 1881.

6 'Walt Whitman', *The New Quarterly Magazine*, x (Oct. 1878), 461-81; reprinted in *Familiar Studies of Men and Books* (Chatto & Windus, 1882).

7 *Walt Whitman, A Study* (John C. Nimmo, 1893), p. 9.

8 Brown, *Letters, op. cit.*, p. 123.

9 *Memories and Portraits* (Chatto & Windus, 1887), p. 164.

10 Symonds praised Thomas Heywood because his characters were 'all gentlemen' (*Thomas Heywood*, ed. A. Wilson Verity, Vizetelly and Co., 1888, p. xxi). Of Tiepolo, he said: 'In addition to his other qualities, Tiepolo painted like a great gentleman. There is an unmistakable note of good breeding in all his work' (*In the Key of Blue*, Elkin Matthews & John Lane, 1893, p. 50).

11 Brown, *Letters, op. cit.*, p. 111.

12 Lockett, *op. cit.*, pp. 191, 192.

13 Edmund Gosse, *Critical Kit-Kats* (William Heinemann, 1896), p. 287.

14 Lockett, *op. cit.*, p. 193.

15 Brown, *Letters, op. cit.*, p. 129.

16 *The Letters of Robert Louis Stevenson*, i, *op. cit.*, p. 237.

17 *Ibid.*, p. 195.

18 *Ibid.*, p. 237.

19 Brown, *Letters, op. cit.*, p. 201.

20 *Memories and Portraits* (Chatto & Windus, 1887), p. 165.

21 MS. letter, Davos Platz, 5 April 1882 (British Museum).

22 Horatio F. Brown, *John Addington Symonds, A Biography* (Smith, Elder & Co., Second Edition, 1903), pp. 407, 408.

23 Lockett, *op. cit.*, p. 198.

24 *Letters of Robert Louis Stevenson*, ii, ed. Sidney Colvin (Methuen & Co., 1911), p. 76.

25 Brown, *Letters, op. cit.*, p. 267.

26 *Letters of Robert Louis Stevenson*, IV, p. 178.

27 Margaret Symonds, *Out of the Past* (John Murray, 1925), p. 21.

28 MS. letter, Milan, 5 June 1879 (Dakyns Collection).

29 MS. letter, Geneva, 12 June 1879 (Dakyns Collection).

30 MS. letter, Davos Platz, 24 September 1879 (Dakyns Collection).

31 MS. letter, Davos Platz, 13 January 1880 (Dakyns Collection).

32 MS. letter, Davos Platz, 1 February 1880 (Dakyns Collection).

33 MS. letter, Davos Platz, 16 July 1881 (Dakyns Collection).

34 MS. letter, Davos Platz, 8 September 1881 (Dakyns Collection).

35 MS. letter, Davos Platz, 10 April 1882 (Dakyns Collection).

36 *Ibid.*

37 MS. letter, Davos Platz, 9 November 1884 (University of Bristol).

38 MS. letter, Davos Platz, 6 November 1883 (Dakyns Collection).

39 MS. letter, Davos Platz, 30 July 1882 (University of Bristol).

40 *The Westminster Review*, N.S., LXVII (Jan. 1885), 284.

41 MS. letter, 24 March 1895 (The Ashley Collection, British Museum).

42 MS. letter, Davos Platz, 6 December 1886 (Dakyns Collection).

43 MS. letter, Davos Platz, 19 February 1880 (Dakyns Collection).

44 MS. letter, 1882 (University of Bristol).

45 *The Pall Mall Gazette*, L (27 May 1890), p. 2.

46 *The Pall Mall Gazette*, L (5 June 1890), p. 7.

47 MS. letter, Siena, 8 May 1880 (University of Bristol).

48 MS. letter, Davos Platz, 6 October 1884 (University of Bristol).

49 MS. letter, Faido, 19 September 1884 (University of Bristol).

50 MS. letter, Davos Platz, 7 January 1885 (University of Bristol). The review appeared in *The Academy*, XXVII (31 Jan. 1885), 71.

51 MS. letter, Clifton Hill House, 15 August 1880 (University of Bristol).

52 MS. letter, Davos Platz, 28 March 1882 (Colby College).

53 MS. letter, Davos Platz, 17 October 1883 (University of Bristol).

54 MS. letter, San Remo, 4 April 1884 (Colby College).

55 MS. letter, Davos Platz, 30 March 1885 (University of Bristol).

56 MS. letter, Davos Platz, 18 November 1879 (The Brotherton Collection).

57 MS. letter, Davos Platz, 15 November 1879 (The Brotherton Collection).

58 MS. letter, Southampton, 22 December 1884 (The Brotherton Collection).

59 MS. letter, Davos Platz, 9 February 1885 (The Brotherton Collection).

60 MS. letter, 17 Sumatra Road, 10 November 1885 (University of Bristol).

61 MS. letter, Davos Platz, 31 July 1886 (The Brotherton Collection).

62 Brown, *Letters*, *op. cit.*, p. 147.

63 MS. letter, Residence, British Museum, 12 October 1883 (University of Bristol).

64 MS. letter, Davos Platz, 6 November 1883 (Dakyns Collection).

65 MS. letter to Miss Poynter, 22 April 1883 (University of Bristol).

66 Melville Anderson, 'Shakspere's Predecessors in the English Drama', *The Dial* (Chicago), v (Feb. 1885), 262-4.

67 *'Shakspere's Predecessors in the English Drama*. By John Addington Symonds', *The Quarterly Review*, CLXI (Oct. 1885), 330-81.

68 MS. letter, 29 October 1885 (University of Bristol).

69 MS. letter, 5 Willow Road, Hampstead, 9 September 1883 (University of Bristol).

70 MS. letter, 28 October 1886 (The Brotherton Collection).

71 MS. letter, Davos Platz, 17 November 1886 (University of Bristol).

72 MS. letter, Davos Platz, 17 November 1886 (The Brotherton Collection).

73 MS. letter, Davos Platz, 26 November 1886 (The Brotherton Collection).

74 MS. letter, Davos Platz, 16 December 1886 (The Brotherton Collection).

75 'Two Biographies of Sir Philip Sidney', *The Pall Mall Gazette* (11 Dec. 1886), p. 5.

76 MS. letter, Davos Platz, 16 December 1886 (The Brotherton Collection).

77 MS. letter, 29 Delamere Terrace, 19 December 1886 (University of Bristol).

78 *Essays and Studies* (Macmillan & Co., 1895), p. viii.

79 MS. letter, Davos Platz, 7 January 1885 (University of Bristol).

80 Edmund Gosse, *The Life of Algernon Charles Swinburne* (Macmillan & Co., 1917), p. 276.

81 *Under the Microscope* (D. White, 1872), p. 45.

82 MS. letter, 21 February 1885 (The Ashley Collection, British Museum).

83 'Whitmania', *The Fortnightly Review*, N.S., XLII (Aug. 1887), 171.

84 *Ibid.*

85 W. S. Kennedy, *Reminiscences of Walt Whitman* (Alexander Gardner, 1896), p. vii.

86 'A Note on Whitmania', *The Fortnightly Review*, XLII (Sept. 1887), 460.

87 Kennedy, *op. cit.*, p. vii.

88 Horace Traubel, *With Walt Whitman in Camden* (Philadelphia: University of Pennsylvania Press, 1953), p. 124.

89 Grace Gilchrist, 'Chats with Walt Whitman', *Temple Bar*, XCIII (Feb. 1898), 210.

90 *Walt Whitman, op. cit.*, p. 9.

CHAPTER X – SYMONDS'S ITALY *pp.* 236-61

1 MS. letter, 1 February 1864 (University of Bristol).
2 MS. letter to Edmund Gosse, Florence, 13 October 1878 (The Brotherton Collection).
3 MS. letter, Venice, 15 April 1883 (University of Bristol).
4 *Letters and Papers of John Addington Symonds*, ed. Horatio F. Brown (John Murray, 1923), p. 102.
5 MS. letter to Miss Robinson, Davos Platz, 30 March 1885 (University of Bristol).
6 *Sketches and Studies in Italy and Greece* (Smith, Elder & Co., 1898), p. 127. This volume, prepared after Symonds's death by Horatio Brown, was a collected edition of all three travel books.
7 MS. letter, Davos Platz, 25 December 1877 (University of Bristol).
8 Brown, *Letters, op. cit.*, p. 248.
9 MS. letter to Dakyns, Venice, 20 May 1891 (Dakyns Collection).
10 Brown, *Letters, op. cit.*, p. 115.
11 MS. letter, Davos Platz, 9 November 1881 (Dakyns Collection).
12 MS. letter to Margaret Symonds, Venice, 11 November 1892 (University of Bristol).
13 Horatio F. Brown, *John Addington Symonds, A Biography* (Smith, Elder & Co., Second Edition, 1903), p. 291.
14 Lena Waterfield, *Castle in Italy* (John Murray, 1962), p. 59.
15 MS. letter to Dakyns, Davos Platz, 26 September 1881 (Dakyns Collection).
16 MS. letter, Venice, 9 November 1890 (The Brotherton Collection).
17 MS. letter to Edmund Gosse, Venice, 12 May 1890 (The Brotherton Collection).
18 MS. letter to Dakyns, Davos Platz, 26 September 1881 (Dakyns Collection).
19 MS. letter, Davos Platz, 9 November 1881 (Dakyns Collection).
20 MS. letter, Venice, 20 May 1891 (Dakyns Collection).
21 Brown, *op. cit.*, p. 437.
22 E. M. W. Tillyard, *The English Renaissance: Fact or Fiction?* (The Hogarth Press, 1952), p. 10.
23 W. K. Ferguson, *The Renaissance in Historical Thought* (Houghton Mifflin Co., 1948), p. 198.
24 Edmund Wilson, *Memoirs of Hecate County* (W. H. Allen, 1951), p. 107.
25 *Letters of Benjamin Jowett*, ed. Evelyn Abbott and Lewis Campbell (John Murray, 1899), p. 211.

26 MS. letter, Davos Platz, 4 January 1891 (Dakyns Collection).

27 MS. letter, Davos Platz, 26 August 1885 (University of Bristol).

28 According to R. D. Brown, the most sensational details of *The Picture of Dorian Gray* were gleaned from Symonds's portraits of the Italian princes in *The Age of the Despots*. See 'Suetonius, Symonds and Gibbon in the Picture of Dorian Gray', *Modern Language Notes*, LXXI (April 1956), 264.

29 MS. letter, Verese, 8 May 1877 (University of Bristol).

30 W. F. Monypenny and G. E. Buckle, *The Life of Benjamin Disraeli*, II (John Murray, 1929), pp. 1445, 1446.

31 T. B. Macaulay, *Machiavelli* (The Holerth Press, 1924), p. 30.

32 MS. letter, Clifton Hill House, 21 January 1863 (University of Bristol).

33 *Renaissance in Italy, The Catholic Reaction* (Smith, Elder & Co., 1886), p. 411.

34 MS. letter, Davos Platz, 18 December 1888 (Dakyns Collection).

35 MS. letter to Charlotte, 3 Victoria Street, 26 January 1875 (University of Bristol).

36 MS. letter, Siena, 8 May 1880 (University of Bristol).

37 The similarities and differences in Burckhardt's and Symonds's work have been analysed in detail by J. R. Hale, *England and the Italian Renaissance* (Faber & Faber Ltd., 1954), W. K. Ferguson, *The Renaissance in Historical Thought* (Houghton Mifflin Co., 1948), and by Mary Jane Loso in an admirable unpublished doctoral thesis, *John Addington Symonds: Nineteenth Century Historian of the Renaissance* (University of Minnesota, 1957-8).

38 *Renaissance in Italy, The Age of the Despots* (Smith, Elder & Co., 1875), p. viii.

39 *Renaissance in Italy, The Revival of Learning* (Smith, Elder & Co., 1877), p. vi.

40 MS. letter, Davos Platz, 26 December 1881 (University of Bristol).

41 MS. letter, Davos Platz, 16 September 1881 (University of Bristol).

42 MS. letter to Miss Robinson, Davos Platz, 29 September 1885 (University of Bristol).

43 *The Life of Benvenuto Cellini*, I (John C. Nimmo, 1888), p. x.

44 *Ibid.*, p. xx.

45 *Ibid.*, p. lxxx.

46 *Ibid.*, p. xxiv.

47 MS. letter, Davos Platz, 27 October 1887 (Layard Collection, British Museum).

48 Brown, *op. cit.*, p. 427.

49 *The Memoirs of Count Carlo Gozzi*, I (John C. Nimmo, 1890), p. ix.

50 MS. letter, Davos Platz, 27 March 1889 (Dakyns Collection).

51 Brown, *Letters, op. cit.*, p. 229.

52 Brown, *op. cit.*, p. 456.

53 MS. letter to Mrs Ross, Davos Platz, 18 January 1891 (University of Bristol).

54 Brown, *Letters, op. cit.*, p. 244.

55 *Ibid.*

56 *Ibid.*, p. 248.

57 MS. letter, Davos Platz, 13 June 1891 (Dugdale Collection).

58 MS. letter, Firenze, 15 November 1890 (The Brotherton Collection).

59 *The Life of Michelangelo Buonarroti*, I (John C. Nimmo, 1893), p. 98.

60 According to Sir Kenneth Clark, Symonds's life of Michelangelo remains by far the best life of the artist from a literary point of view, but his classical and naturalistic standards invalidate his art-criticism today (letter addressed to author).

61 MS. letter, Davos Platz, 18 September 1891 (The Brotherton Collection).

62 MS. letter to Dakyns, Davos Platz, 4 September 1891 (Dakyns Collection).

63 MS. letter, Davos Platz, 18 September 1891 (The Brotherton Collection).

64 *Michelangelo, op. cit.*, p. 273.

65 MS. letter, Venice, 20 May 1891 (Dakyns Collection).

66 MS. letter, Davos Platz, 22 June 1891 (The Brotherton Collection).

67 *Michelangelo, op. cit.*, II: p. 385.

68 *Ibid.*, p. 384.

69 *Ibid.*, p. 383.

70 *Ibid.*, p. 385.

71 *The Fortnightly Review*, III (Jan. 1893), 79.

CHAPTER XI — THE PROBLEM *pp.* 262-94

1 'In Dreamland', Miscellanies III (The Houghton Library, Harvard University).

2 *Ibid.*

3 *Sexual Inversion* (Wilson & Macmillan, 1897), p. 62.

4 MS. letter to Gosse, Davos Platz, 18 September 1891 (The Brotherton Collection).

5 MS. letter to Gosse, Davos Platz, 22 July 1890 (The Brotherton Collection).

6 MS. letter, Davos Platz, 4 January 1891 (Dakyns Collection).

7 MS. letter, Davos Platz, 16 January 1891 (Dakyns Collection).

8 MS. letter, Davos Platz, 27 March 1889 (Dakyns Collection).

9 'The Arabian Nights' Entertainments', *The Academy*, xxviii (Oct. 1885), 223.

10 MS. letter, Venice, 21 October 1892 (University of Bristol).

11 *The Notebooks of Henry James*, ed. F. O. Matthiessen and K. B. Murdock (New York: Oxford University Press, 1947), p. 57.

12 MS. letter, 3 Bolton Street, W., 9 June 1884 (The Brotherton Collection).

13 MS. letter, 6 November 1890 (University of Bristol).

14 MS. letter, Davos Platz, 8 July 1892 (University of Bristol).

15 MS. letter, Davos Platz, 28 February 1890 (The Brotherton Collection).

16 *Sexual Inversion, op. cit.*, p. 19.

17 *Walt Whitman, A Study* (John C. Nimmo, 1893), pp. 6, 7.

18 MS. letter to Dr George Williamson, Davos Platz, 26 December 1881 (University of Bristol).

19 MS. letter, Davos Platz, 22 June 1891 (The Brotherton Collection). *Un Raté* (1891) was the work of Gyp; *Monsieur Vénus* (1884) was by R. F. Talman; and *Footsteps of Fate* had been translated from the Dutch by Louis Marie Anne Couperus for Heinemann's International Library series of which the Editor was Edmund Gosse. In an epilogue to *Footsteps of Fate*, Gosse pleaded for greater emancipation in the subject-matter admitted into English literature.

20 Miscellanies iii (The Houghton Library, Harvard University).

21 MS. letter, Davos Platz (1887?) (University of Bristol).

22 MS. letter (University of Bristol).

23 MS. letter, Davos Platz, 27 March 1889 (Dakyns Collection).

24 *The Autobiography of Margot Asquith*, i (Penguin Books, 1936), p. 176.

25 MS. letter, Davos Platz, 4 August 1890 (University of Texas).

26 MS. letter, Davos Platz, 27 August 1890 (University of Texas).

27 *Brown, op. cit.*, p. 440.

28 MS. letter, Davos Platz, 19 July 1890 (Dakyns Collection).

29 MS. letter, 29 Delamere Terrace, 24 February 1890 (University of Bristol).

30 MS. letter (University of Bristol).

31 MS. letter, Florence, 23 November 1890 (The Brotherton Collection).

32 MS. letter, Davos Platz, 23 January 1891 (Dakyns Collection).

33 MS. letter, Davos Platz, 24 September 1890 (Dakyns Collection).

34 MS. letter, Davos Platz, 23 January 1891 (Dakyns Collection).

35 MS. letter, Davos Platz, 15 January 1892 (Dakyns Collection).

36 MS. letter, 34 De Vere Gardens, 7 January 1893 (The Brotherton Collection).

37 MS. letter, Board of Trade, 5 March 1890 (University of Bristol).

38 MS. letter, Davos Platz, 20 May 1891 (Dakyns Collection).
39 MS. letter, Davos Platz, 23 December 1885 (Ashley Collection, British Museum).
40 MS. letter, Delamere Terrace, 26 December 1885 (University of Bristol).
41 Typescript copy of letter, Davos Platz, 18 December 1892 (Weeks Collection).
42 MS. letter, Davos Platz, 23 February 1891 (The Brotherton Collection).
43 MS. letter, Venice, 20 May 1891 (Dakyns Collection).
44 Havelock Ellis, *My Life* (William Heinemann Ltd., 1940), p. 165.
45 'The Present Position of English Criticism', *Time*, XIII (Dec. 1885), 675.
46 MS. letter, Davos Platz, December 1885 (University of Bristol).
47 *The New Spirit* (George Bell & Sons, 1890), p. 7.
48 Copy of letter, 9 St Mary's Terrace, 10 July 1891 (University of Bristol).
49 MS. letter, Davos Platz, July 1891 (University of Bristol).
50 Copy of letter, 9 St Mary's Terrace, 18 June 1892 (University of Bristol).
51 MS. letter, Davos Platz, 20 June 1892 (University of Bristol).
52 MS. letter, Davos Platz, 20 June 1892 (University of Bristol).
53 *Ibid.*
54 Copy of letter, 9 St Mary's Terrace, 1 July 1892 (University of Bristol).
55 Copy of letter, 19 February 1893 (University of Bristol).
56 MS. letter, Davos Platz, 1 December 1892 (University of Bristol).
57 Copy of letter, Lelant, Cornwall, 21 December 1892 (University of Bristol).
58 *Ibid.*
59 MS. letter, Davos Platz, 29 September 1892 (University of Bristol).
60 Copy of letter, Lelant, Cornwall, 21 December 1892 (University of Bristol).
61 Copy of letter, 3 March 1893 (University of Bristol).
62 Copy of letter (University of Bristol).
63 MS. letter, Athenaeum Club, 21 September 1892 (University of Bristol).
64 *Sexual Inversion, op. cit.*, p. 1.
65 *Ibid.*, p. 39.
66 Sigmund Freud, *Introductory Lectures on Psycho-Analysis* (George Allen & Unwin Ltd., 1949), p. 259.

CHAPTER XII — THE LAST YEARS *pp.* 295-317

1 MS. letter, Venice, 20 May 1891 (Dakyns Collection).
2 MS. letter, Davos Platz, 10 April 1887 (University of Bristol).
3 MS. letter, Badenweiler, 29 April 1887 (University of Bristol).

4 MS. letter to Robert Louis Stevenson, Davos Platz, 27 February 1885 (British Museum).

5 MS. letter, Davos Platz, 26 June 1892 (University of Bristol).

6 MS. letter, Davos Platz, 26 December 1885 (University of Bristol).

7 MS. letter, Davos Platz, 19 February 1887 (University of Bristol).

8 MS. letter, Davos Platz, 6 December 1889 (University of Bristol).

9 MS. letter, Davos Platz, 15 August 1891 (University of Bristol).

10 MS. letter, Davos Platz, 10 August 1891 (University of Bristol).

11 MS. letter, Davos Platz, 10 November 1889 (University of Bristol).

12 MS. letter, Klosters, 29 November 1889 (University of Bristol).

13 MS. letter, 29 September 1889 (University of Bristol).

14 MS. letter, Davos Platz, 10 August 1891 (University of Bristol).

15 MS. letter, Davos Platz, 7 July 1892 (University of Bristol).

16 Copy of letter, 29 October 1892 (University of Bristol).

17 MS. letter, Venice, 19 October 1892 (University of Bristol).

18 MS. letter to Dakyns, Davos Platz, 9 November 1881 (Dakyns Collection).

19 MS. letter, Athenaeum Club, 3 November 1881 (The Brotherton Collection).

20 MS. letter, Davos Platz, 4 August 1883 (University of Bristol).

21 MS. letter, Davos Platz, 23 October 1883 (University of Bristol).

22 MS. letter, Davos Platz, 12 June 1886 (University of Bristol).

23 *The Autobiography of Margot Asquith*, 1 (Penguin Books, 1936), p. 172.

24 *Ibid.*, p. 174.

25 *Ibid.*, p. 175.

26 MS. letter, Davos Platz, 6 December 1887 (University of Bristol).

27 Janet Ross, *The Fourth Generation* (Constable & Co., 1912), p. 210.

28 MS. letter, Venice, 9 November 1890 (The Brotherton Collection).

29 MS. letter, Zurich, 13 November 1891 (University of Bristol).

30 Holbrook Jackson, *The Eighteen Nineties* (Grant Richards, 1913), p. 45.

31 MS. letter (University of Bristol).

32 MS. letter (University of Bristol).

33 MS. letter, Firenze, 15 November 1890 (The Brotherton Collection).

34 MS. letter, Davos Platz, 19 July 1890 (Dakyns Collection).

35 Horace Traubel, *With Walt Whitman in Camden* (Boston: Small, Maynard & Company, 1906), p. 388.

36 *Letters and Papers of John Addington Symonds*, ed. Horatio F. Brown (John Murray, 1923), p. 50.

37 Asquith, *op. cit.*, p. 176.

38 *Essays Speculative and Suggestive*, II (Chapman & Hall, Ltd., 1890), p. 62.

39 MS. letter, Davos Platz, 14 February 1889 (Dakyns Collection).
40 Asquith, *op. cit.*, p. 173.
41 MS. letter, Davos Platz, 8 July 1892 (University of Bristol).
42 MS. letter, Davos Platz, 16 July 1892 (University of Bristol).
43 MS. letter, Davos Platz, 2 July 1892 (Dakyns Collection).
44 MS. letter, August 1892 (University of Bristol).
45 *Ibid.*
46 MS. letter, Davos Platz, 10 January 1893 (The Brotherton Collection).
47 Horatio F. Brown, *John Addington Symonds, A Biography* (Smith, Elder & Co., Second Edition, 1903), p. 471.
48 *Ibid.*, p. 477.
49 *Letters of Thomas Edward Brown*, ed. Sidney T. Irwin (The University Press of Liverpool, 1952), p. 115.
50 MS. letter, Venice, 3 May 1893 (Dakyns Collection).

CHAPTER XIII – AFTERMATH *pp.* 318-27

1 MS. letter (University of Bristol).
2 MS. letter, 2 November 1893 (Dakyns Collection).
3 MS. letter, 24 March 1895 (Ashley Collection, British Museum).
4 MS. letter, Venice, 2 October 1894 (Dakyns Collection).
5 Horatio F. Brown, *John Addington Symonds, A Biography* (Smith, Elder & Co., Second Edition, 1903), x.
6 *St James's Gazette* (1 Jan. 1895), pp. 5, 6.
7 L. E. Elliott-Binns, *English Thought, 1860-1900* (Longmans, Green & Co., 1956), 12.
8 MS. letter, 34 De Vere Gardens, 27 December 1894 (The Brotherton Collection).
9 Copy of letter, Ramsey, 28 December 1894 (Dakyns Collection).
10 MS. letter, Clifton, 13 February 1899 (Dakyns Collection).
11 MS. letter, Cambridge, 20 April 1893 (The Brotherton Collection).
12 MS. letter, 22 April 1893 (The Brotherton Collection).
13 E. E. Charteris, *The Life and Letters of Sir Edmund Gosse* (William Heinemann Ltd., 1931), p. 230.
14 *The Saturday Review*, LXXV (29 April 1893), 456.
15 'In Memoriam John Addington Symonds', *The Spirit Lamp*, IV (4 May 1893), 44.
16 *The Artist*, XIV (1 May 1893), 131.

17 *Black and White*, v (29 April 1893), 503.

18 *Studies in Prose and Poetry* (Chatto & Windus, 1894), p. 34. *The Times*, in an otherwise favourable review, objected to the tone of the passage (6 Nov. 1894, p. 18). Geoffrey Faber believed that although 'calamus' means a reed-pen', Swinburne evidently meant the reader to think of the word *catamite* (see *Jowett*, Faber & Faber, 1957, p. 370). In a reference to sodomy in a letter to Theodore Watts in 1894 Swinburne speaks of 'Mr Soddington Symonds' (*The Swinburne Letters*, iv, ed. Cecil Lang. Yale University Press, 1962, p. 74).

SELECT BIBLIOGRAPHY

The place of publication is London unless otherwise indicated

ALDINGTON, RICHARD. *The Religion of Beauty*. William Heinemann, 1950.

ARNOLD, MATTHEW. *Essays in Criticism*, Second Series. Macmillan & Co., 1888.

The Autobiography of Margot Asquith. 2 vols. Penguin Books, 1936.

BABINGTON, P. L. *Bibliography of the Writings of John Addington Symonds*. John Castle, 1945.

BLODGETT, HAROLD. *Walt Whitman in England*. Ithaca, N.Y.: Cornell University Press, 1934.

BROOKS, VAN WYCK. *John Addington Symonds, A Biographical Study*. Grant Richards Ltd., 1914.

BROWN, HORATIO F. *John Addington Symonds, A Biography*. 2 vols. John C. Nimmo, 1895.

BROWN, HORATIO F., ed. *Letters and Papers of John Addington Symonds*. John Murray, 1923.

—— *Life on the Lagoons*. Kegan Paul & Co., 1884.

Letters of Thomas Edward Brown, ed. Sidney T. Irwin. The University Press of Liverpool, 1952.

BROWNING, OSCAR. *Memories of Sixty Years*. John Lane, 1910.

BURCKHARDT, JACOB. *The Civilization of the Renaissance*. Phaidon Press, 1944.

CARPENTER, EDWARD. *Days with Walt Whitman*. George Allen & Unwin Ltd., 1906.

CHARTERIS, E. E. *The Life and Letters of Sir Edmund Gosse*. William Heinemann Ltd., 1931.

CHORLEY, KATHARINE. *Arthur Hugh Clough, The Uncommitted Mind*. Oxford University Press, 1962.

Poems and Prose Remains of Arthur Hugh Clough. 2 vols. Macmillan & Co., 1869.

Miscellaneous Writings of John Conington, ed. John Addington Symonds. 2 vols. Longmans, Green & Co., 1872.

COULTON, G. G. *Fourscore Years*. Cambridge University Press, 1943.

Davos Platz, by One Who Knows it Well. Edward Stanford, 1878.

Memorials of Albert Venn Dicey, ed. R. S. Rait. Macmillan & Co., 1925.

ELLIOTT-BINNS, L. E. *English Thought, 1860-1900*. Longmans, Green & Co., 1956.

357

ROSS, JANET. *The Fourth Generation*. Constable & Co., 1912.

DE SANCTIS, FRANCESCO. *History of Italian Literature*. 2 vols. Oxford University Press, 1932.

SCHUELLER, H. M. *John Addington Symonds as a Theoretical and as a Practical Critic*. Ph.D. thesis. (University of Michigan, 1941.)

SIDGWICK, A. and E. M. *Henry Sidgwick, A Memoir*. Macmillan & Co., 1906.

SIDGWICK, HENRY. *The Methods of Ethics*. Macmillan & Co., 1874.

SMITH, GOLDWIN. *Reminiscences*. New York: Macmillan Co., 1910.

STANLEY, ARTHUR P. *The Life and Correspondence of Thomas Arnold*. B. Fellowes, Sixth Edition, 1846.

STEVENSON, ROBERT LOUIS. *Essays of Travel*. Chatto & Windus, 1905.

—— *Familiar Studies of Men and Books*. Chatto & Windus, 1882.

The Letters of Robert Louis Stevenson, ed. Sidney Colvin. 4 vols. Methuen & Co., 1911.

—— *Memories and Portraits*. Chatto & Windus, 1887.

SWINBURNE, ALGERNON CHARLES. *Essays and Studies*. Macmillan & Co., 1895.

—— *Studies in Prose and Poetry*. Chatto & Windus, 1894.

—— *Under the Microscope*. D. White, 1872.

The Letters of Algernon Charles Swinburne, ed. Cecil Lang. 6 vols. Oxford University Press, 1959-62.

SYMONDS, JOHN ADDINGTON, THE ELDER. *Miscellancies*, ed. with an Introductory Memoir by John Addington Symonds. Macmillan & Co., 1871.

SYMONDS, JOHN ADDINGTON. *Animi Figura*. Smith, Elder and Co., 1882.

—— *Ben Jonson*. Longmans, Green & Co., 1888.

—— *Essays Speculative and Suggestive*. 2 vols. Chapman & Hall, 1890.

—— *Giovanni Boccaccio as Man and Author*. John C. Nimmo, 1895.

—— *In the Key of Blue and Other Prose Essays*. Elkin Mathews & John Lane, 1893.

—— *An Introduction to the Study of Dante*. Smith, Elder & Co., 1872.

—— *Italian Byways*. Smith, Elder & Co., 1883.

—— *The Life of Benvenuto Cellini*. 2 vols. John C. Nimmo, 1888.

—— *The Life of Michelangelo Buonarroti*. 2 vols. John C. Nimmo. 1893.

—— *Many Moods*. Smith, Elder & Co., 1878.

—— *The Memoirs of Count Carlo Gozzi*. 2 vols. John C. Nimmo, 1890.

—— *New and Old*. Smith, Elder & Co., 1880.

—— *Our Life in the Swiss Highlands* (in collaboration with Margaret Symonds). Adam & Charles Black, 1892.

—— *A Problem in Greek Ethics* (privately printed). 1883.

—— *A Problem in Modern Ethics* (privately printed). 1891.

—— *Renaissance in Italy.* 7 vols. Smith, Elder & Co., 1875-86.

—— *Shakspere's Predecessors in the English Drama.* Smith, Elder & Co., 1884.

—— *Shelley.* Macmillan & Co., 1878.

—— *Sir Philip Sidney.* Macmillan & Co., 1886.

—— *Sketches in Italy and Greece.* Smith, Elder & Co., 1874.

—— *Sketches and Studies in Italy.* Smith, Elder & Co., 1879.

—— *Studies of the Greek Poets.* Smith, Elder & Co., 1873.

—— *Studies of the Greek Poets.* Second Series. Smith, Elder & Co., 1876.

—— *Vagabunduli Libellus.* Kegan Paul, Trench & Co., 1884.

—— *Walt Whitman, A Study.* John C. Nimmo, 1893.

—— *Wine, Women, and Song.* Chatto & Windus, 1884.

SYMONDS, MARGARET (Mrs W. W. Vaughan), *Out of the Past.* John Murray, 1925.

THORNTON, PERCY. *Harrow School and its Surroundings.* W. H. Allen & Co., 1885.

TILLYARD, E. M. *The English Renaissance: Fact or Fiction?* The Hogarth Press, 1952.

TOLLEMACHE, L. A. *Old and Odd Memories.* Edward Arnold, 1908.

TRAUBEL, HORACE. *With Walt Whitman in Camden,* March 28-July 14, 1888. Boston: Small, Maynard & Co., 1906.

—— *With Walt Whitman in Camden,* July 16-Oct. 31, 1888. New York: D. Appleton & Co., 1908.

—— *With Walt Whitman in Camden,* Jan. 21-April 7, 1889. University of Pennsylvania Press, 1953.

TUKE, D. HACK. *Prichard and Symonds in Especial Relation to Mental Science.* J. & A. Churchill, 1891.

VAUGHAN, CHARLES JOHN. *Memorials of Harrow Sundays.* Macmillan & Co., 1859.

WARD, MRS HUMPHRY. *Robert Elsmere.* 3 vols. Smith, Elder & Co., 1888.

—— *A Writer's Recollections.* W. Collins & Sons, 1918.

WATERFIELD, LENA. *Castle in Italy.* John Murray, 1962.

In Re Walt Whitman, ed. by Whitman's literary executors. Philadelphia: David McKay, 1893.

WORTHAM, H. E. *Oscar Browning.* Constable & Co., Ltd., 1927.

YOUNG, G. M. *Victorian England: Portrait of an Age.* Oxford University Press, 1953.